The Journey Takers

LESLIE ALBRECHT HUBER

Art Direction, Design & Production: Studio 6 Sense • www.6sense.net

Publisher's Cataloging-in-Publication data

Huber, Leslie Albrecht.
The journey takers / Leslie Albrecht Huber.
p. cm.
Includes bibliographical references.

ISBN 9780578052144 (pbk.)

1. Immigrants --United States --History --19th century. 2. United States --Emigration and immigration --History. 3. Immigrants --United States --Social life and customs. 4. Church of Jesus Christ of Latter-Day Saints --History. 5. Mormons --United States --Social life and customs. 6. Immigrants --Utah -- History --19th century. I. Title.

JV6451 .H83 2010

304.8/4073--dc22   2010924144

First Printing, 2010

Visit the website at www.thejourneytakers.com

To the thousands of descendants of
Georg and Mina, Edmond and Karsti.
And to descendants of all those who share their story.

Contents

Part One

In Germany: The Story of the Families of
Georg Albrecht and Mina Haker 1

Part Two

In Sweden: The Story of
the Family of Karsti Nilsdotter 79

NOTES ON RESEARCH

The research for this book has been a project that has taken me nearly ten years. I relied on a variety of sources including original records, secondary sources, social and local histories, interviews, and unpublished family papers. I visited libraries and archives across the US and around the world.

I thought carefully on how to present my research. I wanted the documentation to be clear, but never intrusive. My purpose in writing *The Journey Takers* was not to write a scholarly account or even a thorough family history (although I hope it is both of these as well). I wanted to write a story — a narrative. This guided my choices.

Endnotes and a bibliography of sources are located at the back of the book. I chose not to footnote family dates and places. Instead, sources used to find these basic facts are provided in the appendix with the family group sheets. Please note that nearly all of the microfilms used were from the Family History Library of The Church of Jesus Christ of Latter-day Saints located in Salt Lake City. In the endnotes and the bibliography, it is noted as "Family History Library, Salt Lake City." Similarly, "LDS Church Archives, Salt Lake City" refers to the Archives of the Family and Church History Department, Church of Jesus Christ of Latter-day Saints, Salt Lake City.

In the family group sheets, I chose to record place names in a way that would be useful to anyone interested in retracing the research. For foreign locations, I include first the town, then the parish (the town where the applicable church was located and the jurisdiction needed to access records), followed by the state or county, and finally the country. This means that in cases where the town that the event took place in contained the church, the same town name is listed twice. I did not include "Germany" as part of the place name for towns in modern-day Germany since Germany, as a nation, did not exist for most of the time my ancestors lived there. However, in the text of the book, I sometimes use the term "Germany" to refer to the German states just for the sake of simplicity.

Often the dates and places listed on these family groups sheets were found in more than one source. I list only one source for each event, choosing the most relevant genealogical record to include. In most cases, this was an original record created at the time of the event.

Names and even places were spelled a variety of ways in the records. I standardized spellings to reduce confusion. Also, particularly for the German families, people were often given two, three, or even four names. In many cases, they did not go by the first name. Occasionally, my ancestors used longer or shorter forms of a name that was given in their birth record. I often found different versions of my ancestors' names in different records—and sometimes even within the same record! I chose one form of the name to use in order to make the narrative easier to follow. Immigrant ancestors, who often Americanized their names, can be particularly confusing. I note these changes, but only with Johann (John) Albrecht do I actually switch my usage.

One other note on names: I use the actual names of everyone in the story with two exceptions. First, I changed my husband's name from George to David. This was for clarity since one of the main characters in the book is Georg Albrecht, the journey taker from Germany. Also, in the German section I briefly mention a couple who help me visit Neukloster: Jody and Franz. Franz's name was actually Christian, but again there were already enough Christians in my ancestry to get anyone confused.

I employed a mixture of techniques to tell this story. I present careful and thorough research. I weave in events in my life as I learn about my ancestors, describing how these experiences affect me. I also envision my ancestors in fictional scenes. These scenes are clearly marked as coming from my own mind, instead of from the records. I relied on social and family research to create scenes that *could* have taken place. I feel these are an important element of the story. Although I don't know exactly what emotions my ancestors had, I certainly know they had emotions. Telling their stories without these doesn't do their lives justice.

My purpose in writing this book was to breathe meaning into the past, into the lives of my family and the lives of the families of all those who share this story. I hope I have done that.

FAMILY TREE

Georg Albrecht (George)
b. 1837 in Weselsdorf,
Mecklenburg (Germany)

Edmond Harris
b. 1825 in Wingrave,
England

Mina Haker (Minnie)
b. 1840 in Nevern,
Mecklenburg (Germany)

Karsti Nilsdotter
b. 1843 in Vallby,
Sweden

Johann Albrecht (John)
b. 1862 in Benz,
Mecklenburg (Germany)

Chasty Harris
b. 1868 in Spring Lake,
Utah

Earl Albrecht
b. 1890 in Fremont, Utah

Rex Albrecht

Don Albrecht

Leslie Albrecht (Huber)

names of the journey takers are in bold
Mecklenburg refers to the former German state of Meckenburg-Schwerin
See appendix for individual family groups

In Germany

The Story of the Families of Georg Albrecht and Mina Haker

PART ONE

GERMAN FAMILY TREE

Christoph Harprecht
b. 1769 in Garwitz
(m. also Sophia Steker,
Elisabeth Schmalfeld,
and Anna Bulls)

Christina Gienken
b. Abt 1770 in Brenz

Johann Albrecht
b. 1795 in Brenz
(m. also Anne Marie Schulz and
Anna Catharina Garbig)

Christian Haker
b. 1809 in Nevern

Sophia Tiedemann
b. 1806 in Weselsdorf

Dorothea Warning
b. 1813 in Nevern
(m. also Heinrich Engel)

*Georg Albrecht (George)
b. 1837 in Weselsdorf

*Mina Haker (Minnie)
b. 1840 in Nevern

Johann Albrecht (John)
b. 1862 in Benz

*the journey takers in this section
See appendix for individual family groups
All listed births took place in Mecklenburg-Schwerin, Germany

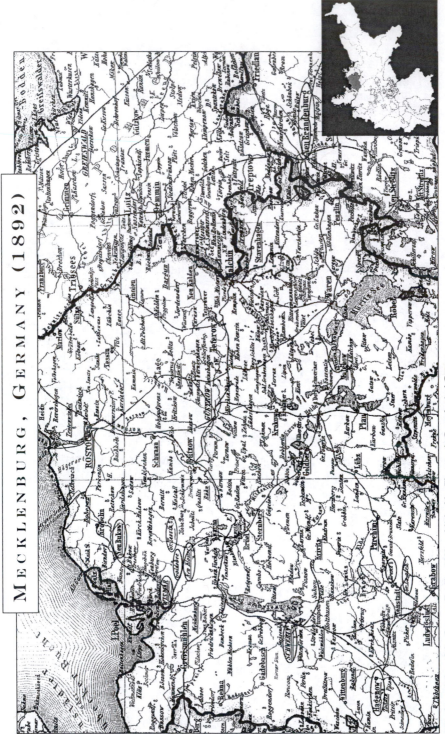

MECKLENBURG, GERMANY (1892)

Map from *Atlas of the German Empire-1892*, published by Thomsen's Genealogical Center

FRAU WOLF (RIGHT) AND ME

CHAPTER ONE

FOUNDATIONS:
EARLY ANCESTORS

We usually don't recognize which experiences in life are important until long after they're over. We need that separation to put them in perspective, to judge what resulted from them. But once in a great while, we know — we sense somehow — even before the experience happens, that it will be significant. We realize that for the rest of our lives we will look back on this experience and know we are different because of it.

That's how I feel about this summer.

I can sense it as I sit here on a bench outside the *Rathaus* (town hall) in Neubrandenburg, Germany, trying to focus on writing a postcard as I wait for Frau Wolf. The view of the old city walls, the sound of people talking in unfamiliar words, but most of all something more vague — a feeling that something important is happening (although really nothing is happening at all) — is already etching a picture in my mind I know won't ever be erased.

I came to Neubrandenburg to do an internship in the city archive for the summer. But it wasn't only the archive that drew me here — it was my family. My family lived not far from Neubrandenburg over a century ago. For the past couple of years, I have learned everything I could about them. I've taken college courses on German history, German language, and even German paleography where I studied each letter in the Gothic script (the handwriting style used in the old records) by writing line after line in a first grade primer. I've searched dozens of microfilmed parish records, locating each event in my ancestors' lives. I've loved the thrill of discovery as I've uncovered new people and linked them into my family tree. I've loved my afternoons spent in the library, coaxing the records' secrets out.

But it wasn't enough.

A trip to Germany seemed like the logical extension of my research to everyone. I wrote essays explaining the reasons I should go for the scholarship committee and the history department so I could get academic credits for my adventures. I spoke with professors and internship advisors to arrange the plans. I explained that I needed firsthand research experience. I needed to look at the real records, see the collections available only in Germany, and improve my language skills. They all nodded in agreement and signed the papers on the line.

But I told my committee only part of the reasons I wanted to go, and not even the important ones. I came here to be near my family—not the living family members, but the dead ones. I longed to walk the paths they walked, to look over the land they farmed, to breathe in the air they breathed. I wanted to not only know about them, but to actually know them—to understand who they were and what mattered to them.

That's what I told myself anyway. But just like I told the scholarship committee only part of the reasons, I also didn't tell myself all the reasons either. Only since I arrived here have I realized what I probably knew deep down all along. My trip isn't only about my ancestors—it's also about me.

I realized it as soon as I stepped off the plane and a feeling of urgency washed over me. The past isn't urgent, but sometimes the present is. People don't start tracing their families because they like to read obscure documents about forgotten events. Family history isn't about what you do; it's about who you are. It gives people a feeling of stability, of belonging to something greater. It provides a sense of identity, an anchor, a foundation.

And now, more than ever, that's what I need. My ancestors can wait, but I can't. If I don't learn about my family and about my past now, it may be too late—it might drift away from me. The past won't change, but with the events ahead, I might.

I look up from my bench outside the *Rathaus* to see Frau Wolf, the director of the city archive, walking towards me, her long brown hair pulled back loosely, her cotton dress swaying with her steps. More than just my employer, Frau Wolf is my host. She picked me up at the airport last week and arranged my accommodations down to stocking my room with food and placing a single flower in a vase on the table.

I've appreciated Frau Wolf's kindness. But even more, I've appreciated her English-speaking skills—uncommon in this area, which belonged to East Germany not that long ago. My German skills, which seemed so impressive in Utah, now seem pathetic. Three semesters of classes barely enable me to order lunch, let alone discuss the important historical events of the past centuries.

"*Es tut mir leid*," she tells me, before switching to English. "I am sorry. My meeting went long. Should we go now?"

Before I can respond, she begins walking briskly down the sidewalk as if our schedule holds an important meeting to which we might be late instead of just an informal walking tour of the city. I glance at my postcard where I've written my almost-fiancé's address, but nothing else, then shove it in my bag and hurry to catch up with her.

Here on these cobblestone paths, the nearness of my ancestors sometimes makes me catch my breath. None of my family actually lived in Neubrandenburg. They lived in villages relatively near it. But perhaps its proximity is good enough. I can feel my family here. Sometimes, when I turn my head, I have the sense that I just missed them. Now as I walk beside Frau Wolf, I can almost see them a few steps ahead of us.

Georg and Mina Albrecht stroll along side by side. Their steps fall in an even rhythm, as if they're just out for an afternoon walk without any real destination or purpose. Once in a while, one of them leans over to the other to say something—either to point something out around them or comment on something one of their children has done. But they mostly just walk in a comfortable silence.

Mina carries the baby, wrapped in a light blanket, in her arms. A daughter, around five years old with blonde hair tied back in a haphazard ponytail, concentrates on trying to skip next to Georg, the pieces of her hair that have managed to escape the ponytail blowing in her face. The other kids, ranging in age from nineteen to two, walk in front of their parents—some talking, some laughing, an older one sometimes instructing a younger one to slow down or speed up.

I watch them for a few more seconds. Then, they turn the corner and disappear.

Georg and Mina are the central characters of the German story—the journey takers—the immigrants, the ones who changed everything. In 1880, they gathered their nine children (another would be born later) and traveled to Hamburg where they boarded a ship and set sail for the US. They forced Germany with its cobblestone paths and cross-beamed homes, into the past.

And yet as I hurry along the path beside Frau Wolf, the cobblestone roads of Germany are no longer the past. They are the present—my present. Here my path nearly intersects with Georg and Mina's path, off only by a hundred years—a hundred years that don't matter now.

At the corner where Georg and Mina's family disappeared, a little girl with blonde hair in a scraggly ponytail peeks her head around. Her eyes meet mine unexpectedly. Neither of us looks away, waiting to see what will happen.

Then she smiles and tilts her head just a little as if to ask, "Are you following me?" And I nod, because of course I am.

As we walk, Frau Wolf asks me what I think about my room, the grocery store, and the city in general. The conversation takes an enormous amount of concentration for both of us. She speaks mostly in simple English sentences, intermixed periodically with German words. I do my best to answer in my awkward, halting German, reducing all my thoughts down to their most rudimentary form. When we get stuck, we pull out my dictionary which I bring everywhere I go.

"You come here at a good time because this summer the city is 750 years old. We will celebrate," she tells me as we come to the stone wall encircling the inner city. "There is much history here—and you can still see it." She motions to the wall near us. "The city has the old wall still up everywhere. It is the best...How do you say it?" She thinks for a second. "Can I say the 'best standing' wall in northern Germany?"

"Best preserved?" I suggest.

"*Ja*," she says, her brow furrowing. "Best preserved."

Standing twenty-four feet high in some places, the wall is an impressive structure. Now that it functions mostly as a tourist attraction, it is also enchanting. The crossbeam houses and stone towers built into the wall add to its almost quaint feeling. But the picturesque houses were originally built as guardhouses and the towers contained dungeons for prisoners. The wall, which once had a deep moat around it, was built to protect—not beautify— Neubrandenburg. For hundreds of years, the only interruptions in the wall were four imposing gates. These gates still stand and earn Neubrandenburg its name of "The City of Four Gates."

"This is the Neues Tor (New Gate)," Frau Wolf says, pausing as we reach the first of the gates. The massive brown structure towers above us, its white and brown bricks forming a stern-looking pattern. "Part of the gate broke in the early 1600s during the Thirty Years' War and they had to build it again."

History permeates everything in Neubrandenburg. The cobblestone roads, the cross-beamed homes, the medieval wall, all remind everyone that we are only the current inhabitants here. This area has a history far more comprehensive and far more enduring than ours. Long before all of this became new and unfamiliar to me, my ancestors walked near here with Frau Wolf's ancestors, sharing the history of war and destruction, peace and progress that this gate has watched over.

"Come," Frau Wolf says. "I want to show you more." We turn and leave the gate behind.

Neubrandenburg and my family's villages were located in Mecklenburg, not far from the Baltic Sea. Germany, as a nation, did not exist during most of the time my family lived here. Modern-day Germany was fragmented into many states, varying in size and power, ruled by semi-independent princes.

Mecklenburg also had a different appearance. The current state, Mecklenburg-Vorpommern, combines Mecklenburg with the western portion of what was historically Pommern (Pomerania in English). Mecklenburg then was made up of two duchies. Mecklenburg-Schwerin, where my family lived, was the larger of the two—although still only the size of Connecticut. Neubrandenburg was located in the other duchy, Mecklenburg-Strelitz. The pages of Mecklenburg's history are filled with tragedy, war, and inept rulers. The duchy often found itself in the middle of Europe's conflicts, not because of a dominant role in European affairs, but because of the bad luck of its strategically important geographic position.

The beginning of Mecklenburg's history, in my mind, is the Thirty Years' War, a war that raged throughout much of Western Europe from 1618 to 1648. I think of this as the beginning because most families have no hope of extending family lines before this war. Few records survived its widespread destruction. Until recently, I also thought my family tree began about this time with a woman named Anna Gävershagen.

Anna was born in 1596 in Garwitz, a small village in the southwestern part of Mecklenburg-Schwerin. She married Jochim Harprecht and had six children.[1] The Thirty Years' War reached Mecklenburg in 1625 when Anna was nearly thirty years old—and stayed there. In fact, the war hit no place harder than Mecklenburg. Here, nearly seventy-five percent of the population was killed through a combination of brutality from the occupying armies, starvation, and disease. Some villages were totally wiped out. Armies marched back and forth across Mecklenburg, burning the farmland and homes, and leaving behind nothing that could sustain life. A Swedish general recorded in his diary: "In Mecklenburg, there is nothing but sand and air, everything laid waste down to the ground. The villages and fields are strewn with dead animals, the houses full of dead people, the misery is indescribable."[2]

One by one, five of Anna's six children starved to death.

The war also widened the gulf between estate owners and peasants in Mecklenburg. With the duke's position weakened and the duchy in disarray, the powerful estate owners took the opportunity to increase their influence and wealth. In 1654, an agreement was signed that legalized serfdom in Mecklenburg. Peasants had no rights, no voice, no power. They couldn't move or marry without the permission of their landlords. Estate owners could buy or sell them with the land.[3]

The Thirty Years' War laid a foundation of hardship for the people of Mecklenburg. For hundreds of years, Mecklenburg would be seen as the most backward of the German states. Some believe it never fully recovered.[4]

Frau Wolf stops walking. "Here is what I want you to see—the Marienkirche." My eyes follow her gaze to the towering Gothic brick church standing in front of us.

"You go inside before?" she asks.

I shake my head. Although the church lies on the path between my apartment and the archive, I hadn't realized it was open to visitors. Frau Wolf opens the door and we walk inside. I'm surprised to see that it's mostly bare—no pews, no altar, no decorations. Only construction tools sit inside a large, empty room.

"The church was built in 1298," she tells me. "Our town is very proud. In 1945, the Russians burned Neubrandenburg—the whole city. It was only a few days before the war stopped. Many buildings burned. This church burned too. It was the biggest disaster for us since the Thirty Years' War. My *Mutter* remembers that she run from the city and turn back to see the church on fire." Her usual crisp, even voice is now animated.

"For years, it was…How do you say it?" She doesn't wait for a suggestion, too intent on her story. "For years, it was a mess," she says simply. "In 1975, they start to build it again. Only now they start to work on the inside."

Her words remind me of a conversation I had recently with an older man. When I told him I had come to Germany to study history, he replied, "If you want to study history, there's something you should know. In Germany, there have only been two wars. After each, nothing of the country remained." When I appeared confused, he clarified. "The first was the Thirty Years' War."

I didn't have to ask what the second war was. Evidence of this war surrounds me. People simply call it *"Der Krieg"* (The War). Signs of it linger everywhere, from the buildings that have never been repaired to the rows of Soviet barracks. Perhaps it's most evident in the reconstruction. Even now, all these years after the war ended, reconstruction remains the theme of the former East Germany. Overwhelming destruction followed by years of a government not particularly concerned with healing and rebuilding have left a lot of projects unfinished.

It's also left a people shaken and scarred from the intensity of their history, not having had the chance to rebuild and recover.

Reconstruction has also been the theme of my family history research. When I began doing genealogical research in college, I inherited a family tree — at least on my Albrecht line. I didn't have to start from scratch, but I did have to do some major renovations.

Eva Balle Albrecht, my great-grandmother, hired a professional genealogist before I was born to trace the Albrechts, her husband's family. Any time Eva had some extra money, she would send it to this genealogist in Germany to continue the research. And so, little by little, he traced the Albrecht line (never deviating to include the wives' lines) back generation after generation until he reached Anna. He could go no further. The Thirty Years' War had destroyed any earlier records.

The family tree, with its branches extending so far back in history, looked impressive. Everyone in the family, at least everyone who cared about family trees, had a copy of it. As I began to learn about my family, I developed an immediate connection with Anna, the woman who had laid the foundation of our family. I learned as much as I could about her life. I read about the war, about Garwitz, about how peasants lived during that period. Then, I wrote an extensive, dramatic history of Anna that I passed out to my family.

In a time when war was flinging death at everyone in its path, Anna lived to be ninety-six. Her funeral sermon described her raising "her shaking hands to God on her deathbed" and singing "*Stärke mich mit deinem Freunden Geiste*" ("Strengthen Me with Thy Sweet Spirit").[5] Her life seemed to radiate strength and endurance. She was a foundation I could build on.

Then I found out she wasn't my ancestor.

It turns out that this professional genealogist took a wrong turn in the 1760s with Christoph Harprecht, the grandfather of Georg Albrecht, the journey taker, and five generations after Anna. My Christoph was born in Garwitz, but not to the parents recorded on my family tree.[6] I discovered this in a family history library while retracing the genealogist's steps (which is, of course, why every good genealogist or any other type of researcher knows it's a good idea to verify the facts yourself—and usually before you write long, dramatic stories about the people involved).

The records in Garwitz go back much further than Christoph's family. They become harder to work with as details that could distinguish families from one another become sparser. Although Garwitz was a small village, there were several Harprecht families having children at any one time. To make matters worse, the Germans relied heavily on only a handful of names. This means it can be next to impossible to figure out which Johann Harprecht is which. I plan to trace the line further in the future, but for now, my family history ends with Christoph.[7]

With this new discovery, my family's foundation doesn't seem so solid anymore. In fact, it feels like it is built on a marsh. The first few levels have already sunk away, and the one left remaining at the bottom is not the one I would have chosen to build on.

Christoph Harprecht, the new foundation, has always intrigued me. Like all of my early ancestors, I know nothing about him personally. What I do know I have learned from parish records; basic recordings of births, marriages, and deaths; or more precisely, of the religious events of christenings, marriages, and burials. Nearly all peasant families exist this way in historical memory. Many of their names are written in no other place. If it weren't for the records of these religious ceremonies, there would be no evidence that these people ever existed.

Parish records and other social history records provide enough insights into Christoph to show a life with some unexpected twists and turns to it. Even with these insights, Christoph remains mysterious to me—not in an exciting way, but in an aloof way. I have never developed that same bond, that same connection I had with Anna (despite the fact Anna and I aren't related).

Christoph is only one of my 128 great-great-great-great-great-grandparents. Yet Christoph's piece of my family's foundation is unique. His piece is the one I have focused my research on. I chose to trace my German family because they were the ones who most needed my help. They were the line with the least amount of information available, the ones who were the most at risk of fading into the abyss of time.

Christoph's piece of the foundation is unique for another reason. This family carries my name—or at least a version of it. Harprecht, Christoph's last name, became Albrecht in the next generation and stayed with my family for centuries until it reached me.[8]

But in a few months, this link will be broken. In a few months, I will no longer be an Albrecht.

"Should we have ice cream?" Frau Wolf suggests as we leave the church. We walk toward a little outdoor café and sit at a table.

I tell her about the man's comment about the two wars in German history.

She considers this for a moment, then nods. "*Ja,* that is true," she agrees. "And both times, we are slow to recover. It took Mecklenburg generations to recover then. And now, it may also take another generation. My generation cannot recover. It is too hard for us to change."

I knew Frau Wolf wasn't referring to herself. She is one of the few here who are unhesitatingly supportive of the new way of life the people of Mecklenburg have been called on to embrace since the Berlin Wall came down.

She shakes her head as we begin our ice cream. "People say they wish they could go back. They do not remember. Before, we had to wait a long time to buy even a telephone. Sometimes the stores had only one kind of fruit. Today, the stores have every kind of fruit. And in a few months, I go to England for the first time."

She smiles, and waves her hand as if dismissing the concerns around her. "And now we will enjoy our ice cream."

Maybe there is something else besides my family's roots that connects me to the people here. The people of Mecklenburg must also understand their past—their foundation—so they can build on it.

A couple of weeks after my walk with Frau Wolf, I board a train to Ludwigslust, a town about ninety miles west of Neubrandenburg, and even closer to the villages where my Albrecht family lived. I've arranged to work in the archive there for a week. As my train rumbles along, I pull out a pen and paper, determined to use the time to write an overdue letter.

"Dear David," I write across the top of the paper, then stop, my gaze drifting to the window and the land rushing by. I've missed David since I left, and I think about him often. Yet, my memories of us together feel fuzzy, almost disconnected. My life before I came here seems part of another world—a world I'm not ready to face yet. The letters I brought to write, the books I brought to read, are all obligations on my checklist from home, a checklist that no longer seems relevant.

Now I can think of nothing more important than looking out the window. I watch the land my ancestors once farmed, coming and going as the train speeds along. With the bright sunlight flooding down on it, the landscape is transfixing. Mecklenburg doesn't possess a dramatic beauty, but instead, a tranquil, serene beauty rests on it. The land stretches out nearly flat, with only a few smooth hills in the distance. Nothing particularly distinctive interrupts its gentle rise and fall.

The colors are what make it striking. Everywhere I look, I see deep, lush green — not just one sweeping brushstroke of green, but a hundred different shades of green, the colors at once blending and contrasting. Scattered clumps of trees, some short and stubby, others tall and intimidating, rise out of the fields of grass. Each tree has its own shade of green. In some places, smatterings of color intermingle with the green of the grass. Flowers, fields of yellow and orange and purple, dominate the scene from time to time.

I'm so engrossed in watching the trees go by that I'm surprised when the train squeals to a stop. Someone meets me at the station and I soon learn that my arrangements are much different than I had expected. I won't be staying in Ludwigslust, but in the nearby town of Hagenow. I'm surprised to learn that I'll sleep at the Freizeit Haus which hosts summer camps for children. I'm even more surprised, and not very excited, to find that I'm signed up as a counselor for one of the camps. I'm not sure if the archive neglected to mention these arrangements or if I had simply not understood when they did.

For the next week, I spend my mornings at the archive. In the afternoons, I have a variety of assignments at the Freizeit Haus. I build towers with playing cards and listen to the kids' jokes and riddles (which I never get because I always miss a word or two vital to the punch line). I go on fieldtrips and scavenger hunts. In the evenings, I help the other counselors prepare dinner. They give me instructions which include words like "sauté" and "mince" that I've never heard in German before. My endless misunderstandings provide amusement for everyone. I tell Frau Porthun, the director of the Freizeit Haus, that her male hairdresser is very friendly when I mean to say her haircut is nice. Her husband replies, "I hope not!" When I look bewildered, the counselors all laugh until tears roll down their cheeks.

My presence at the camp somehow attracts a local reporter who comes to interview me. The next day, the headline of the local paper reads, "An American in Hagenow." When I walk down the street with the kids, old women nudge each other and point at me. Several come up and ask me if I'm the girl in the paper. I almost feel like a celebrity. When the week is over I am much sadder to leave the children than I am to leave the archive.

I had planned to stay at a youth hostel in Schwerin, the state capital, the next week while I do research at the state archive there. But now Frau Porthun insists that I stay at her house instead, and take the twenty-mile train ride into Schwerin each morning. It doesn't take much persuading for me to agree.

The Schwerin archive is closed for the weekend. So, the Porthuns offer to be my tour guides in the meantime. They drive me to Ratzeburg, the first city they visited in the West after the Berlin Wall came down. We also spend a day in Hamburg where we go on a short boat tour of the port. That evening, they ask if there's another place I'd like to see. I immediately know my choice. Brenz, the town Christoph Harprecht lived in most of his life, is only about a thirty-minute drive from Hagenow.

On a sunny Sunday afternoon, the Porthuns drive me to Neu Brenz (we soon learn that Brenz in its original form doesn't exist anymore). Herr Porthun locates the mayor's home and parks in front of it. We haven't even climbed out of the car before the mayor appears to greet us. He smiles and shakes our hands vigorously as Herr Porthun explains why we've come.

"*Willkommen zu Neu Brenz!*" he says enthusiastically as he asks us to follow him around to the back of his house. Here, his family is just sitting down to eat pastries, drink juice and tea, and enjoy the afternoon. He invites us to join them. As we eat, he tells us about Neu Brenz.

Christoph probably made the short move from Garwitz to Brenz in order to buy a small farm. Brenz was a mid-sized village made up of twenty-six tenant farmers and thirty-one small farm owners, or *Büdners*, like Christoph, as well as a cemetery and a church.[9] Here, Christoph married Christina Gienken in 1790.

Over the next twenty years, nine children entered their family. Death and disaster became the constant companions of this growing family. In 1795, Georg's father was born. He was the second of three boys they named Johann Jochim. The siblings on either side of him died as babies—one from a fall at age fourteen months and the other, not quite one month old, from a "stroke," according to the local records.

When Johann was four years old, another tragedy struck. On March 29, 1800, the village burned to the ground. The parish history reads: "In a short time, sixty-four buildings were destroyed. It was probably the greatest misfortune that had occurred here since the Thirty Years' War."[10]

The disastrous fire began at 4:00 p.m. at the home of the Niemann family. By the time it was over, only the church and three other buildings remained standing in Brenz. The fire was unusual only in its magnitude, not in its occurrence. (The history of Neubrandenburg tells that a fire that burned many buildings in 1676 was the seventy-fifth of its kind in the city's history.[11]) Since most of the houses had thatched roofs made of straw and other dried materials, it would take only a matter of minutes once a fire started for the home to be burning ferociously. With even a slight breeze, the fire could easily leap from house to house, spreading its destruction. Without efficient firefighting equipment, the villagers found themselves helpless against the flames. They could do little more than grab the belongings they could carry and run.

Fires were such a problem in some villages and towns that local leaders passed regulations to try to control them. If a fire started, laws required villagers to stay and help try to put it out. The people passed buckets of water down a line as fast as they could. Unfortunately, this method was not incredibly effective. Later, city officials passed laws about how close together and from what materials houses could be built. Although a little more effective, these laws took a while to catch on. Local leaders often didn't enforce the ordinances, and people, not surprisingly, weren't eager to rebuild their homes or roofs in order to comply.[12]

Here, so near their home, I can picture my family on the day of the fire in March of 1800.

Johann stands in the corner of the room, watching his mother and older sister anxiously. His mother's hurried movements are awkward, her eight-month pregnant stomach slowing her down. She grabs their most treasured belongings and thrusts them at Johann's older sister, Sophia, who immediately carries them outside. Johann feels frightened and confused, but he doesn't ask questions.

In the midst of their frantic preparations, his father bursts in, his breathing heavy as sweat runs down the side of his face.

"We can't stop the fire. It's coming this way," he says. Christina doesn't look up but instead hands another bundle to her daughter.

"Christina!" Christoph speaks more urgently. "You must take the children and leave."

"Sophia can take Johann. I'll get some more of our things," Christina says, still not meeting his eyes.

"No!" he thunders. Christina and Sophia both freeze as silence fills the room. Then Christoph speaks again, his voice barely above a whisper. "There's no time. Take the children. Quickly!"

Christina meets his eyes for a long moment, then looks at her children.

"Come, Johann," she says, grabbing his hand. The look on her face makes his heart fill with worry.

"*Mutti*?" he asks as they hurry out the door, his sister following behind them. Christina doesn't answer, lost in her own thoughts. At the edge of their property they stop as Christina stares back at their home. Johann can see the flames ripping at a house near theirs, crackling and spitting as they consume their meal.

"*Mutti*?" he asks again. But his mother only stares, transfixed, at the fire.

The fire was a terrible tragedy for my ancestors. It destroyed their home and ruined or damaged their land and many of their animals and possessions. For a family that based their living on their home and land, a disaster like this could plunge them into a state of poverty that would take a lifetime to climb out of again.

Hundreds of years later, the fire is also a tragedy for me. Besides damaging buildings and land, the fire also destroyed the records. The book that was in current use at the time of the fire was probably kept at the church, and it survived. Because of this, the records date back a few years before the fire. The pastor most likely kept the earlier books at his home. These books, like his home, were lost to the fire.

Neu Brenz was founded soon after the fire. It started when a few people began rebuilding their homes across a brook from where the original town stood. Others soon followed. Before long, almost everyone who had lived in Brenz had shifted across the brook to the site where the town stands today.

"So, all these houses were built after the relocation," the mayor finishes, pausing to sip his juice. "My house—which is nearly two hundred years old—is the oldest house in town. When you finish eating, I'll take you on a tour."

A few minutes later, the mayor proudly escorts the Porthuns and me through his house. After telling us about the home, he points out the church across the road, which is partially covered in scaffolding.

"Our church was built quite a while after the fire," he explains. "But now it sits locked and unused because we don't have a pastor for it. People here always talk about finishing the repairs and hiring a pastor, but it hasn't happened yet."

Suddenly the mayor claps his hands. "My son and his singing group will do a special performance in the church on Thursday night," he tells us. "*Sie müssen kommen* (You must come)."

I glance over at Frau Porthun who has seemed amused by much of the events of the afternoon.

"That would be lovely," she replies.

As we leave Neu Brenz, I look out over the town. *One of these plots of land was the site of the Harprecht's new home,* I think. Their first few years in this new home provided no respite from trials, though. Almost immediately after completing it, Christoph and Christina were forced to share it with uninvited guests—French soldiers.

Napoleon had begun his military campaigns soon after his assumption of power in France in 1799. Over the next few years, his armies defeated Austria and Russia. War grew closer to my ancestors when Russian troops passed through Mecklenburg in 1805 leaving only destruction behind them. Then in 1806, Napoleon began his interference with the German states, abolishing many of the smallest ones and pressuring sixteen into the Confederation of the Rhine.

In October of that year, Napoleon defeated the Prussian army. In disarray, the army made a hasty retreat through Mecklenburg, marching close to Neu Brenz. No sooner had they left than the French arrived. On November 17, 1806, one thousand troops and fourteen hundred horses were temporarily quartered in Neu Brenz and the nearby villages.[13] Christoph and Christina probably housed some of them.

After the campaigns that season, Napoleon recorded: "Mecklenburg has been equally devastated by French and Prussian troops. A large number of troops whose paths crossed in this province in all directions and in fast marches could only provision themselves at the expense of the province."[14] On November 28, Mecklenburg was declared to be a land under occupation. Because the dukes had allowed the free passage of Russian troops through their lands, they were considered enemies and forced to pay large fines.

Johann spent his teenage years with the shadow of the French hanging over him. The period from 1806 to 1813 became known as the *"Franzosentid,"* or the period of the French occupation. At first some of the people attempted to make friends with the French and even considered it a sign of high standing to carry on conversations in French. But their disillusionment grew rapidly as they felt the heavy burden the French imposed.[15]

Christoph and Christina's family and the other families in Neu Brenz suffered from robbing and plundering at the hands of the French army. French troops took horses, food, and whatever other supplies they needed without any compensation to the people.

The Neu Brenz history records that in May of 1809, a decree went out to the people of the town requiring that ten wagons loaded with straw, certain groceries, and one cow be gathered from the community and sent to the nearby French headquarters.[16] Christoph must have felt resentment welling inside him as he gathered his family's contribution.

During the next few years, peasants were periodically forced to take in troops and provide for them. The French government levied heavy taxes to support the continual warfare and drafted young men into the French army. Prices on common goods increased enormously. Napoleon did bring some "progressive" changes with him though. One of these — more lenient divorce laws — greatly affected my family.

Christoph and Christina had continued adding children to their family — and continued losing them as well. Their seventh and eighth children, Hanna and Sophia (the second daughter that they named Sophia), died young of pneumonia. Hanna lived for seventeen months; Sophia for ten. Four of their nine children didn't live to their second birthdays.

While devastating, the loss of young children was common. But what happened next was nearly unheard of. Sometime after the birth of their ninth child, the couple divorced. Before the introduction of French rule, this would have been nearly impossible. Even during French rule, divorce remained rare. People didn't divorce because they "didn't share the same goals anymore" or because they wanted to "find themselves." They divorced because of adultery, cruelty, or insanity.[17]

There's a story there — a scandal, certainly. The neighbors must have whispered the news to one another. I can imagine them sitting at their dinner tables, commenting to one another that they had seen it coming, that it was a disgrace, that they were glad the one had at last been able to escape the other, that who knew what would become of the poor children now. I see them filling each other in on all the details and developments.

It's a discussion I will never have around my dinner table, though. Whatever the terrible family secret was, I will never know it. Although lots of people must have talked about it, none of them wrote about it. And no record tells me anything more about the divorce than that it happened.[18]

By 1812, Napoleon's strength was at its height with his dominance spreading throughout much of Europe. Soon, he became the head of what was known as the Grand Empire. Only Great Britain remained effectively separate from the new system. Then suddenly, Napoleon turned against Russia, his supposed ally since 1807. In June of 1812, he gathered an army of six hundred thousand, including two thousand men drafted from Mecklenburg, and set off to invade Russia.

The invasion was an astronomical failure. After spending weeks in burned-out Moscow, Napoleon ordered a retreat. Crumbling supply lines, a harsh winter, and frequent harassment from the Russian army created one of the worst military disasters in history. Only thirty thousand men returned from the Russian campaign.

Defeat in Russia represented the turning point of the war. Mecklenburg was among the first German states to switch sides to form an alliance against the French. They took an active part in the War of German Liberation that raged from 1813 to 1815. Neu Brenz also participated, providing sixty-two men to fight in the war.[19] Now eighteen years old, perhaps Johann joined the fight against Napoleon's army.

By 1815, the French had been removed from German soil. Mecklenburg was left alone to nurse her wounds.[20]

Several days later, I sit in the Neu Brenz church with the Porthuns listening to the music of the mayor's son and his friends. The haunting melody floats through the dimly lit room as my thoughts return to Christoph and his family.

The 1819 Mecklenburg census shows Christoph and Christina living in the nearby village of Rastow.[21] Although the records contradict each other on exactly when Christoph and Christina divorced, Christoph had remarried by 1824. He next shows up back in Neu Brenz in 1828 when Sophia Steker, his second wife, died. Instead of being a farmer, he was now an *Einlieger* or *Arbeitsmann*, an agricultural laborer who didn't own land.

One year after his second wife's death, Christoph, now age sixty-two, married Elisabeth Schmalfeld. Their marriage lasted less than two years. According to her death record, soon after Christmas in 1829 someone found Elisabeth outside in the snow near another village. It was a very cold day, and she had become lost during a storm. She never fully recovered and died about nine months later.

Two years after this, in November of 1832, Christoph married his fourth wife, Anna Catharina Elisabeth Bulls. This time, his wife outlived him. Christoph died on July 3, 1838, from "old age." His death record adds a final note of sorrow to his life. In the place for occupation, it says that in his later years, he was supported by the parish poor house.

The music ends and we walk back to the mayor's house. I stay there until late in the night, talking and laughing with the Porthuns, the mayor's family, and the other members of the singing group.

My memories of Neu Brenz will always be of laughter and music. I wonder what Christoph's memories were. The records tell only of death, war, divorce, and hardship. But here in Neu Brenz where my family lived, standing on the foundation they laid so long ago, I know there must have been more. They must have had music and laughter too.

Christoph and Christina are the only Neu Brenz ancestors I have information on. Their son, Johann, moved away. Neu Brenz was only a fleeting part of my family's lives. Now it's a fleeting part of my life too.

Two days later, the time has come to return to Neubrandenburg. In the morning, I say good-bye to Frau Porthun. She hugs me tightly. When I look up, her eyes are red. My emotions jump to the surface and a lump in my throat grows. I've only been in Hagenow two weeks, but it has been an eternity.

Herr Porthun walks with me to the train station. Because of the early hour, we're the only ones waiting for the train. The air is cool and the morning mist still lingers. When the train arrives, I wave good-bye to Herr Porthun and climb on board the nearly empty car.

I watch out the window as Herr Porthun grows smaller and then disappears. A feeling comes over me I've only known in Germany—a feeling as if I'm looking at a photo of this moment. Instead of experiencing it, I'm already remembering it—not in the fuzzy, distorted image of most memories, but in the clear focus of a photo that freezes a moment just as it is.

My eyes drift to the land rushing by again. In my mind, I can see Christoph, now an old man, hunched over in the field, working someone else's land. His weathered hands move slowly, his arms appear weary. He straightens his broad shoulders to watch my train go by. His eyes, impenetrable, stare toward me. Then, without disclosing any sign of emotion, he tips his hat to me before turning back to his work.

I slide out a postcard I bought for David. Our communication has been spotty since I have been in Hagenow. I've had no access to the Internet and only limited access to telephones. And maybe I've preferred it that way. People often worry about the past interfering with the present, but I haven't wanted the present to interfere with the past.

"Dear David," I write, forming the letters slowly.

My eyes wander back to the window. What should I tell him about the past weeks? In these two weeks, I've visited the place where my German family (as I know them now) began, where they laid their foundation. I have come to see a little more clearly what was always there—and will always be there whether or not I recognize it.

I look back down at my empty postcard, take a deep breath, and begin to write.

THE CHURCH IN
NEUKLOSTER, GERMANY

CHAPTER TWO

DIFFERENT WORLDS:
MINA'S PARENTS

I pull my suitcase down off the train and look around the train station in Neubukow. I don't see anyone familiar so I find a bench and sit down, feeling excitement begin to flutter inside me. While there's nothing exciting per se about Neubukow, there is something exciting about the fact that I'm only a few miles from the town of Neukloster and the surrounding villages—the area where Mina, the journey taker, and her family lived for generations. This was the area I wanted to see most from the time I first started planning my trip to Germany.

The professional genealogist my great-grandmother hired focused on Georg's family. Mina's family tree was much less established. The frustration and thrill of discovering this family on my own makes my bond to them feel even stronger.

Despite this, I have been in Germany for nearly two months before taking this trip. Transportation options between little towns in Mecklenburg are few for people without a car—and, at twenty-one, I'm not even old enough to rent one. Then two weeks ago, a couple I met in Neubrandenburg who are not much older than I am offered to help me. The husband, Franz, is from Neubukow and his wife, Jody, is from Utah.

With their help, I planned my trip. I've spent the entire day traveling the ninety miles west from Neubrandenburg to Neubukow. The process involved two buses and a train—and lots of time spent waiting since the buses and trains only come a couple of times a day. Franz and Jody will meet me here at the train station and take me to Franz's parents' house where I'll stay the night. Tomorrow morning, they'll drive me the remaining fifteen miles south to Neukloster.

I have only been waiting a few minutes when their car pulls up. Jody hops out to greet me while Franz throws my suitcase in the trunk. After a short drive to Franz's parents' house, and a detour to my assigned bedroom to deposit my bags, I join them in the living room for some juice. Jody opens the cabinet to reveal at least a dozen different flavors, many that I never knew existed. She makes a big production of helping me select the perfect flavor, then chooses one for herself and settles into the chair next to me. Although my German has come a long way in the past two months, it still feels wonderful to speak without having to concentrate so hard. The conversation wanders from one topic to another as we sip on the room-temperature juice.

"So what are your plans when you go back home?" Jody asks, pouring herself another glass of juice. "You'll graduate in December? Then what?"

"Well, I want to go to graduate school. But that will have to wait a little while because…" My voice trails off as I start to feel awkward.

"Because why?" she prompts.

"Well, because I'm probably getting married… I mean, I am getting married…in December. David still has a year and a half left at Brigham Young University to finish his Master's degree."

"Oh-h-h-h." She draws out the word, her eyes big. "Getting married? That's exciting!" She leans over to examine my left hand more closely. "I didn't think I saw a ring."

"No, you didn't. I guess it's not really official…" I stutter, feeling even more awkward. "Our plan is to get engaged when I get back in August and then get married in December."

"Wow! That's fast," Jody exclaims. "But I guess if you find the right one, why wait, right?" She winks at Franz sitting across the room before smiling at me. I try to smile back.

"Yeah," I agree weakly. "Why wait?"

Later that night as I get ready for bed, my mind replays Jody's question. *Yes, why wait?* I repeat to myself. *And, he is the right one.* From the beginning, David felt right. But lately, the fear that has quietly festered in the back of my mind all along has grown into something much bigger that feels like it might swallow me.

It isn't fear of marrying the wrong person that makes me feel like hyperventilating when I hear the word "marriage." It's fear of marriage itself. It seems to me that my world will be much different once I get married — and not necessarily all in positive ways. Now, I am free to follow my dreams. After marrying, I will link my destiny to someone else's. Where there are absolutes now, there will be compromises. Where I see simplicity and black-and-white choices, I'll find complexity and a sea of gray. Now, I only have to find my own path. After, I will have to balance another path.

As I lie in bed, I turn all this over in my mind as I have dozens of times in the past few weeks. I've tried communicating my fears to David, but they mostly puzzle him.

"Of course, you can still be yourself. You can still follow your own dreams," he says. I know he's sincere. But what if he's wrong?

I know this train of thought is unproductive, so I finally force myself to think about something else. Instead of dwelling on my upcoming marriage, I turn my thoughts to another marriage—a marriage that took place near here and the one I have come to learn about.

Mina's parents, Johann Joachim Christian Haker (who was known as Christian—Germans often went by names other than their first name) and Dorothea Maria Sophia Warning married not far from where I am now in the Neukloster church on November 28, 1833. Their marriage brought together two families who lived in the same area and attended the same church for years, and yet lived in different worlds.

Christian's family had owned land in Nevern, a little village in the parish of Neukloster, for generations. In fact, the Hakers were probably the most well-off of any of my German ancestors (although "well-off" is relative). Christian's father, Christian Frederick Haker (to make things more confusing, the Germans liked to use lots of names—but not lots of different names; they just rearranged the same names in different orders), was a *Vollhüfner*. This meant he owned — or more accurately, had rights to under the jurisdiction of a noble—a full-sized farm large enough to support a family.[1] This put his family at the top of the social order among peasants.

The distinction of owning land had important, and yet limited, consequences. For one thing, owning land anchored families like the Hakers to specific places. Hakers can be found living in Nevern from the time the records began until the time my family left for America and beyond that.

As landowning peasants, Christian's family also enjoyed a higher standard of living than some of their neighbors. They had more stability. They lived in larger and sturdier homes and had more valuable belongings, ranging from better horses to better quality clothing. "Landed peasants," as they are sometimes called, could often afford to hire farmhands or maidservants to help, at least during the most labor-intensive parts of the year. They also had more influence in their communities.

Despite these advantages, the Hakers were still, like everyone around them, peasants. And life for all peasants in Mecklenburg was hard. While their counterparts in other western European countries, and even some western German states, slowly gained a few basic rights, Mecklenburg peasants continued to live under the old social order of serfdom for much of Christian's life. The Haker homestead lay on the estate of a knight or noble who wielded great power and authority over the family. In some places, after paying dues and labor to the estate owners, landowning peasants earned little more than the rural laborers. Christian's father probably operated in deficit some years, increasing his dependence on the estate owner. [2] The entire family had to work hard to keep the family afloat. Even as a child, Christian would still have been expected to contribute to the functioning of the household.

Higher status also didn't protect landed peasants from the other miserable conditions that surrounded them. They faced the same high death rates and illnesses as the landless people did.[3] Christian's family was no exception. His father died when Christian was only thirteen years old.

While the Hakers were at the top of the peasant social order, Dorothea's family, the Warnings, fell at the bottom. Though the Hakers faced hardship, there can be no doubt that Dorothea's family faced more. They had none of the advantages the Hakers did. Dorothea's parents eked out a miserable existence as landless peasants. Her father worked as a *Knecht* (servant), *Tagelöhner* (day laborer), and *Arbeitsman* (workman). He made his living day-to-day, never knowing what work would be available.

Nearly everyone in Mecklenburg was poor; but the landless peasants were the poorest of the poor. And in Mecklenburg, the landless peasants made up the majority of the population. These people had little voice in their communities. Most owned no land, no farm, and often, no home. Sometimes landless peasants built small temporary houses. Other times, they lived in the homes of landowners. Landless families moved often—sometimes every five years, although usually within a small radius—looking for work.[4] Dorothea and each of her three siblings were born in different villages, although all within the parish of Neukloster.

Like other landless families, Dorothea's family faced tragedy often. Her mother died at age twenty-eight when Dorothea was two years old. Her father remarried, but then died only a few years later. By age seven, Dorothea had lost both of her parents.

The records don't reveal what happened to Dorothea after her father's death. Two years later, Dorothea's stepmother married a second time. Perhaps Dorothea continued living in this household, raised by two stepparents. Perhaps another relative took her in. Or perhaps, Dorothea spent the rest of her childhood and teenage years working as a servant in other households.

In landowning families, children were economic assets, providing needed labor on their farms. The same did not hold true in landless families. Instead, these children drained the already scarce resources of the family because their parents had to feed, clothe, and care for them. For these reasons, poor parents hired out their children to work for other people starting from very young ages—sometimes when the children were only six to eight years old. Young boys were often given the responsibility of watching over herds of animals. Girls helped with younger children or worked as household servants for more prosperous peasant families.[5] Perhaps Dorothea began a position like this.

Only my imagination and generalizations based on my knowledge of the area at the time can fill in her childhood years. The next time Dorothea appears in the records is at age nineteen when she married Christian Haker in the Neukloster church. By this time, three, and possibly all four, of their parents had died. They had never known that their families would be linked together.

The next morning, Franz and Jody drive me to Neukloster. At a street corner in the center of town, I pull my bags out of the trunk and thank them for their help. Then I set off on my first task—to locate a place to stay. Before I've walked two blocks, I find a little inn which offers a spacious room with a bed, couch, table, TV, and its own bathroom—all for a fraction of what hotel rooms in the US typically cost. Compared to the youth hostels I've stayed at during other trips and the bare apartment I've been sharing with roommates in Neubrandenburg, the room feels luxurious.

I drop my bags off, grab something to eat at a shop next door, and head out into Neukloster. The town, with its quaint shops lining its main street, instantly enchants me. I wander in and out of the shops, slowly making my way towards the church along a path my ancestors must have taken two hundred years ago.

The feeling of quaintness radiating from the main street vanishes as I get close to the church. Its tall, red brick walls loom over me, intimidating and almost menacing. Dominating everything around it, the church looks unnaturally large in this small community. The tall, narrow windows and sharply pointed roof with its stern, gray spire seem to frown on anyone who comes near.

I walk onto the church grounds which are crowded with gravestones. I lean over and squint to make out the inscriptions, looking for family names. After a few minutes, I notice a middle-aged woman watching me.

Finally, she approaches. "*Suchen Sie etwas* (Are you looking for something)?" she asks.

"My family lived in Nevern a hundred years ago," I answer. "I want to see if any of their gravestones are here." Her eyebrows shoot up in apparent surprise by my thickly accented German which instantly gives away the fact that I'm a foreigner.

"The gravestones rarely go back that far," she explains. "The Communists got rid of most of them. They weren't well cared for and they thought it was a waste of space. You say your family lived in Nevern?"

I nod.

"There's an older couple who lives in Nevern," she tells me. "They know a lot about the history of the village and the people who lived there. You should speak with them." She fishes in her bag for a piece of paper and a pen.

"If you'd like to see inside the church, you should come at ten o'clock on Sunday morning," she adds as she writes down the address on the scrap of paper. "That's when services are held. The church stays locked the rest of the week." She hands me the paper, points me in the right direction, and wishes me luck.

I walk a few blocks to the edge of town where the road that leads to Nevern begins. A little yellow sign informs me that I have two kilometers to go. The warm sun shines down on me as I walk along the road, undisturbed by any people or cars. I smile, feeling immensely content. I can think of few things I'd rather do right now than walk along the road from Neukloster to Nevern, breathing the clear summer morning air. Soon, green fields stretch out on both sides of me. Occasionally I see little farmhouses along the road. I wonder if the Haker homestead looked like one of these.

After a few more minutes, a cluster of homes comes into view. Soon, another little yellow sign tells me I've entered the village of Nevern. I recall from my research that, according to the Mecklenburg census, 158 people lived in Nevern when my family lived here.[6] It looks like even fewer people live here now.

I locate the house with the number that matches the one the woman in the churchyard gave me. I walk up to the small, light-blue, two-story house, and wonder for the first time what these people will think of an American girl unexpectedly at their doorstep.

I take a deep breath and knock. After a few seconds, a window on the second floor opens. A stout, older woman with a scarf over her hair glares down at me.

"*Was wollen Sie* (What do you want)?" she asks briskly, her scowl deepening.

"I understand you know a lot about the people and history of Nevern."

Her expression doesn't change. "I don't know who told you that." She slams the window shut.

"Please!" I call, not sure if she can still hear me, but feeling desperate. I have traveled too far to be intimidated. "I've come all the way from America to learn about my family. Now, I've walked the two kilometers to get to your house because I thought you could help me."

Only silence answers my plea. I sigh, and then turn to walk away. Suddenly, I hear the front door opening.

"*Kommen Sie herein* (Come in)," she says, eyeing me suspiciously. "We'll see what we can do."

I follow her into the living room, feeling like I'm stepping into the past. Even this woman, at least six inches shorter than I am and wearing a dull, blue dress and headscarf, looks like she walked out of a picture taken a hundred years ago. She leads me through a hallway lined with wall hangings and other knick-knacks into the living room. Here, she motions to a worn chair, and I sit down.

A short, balding man appears from the kitchen. He puts on his glasses and stares at me, then looks at his wife. They converse so quietly and quickly that I only pick up the words *"Amerikanerin," "Nevern,"* and *"Familie."* When they've finished talking, the man breaks into a smile and hurries over to get a closer look at me. He introduces himself as Herr Lange, then sits down in a chair near mine.

"So you're American?" he asks.

"Yes."

"You want to know about your family?"

"Yes."

"They lived in Nevern?"

"Yes."

He smiles again, apparently very pleased with the conversation so far.

"What was their name?"

"Haker," I tell him.

Herr Lange nods his head enthusiastically. "Yes, Haker," he repeats as if I've given the correct answer. "I know about Hakers. Half of this town used to be Hakers. What Hakers were they?" Before I can answer, he continues. "Haker One? Haker Two? There were many different Haker families."

Although his recognition of the name excites me, I'm puzzled by his question.

"I don't know what number. I only know their names."

He nods again, contemplating this. "There were so many different Haker families in this area in the old times that they assigned numbers to the big families. They went up to seven," he explains. "I have lots of Hakers in my family. We will look."

He gets out of his chair and leaves the room, returning a few moments later with a stack of disheveled papers that he sets on a table in the corner of the room. He pulls a chair up to the table and motions for me to join him.

"So, where are all these Hakers now?" I ask as he unfolds a large family chart and spreads it across the table in front of us.

He pulls his glasses off and sets them down on the table, then shakes his head. "There is not one Haker in Nevern anymore," he says. "After the war, everyone left. Now, there are only a few families like us with old ties to Nevern."

Over the next thirty minutes, we compare Haker families and talk about the history of Nevern. Although his family line is indeed filled with Hakers, we can't find any matches. Finally, my new friend is convinced we've exhausted all possibilities. He folds his chart up, looking disappointed.

"I haven't been any help," he laments. I assure him that he's provided lots of useful information about the village.

"You must eat something before you leave," Herr Lange announces, standing up.

By the time we reach the kitchen, his wife is already preparing my food. I sit down and she presents me with a bowl filled with fresh strawberries with thick, creamy milk poured over the top of them.

They both sit down at the table with me, apparently content to watch me eat. I feel uncomfortable, but see no other option except to eat the strawberries while they look on. As I eat, they talk, the conversation soon drifting to the problems facing the area since the reunification of Germany. Their voices grow more intense, and their words come more rapidly as they forget their efforts to speak slowly and deliberately.

I find it nearly impossible to keep up, and my thoughts begin to wander. I remember that the church in the town of Goldebee, where Mina Haker, Christian and Dorothea's daughter, and Georg Albrecht married, is also near here. I decide I might as well continue my walk.

"How do I get to Goldebee from here?" I ask my hosts at an appropriate pause.

"Oh, it's just a couple of kilometers down the road," Herr Lange replies. "Are you going there?"

"Yes. My ancestors lived there for a while before they left for the United States," I say.

"How will you get there?" he asks.

"Walk."

He shakes his head. "It's too far. I will drive you."

Before I can object, he has left the room. A few seconds later, he returns with his car keys in his hand. I finish my last bite of strawberries and follow him out to his car.

When we reach Goldebee, Herr Lange drives directly to a house located across the road from the church and parks in front of it. "The church warden," he explains. "He'll have a key to the church."

I walk to the door with Herr Lange. Soon after he knocks, the door swings open, revealing a thin, wiry man who appears to be in his late fifties. He and Herr Lange talk for a minute. Then, the warden turns to me.

"So, your family lived in Goldebee?"

"Yes, my ancestors married here in 1864," I say.

He smiles. "Then, let's go see the church."

The three of us walk around the outside of the plain, red brick church as the warden tells me about the history of Goldebee. I nod as if I understand every word. He asks about my German family—where and when they lived and what I know about them. I tell him that my information is sparse. Only a few family records have survived. Everything else I've learned from parish records.

The warden unlocks the church door with a rusty key and we step into the dimly lit room. I look around at the high ceilings and bare walls as I make my way towards the front, thinking of the day when Georg Albrecht and Mina Haker walked down this aisle to be married.

A simple, black, metal stand and bowl filled with water for christenings catches my attention. Noticing my gaze, the warden explains that this bowl dates back to the 1700s. I reach out to touch it, realizing that Mina and Georg's son, and my great-great-grandfather, Johann Albrecht, was christened here—the last member of my direct line family to be christened into the German Lutheran Church.

Then another thought strikes me. No one in my family has seen this church since the Albrechts left Germany. In fact, none of them even know about this place. I had to search through many rolls of microfilm to discover that Johann was born here. This information had fallen into the vastness of forgotten, unimportant history.

Without warning, I feel my throat choke up. Embarrassed, I glance over at the two older men, hoping my emotions aren't apparent. To my surprise, I see tears in the eyes of both of them.

As if reading my mind, the warden says, "This is where your ancestors stood to be married." He motions to the carpet in front of the altar. "No one from your family has seen it until now." He pauses, looking straight at me. "They were forgotten. But now, you must not forget. You have seen where your family lived. You now have some understanding of what their lives were like. You must go back and tell your family — tell them about their German ancestors. Teach your children about where they came from. You must tell them all so they will never be forgotten again."

For a moment, the language barrier is gone. I understand him effortlessly.

The next morning, I wake up early. I get ready quickly and walk to the Neukloster church. Although I'm early for the service, the church is unlocked. I have to pull with all my weight to open the heavy wooden door. Inside, only a handful of people, mostly middle-aged and elderly women, sit in the pews. Despite the warm weather outside, I find myself shivering as I walk up the aisle toward the front of the church.

My footsteps seem to make an extraordinary amount of noise, disturbing the intense silence of the room. I crane my neck to look at the decorated arches above. Dusky light filters down from the lamps along the walls of the church and from an intricate gold chandelier filled with white candles hanging from the ceiling. At the front, more candles shine on a small, gold statue of Christ's crucifixion. Not far from this sits a simple stone christening bowl filled with colorful flowers.

I find an empty pew in the middle of the church and sit down. As I wait, an unexpected thought jumps into my mind: *I wish David were here.* I wish I could lean over and whisper in his ear. I want to tell him about Nevern and eating strawberries and milk. I want him to see this church I'm sitting in now. *I'll tell him about it eventually,* I remind myself. When I get back to my apartment, I will send him an e-mail. A few days from now, I'll try to call him like I do once a week. *But it's not the same as having him here with me,* I think again.

Before I can chase away these thoughts, I feel an unfamiliar twinge of homesickness — not for my home in Texas, or my college apartment in Utah, but for the place on my couch where David and I sat for hours talking about my upcoming trip and about everything that mattered to me. It startles me to think that even here, in a place I have dreamed of seeing for so long, this feeling can find me.

In the midst of my thoughts, the pastor enters the room and climbs up the small, winding staircase to his position looking over the tiny congregation. We pray and stand up and sit down a few times, and then the pastor begins his sermon about the lamb and the lion lying down together.

I look around the church as he talks, picturing Dorothea Warning and Christian Haker making their way here on their wedding day.

Dorothea walks nervously towards the imposing Neukloster church, the crisp, late-November air nipping at her face and hands. She has no mother or father to accompany her on this important day. Instead, a trusted friend makes the journey with her. A light dusting of snow covers the ground, adding a dreamlike touch to the scene. This familiar church that she has attended her whole life now seems almost mystical and enchanting as she enters. Dorothea smoothes down her hair again and touches her dress self-consciously, feeling her heart racing.

I can only imagine the design of her dress, the arrangement of her hair, and the features of her face. No record of these details exists. But there is one thing I know about her appearance. As Dorothea stood waiting for the ceremony to begin, her most notable characteristic was her bulging tummy. Dorothea was expecting. No carefully chosen dress could conceal that fact. Dorothea and Christian's first child would be born five days after the wedding.

Their marriage may have raised a few eyebrows. Maybe the neighbors felt Christian should have found a bride from a more respected family. Perhaps his siblings felt he had been trapped by the circumstances. But I like to think that Christian, as he made his way to the church that day, felt his heart race with excitement too.

Dorothea's stomach may have raised a few eyebrows, but her unwed pregnancy would have hardly shocked the neighbors. In fact, illegitimate births were common. Illegitimacy rates for the German states as a whole at that time fell just below twelve percent of all live births.[7] For Mecklenburg, illegitimacy rates reached nearly twenty percent.[8]

While many children were born (or conceived) out of wedlock, most weren't born without a father around. In fact, Christian and Dorothea may have already lived together and considered themselves a family, having made the decision to get married before Dorothea got pregnant.

Dorothea and Christian may have delayed their marriage for several reasons. Perhaps they didn't have the money to pay the marriage fee. They may have felt the restraints put on marriages by many German states in an effort to control the booming population.[9] Or perhaps, Dorothea and Christian simply didn't feel much concern about whether marriage or children came first. Before the Lutheran Church gained a prominent role, peasant society had its own marriage customs. The community viewed living together, making a commitment to one another, and especially having children, as equivalent to getting married.[10] Despite valiant efforts made by the Lutheran Church, stamping out old traditions and convincing people to first perform the marriage ceremony in a church proved difficult.

Tragedy struck quickly for Dorothea and Christian. That first baby, who arrived on December 3, 1833, was stillborn. The child was never given a name and never baptized, never experiencing even that first breath of life. The pastor didn't even bother recording if the baby was a boy or girl. Dorothea never heard that first content sigh or felt the little fingers wrap themselves around hers.

Christian is listed as a *Knecht*, or servant, in the birth record of this first anonymous child. Eighteen months later, Christian and Dorothea christened their first living child, Johann Carl Christian (who went by Carl). This time, Christian was a *Hauswirt*, or house owner, of the Haker homestead.

Land records, or more specifically *Hauswirt Dokumenten* (home-owner documents), give tantalizing glimpses into the Haker family that are not available for my other ancestors. These describe the line of inheritance, the logic of which I don't always follow. The papers show that, of Christian's ten brothers and sisters (some from other marriages of both of his parents), somehow Christian was the one chosen to inherit the Haker homestead. When his stepfather passed away in 1835, the land went to Christian.[11]

This inheritance made all the difference to Christian and Dorothea —and later to Mina when she came into the family. Neukloster was feeling the same pressure as other communities at the time. Poverty and desperation filled the town. A local pastor wrote about beggars lining the roads. He described landless peasants' homes being made from flimsy materials with small, simple rooms and straw roofs so low that people entering had to duck their heads to avoid hitting them. He wrote that some laborers, and even their entire families, slept in the lofts of homesteads or in the corners of rooms on hay laid out on the floor.[12] This was the life Dorothea had grown up in, and it would have been the life ahead for them had Christian remained a *Knecht*.

Maria Mina Elisa Frederica, my great-great-great-grandmother, was born in the Haker homestead on February 27, 1840 and christened in the towering church in Neukloster. She was the third of their children who lived. A sister, who was less than three years older, was also named Maria. My ancestor went by "Mina" or occasionally "Wilhelmina" in Germany and "Minnie" once she arrived in the US.

Little snippets have survived to give me insights into Mina's life as an adult, but no record gives me any personal insights into her childhood. Now, here in Nevern, I can imagine her clearly on a summer day much like this one.

Mina stands beside her mother in the kitchen, watching her chop potatoes. She keeps her eyes on the growing pile of potato pieces, knowing that once it gets big enough, it will be her job to throw them into the pot with the cabbage and the other vegetables that they grew in their garden. Mina loves that it is just the two of them together now—something that doesn't happen very often. She spends a lot of time at her mother's side in the kitchen since the family eats five times a day and Dorothea is often either cooking or giving cooking instructions to others. Usually, her older sister and a hired girl help as well. But today the hired girl is home visiting her family and her sister went out to the garden to gather a few more vegetables.

Her mother hums as she works. It's an old folk song that Mina recognizes. Mina watches her, noticing her rosy cheeks and the speckles of soot in her hair—both from working over the wood-burning stove. Dorothea nods at Mina, a sign Mina understands to mean she should throw the potatoes in the pot. As she does, Dorothea cuts some ham to put in the soup too. Mina remembers her mother telling her that when she was a child they only ate meat once a day.

Mina hears the front door open and knows that her brother, father, and the two farmhands have come inside. Forgetting the potatoes, she runs to the kitchen door and looks out, seeing her father urging the horses into the main, large room of the homestead. A farmhand closes the doors behind them as Christian leads the horses over to their stalls, connected to this main room. The horses sleep only a few doors down from her, and directly next to the farm servants' room. This arrangement keeps the animals warm in the winter. It also keeps the stench of animal manure in the home. Mina hardly notices it—it's all she's ever known.

Christian ties up the horses and then walks into the room next to the kitchen—the family's main living quarters, a multipurpose room that functions as a kind of living room and dining room in one. Mina can tell he's weary by the way he walks. Carl follows behind his father, also looking weary. She peeks around the corner, waiting for her father to notice her. He sinks into one of the wooden chairs, stretching out his feet and pulling off his boots. Carl sits down next to him, mimicking his father's every movement. When Christian looks up, he catches sight of his daughter for the first time.

"Well, who do we have here?" he teases her, holding out his arms. She runs and jumps onto his lap.

"I'm helping Mother make soup," Mina tells him, her voice solemn to convey the importance of her responsibility. "I get to put the potatoes in."

"Oh, I see." He nods knowingly. But then he looks confused. "Then what are you doing peeking around the corner at us? How will your mother get the potatoes in the soup?"

Just then Mina hears her mother's voice from the kitchen. "Mina! Where are you?" Mina looks alarmed and Christian laughs.

"I'd better go, *Vatti*," she says, jumping off his lap and scurrying back to the kitchen.[13]

In the images I have in my mind of Mina with her family, Mina is always very young. My idealistic vision can only apply for a short time. One month after Mina turned four, her father died. In the record, the column for his cause of death is left blank. He was thirty-five years old. Christian left behind a young, grieving wife, three small children, and a large farm. It was tragic, but not unusual. The average life expectancy at the time in the parish was approximately thirty-three years. If a person survived the first dangerous year of life, his life expectancy increased to a little over forty years.[14]

Dorothea probably began looking for a new husband almost immediately. She simply couldn't provide for her family alone. Harsh peasant life demanded two parents. During the time she spent without a husband, she would have relied heavily on hired help—a luxury only the relatively well-off could afford.

While having three children at home didn't help her marriage prospects, Dorothea had other things going for her. She could offer a homestead and a farm—and the life of a landed peasant. Just over a year after Christian's death, Dorothea married Johann Heinrich Engel (who went by Heinrich). Dorothea was thirty-one. Heinrich was twenty-five.

Mina became part of a stepfamily at age five. Although she probably had a few memories of Christian, Heinrich would be the one who filled the father role in her life. Many children at that time experienced similar situations. Stepfamilies abounded—not because of divorce, but because frequent early deaths left many young widows and widowers. In fact, parish records show that nearly twenty-five percent of marriages in Neukloster were second or subsequent marriages. Their ages were also representative of the trends around them. Often the person marrying for the second time, whether male or female, married a younger person.[15]

Dorothea's second marriage started out with the same heartbreak her first marriage had. In August of 1846, their first child was stillborn.

After the church service, a family invites me to join them for lunch. As we eat, they talk to me about the history of Nevern and about the high unemployment rate Mecklenburg faces today. By the time I leave, I have only enough time to pack up my things before meeting Franz and Jody in our designated spot for the ride back to Neubrandenburg. The weekend has passed too quickly.

By the time I get back to my apartment, darkness has descended on Neubrandenburg. My arms are sore from dragging my bags from the train station to my apartment and up the six flights of stairs to my room (there's no elevator). I'm starving and exhausted. But when I walk by the computer room and see the door open, I can't resist stopping in.

I log into my e-mail and see a message from David. I read about the test he took yesterday, the battery in my car (which he's driving) dying, and his roommate getting engaged. "I can't wait to see you in just one more month," the last sentence reads. I stare at the computer. One month?

I go back to my room and sit on my bed. I absently munch on hard rolls and Nutella (the only food available since the apartment's little kitchen was torn out for remodeling, leaving me with no refrigerator and no oven). Then, I lie down and stare at the ceiling. *I'm going to go home and get married,* I repeat to myself several times. *Nothing will ever be the same.*

The next week I travel with Frau Wolf to Schwerin. She will attend meetings in the *Schweriner Schloß* (Schwerin Castle), while I visit the archive again. Nearly all the parish records here are available on microfilm in Salt Lake City. But, spinning the microfilm reel can't compare to turning the pages of the church books—the actual pages where my ancestors' names were written.

My first morning, I fill out a form listing which records I need. Then, the archivist directs me to a long, deserted table. A few minutes later, he plunks the large Neukloster parish book down beside me. I open it slowly and breathe in the musty smell of old, forgotten pages. I run my hand over them. The pages, with their yellowed corners, crinkle as I turn them, extracting more of my family's story.

Dorothea and Heinrich had six more children between 1847 and 1857: three girls, two boys, and another stillborn with no indication of its gender. The two boys died as children, one living three and a half years, the other living one day short of one year. Mina spent her childhood then with her brother, sister, and three half-sisters.

Running her household and caring for her growing children consumed nearly all of Dorothea's time and energy. Besides, her participation in decisions or occurrences outside her home wasn't welcome. Dorothea stayed under the authority of a man throughout her life, never being treated as a fully independent person. Until she married, her father — or the father figure in her house since her father died when she was seven — had authority over her. Once Dorothea married, she became subordinate to her husband. Throughout the eighteenth century, and often beyond, German law even condoned a husband's right to use physical force against his wife.[16]

This second-class status also meant that most German states didn't recognize women's right to hold property. Because of this, the Haker homestead never passed to Dorothea. When Christian died in 1844, the farmstead was meant, not for his wife, but for Carl, his oldest son. Dorothea oversaw it while he was young. When Dorothea married Heinrich, Heinrich became the "interim" farmer of the land. Dorothea only appeared on records as his wife — not as the property holder.

In 1861, the land passed to twenty-six-year-old Carl.[17] After living in her home for twenty-eight years, Dorothea no longer had rights to it. Having worked as a farmer for sixteen years, Heinrich no longer had land to farm. They had no choice; they had to move out.

Dorothea and Heinrich packed up their belongings and left Haker farm No. 7 (after carefully studying the *Hauswirt Dokumenten,* I finally figured out which number my Hakers were). Mina, now twenty-one, had temporarily moved a few miles north to the village of Bäbelin to work for a farmer there. Her older sister had recently married. But Dorothea and Heinrich still had three children at home: Elisa, age thirteen; Anna, age ten; and Dorothea, age six. Sometimes I think of them on that day in 1861.

Heinrich secures their belongings on the wagon. Elisa, Anna, and little Dorothea stand beside the wagon, watching their father, then turning to look at their mother. Dorothea hesitates, staring at her home one more time. She looks at the gardens and the flowers, and then at her son's wife, standing at the doorway, looking awkward. When Dorothea's eyes fall on Carl, he looks away, unable to return her penetrating gaze. At last, she turns and walks out to the wagon.

"We knew this day would come," Heinrich reminds her gently.

"I know," Dorothea says. *But that doesn't make it easier,* she adds silently. They're only moving a few miles away. Her son will still live here. She will be back — but as a visitor. This won't ever be hers again.

She is forty-seven years old. In her adult life, she has known nothing besides this home—and the life of a landed peasant's wife.

Heinrich reaches his hand out, and helps her into the wagon beside him. Their new home is only a few minutes ride, but it is an eternity away.

Dorothea and Heinrich made their home in Benz in the parish of Goldebee, the town in which Mina would later marry Georg and christen their first two children (although not in that order). Records from that point on describe Heinrich as a *Kätner* (cottager), someone with a small house, a garden, and perhaps a little land for animals. Their economic status and well-being had taken a significant plunge—one from which they never recovered. When Heinrich died thirty-three years later, he was still a *Kätner* in Benz.

Dorothea lived almost as long in Benz as she had in Nevern. She watched her children grow and marry. This home in Benz would be the one where Mina would bring her children to visit their grandmother and the one where she would tell her parents that she had decided to cross the ocean to America. This is where Mina would hug her mother and stepfather good-bye for the last time.

Dorothea died on December 4, 1886, on her seventy-third birthday. The death records from Neukloster and Goldebee list her, both claiming she died there. I like to think Dorothea died while staying at her old home in Nevern. I imagine her husband, grown children and grandchildren sitting by her bed, stroking her hand, and talking softly to her as her time drew to a close.

Even though Dorothea had given birth to eleven children, only three, at the most, gathered around her bed in her last hours. She had already bid good-bye to eight of her children. Five had died as children; two had died as adults; and Mina had emigrated. Dorothea must have held the hands of so many as they took their last breaths. I hope someone held her hand when she took hers.

During the next month, I continue doing research, traveling all over Mecklenburg to use records in other cities. I visit Gdańsk, Poland, with a German group that performs *The Tempest* there and Leipzig, Germany, where I see Johann Sebastian Bach's grave. I work on translating a history of Neubrandenburg into English and eat lunch with the women at the city archive. And then, suddenly, it's time to go home.

On my last night in Germany, I sit out by the shore of Lake Tollense, the lake visible from the window of my Neubrandenburg apartment. I watch the water rippling in the wind. In the background, I hear the chatter of families talking to one another.

I've only been in Germany for three months, but I will go home a different person. Over the past month, my panic about getting married has gradually decreased. This summer has given me a deeper understanding of my family, their lives and experiences. It's also given me a greater understanding of myself. As I've searched out my background here all on my own, my confidence in my ability to recognize and follow my path has grown.

I look at the deep-green trees all around the lake and notice the sleepy fishermen on their boats. *Will I ever sit here again?* I wonder.

I will. I must. But, I realize, it might not be for a long, long time.

The dark of night begins to fall around me. I watch as families gather up their children and belongings and leave the beach behind. Finally, I must bid good-bye to the lake, too.

That night, I finish packing my bags, finally resorting to sitting on them and pulling with all my might to force the zippers closed on the overstuffed suitcases. I check and recheck my tickets. Then, I sit in bed unable to sleep—partly out of fear that my untrustworthy alarm clock won't really go off at 3:30 a.m. like it's supposed to, partly out of sadness for leaving, and partly out of nervous anticipation for what lies ahead.

Frau Wolf and her husband pick me up the next morning and drive me to the airport in Berlin. As I watch the trees speed by the window, I think back to when Frau Wolf drove me to Neubrandenburg for the first time. I remember watching these same trees and saying over and over again in choppy German, "*Es ist so grün heir* (it's so green here)," because I could hardly say anything else. Now, we laugh and talk about Frau Wolf's upcoming vacation to England (she's concerned that her husband will drive on the wrong side of the road) and my return to the oppressive humidity of Texas.

We arrive at the airport late. I grab my bags and rush toward the check-in counter with hardly a moment to say good-bye. As I enter the line to go through security, I turn around to see Frau and Herr Wolf watching and waving, their faces stoic. Fifteen minutes later, after passing through security, I turn around again. They're still standing there, watching me leave.

After a long and uneventful flight, my plane lands in Houston. I gather my bags and walk slowly through the gate into the terminal, scanning the crowd for my parents and David. As I spot them, a thought strikes me: *I'm back. My summer journey has ended.*

Then, my parents are hurrying towards me. David is right beside them, beaming at me. He steps forward and engulfs me in a big hug.

"I'm glad you're back," he says.

"So am I," I say. And I really mean it.

CHAPTER THREE

WINDS OF CHANGE:
GEORG'S PARENTS

MARRIAGE RECORD OF JOHANN ALBRECHT
AND SOPHIA TIEDEMANN

"I'm going to do it," I tell David as I get in the car. "I'm going to quit today."

"Good," he says.

"I'm just going to explain the situation. I'll say I've enjoyed working here, but I found something that fits my...." My voice trails off as David backs down the driveway. He's driving me to the bus stop across town as he does many mornings to shorten my hour-long bus ride from our student apartment in Provo to the Family History Library in Salt Lake City.

He looks at me with an amused expression.

"What?" I demand.

"You're awfully nervous," he says. "What's the worst that can happen? They can't fire you. You're quitting."

In the past eight months since I graduated from college and got married, I have been working as a professional German genealogist for a company in Salt Lake City. I love genealogical research, but I don't love this job. Sometimes I make exciting discoveries — but sometimes it's dreadfully dull. I spend hours reading faded passenger lists or parish records line by line without finding a hint of the correct family. Worse still, I find it unbearably lonely. I speak only a few dozen words all day — perhaps to get a second opinion from someone behind the desk on a difficult word, perhaps only to get change for a dollar to put in the vending machine. Otherwise I sit at a microfilm reader by myself.

I always knew this was a temporary job. I thought I would work here for a year and a half while David finished his Master's degree. Then, we would both continue school somewhere else. Two things made me change my mind. First, looking into graduate schools convinced me that I needed work experience related to Public Affairs, my intended field of study. Second, I finally admitted to myself that I really don't like my job.

So, I applied for another job in town working as a volunteer coordinator for a nonprofit agency. They offered me the job last Friday, and requested that I start as soon as possible. That leaves only one task — quitting the job I have.

"But I've never quit a job before," I explain to David.

He raises his eyebrows. "You're not still serving french fries are you?"

"Well, okay. I've never quit a *real* job before."

As we drive, I make David pretend to be my supervisor as I practice quitting to him.

"I never thought I'd tell you this, but I think you make a wonderful quitter," he says as I get out of the car at the bus stop.

I smile wryly. "Thanks."

An hour and a half later, I call David from the Family History Library.

"I'm now officially an almost un-employee — or I will be after I finish up the projects I'm working on now." I tell him about the conversation. My boss had seemed unruffled by my news. He told me most people quit after less than a year.

"Great," David says when I'm finished. "I bet they never heard such an eloquent, well-rehearsed quitting speech."

I choose a microfilm reader and sift through my stack of projects. I select one that looks promising and start clocking my time. I'm anxious for the hours to pass because there's another project I want to work on today — a project on my own family tree. I want to tie up some loose ends on Johann Jochim Harprecht, Georg's father, and Christoph's son.

Johann Harprecht, my great-great-great-great-grandfather, was a man of change, although not necessarily by choice. During his lifetime, he changed states, wives, occupations, and even names. Yet, in the end, his generation proved to be the last in my German line to stay the same — living their lives much as their parents had, dying in a world very similar to the one in which they had been born. They may have felt the winds of change blowing through, but it wasn't until the next generation that the wind carried my family with it.

Christoph had made his living as a small farmer. Johann took another path. He became a craftsman — a bricklayer. Becoming a bricklayer required specific skills and experience. Johann's training probably began when he was about fourteen, although it may have started much earlier. Law required him to first attend a general primary school until this age. The law, however, was enforced with varying degrees of zeal in different places.

Sitting in the library, my mind drifts to Johann. I imagine him as a skinny, little boy with floppy brown hair sitting in his desk in a small classroom. His classmates, ranging in age from five to fourteen, sit in desks around him. He fidgets in his seat, trying to pay attention, but his eyes keep darting to the sunshine streaming through the window. The lessons will be shorter than the usual six-hour block. The parents need their children's help in the fields today.

"Johann, your turn," his teacher says.

Johann stands beside his desk, trying to swallow his nervousness. He recites the Bible verses he memorized the night before, his words running into each other as if he has to get them out before he forgets them. He smiles when he's finished. He remembered them perfectly.

"What does that mean?" the teacher asks. "And please speak more clearly."

Johann takes a deep breath. He had hoped this question wouldn't follow. But he's not surprised. He knows that the purpose of school isn't just to learn to read the Bible, but to understand it so he can grow up to be a good Christian.

"This verse teaches us.…"

Towards the end of Johann's schooling, the approach to education shifted. Prussia's humiliating defeat to Napoleon in 1806 demonstrated to many the need for far-reaching changes. Prominent leaders and influential reformers began to recognize the potential and value of education. Some idealistically declared that with universal, high-quality education, they could end poverty and crime.

Prussia and other German states started revising their educational systems. Johann may have begun to study a wide variety of subjects including history, science, and geography out of newly introduced textbooks instead of only the Bible. New teachers with training may have come to teach at the school. And classes may have begun being divided by age. New teaching methods might have challenged Johann and others to think freely for the first time.

The changes didn't last though. A backlash began as early as 1822. Sucked in by the conservative rhetoric building throughout Europe, King Frederick William III of Prussia decided that changes had gone far enough. He began to fear that the people were now receiving too much education. He believed that a thinking man was a dangerous man. After all, what need did peasants have of these advanced subjects? In fact, his reasoning continued, the expanded curriculum made peasant children unfit for the reality of their future occupations.

This attitude culminated in the Regulations of 1854 which aimed to restore things to how they had been before the reforms. Religious training, reading, and writing could be taught in schools. Simple arithmetic was also permitted, but only as much as was needed for domestic use—no square roots, fractions, or decimals were allowed. The Regulations forbade the teaching of history, geography, and science. These subjects were deemed unnecessary. Training colleges for teachers were closed and memorization resumed as the major method of instruction. Further progress in education didn't occur until 1870. Instead of being the first to benefit from an improved educational system, Johann's cohort was the exception.[1]

After Johann completed primary school at age fourteen, he had several options. He could attend a secondary school which would prepare him for the university. Mostly middle-class and upper-class students—not children of rural peasants—pursued this track. Instead, peasant children who received any additional training did it by learning a trade.

Trades were organized into a system of guilds, or professional organizations. To become a craftsman, Johann began as an apprentice. The quality of his experience depended on the person for whom he worked. Some master craftsmen made a conscious effort to ensure their apprentices learned and understood the trade, giving them important opportunities to practice. Others took advantage of the apprentices, using them as little more than slave labor. The length of service was usually determined by a contract and could last around four years.

Next, Johann advanced to the journeyman stage. While most people worked as apprentices for masters in or near their hometowns, this next step required young men to leave home. They packed up some belongings, said good-bye to their families, and struck out into the world. They spent the next two or more years working for a master or series of masters in another town or towns, perfecting their skills and learning more about their craft—and the world.[2]

Sometimes I think of Johann setting out on this adventure. He's no longer a skinny, little boy, but a young man, his floppy brown hair now slightly disheveled and his eyes restless. He ties his brightly colored rucksack tightly around his few possessions, then flings the bag over his shoulder as he walks towards the door. He hugs his sister who has come to say good-bye. She wipes away her tears as she embraces him, but he has no matching tears to wipe away.

Then, he starts down the road that leads out of Neu Brenz. He's not sure which way he will turn when he comes to the road's end.

And it feels wonderful not to know. He has control of his future—and the possibilities seem endless.

Johann's travels eventually brought him to Osterburg, a town in the Prussian province of Saxony located about fifty miles from Neu Brenz, a significant move at that time. Johann left something important behind when he made this move—he left his name. He was christened Johann Harprecht, from a long line of Harprechts. In Osterburg though, he would first be Abprecht and then soon Albrecht, the name he would pass on to his children and their children—and me.[3]

When I finally complete my projects for the day, I pick up my family's research at the point Johann arrived in Osterburg. From later records, I know he married and had at least two children there. Today, I want to see what else the Osterburg records can tell me.

Johann found opportunities in Osterburg that he couldn't find in his small, rural hometown. Osterburg, though not a city, was at least a respectably sized town. During the time that Johann lived there, it claimed nearly 1,700 inhabitants, including a variety of craftsmen. This setting greatly affected how Johann felt the rustlings of the next few years.

After the defeat of Napoleon in 1815, many European governments began looking inward, determined to squelch out the liberal ideas that had started the French Revolution. But the conservatives couldn't halt the changes that had already begun in agriculture. As with education, leaders across the German states had recognized that agricultural development and production lagged behind many other Western European countries. Progress began with Prussia passing the October Edict of 1807 which declared that all peasants with a certain amount of land were free. Serfdom was abolished, undoing the chain of obligations that had bound peasants to their landlord nobles. Peasants could move or marry as they pleased. Under a complicated system of requirements, they could also buy the land on which they lived (or part of it).

Other German states followed suit. In 1820 after Johann had made his home in Saxony, the dukes of Mecklenburg took action, formally putting an end to serfdom. But in Mecklenburg and other places where the paternalist relationships of serfdom had the most extensive grip, the expected jump in the quality of living didn't occur. In fact, gaining freedom may have only worsened the circumstances of my ancestors.

With few resources and no preparation for land ownership, many peasants saw no choice but to sell their land. The main purchasers of the land were the nobles and landowners. The peasants then went back into the service of the landlords, working as wage laborers on the same land they had worked before. But now, the abolition of serfdom had erased any obligation the estate owners had to them. This meant that many estate owners no longer provided employment for day laborers or gave the farmers assistance during hard times. A collapse of the market in the 1820s accelerated the trend. In the end, the number of peasants living on or renting a plot of land of their own actually fell after the land reforms.[4]

The turbulence of those years probably affected Johann a little differently. Johann was trying to make a life in a more urban circle. In 1819, he married Anne Marie Louise Garbig, the daughter of a wheelwright. Later that year, his first child was born. Both records describe Johann as a day laborer.

Johann had managed to secure a position as a journeyman to a master bricklayer by 1821. The records show his growing connectedness to the community. Day laborers appear as witnesses in the christenings of his first two children. After this though, Johann and Anne Marie almost exclusively invited craftsmen to be witnesses in their children's christenings. Other bricklayers, journeymen and masters, as well as a brewer, schoolteacher, shoemaker, carpenter, and even a head master of a guild served as witnesses in these most personal events.

As a member of this urban crowd, and as a journeyman specifically, Johann felt the frustration around him. Few, if any, groups were more radical than journeymen. The journeyman position by nature bred frustration. Rules set by the guilds governed every aspect of their behavior, yet journeymen had little power themselves. Groups of journeymen, often transcending occupational barriers, banded together in increasingly militant groups to demand more power and economic security. Perhaps Johann belonged to a group like this.

Frustration built as the guild system, which had been around for centuries, slowly started crumbling. Governments began placing more limitations on guilds, partly in an effort to end some of the reported abuses and partly to consolidate more power within the government. About this same time, markets began opening up beyond single communities causing craftsmen to lose their local monopolies. With declining markets and more independent people setting up shops, many journeymen found it impossible to take the final step in the process and become a master.[5] Johann was one of these. As far as I can tell, Johann never became a master bricklayer.

Widespread resentment towards the rampant inequality in society combined with desperation brought on by hunger and other suffering propelled both the urban and rural masses to action. The first wave of eruptions broke out in 1830 in France. Tremors from the events in France spread outward. Nearly all of the German states felt them as riots and protests broke out within their borders. Peasants and other workers marched against their local leaders, sometimes attacking and burning manors. Maybe Johann marched in Osterburg.

Yet, the outbreaks largely remained isolated and disorganized. The conservative forces quickly and easily restored order. Although some German rulers were forced to make limited compromises, others escaped with little damage to their position.[6]

I glance up at the clock, suddenly realizing how much time has passed. I have twenty minutes until the late bus comes. I hurry to copy the records I've found — six christenings of children to Johann and Anne Marie and almost as many deaths. Their first child suffered a "stroke" at age six. Their second child lived a week before dying of "epilepsy." They lost their third child to pneumonia at age seven and a half. Their fifth child died at seven months. Then in May of 1828, Anne Marie died at age thirty-one. One by one, the records that tell the story of Johann's family roll out of the microfilm printer.

I shove all the papers into my backpack and run up the stairs and out the door. I run all the way to the bus stop, barely climbing on before the doors close. I sit down in the first empty seat, breathing heavily.

As soon as I catch my breath, I pull out the stack of documents. I flip through the papers, pausing at the death entry for each child, the papers feeling heavy in my hands. When I get to the death record of their seven-month-old baby, I stop, unable to turn further for a moment.

Although people today like to think that losing children was somehow not so difficult back then, the few records that provide glimpses into the emotions of nineteenth-century parents show this wasn't the case. Parents then loved their children intensely and worried over their well-being just as parents today do.

There was a fundamental difference, though. From the time a child was born, parents knew their time together was uncertain and fragile. Instead of making death easier, this may have only made life harder. A child's sickness couldn't be taken lightly. Common colds developed into pneumonia. Smallpox and other now-extinct diseases laid their claim. When children became ill, parents were often gripped with fear as they sat awake at their children's bedsides, unable to intervene with the diseases taking hold on them.[7]

Here, as I sit on the bus in the dark, I think of my ancestors.

Anne Marie and Johann sit awake in the dark also. Anne Marie holds the baby, heavy and hot against her chest. Her long, blonde hair hangs limp and matted—she has had no time to wash or even brush it. Her eyes are red and puffy and creases of worry line her face. She looks down at the little bundle she holds, exhaustion blurring her vision. She has sat awake with this baby for three nights now, but his condition only worsens.

Johann brings her a cool, damp cloth and lays it across the baby's forehead. Then he gets up again and returns to pacing the floor, a feeling of panic beginning to well up inside him. He sees the despair and desperation in his wife's face. The loss of their little Carl Andreas, not quite seven years old, only a few months ago still pierces them so sharply. He can't stand the thought of burying another child. *Please God*, he begs, *let this one live.*

I turn to the next copied page—Anne Marie's death, only a year and a few months after this baby's death. I pull it closer to my face, trying to decipher the note the pastor added with only the dim light on the bus. I study the handwriting, making out the words that tell me that on this day, at 6:00 in the evening Anne Marie died of a fever after being attended to by a doctor. She left behind "a good man and three children"—a three-month-old baby girl, a three-year-old boy, and a five-year-old boy (who would die two years later).

Something about the pastor's description of Johann as a "good man" makes me catch my breath. I tell myself that the adjective doesn't mean anything personal or unique to Johann. The pastor surely didn't consider Johann's goodness or badness when writing the entry. But the word reminds me that Anne Marie didn't leave behind a list of names. She left behind real people, three small children that loved and needed her, and a husband who must have felt a depth of loneliness and loss that I can't even begin to comprehend.

The other thing that strikes me about Anne Marie's death record is the noted presence of a doctor. Although death was part of life for my German ancestors, usually doctors weren't. By the beginning of the 1800s more doctors were receiving training as the medical profession grew more regulated, but most of these doctors catered to wealthy and middle-class people in the cities. Peasants in the countryside usually couldn't afford their services even if they were available.[8] Anne Marie probably received the care of a doctor because the family lived in a town and, as part of the craftsman class, had the resources and knowledge to call for him.

My ancestors usually cared for their sick at home. Caring for sick children fell under the jurisdiction of women, meaning that Anne

Marie provided the primary care for the children she and Johann lost. Anne Marie would have relied on herbal remedies, ointments, and other natural treatments that she had learned from her mother and other women in her hometown. In rural areas, when a child became gravely ill, families may have called on a local healer to assist. These healers usually had no formal training, but instead had learned their skills from watching other local healers or perhaps even from reading books. Trained doctors complained that these healers were ignorant and even dangerous. But rural peasants had no other options.[9]

Childhood was a dangerous time, as the records for Johann and Anne Marie's family indicate. In Germany as a whole, the infant mortality rate in the mid-1800s was just under thirty percent, meaning nearly three in ten babies died before reaching their first birthdays.[10] Much more important to an infant's chance of survival than if a doctor lived nearby was if the baby was breastfed. In areas where mothers didn't breastfeed their babies, infant mortality rates soared.

Beliefs about breastfeeding differed greatly between areas, sometimes even between villages. Peasant women were influenced by authority figures such as doctors and pastors who expressed doubts about the value — and even morality — of breastfeeding. Many wealthy women hired wet nurses to avoid having to do the questionable task themselves. Peasant women couldn't afford wet nurses. In some areas, the majority chose not to breastfeed at all. Even those who intended to breastfeed had a difficult time juggling it with their chores which often required them to work in the fields much of the day.

Peasant women who didn't breastfeed turned to artificial feeding. But in nineteenth-century Germany, there was no high-tech, carefully researched baby formula. Mothers fed their babies undiluted cow's milk, sucked through a cloth or quill that had received little or no cleaning. Some mothers offered a form of solid food to their babies when they were as young as two months old. This often consisted of chewed up adult food wrapped in a cloth for the newborn to suck. Not surprisingly, these feeding practices spread disease and disrupted the newborn's developing digestive system, causing sickness and even death.[11]

Unsafe feeding practices were only one factor that led to high mortality rates among children. A number of serious diseases also played a role. Because people had a limited understanding of hygiene and how diseases spread, one case of a contagious disease could soon create an epidemic in the community. Until a vaccine developed at the end of the eighteenth century eradicated it, small pox had been the most lethal epidemic disease.[12]

The rudimentary understanding of disease and lack of medical care makes it difficult to determine exactly what my ancestors actually died from. In Mecklenburg during this period, the broad category of "chest infections" occupied the position of the leading killer, with pneumonia and other serious infections overcoming people of all ages. "Fever," Anne Marie's listed cause of death, also appeared often. Accidents claimed many lives as well. Parish records categorized the cause of less than ten percent of deaths as "old age."[13]

Childbirth also presented serious hazards to both mothers and babies. Many women feared it—and with good reason. The cumulative probability of dying during childbirth came to between five and ten percent for a woman during her life.[14] Most of my ancestors delivered their babies at home, probably with the help of another female family member such as a mother or mother-in-law, as well as a community midwife. Midwives, the closest thing to an expert available to most of my ancestors, often had only the training of experience. Some had read a book before beginning their practice.[15]

These risk factors together meant that almost no family escaped the sting of losing a child. Nothing could completely take away the pain it caused parents. Yet parents did develop coping mechanisms. Besides relying on their family and community for comfort, parents also turned to religion. When medicine offered no more hope, they could still plead with God for their child, easing their feeling of helplessness in some way. They found peace in the belief that God still watched over them, that everything, even life and death, remained in his hands.

"The Lord gave and the Lord hath taken away," they reminded each other when they lost a baby. Small, innocent children, having so little of this sinful world on them, were certain to return to heaven, they believed. And wasn't heaven, a paradise where they could live with God, a much better place for a child than this wretched world of sorrow and suffering? Their faith gave them hope that despite the injustices and heartbreaks of life now, something greater awaited them.[16]

For the next two weeks, I attempt to work two jobs full time since I've started my new job but haven't quite finished my old one. David has gone to Belgium for ten days to present a paper at a conference. For the first nine of those days, I hardly notice he's gone since I spend every waking moment working. But the day before he comes back, that changes. I have some news to share with him—news that makes it difficult to concentrate on anything else.

As I wait at the airport to pick him up I think of creative ways to make my announcement. I watch impatiently as his plane pulls up to the gate, my heart beating faster. At last, the doors open and passengers file out into the terminal. Towards the end of the line, David appears, his feet dragging and his eyes glazed. I run up and hug him.

"How was your trip?" I ask absently, my mind on my news.

"I haven't slept in twenty-four hours. I'm wiped out."

I don't even hear him. "Guess what?" I say, completely forgetting my elaborate announcement plan. "We're going to have a baby."

He stares at me blankly. I wait, ready for an enthusiastic reaction.

"Oh," he says after a moment, his voice still dull. "That's nice."

I stare at him, stunned.

"That's nice!" I repeat. "That's all you have to say? Our entire lives are about to change and you say, 'that's nice?'!"

"I mean, that's great," he tries again, summoning a little more animation in his voice.

"That's great?" I narrow my eyes at him before turning to walk towards the baggage claim.

He hurries after me. "Leslie, I'm just really tired," he says when he catches up.

I stop walking and look at him.

"I'm excited," he says in a less-than-excited-sounding voice.

I raise my eyebrows.

"I am."

As we pick up his bags and load them in the car, David continues to profess how thrilled he is. Still, after about ten minutes in the car, he's sound asleep. I turn and glare at him every couple of minutes, but soon find that I get little satisfaction out of being irritated at someone who's sleeping.

With a thirty-minute drive still ahead of me, I switch my thoughts to my family. Despite my busy schedule lately, I couldn't resist squeezing in some research on Johann's life in Osterburg. In these quick and disjointed searches, I found that Johann married again in September of 1828, only four months after Anne Marie's death. His new wife, Anna Catharina Louise Schulz, was the twenty-eight-year-old daughter of a shoemaker. Within two years, they had a stillborn daughter and a little girl named Augusta. Then in 1833, Anna Catharina died.

In his fourteen years in Osterburg, Johann buried two wives and five children. Not long after his second wife's death, Johann left Osterburg. He made his new residence in Weselsdorf, a small village in the parish of Gross Laasch, only minutes away from his hometown of Neu Brenz. Perhaps he thought he could find more support in caring for his children nearer to his family.

As we drive down the dark interstate towards home, my mind drifts to Johann making his way home in the spring of 1833.

Johann stares ahead, trying to guide the horses forward on the dusty road in the thickening twilight. Beside him, his two daughters sit squeezed together, Anna Catharina with her mother's light hair and high cheekbones and Augusta with her mother's darker hair and matching long, dark eyelashes. Little Anna Catharina's eyes droop as she struggles to fight the sleep threatening to overcome her. She leans her head against her brother, who sits stiffly upright on the bench. Friedrich's solemn expression makes him look older than his eight years. He takes his role of big brother and his father's helper very seriously. After all, it's just them now. Only his eyes give away his weariness.

Johann hurries the horses along in a race against the approaching darkness. The wagon, piled high with their possessions, rattles and bounces as the miles fade behind them. They round another large bend, and then at last, the road starts to look familiar. *Not much has changed,* Johann thinks looking around him.

And yet, everything has changed. Glancing at the children beside him, he feels as if he has aged much more than fourteen years. His brown hair already shows traces of gray and his shoulders droop. He left here a young man, anxious to explore the world. He comes home nearly middle-aged, with three children, but no wife.

Johann probably met Sophia Maria Elizabeth Tiedemann soon after arriving in Weselsdorf. Sophia had been born in the village and her family had lived within the parish of Gross Laasch for generations. They married at the end of 1833, ten months after the death of Johann's second wife. Johann was thirty-eight, marrying for the third time. Sophia was twenty-seven, marrying for the first time and instantly becoming the mother of three children.

When Johann and Sophia married, the area around Weselsdorf was growing rapidly. In 1820, 433 adults along with 140 schoolchildren and 98 children under five lived in Gross Laasch. Twenty-six years later, the village had 692 adults, 452 schoolchildren, and 289 children under five. Between 1835 and 1840, the village had to build another school to accommodate all the children.[17]

The boom was representative of a trend sweeping all of German-speaking Europe. Between 1817 and 1865, more births than deaths occurred every year as the population climbed. A slightly lower mortality rate, lengthening life spans, small improvements in health care, and fewer epidemics all contributed to it. The growing population added more pressure to the already tight conditions on the land.[18]

Johann and Sophia's children were part of the baby boom. Their first child, Magdalena Sophia Maria, was born in 1834, followed in 1837 by Georg Ernst Frederick Ferdinand, the journey taker and my great-great-great-grandfather, and finally, Sophia Dorothea Maria in 1841. Sophia didn't survive her first year. She died in February of 1842, only eight months old.

Georg became the baby of the family, the last child to make it past his first year. By the time he entered, the family's history was already long and winding. His father, who had turned forty-two eight days before his birth, had experienced more than most people do in a lifetime. This winding path had shaped Georg's family, but not Georg directly. Georg wouldn't experience the family upheaval his older half-siblings had.

The absence of upheaval also means an absence of records. No more birth, deaths, or moves entered the family's story during Georg's childhood—so there was little reason to create records. The Weselsdorf parish records give only the tiniest glimpse of the family in the form of confirmation records. These records, created at a child's confirmation at about age fourteen, assure me the family is still there, going about their day-to-day lives.[19]

While peace and tranquility may have settled over Johann's family during Georg's childhood, it hadn't settled over their political environment. Discontent continued stirring throughout much of Western Europe. Bad harvests, expanding depression, and rising unemployment led people everywhere to simmer with frustration. The restlessness gathered momentum, first arriving in distant cities, then sneaking in closer to Berlin and the nearby port town of Rostock until finally reaching the small, remote village of Weselsdorf where Johann felt the tremors at his front door.

Events in Paris once again provided the catalyst to turn rumblings into explosions. In February of 1848, liberals in France declared the end of monarchy. As news of this spread to other countries, people took to the streets in masses. Monarchies around Europe began to tremble and then collapse. In Prussia, King Frederick William IV promised to allow a liberal constitution and to work to form a unified German state. A group of self-appointed liberals met in Frankfurt with the goal of writing a federal constitution for this new German land.

The spirit of revolution left almost no corner, no village, untouched. The short Gross Laasch parish history doesn't mention the events (noting only a fire that took some villagers' lives that year), but the Neukloster history shows the reach of revolution. There, some villagers joined together, voicing their frustrations to the local leaders, landowners, each other, and anyone else who would listen. Twenty men got together and traveled to the nearby town of Warin where, as the pastor wrote, "they fussed over this and that." In response to the growing chaos and disorder, a citizen's protection organization was set up to keep the peace. It operated as somewhat of a volunteer police force. With picks as their arms, the group met and practiced.[20]

As before, revolution proved hard to sustain. The coalition of educated middle-class liberals and the more volatile and desperate lower-class peasants couldn't hold together. While the middle class spoke of ideals and theories, the peasants demanded food and freedom. And as chaos and violence grew, people began turning back to the conservative governments to reestablish stability. The monarchies that had fallen one by one throughout the spring of 1848 began regaining their positions that summer.

In the German states, rulers reasserted their power, crushing the revolutionary forces. The Frankfurt Assembly completed their liberal constitution for a unified Germany. They elected King Frederick William IV of Prussia as the emperor in October of 1849. By then, Frederick had already reclaimed his position in Prussia. He refused to accept their offer, calling it a "crown from the gutter" and instead declared that he ruled by divine right.[21]

The winds of change had blown through. Now, they blew out again.

Several months after my airport announcement, I sit at home on my couch, books strewn out around me. David has left to run some Saturday errands. I stayed home, intent on wading through the Gross Laasch parish history—something I had expected to finish weeks ago. The project has proved more difficult than I expected. The technical and slightly archaic vocabulary would have challenged my German even at its best. Now, with my language skills slipping, I find reading the history to be frustrating and slow. I have to look up at least one word in nearly every sentence.

My less-than-stellar German skills have not been the main impediment to my project though. Pregnancy has. I expected having a baby to be a life-changing event. What I didn't realize was that it would turn my life upside down from the beginning of pregnancy. Morning sickness (which for me doesn't limit itself to morning) controls my life. On good days like today, it's an unpleasant, unrelenting backdrop for everything I do. On bad days, it's nearly impossible to think about anything else. I struggle to keep any food down. Reading or even walking short distances makes me motion sick. I have spent many of the evenings I had intended for research lying in bed instead.

The sound of the door rattling startles me. Looking at the clock, I realize two hours have passed. David walks in, his dark hair wet and ruffled from the chilly, windy March rain. I watch him remove his glasses and dry them on his jacket. Then I notice something — a stack of letters in his hand.

"Oh!" I say, jumping up — or at least as close to jumping as I can manage with my pregnant stomach. "You got the mail?"

He nods, but doesn't say anything as he begins looking through the stack.

"So?" I ask, trying to read the envelope labels.

"What?" he asks, pretending to have no idea what I want. He turns his attention back to the letters, sorting them in slow motion as he holds them at an angle out of my view, enjoying my anxiety.

"Anything interesting?"

"Yep."

I feel my heart skip a beat.

"There's a phone bill. Then, there's a credit card application. And here," he holds up the paper so I can see, "is a coupon for a free drink when you buy a large pizza."

I groan. Several months ago, we sent out applications for graduate school. I am planning to get a two-year Master's degree, while David will get a five-year (or more) PhD. Any day now, we should receive news on whether we have been accepted to these schools. Evidently, today's mail doesn't include any responses.

David smiles, pleased with his ability to get a reaction out of me.

"I'm glad you find yourself so amusing," I tell him, rolling my eyes. Then I add, "Are you sure you really want to go to graduate school anyway?"

David looks surprised as he takes off his jacket.

"We could just stay here. I could keep working at my job. You could get a job somewhere. I think I saw a sign that the grocery store needs more check-out clerks," I continue.

He makes a face. "Sure, sounds good to me."

I flop back down on the couch next to my stack of books. Going to graduate school has been part of my plan since before I finished high school. But as the time approaches, its appeal seems to decline. For one thing, I love my new job. Even Provo, my home for the past four and a half years, has started to grow on me. Yet, I know we can't stay. Everything about our lives now is temporary. We live in a student apartment, I work at a job with a one-year appointment, and David goes to school. At the same time, change seems so... uncomfortable.

David walks into the kitchen to throw away the stack of useless mail. I pick up the Gross Laasch history again and try to focus on Johann and his family's lives.

Little probably changed for Johann's family over the next few years. Although the family certainly experienced the challenges that everyone did in Mecklenburg, they likely enjoyed a relatively comfortable lifestyle as respected members of the community. Craftsmen's families varied greatly in their economic well-being making it hard to predict how Johann and Sophia fared. Craftsmen in rural communities didn't become wealthy, but they were also not usually numbered among the poor.

Since Johann never reached the status of master bricklayer, he likely didn't employ assistants. Instead, he relied on the help he had available—his sons, first Friedrich, then later, Georg. This skill, first learned from his father, would be something Georg carried with him to his new home across the ocean. Sometimes I think of them together.

"Hand me that stone, Georg," Johann says, wiping away the sweat beginning to trickle down his forehead. The afternoon heat has reached its peak and Johann can feel it draining his energy.

Georg, about ten years old, looks at the pile of stones at his feet and wonders which one his father means.

"Georg," his father says, his voice impatient. "I need that stone."

Georg runs his fingers through his blond hair and bites his lip. His father would know exactly which stone would fit, but he doesn't. He grabs one at random and hands it to his father.

Johann takes it without glancing away from the wall, holds it up, then hands it back to Georg.

"The bigger one, Georg. This one won't work." Johann sighs.

Georg sighs too, his sigh sounding even wearier than Johann's. Johann looks over at his son who is studying the pile of stones intently. A smile creeps into the corners of his mouth.

"Georg," he says again, the edge gone from his voice. "You'll get it."

Georg may have worked at his father's side for the rest of Johann's life. Georg could receive the apprentice training he needed, and Johann could have the assistance he needed. No records tell me this though.

The next peek into the family's window that the records give is in 1859 when Johann died in Weselsdorf of a stomach illness at age sixty-three. He probably worked until sickness made it impossible. His wife's story remains open-ended. I haven't yet located her death record.

Sometimes I think of Georg sitting at his father's bedside as Johann's illness worsens. Georg may have told him about events in town, or reported on how their business was faring. He may have listened to his father share stories of his life, of that long, winding path he had walked—the heartbreak he had experienced and the joy that had made it all worth it.

Georg's own story would stretch out far ahead, just as long and winding as his father's had before him. I wonder if when Georg's journey got complicated, when the path was muddled or the inevitable obstacles appeared, if Georg thought of Johann and remembered the words of wisdom his father had passed on to him perhaps during their hours working together or in those final moments before Johann slipped away. I like to think his father's journey strengthened him on his journey.

I sit up in bed, feeling momentarily disoriented. Then I remember. We are in a hotel room in Madison, Wisconsin, where we have come for a recruiting visit hosted by the university. We are here to make our decision.

The dull, constant nausea settled in the pit of my stomach makes it apparent I won't be falling back asleep. So, I climb out of bed and walk over to the window. I move the curtains aside to peek out. Snow falls all around—not little flurries, but thick flakes blown fiercely by the howling wind. It looks like a blizzard—the kind that should only come in January. But it's not even winter anymore. It's the first weekend in April. *Welcome to Wisconsin,* I think.

I feel like I have been on an emotional roller coaster for the past month as we've struggled to decide where we should go. Both of us were accepted to four of the five schools we applied to (and luckily even the same four). Each school has its own unique list of positive and negative characteristics, making none an obvious answer.

We had applied to one school near each of our families. But Wisconsin was near to nothing. And now, watching the snow fall on this April weekend is doing little to ease my concerns. *I grew up in Texas,* I remind myself. *I wasn't meant to live in a place with blizzards in April.*

Yet all along, from somewhere inside me came the feeling that we would end up here. Yesterday when we arrived, we both felt it—this was the place for us. The school offered strong programs for both of us, good funding, great insurance, and a flexible schedule.

I glance at the clock and see that it's 7:00 a.m. *I should wake David*, I think. We're supposed to meet someone at 8:00 for breakfast.

Turning away from the window, I catch a glimpse of my profile reflected in the window. I turn back to study it. I pull my T-shirt tight to show my seven-and-a-half-month pregnant stomach poking out, a sight that continues to surprise me.

The next time we're in Wisconsin, we'll have a baby, I realize. I'll be taking economics and statistics classes during the day and rocking a baby to sleep at night in a little (and "little" is not a term of endearment here—but a reality) apartment in student housing.

So many things will change.

MINA HAKER

GEORG ALBRECHT

CHAPTER FOUR

A NEW IDENTITY:

GEORG AND MINA'S JOURNEY

"David, wake up," I say, turning on the light in the bedroom as I rummage through the closet for something to wear.

David groans and turns over in bed. It's 4:30 a.m. on a Tuesday morning.

"We need to go to the hospital," I continue, pulling out a long shapeless cotton dress — one of the few things that still fits.

He sits up, instantly alert.

"What?" He stares at me. "You're in labor?"

"I am *not* in labor," I tell him, now searching for some shoes. "I'm just not feeling so good. I called the hospital and they want me to come in so they can check everything out."

He rubs his eyes. "Are you sure you're not in labor?"

I sigh. "I would *know* if I were in labor. Anyway, the baby isn't due for three weeks."

Thirty minutes later, I lie on an examining table.

"Well, it looks like you're having a baby today," the nurse says. When neither David nor I respond, she clarifies, "You're in labor."

The morning passes in a whirlwind. Despite the nurses' predictions that we won't have a baby until this evening at the earliest, five hours later Rachel Shayla Huber is born. The nurse wraps her in a little blanket that almost swallows her, puts a tiny white hat on her head, and hands her to me. My new baby stares at me with big, calm, inquisitive eyes. I stare back, my eyes just as big, but much less calm.

I'm still staring in amazement at this little person in my arms, when the doctor announces that he has to take her. He says something about giving her a little oxygen, but assures me there's nothing to worry about. My brain seems to operate in slow motion, and I find it difficult to follow what's happening. David decides to go with the doctor to make sure Rachel is okay. One of the nurses leaves to assist with a delivery down the hall. Another nurse goes to find out where she's taking me next. Suddenly my room, which only a few minutes ago was bustling with energy and people, is now empty and quiet.

I lie back down and stare at the ceiling, too exhausted to move. My only thought is that I'm famished. *I wish someone would bring me some food*, I think. I haven't eaten since last night, and for the first time in months, I don't feel nauseated. I begin conjuring up images of different foods, happy to find that they all sound appealing.

I'm in the middle of picturing a thick lasagna with layers of meat and cheese when the door opens and one of the nurses walks in.

"Oh." She seems surprised to see me. "Hasn't anyone come back to get you? They didn't even let you know about your baby?" She seems to be talking more to herself than to me. "You must be getting so anxious. Oh — don't worry. She's just fine."

Baby? I think. *What I really want is some lunch.* I can tell motherhood is going to take some getting used to.

After a two-day stay in the hospital, we dress Rachel in her "homecoming outfit," which is ridiculously too big for her six-pound body, pack up the binders of baby care instructions, and leave the hospital. I feel uneasy, as if the nurses should first give us a quiz on all the information in those binders with questions on how to clean umbilical cords and how to wrap those receiving blankets so tightly before letting us leave with her.

That night, I crawl into my own bed feeling run down and overwhelmed. I find it hard to relax. Every time I close my eyes, random thoughts drift through my mind about hospital gowns, lactation consultants, and miniature diapers. My stay at the hospital seems to have stretched for weeks, months, maybe even years. I can hardly remember what my life was like before this little baby arrived. I have transformed into a different person with a new identity. I have become a mother.

More than any of my German ancestors, Georg and Mina took on new identities. They were both born in small farming villages in Mecklenburg. They were christened in or near the churches in which their families had been christened for generations. They spoke the same local dialect and attended the same Lutheran Church that their ancestors had.

When Georg and Mina died, they were buried in a small farming town thousands of miles away from the ones in which they had been born. Their children spoke English and attended a new church. Georg and Mina had embraced a new life. Before long, their descendants would hardly remember that there had ever been an old one.

Long stretches of time exist between Georg and Mina's generation and the generation of their parents. Although no one alive today remembers Georg and Mina, there are those who remember people who knew them well. I grew up hearing stories about "George and Minnie" (the Americanized names they used after arriving in the US)—the immigrants.

A thick, mysterious void lay beyond them. Probably all of my dad's brothers and sisters and many of my cousins know that Georg and Mina are their immigrant ancestors. But I would be surprised if any of them could go one generation further back. When I was growing up, Georg and Mina seemed to be the beginning of the family. My dad grew up down the road from where Georg and Mina spent the last half of their lives. Every member of my family since Georg and Mina has been to Fremont, Utah, where they died. But I am the only one who has visited Nevern or Weselsdorf where they were born.

Georg Ernst Frederick Ferdinand Albrecht was born and raised in Weselsdorf. Sometime before he turned twenty-five, he made an important move—one that would link together the two sides of my German family. Like his father, Georg moved just over fifty miles away from his hometown. Unlike his father's move, this move was just the jumping off point for greater changes for Georg.

Georg continued down the path he had begun as a child working beside his father. He probably worked in his hometown as an apprentice bricklayer. When he had completed those requirements, he set out as a journeyman, as his father had years before. By 1862, he had come to Züsow, a small town northeast of Benz.[1] He probably worked as a journeyman bricklayer there.

Maria Mina Elisa Frederica Haker lived in Benz with her mother, stepfather, and three half-sisters when Georg arrived in Züsow. Eventually, their paths crossed. Although I don't really know when or how, I sometimes imagine what this first meeting may have been like.

Mina shifts her weight from foot to foot impatiently, looking down the road for Elisa, her half-sister. Elisa had done some mending for an older woman in Goldebee and needed to return it today. Their mother had asked Mina to go with her to town. Mina had decided to wait outside while Elisa delivered it, but now she wonders what could be taking her younger sister so long.

Mina glances up at the sky, noticing that the storm clouds seem to be getting closer. She walks towards the house where Elisa is, considering whether she should knock on the door. She stops at the building next to the house, noticing it for the first time. Last time she was here, there had been only the beginning of one brick wall. Today, the building appears almost finished.

"What do you think of it?"

The voice makes Mina jump. She hadn't noticed anyone approaching. She turns to see a young man with blond hair, broad shoulders, and striking, deep-blue eyes, smiling at her.

"You were looking at the building I've been working on. I just wondered what you thought of it." His voice is soft and even, but not timid, and he seems almost amused at her surprise.

"Oh," she says looking away from his intense eyes to the building again. "It looks…nice," she finishes lamely. She can't think of anything clever to say about a brick wall, especially while he's looking at her.

When he doesn't say anything else, she adds, "I don't think I know you."

"No," he answers. "I don't think you do either. I'm not from here. I'm Georg Albrecht, a journeyman in Züsow. And you?"

Just then, Elisa tugs on her arm.

"Mina, it's going to rain soon. We should hurry home," Elisa tells her older sister, ignoring Georg.

"Rain?" she repeats absently. Then clearing her head she says, "Yes, rain. You're right. We must get home right away."

"Nice to meet you, Georg," she says before turning to walk away with her sister.

"Your name," he calls after her. "I didn't get your name."

She smiles, pleased he cares. "Mina," she calls back over her shoulder. "Mina Haker."

Mina and Georg's names are linked together for the first time in 1862 in the birth record of my great-great-grandfather, their oldest child. This child was christened in the Goldebee church as Johann Christoph Haker because, as the christening record notes, he was illegitimate. Two years later, on Mina's twenty-fourth birthday, the couple had their second son, also in Benz. Then, on June 24, 1864, with two-year-old and four-month-old sons, Georg and Mina married. The sons then became "Albrechts"—the surname they used throughout their lives. The marriage record states that while Georg lives in Züsow, the family will soon be in Wismar.

Although less than six miles west of Benz, Wismar was a world away. Wismar's port on the northern coast had propelled the city into prominence hundreds of years earlier. During the 1800s, the population doubled from around ten thousand to nearly twenty thousand. With its spacious central square, prominent red brick churches, and homes of wealthy merchants, Wismar had been enchanting visitors for centuries.

Wismar offered more employment opportunities for Georg. While mostly farmers and day laborers lived in Weselsdorf or Benz at that time, 11 clockmakers, 6 bookbinders, 128 merchants, 152 fishermen, 4 masons, and people working at a variety of other occupations resided in Wismar.[2]

The Albrechts attended services at the massive red brick St. Nicholi Church located near the center of the city. St. Nicholi, which now draws more tourists than worshipers, dwarfed the churches both Georg and Mina had attended previously. Here, they christened four more children, two girls and two boys. They also buried a six-month-old daughter on the church grounds.

One of the most important events of German history happened while the Albrechts lived in Wismar. In 1871, a new constitution proclaimed the King of Prussia to be the emperor of a united Germany. At first, the states retained significant autonomy and much of their distinct character. For Mecklenburg, this meant that unification didn't erase its backwardness. Conditions for peasants there continued to lag behind those in other German states. The Albrechts probably felt few changes in their lives.

After about ten years in Wismar, the Albrecht family moved again. This time, they settled in Gross Tessin, a village about twenty miles east of Wismar. Emma, their fifth child who was born in 1871, wrote a short history describing her life there—the first personal description I have of my family in Germany. Emma wrote that while her family wasn't wealthy, they established a comfortable life in Gross Tessin. They owned a home and stables, as well as a cow, a pig, and some geese and ducks. Their meals were simple, consisting of rye bread, butter, dried fruit, milk, and, once a day, some meat. They ate biscuits with raisins for a special treat on Christmas.

To supplement Georg's work as a bricklayer, the family also ran a small farm. Johann, Karl, and Heinrich, the three oldest children, helped their father with his trade and with the farm. Mina spent many days working in the fields, relying on her older children to take care of the younger ones. Since the three oldest children were boys and the fourth child died as a baby, this responsibility fell on Emma. By the fall of 1877, Mina left Emma in charge of her four-year-old brother Georg, two-year-old sister Wilhelmine (who also went by Mina), and baby sister Meta. Emma was six years old. Mina didn't allow Emma to pick up the baby from the cradle. When Meta cried, Emma gave her a bottle filled with milk mixed with coffee that her mother had prepared.

The children attended school in Gross Tessin. Johann completed a shoemaking apprenticeship. Karl and Heinrich also began learning trades. Emma wrote that during her first year in school she learned to knit. The second year, she worked on improving her sewing skills. The Bible served as her only textbook. Each day, she had to memorize three verses. If she came to school without knowing her verses, she "received a licking."[3]

Life in Gross Tessin wasn't much different than it had been in other places, or in previous generations. Then after about six years in Gross Tessin, the Albrechts moved again. This time, everything changed.

A little cry pierces the silence of our apartment. *How can she be hungry already?* I think as I roll over and look at the clock. It's 2:00 a.m. Only two hours have passed since the last time Rachel nursed. I'm not even sure I have slept in those two hours.

Rachel's little cry grows into a full-fledged shriek as I drag myself out of bed and over to her bassinet. Rachel kicks her feet in distress, her mouth making furious sucking noises as if she hasn't eaten in days. I pick up the tiny bundle and walk into the living room. I turn on the light, sit on the couch next to my stack of books, and begin to nurse my starving baby. David's college calculus textbook sits on the top of the stack. I groggily open it to a page near the front that explains how to find derivatives.

Just recently, David and I sent in the papers officially committing ourselves to graduate school at the University of Wisconsin. Most of the time, I feel excited about going back to school. But sometimes, I feel scared. For one thing, I don't seem to be a natural at this motherhood thing. I can't help wondering how I'm going to balance a baby and school.

I also feel woefully unprepared for graduate school. The first semester begins with the assumption that all students have a basic understanding of calculus and economics. The classes I took five years ago as a senior in high school fulfill the prerequisites. But to say that I have a "basic understanding" would be a stretch. I have decided that my only hope is to somehow teach myself calculus and economics during the summer. So, I've begun nightly calculus lessons. While Rachel nurses in the wee hours, I attempt to learn calculus in twenty-minute segments.

Tonight my brain is foggy and seems unable to grasp the concepts. After a few minutes of staring blankly at the calculus book, my eyes wander back to my baby. With her eyes closed, she lets out a sigh of perfect contentment. I listen to her breathe and swallow, fascinated by these simplest of tasks. I find myself amazed for the hundredth time that a person can be so small and yet so whole, so complete. I reach my hand out to touch her—feeling as if I'm reaching into the future.

As I do, another thought slips into my mind—the echo of words, the forming of a scene. I'm back standing inside a church in Goldebee with the church warden and the man from Nevern. I reach my hand out again—this time to touch the christening bowl where Georg and Mina christened their first child, my last ancestor to be born in Germany. I reach out to touch the past.

Then I hear a voice.

"Your family has been forgotten," the church warden says. "But now, you must not forget. You must go back and tell your family— tell them about their German ancestors. Teach your children about where they came from. You must tell them all so they'll never be forgotten again."

As I hold my new baby, I wonder: *What should she know about her ancestors, about her past? What should I teach her about her family that will someday matter to her?*

One basic fact nearly all of Georg and Mina's descendants know about them is that they were the ancestors who first joined the LDS Church. The Church of Jesus Christ of Latter-day Saints, the official name of the church more commonly known as the Mormon or LDS Church, began in New York during the Second Great Awakening, a period of religious revival in the US in the early 1800s. Here, fourteen-year-old Joseph Smith proclaimed that he had seen a vision in which God the Father and Jesus Christ appeared to him. According to his history, several years later, in 1827, an angel directed him to retrieve golden plates with ancient engravings on them from a nearby hill. He translated these and published them as the *Book of Mormon*. Smith officially organized this new church on April 6, 1830, in a log cabin near Fayette, New York.

Over the next decade, the members of the LDS Church (called "Saints" among themselves) wandered from place to place unable to find a home. Persecution followed them wherever they went. Between 1831 and 1839, church members moved from Kirtland, Ohio, to Jackson County, Missouri, and then to Nauvoo, Illinois. They enjoyed several years of peace and prosperity in Nauvoo until June of 1844 when Joseph Smith was murdered while imprisoned in nearby Carthage. Soon after, mob violence and pressure forced the members to leave Nauvoo. On a frigid day in February of 1846, they began their journey to Utah, which was at that time located outside the boundaries of the US. Here, they found a place they could live in peace.

While the Church was still in its infancy, LDS leaders launched an ambitious and far-reaching missionary program. Early members served missions, which could last a year or longer, in the nearby areas and eastern states. Only seven years after the Church's organization, leaders moved their efforts to win converts to an international level. In 1837, missionaries arrived in England where converts streamed in by the hundreds. As the Church expanded into other Western European countries though, they found the success in England to be unique.[4]

The LDS Church reached the German states in 1851. Missionaries immediately had to contend with German authorities. Lutheran pastors and Catholic priests alike condemned the Mormons, but local government leaders proved the most problematic. They arrested and banished missionaries.

Despite this, growth of the LDS Church in Germany limped forward. By 1880, the LDS Church was still small, struggling, and unaccepted, but it had proved it could endure after surviving in Germany for almost thirty years.[5]

I close the book I've been holding (but not reading) and look down to see that Rachel has fallen sound asleep. I lay her back in the bassinet and climb into my own bed. David snores softly, unaware that the baby ever woke up. I concentrate on thinking about nothing so I can fall asleep quickly. It doesn't work. Instead I remember a story about my family in Germany that has been passed down through the generations. In my mind, I imagine how it took place.

Georg walks down the dirt road leading to his house, humming as he goes. Business was good today. The crisp, coolness of the air tells him that autumn has arrived—his favorite time of year.

Suddenly, he stops walking. Ahead, he sees a group of men gathered in a circle. Their angry voices hurl accusations towards the center at people he can't see.

"Go home!" yells one man from the crowd. "You don't belong here."

"We won't listen to your lies!" another calls out. "We don't believe your stories about boys seeing God."

Georg hurries toward them. As he gets closer, he can see they have surrounded two young men. Georg watches in astonishment as someone from the crowd picks up a rock from the ground and throws it at one of the men in the center. It hits his target with a solid thud. Evidently inspired by his example, several other men bend over to retrieve rocks.

Georg's eyes meet the wide, frightened eyes of one of the men in the center. The young man's eyes plead for help. Just then, another rock hits him on the leg and then another on the side of the head. Georg can tell the group is getting out of hand.

"Stop." Georg steps forward into the crowd, his voice low but firm.

Several people in the crowd turn to look at him, surprised.

"What's going on here?" Georg asks.

"These foreign boys have come to teach us about Jesus," sneers one of the men.

Georg raises his eyebrows. He had heard there were some missionaries in town. "So, you throw rocks at them?" he asks.

Several of the men look sheepish. "We were just letting them know they're not welcome here," the same man begins. "We don't need these strangers wandering our streets…"

As he talks, Georg looks more closely at the two men in the middle. Their clothes are scuffed and their faces weary. A feeling of shame for his neighbors rises up in him.

"Have you eaten dinner?" he asks the two men quietly, as the angry man in the crowd continues ranting.

"No," one of them answers.

"Are you hungry?"

"Yes," the other says.

"They won't be wandering the streets anymore tonight," Georg announces to the crowd, interrupting the man still hollering. "You can all go home," he says when nobody moves. "They'll be joining my family for dinner."

He pushes through the crowd and continues down the road towards his home. The two young men look at each other and then hurry after him.

That may have been the first of many nights that Georg and his family spent listening to the missionaries and asking questions.[6] On January 4, 1879, Georg was baptized into the LDS Church.[7] It was probably the most significant decision of his life. The Church was not approved of in Germany, was not popular with the neighbors, and it asked converts to do something monumental. They were supposed to move to Utah.

Many of the beliefs of the LDS Church were new to Georg and Mina. But few affected them as much as the "doctrine of the gathering." *Gathering* basically meant that new converts should move to one central location. They called this location "Zion"—a place where they could worship together undisturbed by outside influence or persecution. Church leaders believed that keeping members together in one place would lend strength and support to individuals as well as to the Church as a whole.

Missionaries taught the idea of gathering from the very earliest days of the Church. New converts gathered in Ohio and Missouri, then Illinois, and finally, Utah. Gathering wasn't viewed as a voluntary option for those who were interested, but as a commandment from God. It was expected of all faithful members. Not until 1898 did Church leaders make an effort to limit immigration. The gathering didn't officially come to an end until twelve years later when the Church issued a decree urging members to stay in their homelands and seek to establish congregations there.

The financial cost of gathering to Utah was staggering. Converts scrimped and saved for months, sometimes years, and even sold their land and possessions. Despite these efforts, many converts found themselves unable to come up with the resources needed to make the journey. Church leaders set up a program called the Perpetual Emigration Fund, or PEF, to assist. Through the PEF, converts could borrow money from the Church to finance their journey. Once they arrived, they were expected to pay off their debt in full.[8] The Albrechts, although not wealthy, managed to pull together enough money to pay for the journey without relying on the PEF.[9]

I can only wonder how Georg and Mina arrived at their decision to go to Utah. Maybe they eagerly embraced the life offered (and required) by their new religion. Perhaps they felt that Utah provided more opportunities for their children than Mecklenburg could. But maybe they didn't want to leave their family and friends. Perhaps the idea of crossing the ocean, of arriving in an unfamiliar land, frightened them. Maybe they struggled with the decision. Many others did. Prior to 1894, barely half of the German LDS converts moved to Utah. Some couldn't make the journey because of financial or health limitations. Others simply chose not to leave their homes.

Georg and Mina must have felt very alone as they began this path. They would have had only a small support group. In any given year, usually only a couple dozen Mormons emigrated from Germany. When Georg and Mina left in 1880, twelve Mormons made the trip. Even this number was enough to wipe out most of the membership of the LDS Church in Germany that year.[10]

While only a few German LDS members took this particular path, thousands of others took similar journeys away from their homelands. In fact, Georg and Mina joined a massive wave of immigrants coming to America. Five million people from various countries arrived during the 1880s. Nearly 1.5 million people left Germany that decade.[11]

Only a small proportion of the emigrants left for religious reasons, like the Albrechts did. The majority had economic motivations.

Mecklenburg had the highest percentage of emigrants of any of the German states. After living in oppressive poverty with limited freedom and few opportunities, many Mecklenburg peasants saw emigration as a new chance at life. In some periods, one percent of the population left each year.[12]

For the great majority of these emigrants, including Georg and Mina, their journey overseas began in Hamburg.

I have two images of Hamburg. The first is a fuzzy memory from the day I took the boat tour around the port with the Porthuns. I don't remember what the boat looked like, or even much about the deck. I have a record of that day: a clear, sharp photograph. In it, I'm wearing tan corduroy overalls, my short blonde hair blowing in the wind. I'm laughing, excited to experience the place I have read so much about.

I have another record of Hamburg from a different day, a day in October of 1880. It's not a photo, but a fuzzy copy of a microfilmed passenger list—the page with my family's names all listed one after another. While the record is fuzzy, the image it evokes in my mind is clear—clearer than the memory of the day I was there and just as real.

Georg and Mina stand on the deck of their ship as it pushes away from the port. Georg grips the rail with both hands as he stares into the distance, his blue eyes watering from the wind and from the emotions that are stirring inside him. Mina stands next to him clutching a baby in her arms. She looks around again, checking on her seven other children. Three-year-old Meta, her wispy blonde hair blowing across her face, holds onto her dad's leg. Little Mina, almost five, links one arm through Johann's arm while she holds a well-worn cloth doll close to her body with the other arm. The other children, ranging from seven-year-old Georg to sixteen-year-old Heinrich, all stand near the railing on the deck, watching the people on the pier as they shrink and finally fade away completely.

Little Mina bursts into sobs, the big tears rolling down her cheeks as they often have throughout the past week. She could hardly bear to say good-bye to her grandmother, aunts, uncles, and cousins. Nine-year-old Emma sniffles a little too. Little Georg grins, excited for the new adventure. The three older boys are stone-faced, trying not to let their apprehension show as the ship rocks in the waves.

Georg turns to look at his wife. She stares back silently, not needing words to convey how she feels. After nearly twenty years together, their eyes communicate the range of emotions bubbling inside them.

The Albrecht's ship, the *Wisconsin*, first docked briefly in Liverpool. While there, other passengers boarded, swelling the group to 258 people, including 188 people from England, Scotland, and Wales; 23 Swiss and Germans; 22 Scandinavians; 10 Italians; 2 Dutch; 12 returning missionaries; and 1 visitor.[13] At that time, Church leaders commissioned ships to bring LDS immigrants across the ocean. Probably all of these passengers were Mormon converts on their way to Zion.

Traveling in the late 1880s meant that the Albrechts enjoyed some important improvements in travel conditions as compared to what earlier emigrants endured. For one thing, they made their voyage by steamship. Steamships began to replace sailing ships as early as 1850, although some emigrants continued to choose to travel by sailing ship for the next thirty years because of the cheaper fares. The Albrechts didn't have this option, though. The last sailing ship left Hamburg in 1879. The switch to steamships cut the time at sea from an average of forty-three days in the 1850s to only twelve to fourteen days by the late 1870s.[14]

The Albrechts, and all those who traveled after 1869, enjoyed another immense advantage—the transcontinental railroad. LDS immigrants could take a train all the way from New York to Ogden, Utah, in a matter of days. This portion of the trip had taken earlier pioneers—who had to rely on a combination of train, boat, and walking—months to accomplish. Even with these improved conditions, the trip was still difficult and uncomfortable.

After only two days at sea, the ship encountered a terrible storm. The winds blew and the waves rose dangerously high. John Nicholson, the LDS leader on the voyage, wrote, "The scene during the storm was indescribably grand, the waves lifting their crested heads to a tremendous height, and breaking with a terrific roar."[15] The storm didn't impede the progress of the ship, though. The wind blew in the right direction, and the *Wisconsin* hurried on her way toward America.

Johann, my great-great-grandfather, passed down only one detail of the ship voyage. He told his grandchildren, that although it might sound babyish for an eighteen-year-old boy, he was so sick that he begged his parents to throw him overboard and end his misery.[16] He wasn't alone. James Bowler recorded, "Every member of our company were seasick excepting Elder Nixon and myself and instead of our usual evening meeting of singing and prayer, could be heard moaning in all the berths."[17]

Calm returned to the sea for a couple of days. Then, on the morning of October 31, another storm struck. This time, the winds blew in the opposite direction, making progress impossible. A torrential rain lasted all day and into the night. By midnight, the boat was taking in about three feet of water an hour. The crew began to worry that they were going to have to lower the lifeboats. The Albrechts and most of the other passengers probably slept, unaware of the growing crisis. After a few hours, the pump began to work again and the danger passed.[18]

Another, more personal, crisis struck the Albrecht family while on the ship. Frederick, the baby of the family who celebrated his first birthday while at sea, became sick. His condition grew worse until the family began to worry that Frederick wouldn't survive the journey. Mina must have spent many nights on that ship walking up and down the constantly swaying floor between the crowded rows of bunks holding her feverish baby. She later wrote that her greatest fear was burying a child at sea.[19] As she held him close trying to calm his restless stirring, she pleaded with God to let Frederick live until they reached land. Mina's request was granted. Frederick's life was spared — temporarily.

Passengers on board the *Wisconsin* shared cramped and unpleasant quarters and suffered other discomforts. Yet their common beliefs and experiences drew them together. Emma's most vivid memory of the voyage wasn't of the small beds, the bland food, or even the endless motion of the ship. It was of dancing. Once, a giant wave washed overboard, drenching the dancers on deck and leaving them standing in water up to their knees.[20]

The Albrecht's ship arrived in New York on November 2, 1880 after ten days at sea. From here, the group took a boat across the port to the train station where they boarded the Pennsylvania Railroad. During the next week, the family traveled across the country, watching through the windows of the train as the changing landscape rushed by. At one point, they saw a prairie fire which made it appear "as though the whole world was in flames and we were hastening into the conflagration," as James Bowler described. Bowler also recorded catching glimpses of "real Indians with garb and feathers something similar to pictures printed in books."[21] Emma wrote that the sight of the American Indians "frightened me terribly." She also remembered watching buffalo roam across the grass.[22]

The Albrecht family arrived in Ogden, Utah, on November 11, 1880. After a brief stop, they continued on to Salt Lake City. Just as I can imagine them on the departing ship, I can also imagine them on the arriving train.

Mina sits up suddenly, sensing the slowing motion of the train. She hadn't realized she had fallen asleep. The disruption of all of this travel combined with the weary task of caring for a sick baby has made sleep difficult to come by in the past few weeks. She looks down at Frederick limp on her shoulder, his eyes closed in a merciful moment of sleep.

We're in Salt Lake City, she thinks. The wave of joy she had expected doesn't come. She feels only relief. She's too tired to feel anything else.

"We're here!" seven-year-old Georg exclaims, jumping up.

"Sit down, son," his father tells him.

But his enthusiasm has already spread to his brothers and sisters who whisper back and forth to each other as they strain to see something out of the dark windows. As Georg watches his children, the fullness of what they've done suddenly presses down on him. They have arrived in this new place so far away from anything familiar. He made this decision to bring his family here and now he feels the responsibility lying heavily upon him.

"*Vatti,* where are we?" Meta asks, looking up at him.

No time for doubts now, Georg tells himself. This was the right choice for their family. At one point, he had known that as surely as he had ever known anything in his life.

"Home," he tells her.

When Georg and Mina and their children climbed off the train with the other immigrants, there was nobody to welcome them to their new home. Church leaders had thought the train wouldn't arrive until the morning. The travelers had to stay the night in a small Church-owned building nearby.[23]

As the morning light shone over Salt Lake City, the Albrechts viewed their destination clearly for the first time. Although the distant scenery was awe-inspiring, their immediate surroundings were far less impressive. The trees had begun to lose their leaves. Brown surrounded them on every side. Even the grass (unless it was well watered and cared for) grew only in shades of brown. If there had been an early snow, a gracious white coating might have covered the dreary land. Vegetation didn't abound this time of the year, or really any time of the year, without a lot of prompting. After all, they had arrived in the middle of the desert, a stark contrast to the lush green of Mecklenburg.

That first day, Meta may have cried for her grandma. Johann may have thought of the friends he had left behind. And Georg may have wondered how a man could ever farm here. But I think they also laughed and hugged each other and celebrated the beginning of their new lives.

Salt Lake City was not the final destination for the Albrecht family. Instead, they received an assignment from Church leaders to go south to the town of Manti. The people in Manti were building a temple. Georg had experience as a mason and could provide needed skilled labor.

Manti was one of the more established towns in Utah when the Albrechts arrived. Mormons first settled the area near Manti in 1849. Despite a rough start due to harsh weather, parched farmland, and hostile American Indians, Manti still flourished.[24]

Georg and Mina reached Manti on November 15, 1880. The next day, Frederick died. Mina believed God had shown her mercy by sparing her baby's life at sea. Still, she must have felt her insides ripped apart as they laid Frederick's little body in the ground in the Manti cemetery.[25]

Georg began working on the Manti temple with his son, Karl, helping him. Johann and Heinrich herded sheep. The younger children attended school where they learned English and, as Emma noted, "forgot German."[26] Their connection to their German heritage quickly began to slip away. To conform to their new identities, many immigrants felt they had to shed their old ones. Some never looked back, not even teaching their native language or customs to their children.

After two years of working on the temple, Georg and his family moved to the small town of Dover located not far from Manti. Although small, unspectacular communities dotted the area near Manti, Dover was even smaller and more unspectacular than most. The surrounding scenery spread out brown and barren around them, without even mountains of any note nearby to brighten the view. The family attended church services in the nearby town of Fayette. At the turn of the century, these two communities together could only claim about three hundred inhabitants. The lone store in the area was located in Fayette.[27]

The Albrechts built a small house from handmade adobe bricks and tried to make a living from farming the arid ground. The children helped on the farm and tried to find work outside their home as often as they could. Emma did housework in Fayette, earning fifty cents to a dollar per week. After six weeks, she had saved up enough money to buy a pair of shoes and an apron. In the winter, the children had to walk four miles each way to attend school.

After living in Dover for about a year, the family's adobe house caved in. Mina and her daughter, Mina, managed to stay beneath the stove which protected them. They crawled through a window to escape. Emma was buried in nearly three feet of mud and willows. It took her family and neighbors several hours to dig her out. Nearly all of their possessions were ruined, destroyed by the collapsed roof.

The family spent the next summer preparing to rebuild their home. Georg, Mina, and their children threshed grain and made new adobe bricks. Other hardships soon followed. Mina's hands broke out in running sores. For nearly four months, she could hardly use her hands and had to rely on her older children to run the household.[28]

Georg and Mina added Jacob Joseph, their tenth, and final, child to the family in June of 1883. As in Germany, Mina had little time to care for the baby. Instead, Emma looked after him and the other young children while Mina worked.

When I read about the family in Dover, I sometimes wonder if they ever wanted to quit. I wonder if Mina ever lay in bed at night and cried into her pillow when her children couldn't hear her. I wonder if discouragement ever grabbed hold of Georg, threatening to overwhelm him completely. I wonder if they ever questioned their decision or thought of their lives in Germany with regret. Sometimes I long to know how they dealt with their challenges. What enabled them to keep going?

But sometimes I think I already know. I have something of Georg and Mina's that gives me this insight—something I don't have for any ancestor before them. It's not a diary or even a letter. It's a photo of each of them.

The pictures are small, only about one square inch. The black-and-white images appear slightly out of focus, the result of being photocopied repeatedly. Even in these tiny photos, the intensity in Georg and Mina's eyes catches me off guard. Both of them are middle-aged, having already experienced their share of life's trials. Georg, with his light-colored hair, mustache, and beard, and his deep-set eyes, stares forward, his gaze strong and certain. Mina's hair is parted down the middle and pulled back, her mouth drawn downward. Yet, her eyes seem to convey compassion and worry, hardship and triumph. In these small, blurry pictures I see the determination I know they must have had.[29]

It took five years for the Albrechts to decide that Dover wasn't the place for them. Periodic droughts and floods ruined their crops year after year. In April of 1887, they packed up everything they had including pigs, horses, chickens, seven cows, and two wagons and headed off to the little town of Fremont, now in Wayne County, Utah. Johann, their only married child also came with his wife, Chasty, and daughter, Rosetta. Georg and Mina were both nearly fifty years old by this time. In Fremont, they would have to start over again.

The trip, which now is about eighty miles by road, took them nine days. Settlers had only arrived in Fremont ten years previously. The area, filled mostly with sagebrush and American Indians when they arrived, was at least as isolated as Dover.[30] The family bought a one-room house where they lived while Georg and his sons built a new home, this time made of rock.

Day-to-day life proved no less difficult in Fremont. To keep his family afloat, Georg worked in a variety of occupations. He did some masonry work in the community, including directing the building of a rock church and schoolhouse. He also built a sawmill to supplement the family's income while they cleared away land for farming.[31]

Georg and Mina spent the rest of their lives in Fremont. Their children left home one by one as they married and started families of their own. Most of them didn't go far. Just as generations had lived near one another back in Germany, many of Georg and Mina's children and grandchildren stayed nearby in Utah.

Georg died in 1914 of "old age" after a lingering illness. Mina died two years later.

Before we leave Utah for our move to Wisconsin, we decide to make one last trip to Fremont to visit my grandma. After talking to my grandma for a few hours, I drive out to the Fremont cemetery alone. I want to take some photos of the gravestones. I don't know when I will have another chance.

I park my car and get out, glad to see that there's no one else here. The day is pleasant and breezy as I enter the grounds with my camera slung over my shoulder. I take my time as I wind my way through the rows of graves. Walking through the Fremont cemetery is like attending a family reunion, only of course, all of the people are dead. I see family members — ancestors — nearly everywhere I look.

I find the gravestone of my grandfather, Rex LeRoy Albrecht. It sits alone without my grandma. I look at it for a minute, imagining my dad, aunts, and uncles gathered around for his burial. I wasn't there. Now, I take a picture to remember.

I go a few more steps and then pause to take another photo. This gravestone takes the next step back in time. Across the top of the flat, white plaque in big letters, it reads, "Albrecht" as do many of the gravestones here. "Mother: Evalena Balle, Mar 10 1889 — Feb 21 1980, Father: Earl LeRoy, May 13 1890 — May 10 1968." These are my great-grandparents.

I find the next generation not far from them. An older, plain, gray tombstone marks the site of John (the name Johann used once he arrived in the US) and Chasty Albrecht, my great-great-grandparents. I can also see the tombstones for other children of Georg and Mina. Of the ten Albrecht children, two died as babies. Six of the remaining eight are buried in Fremont. I take pictures of all of their tombstones.

I keep walking, knowing there's one gravesite I haven't seen yet. Towards the back of the cemetery sits a large, curved tombstone with leaves carved across the top. It's the tombstone of Georg and Mina. On the left side, the words say, "Wilhelmina Albrecht, Feb 27 1840 — Apr 4 1916, Mother."[32] On the right, it reads, "George F. Albrecht, Dec 20 1837 — Mar 1 1914, Father."

I snap my photo and then squat down next to the gravestone to get a closer look. Georg and Mina each have only one word to describe them—"mother" and "father." This seems appropriate. They crossed the ocean, leaving the past behind. They were the founders of their American family. Georg and Mina are the "mother" and "father" of the Utah Albrecht family, a family with members now numbering in the thousands. Their choices, their new identity, shaped all of those who came after them.

In my apartment back in Provo, I sit up and stretch my back, trying to get rid of the soreness from sleeping on the floor. I look at my watch—6:15 a.m. David and Rachel are both still asleep. I get up and wander around the apartment, looking in each of the empty rooms. *Today is really the day,* I think. In only a few hours, we'll pull out of our driveway, never to pull back in again.

Almost everything is already packed in the moving truck that sits in front of our apartment. Yesterday, David and our neighbor spent all afternoon loading stacks of boxes and our few pieces of furniture into the truck. Then, after several frustrating attempts, they managed to hook our car up to the truck so we can pull it behind us. Last night, David and I slept on the floor with a few blankets that we could throw in the truck this morning. We plan to leave as soon as we can get up and eat breakfast. It will be a long drive, especially with a not-quite-three-month-old baby riding between us.

I sit back down in a corner against the bare wall in the living room. I think of the changes that have occurred in my life during the years I've lived in Utah. When I arrived here, I was eighteen, fresh from high school, having never lived away from home before. Now, as I leave, I'm twenty-three, a college graduate, married, and the mother of a baby girl.

Although we are only going to continue school, I still feel like we are entering the real world. Moving to Utah seemed comfortable and safe. I was born here and had visited here many times since I was a child. My grandparents and every aunt and uncle on both of my parents' sides lived here. Wisconsin is different. Until our visit in April, I had never been to the state—or even met anyone from Wisconsin. Now, we will start a new life there.

A few minutes later, David wakes up, groaning as he, too, tries to stretch the stiffness from his body. We scurry around the house, getting ready and finishing the last-minute details. Finally, we're ready to leave.

As I put on my shoes, I hear a knock at the door. I open it to find my neighbor standing on our front step in her pajamas. She hands me a heavy, brown paper bag.

"I figured you could use something to eat," she says. "I made breakfast burritos for you." I peek in the bag and feel the warmth of the freshly cooked potatoes and sausage floating up to my face.

I start to tell her that it smells delicious, but find myself unable to speak. Instead, I hug her, and choke out a "thank you" once I've regained my composure.

With the bag clutched in one hand, I climb into the front seat of the moving truck, buckling Rachel into the car seat in the middle. Our truck seems to move in slow motion as we drive down the street. Yet, I don't cry. My memories of my time here don't leave me with sadness, but with a feeling of satisfied contentment. I have been happy here.

I will miss Utah. But, as our apartment disappears from view, I know the time has come for us to move on.

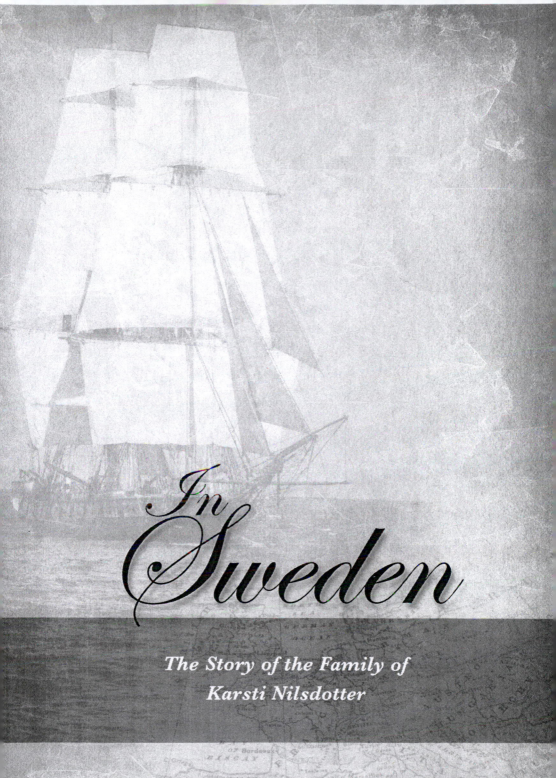

In Sweden

The Story of the Family of Karsti Nilsdotter

PART TWO

SWEDISH FAMILY TREE

Nils Jeppson
b. Abt 1734 in Svinarp
*(m. also Kirsti Pehrsdotter and
Kirsti Olofsdotter)*

Nils Nilsson
b. 1763 in Blentarp
(m. also Kerstina Andersdotter)

Marna Pehrsdotter
b. 1755 in Veberöd

Karna Larsdotter
b. 1761 in Bosarp

Nils Nilsson
b. 1786 in Svinarp

Lisbeth Nilsdotter
b. 1799 in Everlöv

*Karsti Nilsdotter
b. 1843 in Vallby

*the journey taker in this section
See appendix for individual family groups
All listed births took place in Skåne, Sweden

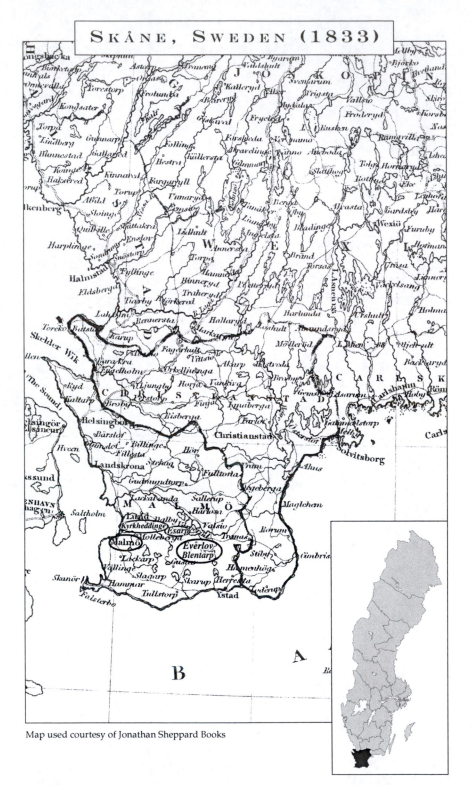

SKÅNE, SWEDEN (1833)

Map used courtesy of Jonathan Sheppard Books

CLERICAL SURVEY RECORD OF NILS NILSSON AND
KARNA LARSDOTTER'S FAMILY

CHAPTER FIVE

ORDINARY LIVES:

KARSTI'S
GRANDPARENTS

The condo is silent except for the sound of soft snoring coming from Taylor, my one-year-old, as he sleeps with his head resting on my shoulder. I have been sitting in this position, rocking him in this rhythm for thirty minutes now, afraid to do anything that might disturb him. But now my desire to stop the monotonous back-and-forth motion has overcome my fear of waking my sick son. I hold my breath and stop rocking. Taylor doesn't stir.

I let my breath out slowly as my body sinks into the rocking chair. We're in a rented condo in Park City, Utah, attending David's family reunion. It's our first time back to visit Utah since we moved to Wisconsin nearly three years ago. David and Rachel have left to go to dinner with his family. I've stayed behind, as I have throughout this past week. Both David and my sister-in-law offered to stay with Taylor so I could get out of the condo. But I declined. I didn't want to leave Taylor and I was too worn out to be social anyway.

Taylor has been sicker than he has ever been before. For the past five days, he has thrown up almost every piece of food and every ounce of liquid we've given him. My week has been filled with changing his clothes, my clothes, and the bed sheets, rushing him to the bathroom, offering him liquids one teaspoon at a time, talking to our nurse on the phone, and worrying. David's uncle is a doctor and has checked Taylor periodically for dehydration. Only this has prevented us from taking him to the hospital.

Besides taking care of Taylor, I have spent my time talking to my mom on the phone. She's also in Utah, about an hour away at the hospital in Salt Lake City with my grandmother. Last week, my grandma's doctor found a cancerous lump near her collarbone. They scheduled surgery immediately.

It hasn't exactly been a relaxing vacation.

After soaking in the stillness for a few minutes, I reach for my binder filled with family history papers that's lying on the floor, careful not to jostle Taylor as I do. Tomorrow morning, I'm going to the Family History Library in Salt Lake City. Both distance and busyness have prevented me from visiting the library since we moved to Wisconsin, and I'm excited to return.

For our first two years in Wisconsin, I juggled graduate school and parenting. I finished my Master's degree a year ago, just one month before Taylor was born. While I was in school, I filed away all thoughts of my ancestors. I could hardly find time to brush my hair between renditions of "Ring-Around-the-Rosy," late-night fights with the statistics computer program, and trying to cope with endless morning sickness. Tracing my family tree was out of the question.

I spent the first few months after finishing school adjusting to life with a new baby — and life without school or a full-time job. As soon as I started getting enough sleep not to run into the walls when I got up with Taylor in the middle of the night, a restless feeling began to come over me. I needed something else in my life. I had plenty of things to fill my time — grocery shopping, fixing dinner, cleaning up messes, changing diapers, driving children to doctors' appointments, and so on. But I needed something else — something outside of my children.

My thoughts turned immediately to family history research. It had been my passion before. Maybe it could fill the gaps now. I dug through my old files and folders, searching for a person or a family line to focus on. Finally, my attention settled on another journey taker: Kerstina Nilsdotter, the mother of Chasty Harris, Johann Albrecht's wife. Kerstina (or Karsti as she went by) took her journey to the US from Sweden alone at age seventeen.

Over the last few months, I had ordered microfilms of parish records to my local Family History Center, looking for any trace of Karsti in Sweden. I soon realized that I had to first sort out their naming system. Just like the Germans, the Swedes used only a handful of names, but they complicated things even further by using a patronymic naming system. In this system, a child's last name was based on the first name of the child's father with either "son" or "dotter" added on to the end. Last names changed every generation. Half of the people in a village could have the last name Nilsson but not be related to each other at all. They just happened to all have fathers named Nils.

After a few false starts, I found Karsti's birth in the parish records of Kyrkheddinge, a small town in southern Sweden, only about fifteen miles from the western coast. But I knew this couldn't be my starting point. To understand Karsti and her journey, I had to go back even further—to her roots.

Then several weeks ago, my family tree suddenly plunged hundreds of years further back into the past. I stumbled onto another family tree, one I hadn't known existed. A distant cousin had hired a professional genealogist to trace the family. But I had learned my lesson with Christoph Harprecht. I intend to verify this family tree carefully. On this trip to the Family History Library, I will focus on Karsti's parents' families.

As far back as I know, and probably much further than that, my Swedish ancestors lived as peasants in what was then Malmöhus County, one of two counties in Skåne, the southernmost province of Sweden.[1] Although my Swedish ancestors lived just across the Baltic Sea from my ancestors in Mecklenburg, Germany, my Swedish ancestors' homeland was far removed from Mecklenburg in many ways. While Mecklenburg was backwards, Skåne was forward-looking. While Mecklenburg was one of the poorest German states, Skåne was the "breadbasket" of Sweden. Mecklenburg was one of the least-populated areas of Germany. Skåne was the most densely populated part of Sweden. Mecklenburg lagged behind all the German states. Skåne was the success story of Sweden.

The comparisons can be deceptive though. The discomforts and tragedies of peasant life were, perhaps, universal. Karsti's family, like Georg and Mina's in Mecklenburg, were peasants. In fact, ninety-five percent of Swedish society lived as common people, or peasants. "People of status," including nobles, members of the clergy and educated professionals such as doctors, lawyers, and military officials, comprised the other five percent. As in Mecklenburg, the amount of land people owned determined their position in the peasant social hierarchy.[2]

Landed peasants, at the top of the peasant social order in Sweden, owned enough land to support their families comfortably. In early times, this meant owning at least one *mantal* of land. A *mantal* wasn't an exact measure of land, but instead a relative amount that varied from place to place. Developed centuries earlier, a *mantal* supposedly represented the minimum amount of land a farmer needed to support his family. As time passed, farmers divided their holdings into smaller and smaller pieces in order to pass them on to multiple heirs. Eventually, it became rare for a peasant to own an entire *mantal* of land. Small improvements in agriculture also meant that a farmer needed less land to support his family. During Karsti's grandparents' lives, a family could live decently on 1/16 of a *mantal*, making this the arbitrary division historians now use to place a family in the landed peasants group.[3]

Karsti's father, Nils Nilsson (Nils was one of the handful of names that the Swedes liked — both of Karsti's grandfathers and her brother were also named Nils) grew up in a landed peasant family. With 3/8 of a *mantal*, Nils' parents, Marna Pehrsdotter and Nils Jepsson, likely enjoyed a relatively comfortable lifestyle.[4] They probably employed young people to assist with farm and household tasks. The male head of household in landed peasant families in Skåne developed a reputation for being fat and lazy. Nils Jepsson may have performed little hard labor himself, but instead directed tasks among his family and hired help. Nils Jepsson might have spent a lot of time drinking home-brewed alcohol, eating, or sitting around smoking a pipe.[5]

As in Germany, landless people fell at the other end of the economic spectrum. These people subsisted mostly by working as day laborers on other people's farms. Their situation wasn't as dire as their counterparts in Mecklenburg, but they still lived in unpleasant conditions and struggled to obtain the basic necessities.[6]

Karsti's mother, Lisbeth Nilsdotter, grew up in a family that fit between these two groups. Lisbeth's parents, Karna Larsdotter and Nils Nilsson (Karsti's maternal grandfather will always be referred to as Nils Nilsson here to distinguish him from Karsti's father and Lisbeth's future husband who is also named Nils Nilsson, but will be referred to only as Nils), owned 1/32 of a *mantal*.[7] Families with less than 1/16 of a *mantal* fell into the category of "semi-landless peasants." These peasants did own land, but not enough to support their families fully. They had to supplement the family's income by working on other people's land as day laborers or by performing a trade on the side. Nils Nilsson chose another occupation to make ends meet for his family.

Although little information survives about Karsti's parents' families, I can still describe their lives because of one simple fact — their families were ordinary. On one hand, I find this convenient. Since nothing distinguished them from the masses of people around them, what I learn about the population in general I can also apply to my ancestors.

But sometimes I wish I could find something that indicated they were different — that my ancestors were special. Sometimes I find their ordinariness a little disappointing.

As I flip through my notes, the front door flings open. The condo fills with commotion as David's family bursts in, oblivious to my efforts at shushing them.

"How's Taylor?" my sister-in-law asks as she runs over and kisses him on the head. He squirms and lifts his head, sleepily opening his eyes to look at her.

"Mommy, guess what?" Rachel jumps up and down. "They played some music and I danced so beautiful." She twirls in a circle to demonstrate.

Their voices, laughing and talking about the evening, envelop the room. I listen for a few minutes, until Taylor's whimpers develop into a full cry.

"Did you bring me something to eat?" I ask David.

"Oh." He pauses. "I forgot." He looks apologetic for a moment, before his attention returns to the conversation. I try not to show my irritation as I get up to take Taylor upstairs. Rachel follows at my feet, holding an open package of animal crackers she found on the floor.

"Mommy, why did Taylor get a cracker and I didn't?" she asks.

Upstairs, I try to lie Taylor down in the portable crib we brought with us. This only makes him cry harder. Instead, I hold him in one arm as I struggle to help Rachel put her pajamas on with my other arm. My moment of peace feels long ago already.

"I want Aunt Julie to read my stories," Rachel cries, rubbing her eyes, worn out from the excitement of the day. After telling me she doesn't want to wear these pajamas, she doesn't want to brush her teeth, she doesn't want to sleep "all alonely" in the room before anyone else comes to bed, she's too thirsty to fall sleep, too scared to stay there, and not tired at all, she falls asleep just minutes after I leave her room.

Two hours later, I climb into bed next to David. Taylor, who still refuses to sleep in his crib, lies between us. I close my eyes, my whole body ready for this day to be finished.

A sound that has grown too familiar wakes me up—Taylor gagging. I grab him and run for the bathroom, only able to think that I don't want to have to wash the sheets again. In my haste, I run full-speed into the television set protruding from the wall, fortunately hitting it with the arm that is not holding Taylor. I stumble into the bathroom, but not in time. Taylor's little body convulses as he throws up all over me.

I sit down on the floor, my arm throbbing from my crash with the television. David runs in behind me, looking disoriented. He surveys the scene and quickly takes Taylor. Although I've been relatively calm throughout the week, without warning, I begin to cry. David cleans up the mess and somehow manages to put Taylor down in his own bed while I sit on the bathroom floor, tears streaming down my cheeks. After a few minutes, I pull myself together enough to change my clothes and wash off my arms. Then, I walk slowly through the dark room to my bed, making sure to avoid the television this time.

"Are you okay?" David asks tentatively as he climbs into bed next to me.

"I'm fine," I answer, not wanting to talk. He knows not to push it further. When he's convinced I'm not going to say anything else, he rolls over to go to sleep.

Alone with my thoughts, that unwelcome restless feeling that has been festering near the surface washes over me again. I try to think of what the feeling is, but it doesn't seem to have a name. It's a nothingness—a feeling of being in a narrow, long hallway with no room to stretch.

I suddenly realize what it is. It's a feeling of ordinariness.

To me, few labels cut deeper than "ordinary." My greatest desire is to reach beyond ordinary, to do something that matters. When my descendants describe me, I would rather them use almost any adjective besides ordinary. Yet, as I lie in my bed tonight, I feel the strong pull of ordinary life.

I think of my assumption that Karsti's grandparents were ordinary and I feel a twinge of guilt. It seems harsh to place this label on people I know so little about. Perhaps Marna showed others in the community great kindness, and made a lasting impact on many lives. Perhaps Nils Jeppson came up with innovative techniques that he used on his farm that had never been used before. Maybe Karna possessed amazing artistic talent and could weave rugs that brought people from miles around to admire. Maybe Nils Nilsson studied everything he could get his hands on, and was the most knowledgeable person in the area. Perhaps, my ancestors weren't ordinary after all. But, if they weren't, no evidence has survived of it.

Now, I wonder, will there be any evidence that prevents my descendants from drawing the same conclusion about me?

The next morning, David drops me off at the Family History Library at 8:00. I plan to spend the day looking for more information about the family of Karsti's father, Nils.

Nils's name falls near the end of his family's chart. When his father, Nils Jeppson, married his mother, Marna, in 1777 he was marrying for the third time. He brought four children ranging in age from three to fifteen to the marriage. Marna was twenty-one. With a forty-three-year-old husband and a fifteen-year-old stepdaughter, Marna almost fit in better as a child than a mother in the family. The couple settled in Nils Jeppson's home in Svinarp, a tiny village that belonged to the Esarp parish, only minutes away from Kyrkheddinge. Marna and Nils Jeppson soon began adding children of their own to the family. Their fourth child, Nils (Karsti's father), was born in 1786.

As with many of my ancestors, I have an image of Nils's childhood. For this one I can rely on a record I don't have for most of my ancestors—one that gives such an intimate look at the family that I almost feel like I'm intruding on their privacy as I read it. It's not a diary or a stack of personal letters. Instead it is Marna's probate record which includes a list of the family's possessions, down to the design on the bed sheets and the clothing in Marna's wardrobe at the time of her death.[8] As I wind my first microfilm on the reel, I think of their family.

In the early hours of the morning, before the first rays of sunlight break through, the homestead lies still. With cross-beamed mud walls and a thatched straw roof, the home looks quaint—from the side view. The front view gives a different impression. Large piles of animal dung, which are for later use as fertilizer, spill over near the entryway.

The homestead wraps around a large, open courtyard, with the buildings joining together to form a square. Many of the family's animals, which include fifteen pigs, seven geese, eleven horses, seven cows, three calves, two oxen, seven bulls, thirteen sheep, one ram, and two lambs, sleep in their stalls just inside the front and side of the homestead.

Next to the animals, the family has a barn. Here, Nils Jeppson keeps an assortment of tools including two harrows, several carts, two sledges, three wheelbarrows, a wood ax, a bucksaw, two chisels, two ploughs, three iron hay forks, two hay hooks, one shackle, a pair of leather harnesses, four scythes, and one hoe—just to name a few. Other rooms in the homestead include a threshing floor, food storage room, salting room, and peat (a mixture of decomposed plant material that was used for fuel) storage room. Several maidservants and farmhands, all in their late teens or early twenties, sleep in their rooms located on the back sides of the house.

The sunlight begins to trickle in the small window in the back room where Nils Jeppson, Marna, and their children sleep. Sensing the sunlight even in their sleep, Marna and Nils Jeppson begin to stir in their large pinewood bed covered with linen sheets and a large, down quilt.

Nils Jeppson stretches his back, his muscles stiff. Marna climbs out of bed, careful not to disturb baby Nils, only a few months old, sleeping snuggly in their bed. She opens the heavy wooden chest on the floor and sorts through some clothes before selecting a practical, green, homespun shirt with four pairs of silver fasteners and a black skirt, also with silver fasteners. She wraps a linen head covering over her hair, then pulls out a newly washed white apron.

The children slowly roll off their mattresses that are laid out on the floor. They moan a little to each other, but know better than to complain to their parents about their morning chores. The older ones help the younger ones get ready. Marna wraps Nils in a sling so Nils Jeppson can stack their beds against the wall. They'll need the space for the other activities that will take place in this room. The first is breakfast.

Once she's ready, Marna goes to the kitchen, next door to the room where they slept. Here, she oversees the breakfast preparations done mostly by the maidservants. The room is filled with her kitchen tools—a heavy iron-tiled stove, a cauldron, various pots and pans all made of iron or copper except for one more expensive bronze frying pan, fourteen pewter plates, several wooden jugs, and various baskets, bins, and tubs for storage.

The women prepare a typical breakfast of sandwiches. Later they will prepare barley porridge or some kind of soup, as well as sausage, cheese, and sourdough bread spread with pork fat. They also bring the *aquavit*, or home-brewed alcohol, to the table. It will accompany breakfast, as it does nearly every meal. The copper still that turns grain or potatoes into *aquavit* is one of their most valuable possessions after their animals.

When the women have finished the preparations, the family and their hired help sit down to eat at the pinewood table that they pull out from the wall in the main room. Five of them sit on wooden chairs with plaited straw seats. The others sit on makeshift benches.

Everyone finds his or her designated place. Nils Jeppson sits at the head of the table with Marna to his right. The senior farmhand sits to Nils Jeppson's left. Other farmhands, male children, and the younger daughters sit in descending order by age (and seniority in the case of farmhands) from Nils Jeppson. The older daughters and maidservants take their meals standing in order to serve those at the table. Children and lower-ranking help remain silent throughout the meal.

The day's work begins after breakfast. Each family member, farmhand, and maidservant has an assigned task—a part to play in making the home and farm run smoothly.[9]

Farming for Nils's family wasn't much different than it had been for his father's family or his grandfather's family. If anything, it had become more complicated. In order to divide the land fairly between heirs and to allow plots of land to connect to water sources, farmers had divided their land into long narrow strips for generations, sometimes narrower than the plow itself. This strip system has led some to speculate that Skåne had the most poorly used land in the world.

The continual buying and selling, dividing and inheriting, of these long, narrow pieces of land meant that farmers with significant landholdings, like Nils Jeppson, often owned many — sometimes over a hundred — pieces of unconnected land scattered throughout the area. Some of the family's holdings were probably an hour's walk from their home. Because of this, they left some land dormant; the strips being too far away to make planting and harvesting there practical. The division of land into narrow strips also made it impossible for Nils Jeppson to harvest his land without disturbing the land that surrounded his. To combat this problem, village associations often assigned days for planting and harvesting.[10]

Tasks on the family farm coincided with the calendar. Plowing took place in spring, followed by planting. Haymaking occurred in July. In August and September, the household focused on harvesting grain. During harvest time, work continued nearly around the clock, sometimes beginning at 4:00 a.m. and not finishing until after midnight (although they often took an afternoon rest). After harvesting, Nils Jeppson and his help concentrated on threshing, usually for twelve to thirteen hours a day. Other tasks included repairing fences, caring for livestock, and milking cows. As soon as he was old enough, Nils probably also helped with these tasks.

Marna may have helped in the field from time to time. She also cooked, spun, wove, mended, and oversaw the household. Because the family had the financial resources to employ help, Marna probably was able to spend some time with Nils and his siblings when they were young. Still, she often had to turn the task of watching the young children over to others.

During the summer and intense planting and harvesting times, the family had little energy or time for anything besides the necessities of life. Long hours of daylight meant long hours of work. When the days grew shorter though, the men sometimes relaxed after the sun went down. Nils Jeppson may have smoked his pipe, told stories, and played with his children. Marna likely gathered with other women in the community in the evenings to spin or weave and chat.[11]

In this way, days blended into weeks and weeks into months as the rhythm of daily life continued. Nils Jeppson planted, drove the plow, and threshed the hay the same way over and over again. Marna cooked meals, spun cloth, and watched children, with each day not much different than the one before. The same tasks filled their lives hour after hour, year after year.

I have managed to squeeze one more half day at the Family History Library into our Utah itinerary. The night before my second visit to the library, my mom calls to ask if I can spend a few hours sitting with my grandma in the hospital. The anesthetic from her surgery has affected her short-term memory, making my grandma confused and unable to be left alone. I haven't seen her since her surgery because she didn't want to be exposed to Taylor's illness, even indirectly. I decide to sit with her in the afternoon and then walk over to the library, located only a few blocks from the hospital.

My brother, Scott, greets me in the hall outside my grandma's room the next afternoon. He has taken the first shift sitting with her today.

"It's bad," he whispers at the doorway. "She basically ran me out of the room. She kept asking if my kids were still sick." My brother, who is still in college, doesn't have any children.

I take a deep breath and walk into my grandma's room. I try not to look alarmed as my eyes meet hers. She sits in her bed, surrounded by cables and wires connecting her to various machines and monitors. Her face is pale and thin, but she smiles when she sees me. Then her smile fades.

"You've been sick?" She looks at me suspiciously.

"Taylor was sick, Grandma. But he's better now," I explain.

"Well, maybe you should sit over there." She motions to a chair on the other side of the room. I sit down obediently.

She tells me about the nurses and the food, her eyes never quite focusing. Her sentences jumble together and she keeps asking every few minutes if I've been sick.

"I'm really tired. I need to take a little rest," she says finally.

"Sure, go ahead," I say.

"Come over here and sit by me," my grandma instructs. I sit on the edge of her bed. She smiles at me as she pats my hand.

"There's something I need to tell you," she says earnestly, her voice barely audible.

I lean closer to hear what she'll say.

"You're special, do you know that?" She pauses as if I should answer, her eyes intent and her voice clear for the first time all afternoon.

I blink back tears, unable to respond.

"I've always known that about you."

She grabs my hand tightly and closes her eyes.

At the library that evening, I scroll through more rolls of micro-filmed records of the Lutheran Church, trying to follow Nils's family. I locate a record that shows that his mother, Marna, died of an inflammatory fever in 1791 at age thirty-six. Her probate lists the names of her sons, including: Anders, age ten; Nils, age five; and Pehr, age "1/2," as the record says. Marna also left behind two daughters: Kirsti, nearly eight years old, and Ingar, only two. For the third time, Nils Jeppson buried a wife who had children who wouldn't remember her. As I look at the record, I can see the family standing in front of the Esarp church to say good-bye to their mother.

Nils stands near his mother's grave, his older sister's arm around him as if to shield him. He looks around at his family. Big tears stream down Kirsti's cheeks as they have all day. Anders stands off by himself, his face white and his eyes red and swollen. His father, with the baby in his arms, stares blankly ahead, no expression on his face.

Ingar huddles at her father's feet. All morning she has been asking their father where their mother is. Their father told them God had taken her to live with him. Ingar doesn't understand, but Nils does. He just doesn't understand why. He asked his father why God needed her more than they do, but his father had just said that there were some things even fathers don't understand.

Nils Jeppson never remarried. Nils's stepsister, Anna, twenty years older than he was, likely filled the mother role in his life.

I put the Esarp parish death records on the microfilm machine and wind carefully through them. At last, I find what I'm looking for: Nils Jeppson's death record. Nils Jeppson died on January 24, 1806, almost fifteen years after Marna. Karsti's father, Nils, was nineteen years old at the time. Far from the oldest, Nils didn't inherit the family homestead. Instead, he probably took his portion of the inheritance and struck out on his own.

Nils Jeppson's death is listed in the records on a page with a half a dozen other deaths. Poor handwriting makes it difficult to even recognize his name. The record gives his age as seventy-four, but I can't decipher the cause of death. Nothing in this record — or any other records of Nils's family — sets them apart from the people around him.

I think of my grandma's words at the hospital. Every grandmother thinks her grandchildren are special. But I want her words to be true.

Since we now live in Wisconsin, my trips to the Family History Library in Utah are rare and wonderful occasions. But only a month after this trip to the library, I get to make another visit. One of my best friends from college is getting married in Salt Lake City. At the last minute, I decide to go to the wedding and stay a few extra days to do research. This time, I will focus on the family of Karsti's mother, Lisbeth Nilsdotter.

First, I have to figure out what to do with my children. David can't take the week off from his studies, so I have to come up with another plan. I succeed in convincing my mother-in-law to come to Wisconsin to entertain Rachel. But, I fail to interest her in chasing a wild thirteen-month-old. I have no choice. Taylor has to come with me.

I'm determined not to let this minor kink disrupt my research plans. Instead, I call everyone I know in Utah in search of babysitters. With a great deal of effort, I arrange a complex schedule. During the times I can't find a babysitter, I decide I'll bring Taylor with me to the library. I'm aware that research libraries aren't the natural habitats of thirteen-month-olds. But, I have a plan: the baby backpack. I'll carry Taylor around with me while I gather information.

By the time I get off the plane and to the baggage claim area at the Salt Lake City airport, my brother, Scott, is already there waiting for me. He has agreed to take the first babysitting turn. I hand him Taylor and the diaper bag, wish him luck, and head straight to the library. As I walk, I consider what I already know about Lisbeth.

Like her husband, Lisbeth entered her family well into their story. Her parents had married in 1780 in Everlöv, a village about ten miles east of Kyrkheddinge. Although Lisbeth wasn't around yet to experience it, her parents' lives together had gotten off to a shaky start. On their wedding day, her father, Nils Nilsson, was sixteen years old. Her mother, Karna, was nineteen—and seven months pregnant.

For people in the parish, the unusual part of the marriage wouldn't have been the obvious baby on the way. As in Mecklenburg, illegitimate births and births from prenuptial conception (or children born to married couples, but conceived before the marriage) were common.[12] But, their ages would have given townspeople something to talk about. The average age at marriage in Skåne was twenty-nine for males and twenty-seven for females. A marriage between two teenagers was nearly unheard of. In fact, less than three percent of marriages included a groom younger than twenty years of age.[13]

Most peasants didn't marry until they had some way to provide for themselves. For landed peasants, this usually meant waiting until their parents retired and passed the land on to the next generation.

Although all the children couldn't inherit the homestead and land, they still received a portion of their parents' wealth and belongings. Those who stood to inherit little from their parents worked for others until they had saved enough to establish an independent household.

Neighbors didn't expect a couple to wait until marriage to conceive a child. But they did expect them to wait until the child could be brought into a financially stable home. As mere teenagers, Nils Nilsson and Karna would not have established their own household yet, and had little hope of providing adequately for their child.

Nils Nilsson had few options available to him. At age sixteen, he was married and a father-to-be. He had a family depending on him — but no land, no money, no home, and few skills. So, Nils Nilsson chose an occupation that could provide something for his family immediately. He joined the military as a cavalryman.[14]

Becoming a cavalryman guaranteed the family some way to make a living, but only a meager living. The military system mandated that people living on a farm or a combination of farms of a certain size had to contribute one soldier. The people provided the soldier with a little cottage and a plot of land as well as some other basic provisions. Those in the cavalry also received a horse. During peacetime, Nils Nilsson farmed his land and hired himself out to other farmers in the area as a day laborer. He also attended military training for several weeks of the year. In times of war, Nils Nilsson would be away for months, leaving Karna to take care of their family alone.[15]

Joining the military wasn't a decision to take lightly. Sweden spent a large amount of time at war which made the risk of death for Nils Nilsson very real. And, the military required no small commitment. Records indicate that Nils Nilsson served in the cavalry for at least twenty-five years, a length of time that would not have been unusual. Nils Nilsson managed to spend most of those twenty-five years at home as Sweden's wars began to slow down.

Nils Nilsson and Karna made their home in Östarp, a village that belonged to the Everlöv parish. There, they had a child every two or three years for the first twenty-one years of their marriage for a total of eleven children. Lisbeth was the ninth child, born in 1799. Of the eleven, two died as children.

The higher survival rate of Nils Nilsson and Karna's children was consistent with a decline in mortality that was spreading across Europe. The discovery of a vaccine for smallpox by English physician Edward Jenner in 1796 as well as other medical advances contributed to longer life spans. Improved nutrition kept people healthier. Hygiene took some important steps forward, decreasing the spread of disease. Perhaps most notably, the introduction of the potato provided peasants with a cheap, healthy, mostly dependable source of food that became a staple in many of their diets. Nearly all of these innovations occurred in northwestern Europe first, where the standard of living was already higher.

Although mortality rates were shrinking, a decline in fertility didn't occur until nearly the turn of the twentieth century. This resulted in larger families.[16] Karna and Nils Nilsson's family was larger than average—mostly because of their younger ages at marriage. Karna had her first child at age nineteen. She was forty-three when her last child was born.

Today in the library, I try to collect all the records I can about Lisbeth's childhood. I have more than the parish birth, marriage, and death records to rely on to tell her story. I have another type of parish record available—clerical survey records.

Clerical surveys functioned almost like census records, listing everyone in a village in their family group every few years. These thorough records contain much more than names—they also record birthdays, marriages, deaths, occupations, addresses, and who moved in and out of the parish. In a column for remarks, the pastor could write down other information as well.

Although genealogists use the clerical surveys for the dates and places, these records contain another piece of often-overlooked information. Clerical surveys show the results of a religious quiz. The records were created as the parish pastor visited each family in their home. He had them recite Martin Luther's Catechisms and then asked them questions to assess their understanding of them. He evaluated their knowledge and marked the records accordingly.

The surveys offer an opportunity to know something individual about my ancestors. I can know how well they knew the catechisms (at least in theory—in practice the marks are difficult to read or interpret). More interesting than what their grades tell me about them is what the existence of these quizzes tells me about their way of life. The information contained in Luther's Small and Large Catechisms and other of Luther's writings shaped the very character of Swedish society.

The Small Catechisms in Sweden consisted of five parts (in most other countries there were six parts). These included the Ten Commandments, The Creed, The Lord's Prayer, Holy Baptism and Confession, and The Sacrament of the Altar. At the end, Luther included a Morning Prayer and Evening Prayer. Luther intended for people to memorize the Small Catechisms. The Swedes took this seriously, as the clerical survey records demonstrate. Luther indicated that fathers should use the Small Catechisms to instruct their families. The Large Catechisms, with more thorough instruction and detail, were meant for pastors and other teachers.

The catechisms reinforced the prevailing social order. First, they reminded peasants of their complete dependence on God for their daily bread, their protection from evil, and their ultimate salvation. This visit by the local pastor also emphasized his position of authority in their lives. The pastor could rebuke the head of household for not teaching his family correctly, or for not following other church rules. Finally, the catechisms reinforced the idea of women's subservience to men. Many pastors required girls to recite "God has placed man in the world to head woman."[17]

As I look at the coded marks in the columns for the catechisms and prayers in the entries of Lisbeth and her siblings, I imagine the pastor sitting in their home. Lisbeth sits near the end of a long row of girls, interspersed with a couple of boys. She concentrates on not fidgeting as she listens to the pastor asking her sister some questions. She catches her father's eye across the room. He frowns just a little, and she sits up straighter, remembering that she must represent the family well.

After sucking all the time I can out of Scott, there are still two more hours remaining until the library closes. After thanking my brother for his help, I hike back to the library with Taylor in the baby backpack and a stack of binders in my arms. I head for the Scandinavian counter that is staffed with research experts. I'm hoping to get help reading a town name recorded in one of these clerical surveys.

As I wait by the counter for my turn, Taylor discovers a new game. From his strategic place in the baby backpack, he takes hold of a fistful of my hair and yanks with all his might. I gasp and reach back to grab his hand in an effort to protect my scalp. Without letting go of Taylor with my left hand, I try to pull the document out of my binder with my right hand.

"Can I help you?" a stern-looking, older woman asks me.

Just at that moment, Taylor seizes a clump of my hair with his other hand and shrieks gleefully as he pulls out another fistful.

"Yes," I say trying to keep my voice even. "I need help with this record."

I hand her the document and point out the word I can't read. She studies it for a moment, then pulls out a magnifying glass to get a closer look.

Having grown bored of pulling out my hair, Taylor now throws himself from one side of the baby backpack to the other, grunting and reaching for the floor as he hits each side. His grunts grow louder and more intense with each passing second. He's not going to tolerate confinement any longer. In resignation, I sit the baby backpack on the floor and pull him out.

"Dadada," he chatters, instantly in better spirits.

"It looks like these first three letters are *G-U-V*," she says, pointing. I lean over to look. Taylor makes a lunge to grab the record.

"Yes, that's what I thought," I agree, absently sitting Taylor on the floor where he can't reach my paper.

As soon as Taylor's feet touch the floor, he takes off toward the nearest bookshelf, his pudgy little legs stumbling and lurching as they struggle to keep up with the rest of his body.

The woman pulls out a reference book. "There isn't a town with a name like that in this parish," she tells me.

That I know.

"There isn't a parish in Malmöhus County with a similar name either."

That I also know.

"Let's see…" she pulls out another book. Taylor catches sight of a shelf filled with pamphlets and flyers and heads toward it at full speed, babbling and drooling as he goes. When he gets there, he pauses long enough to smile sweetly at me.

"Maybe it's *G-A-V*."

Taylor grabs a handful of flyers and begins scrunching them up and flinging them around. I snatch him up, stick him back into the baby backpack, and struggle to put my arms through the straps.

"I don't see that either." She shuts the book and peers at me over the edge of her glasses. "I don't know what it says."

Taylor, realizing he's confined again, lets out a bloodcurdling shriek. I know just how he feels.

Back at my aunt's house that night, I lay out the clerical survey and parish records, trying to shape the timeline of the family. Before Lisbeth's birth, her father likely served in a war. Then, when Lisbeth was not quite ten years old, Nils Nilsson's role in the cavalry may have interrupted their family again.

As countries joined Napoleon's Continental System one by one, Sweden clung to an alliance with England against Napoleon. In February of 1808, Russia, an ally of France, attacked Finland (then part of Sweden) using Sweden's support of England as their justification.

More likely, Russia was simply taking advantage of an opportunity to incorporate Finland into Russia.

The resulting war was one of the biggest disasters in Swedish history. Defeat in Finland came quickly. The troops, of which Nils Nilsson may have been a part, suffered more from the conditions than the fighting. Poor planning, limited supplies, and inadequate training led to thousands of soldiers dying of cold, hunger, and disease.[18]

Looking at the records of Lisbeth's life, my mind drifts to a scene.

Lisbeth opens her eyes in her bed. Next to her, her sisters breathe deeply, their faces relaxed in sleep. Lisbeth looks around the room, trying to find what woke her. Then she sees her mother in her dressing gown, her hair tied back, looking out the window.

She has woken to this before and knows that every night before her mother goes to sleep, she checks out the window. When Lisbeth asked her about it, her mother had smiled and then sighed.

"It's silly, isn't it?" she said to Lisbeth. "I just have to look one more time for your father before I can sleep."

But Lisbeth doesn't think it's silly. Her father has been gone for months now—Lisbeth can't even remember how many it has been. The news that comes back from the war front is always bad—people sick and dying. They all worry about what will happen to their father.

Lisbeth sees her mother stand up and walk to her bed. Before climbing in, she kneels to pray. Lisbeth knows what she's praying for and she also says a little prayer in her heart that God will bring her father home again.

At the beginning of 1809, Russian troops descended on Sweden. Russia's allies, Denmark-Norway and France, became involved. Sensing impending collapse, a Swedish general, with support from much of the army, walked into the king's room and arrested him. A temporary government tried to salvage the situation, making peace with everyone. In the end, Sweden had to cede over a third of its territory and join Napoleon's Continental System.

Over the following months and years, Sweden struggled to find solid footing again. It took only two weeks for a drafting committee to put together a new constitution that lasted, with only a few revisions, until 1970. Sweden also needed a new ruler. After considerable maneuvering and mind changing, the temporary government settled on an unusual candidate—Jean Baptiste Jules Bernadotte, a French general. The royal family adopted Bernadotte, who assumed the more Swedish-sounding name of Karl Johann.

Nils Nilsson likely found himself called upon to prepare for battle once again. When Napoleon's troops began to weaken, England and her allies saw their chance. Although Nils Nilsson was a middle-aged man by that time, he may have followed Karl Johann as he led Swedish troops into his former homeland.

That was Nils Nilsson's — and Sweden's — last war. In 1814, Sweden settled into a period of peace — the longest continuous period of peace for any country in European history. In part, Sweden just didn't have the strength or resources to wage war anymore.[19]

My friend's wedding is the next day. I dash back to the library briefly between the ceremony and the luncheon, but I have no other time for research. I'm counting on Thursday being my big day. Thursday morning though, I learn that the first of my two babysitters is in the midst of a family crisis and she is unable to watch Taylor. I decide instead to take Taylor with me to some history museums downtown.

On the drive, Taylor falls asleep. This gives me new hope. Perhaps, I think, he'll sleep in the baby backpack. Despite the unpleasantness of my last attempt, it seems worth a try. So, I park the car, carefully lift Taylor, still asleep, into the baby backpack and set off for the library.

Once I'm downstairs on the international research floor, I shuffle through my papers until I find the page I need. After thirty-three years in Östarp, Lisbeth's family moved to Kornheddinge, a village in the parish of Kyrkheddinge.[20] Lisbeth was thirteen when they moved. Nine years after their move, Karna died. This page gives the information I need to locate Karna's probate record.

I find a deserted area and pull the baby backpack off. The second I set it down, Taylor's head perks up. In only minutes, it becomes apparent that there's no hope of keeping him in the baby backpack. So, I put him on the floor, determined to find the probate as quickly as possible.

Taylor wanders between the readers, jabbering to the other patrons. Every sound he makes echoes off the walls of the otherwise silent library. After bouncing him on my knee, turning the reel while standing up, and chasing him down several aisles, I locate the record. I copy it and rush out of the library, clutching Taylor with one hand and the document with the other. I feel as if I have finished a wrestling match.

I pull out the probate when I get to the car. Like Marna's probate, Karna's probate gives a long, detailed list of the family's possessions. It shows that despite their difficult start, Lisbeth's parents created a solid life for their family. For one thing, they had acquired more land than the small soldier's allotment in Östarp. The probate also shows that Nils Nilsson had assembled a large collection of carpentry tools over the years—evidently having done carpentry work on the side. There is also a list of people who owe the family money which suggests that Nils Nilsson and Karna may have loaned money to people in the community as a business, charging interest until the people repaid the loan.[21]

Karna's probate also records that when she died, all of her children gathered in Kornheddinge to receive their inheritance and pay their respects to their mother. Many made the trip from nearby towns. Lisbeth was twenty-two when she joined her brothers and sisters for the funeral of their mother. Five of Lisbeth's older siblings had already married and begun families of their own. They probably came with their spouses and perhaps their children too.

I like to think of all of them gathered in the family home after the funeral service. I imagine them hugging one another, crying together, and comforting their father. Mostly though, I picture them sitting together sharing stories—personal, meaningful stories of their mother. To everyone else, Karna may have been ordinary. But Lisbeth and her brothers and sisters must have known what made her special.

After finishing my research that night, I pick Taylor up from my aunt's house. We drive to another relative's house where we'll spend the night. We're both exhausted. After a few minutes of screaming, Taylor falls asleep in the car. I turn the radio off and drive in silence. Pulling the rearview mirror down, I glance at my sleeping son in the backseat. His head tips to one side and his blond hair curls around his ears. He looks so peaceful. I feel so frazzled.

In the quiet of the drive, the emotions and events of the last few days flood through my mind. Although I have never tried to bring a toddler to a research library before, it symbolizes a theme in my life. It's a theme of trying to juggle—of trying to fit together things that don't really go together.

In my heart, I believe my family should be the priority in my life. And I truly believe that raising my children is the most important, most valuable thing I can do. But, at the same time, I feel like something is missing in my life. I don't feel complete. I don't feel satisfied. My life seems unacceptably ordinary. I want more—without letting go of anything I have.

After my trip to the library though, I wonder if my only alternative to ordinary is frazzled.

THE CHURCH IN
KYRKHEDDINGE, SWEDEN

CHAPTER SIX

CHOICES:
KARSTI'S PARENTS

After a long and dreary winter (as winters tend to be in Wisconsin), today feels like spring. For the first time in months, I can go outside without a coat. A day like this would normally be the cause for much celebration from me, an avid winter-hater. But today, my focus is elsewhere. By the time night falls, I will see the village of Vallby, Sweden — Karsti's birthplace.

"Taylor, Mommy is going to Sweden today," I tell him, pulling up the sunshade on his stroller so I can see him as we make the short walk to Rachel's preschool.

"Oh. Wee-den?" he repeats.

Then he points to Rachel speeding ahead of us on her little bike. "Cha-chel, wait 'a me!" he calls, his interest in my announcement already passed.

He cranes his neck backwards to see me. "Mama!" he calls wanting me to notice Rachel. But I hardly hear him — my attention consumed by thoughts of Sweden. When I don't respond, he tries again, his voice louder. "Mama! Urry!"

"Okay, okay," I say, quickening my pace to catch up with Rachel.

When we arrive at the preschool a few minutes later, I absent-mindedly unfasten Rachel's bike helmet. Taylor jumps out of the stroller and runs after her into the building. *I'm really leaving my children for a week*, I think as I follow them.

"Mommy!" Rachel engulfs me in a tight hug. "Have a fun time in Sweden. Bring me a surprise, okay?" She kisses my cheek before disappearing into the crowd of three- and four-year-old children.

Back outside, I hug Taylor before buckling him into a friend's car. "Bye, Taylor. I love you," I tell him as I kiss his forehead.

"Hannah!" he answers, pointing to my friend's little girl who is sitting next to him in her car seat. He kicks his feet back and forth in excitement, oblivious to my good-bye.

Will they be okay without me? I wonder as I close the car door. I wave one last time through the window, then turn to walk back home.

For the next two hours, I scurry around my apartment, pretending to be productive. I look through my bags and recheck my ticket, going over every detail in my mind again and again. At last, the time comes for my mother-in-law to drive me to the University of Wisconsin campus where I catch a bus to the Chicago airport. There, I wait three more hours for my flight. I haven't spent this much time alone in months — and I haven't even gotten on the plane yet.

When I finally board the plane, I find myself comparing this trip to my trip to Germany six years ago. Then, I was twenty-one and single. For three months, I wandered around the country, soaking everything in. The world stretched out before me, full of choices and with few ties to constrain me.

This time, I will spend one carefully planned week in Sweden. The week had to fall when I wasn't nursing a baby or miserably ill from pregnancy; when the weather was warm enough for me to walk around outside, but before the travel season kicked in, forcing the prices of plane tickets out of reach of our graduate student budget. After months of checking prices, I bought my ticket for the last week of March. One week is so short, and yet it feels like an eternity to be away.

My heart races as the plane takes off. My emotions mix together in an unrecognizable mush. But as I look out the window at the ground spread out under me, I feel free. The walls of confinement that sometimes press on me are far below now. The world, at least for a moment, looks limitless again.

Many hours later, I breathe a sigh of relief as I pull my rental car onto the highway. I've taken a bus, two planes, and a train. After I arrived in Malmö, a city on the southwestern coast of Sweden, I had to drag two suitcases filled with books and binders, a pillow, a sleeping bag, and a backpack for several blocks from the train station to the car rental agency. Now, at last, I drive east towards Blentarp, the village where Karsti's ancestors attended church for hundreds of years and where I will spend my first four nights in Sweden. I'm exhausted from nearly twenty-four hours of continuous travel, and in desperate need of a shower. But as I drive the final hour of my trip, the sight of the green farmland through the window refreshes me.

Not far out of Malmö, I see signs pointing to Kyrkheddinge, the village where the residents of Vallby, including Karsti and her family, attended church. As if on autopilot, I pull off the highway. Kyrkheddinge and Vallby are the places I've dreamed of seeing most.

The exit road winds around onto the center street of Kyrkheddinge. After driving past a row of little houses that look like they could have come out of a storybook, I see the church on the right side of the road. A wave of excitement washes over me. It was here that Karsti's parents, Nils (son of Nils Jeppson and Marna Pehrsdotter) and Lisbeth (daughter of Nils Nilsson and Karna Larsdotter) married. In this church, Karsti and all of her siblings were christened. After reading so much about the area, looking at stacks of documents of events that took place here, and even seeing pictures of the church on the Internet, I feel like I've come across an old friend. I park in the lot next to the church to get a better look.

A scene unfolds in front of me as I stare at the white, clay building. The grounds bustle with villagers dressed in their Sunday best arriving for church. Nils and Lisbeth smile and greet their neighbors as they walk down the short dirt path to the church. Lisbeth glances at the baby in her arms, pulling on the blanket to make sure it shields the baby's face from the cool, spring breeze. Her long, thick, dark skirt and fitted jacket almost succeed in making her look solemn. But, her brightly colored hair scarf and rosy cheeks hint at another part of her personality. Nils walks beside her, his sandy hair and fair skin contrasting with his dark coat. His greetings are soft, yet cheerful, as he tries to keep his family moving towards the door.

Their children follow behind them, their clothes simple, yet clean and orderly. All of the girls — from the oldest who is nearly as tall as their mother, to the youngest who barely comes to her waist — have their hair pulled back neatly. I watch as they reach the church door and then disappear one by one into the dimly lit room.

My gaze lingers on the church for a moment before I steer the car back to the main street. Instead of returning to the highway, I decide to drive a little further into Kyrkheddinge. I've gone about a block or two when I catch sight of a sign I can't read that points down a side road. *Maybe this goes to Vallby,* I think as I turn onto the road.

After driving for several hundred feet, I realize I'm actually following a bike path — and it's quickly growing too narrow for my car. There's no room to turn around. I have to back out. I try putting the car into reverse, then tap the gas. I move forward. I try again. I move forward again. Ten attempts later, I've failed to move one inch backwards.

I get out of the car, feeling slightly like an idiot, and consider what to do next. I notice a woman walking her dog along the path a little further up. When she gets closer, I ask if she speaks English. She looks at me oddly and nods yes. (I soon quit asking since virtually everyone speaks English.) I explain my predicament and she laughs.

Without hesitating, she and her dog climb in my car. She backs it out easily (and shows me the simple trick for getting it into reverse), then introduces herself as Yvonne, a longtime resident of Kyrkheddinge. After I explain why I have come from America to drive down a bike path in a Swedish village, she offers to be my guide around the area two days from now. I arrange to pick her up on Sunday afternoon.

Back on the highway, I see a sign for Vallby. I steal glances out of the window as I drive. But all I see is flat, green farmland dotted with little houses. Reluctantly I keep driving, determined to get to Blentarp before dark. I will have to wait until I come back on Sunday to get a closer view.

I think of Vallby as the centerpiece of my Swedish family's story. In Vallby, my family made their last Swedish home. And in Vallby, Karsti made two important choices — choices that would affect my life 150 years later. Vallby as the setting was no coincidence. The choices, perhaps, wouldn't have happened anywhere else.

Maybe in Vallby, I can find the answer to the question I've had since I started this research: Why did Karsti make these choices?

Vallby first entered my family story sometime before 1817 when Nils arrived there. He may have originally come to work as a farmhand. By the time he married his first wife, Anna Jonsdotter, on November 29, 1817, he was an *åbo*, or tenant farmer, with lifetime rights and inheritance rights to his land.

Nils and Anna settled on Nils's farm at No.1, Vallby. Here they had two children before Anna died of a "fever." Only seven months later, Nils married Lisbeth Nilsdotter. Nils had probably known Lisbeth for some time since her family lived nearby and attended the same church in Kyrkheddinge. When they married on November 2, 1823, Nils was thirty-seven and Lisbeth was twenty-four. Lisbeth moved into the home at No. 1, Vallby.

Vallby would remain the backdrop of my family story for the rest of their time in Sweden. In their home in Vallby, nine children all took their first breaths. And even before Karsti's birth, two children had also taken their last breaths there.

When Nils and Lisbeth began their family, Vallby was a small community made up of fifteen farms, with one to five families living on a separate section of each of the farms. Nearly every one of the heads of households was an *åbo* or a *dräng* (a farmhand).

Nils and Lisbeth lived on 1/32 of a *mantal,* or approximately seven to ten acres, putting them in the category of semi-landless peasants.[1] At one time, a plot of land this small would have meant they fell towards the bottom of the social order. Because of the shifts taking place in the Swedish population though, most of their neighbors also owned plots of similar size.

The group of landed peasants had begun to shrink rapidly by the beginning of the 1800s. A dramatic increase in the Swedish population was part of the cause. The land simply couldn't absorb the additional people. This left many young people with either no land or only a small piece of land that had been subdivided from their families' plots.[2]

On Sunday afternoon, I head back to Kyrkheddinge to pick up Yvonne. I find myself thinking about my children as I drive. Besides a short conversation soon after I arrived in Sweden, I haven't had any contact with my family since I left. Locating a phone and a reasonably-priced international phone card has proved challenging.

Although I miss my kids, there are things I don't miss. My life has been easier this week in ways that are both dramatic and expected. I have been free to go where I want, when I want, without worrying if my destination can hold the attention of a three-year-old or if my plans will interfere with naptime. I am able to get ready in the morning in thirty minutes instead of our usual two hours. I can wake up when I choose — which doesn't include several times in the middle of the night.

There's an exhilaration that comes with this newfound freedom. But after that initial rush, there's also something I didn't expect — an emptiness.

Besides, I'm inclined to think my children are withering away without me. A nagging sense of guilt has stayed with me — a worry about how my children will survive for over a week without me. There is no doubt that David is a fabulous dad, but everyone knows children *need* their mothers. I'm the only one who knows the right spot in Rachel's bed for each of her stuffed animals and exactly how Taylor likes his "night-night" arranged in his crib.

I've just conjured up a picture of my children sitting on their beds crying for their mother when I spot the Kyrkheddinge exit. I push the image out of my head and instead focus on locating Yvonne's house (a task that requires all of my attention — directions have never been my forte). After only one wrong turn, I find it. Yvonne, who is waiting out in front of her house for me, climbs in to the passenger seat before I can even get out to greet her.

Yvonne tells me about the area as she directs me through the small, unlabeled roads to Esarp, Alberta, and Orup, all villages where members of my family lived. She finds these places without much problem, but locating Svinarp, Nils's birthplace, proves difficult even for her. We drive back and forth near where she thinks it should be, but we don't see any sign of Svinarp.

"Pull over and I'll ask him," she says finally, pointing to a man working on the road. I stop the car next to the man and Yvonne rolls down her window. They talk for a moment in Swedish and then Yvonne bursts out laughing.

"No wonder I couldn't find it," she says to me. "Svinarp only has one house in it now."

With the man's directions, we locate the one-house village. Yvonne insists we knock on the door. The family who lives in the house invites us in, gives us the grand tour, and invites us to join them for ice cream. By the time we extract ourselves, evening is settling in, and Yvonne must return home. I still haven't seen Vallby.

"I'll show you where Vallby is, and then you'll have to look for the house alone," Yvonne tells me.

She directs me out into the countryside near Kyrkheddinge. "All of this is Vallby," she explains, "and on the other side of the highway — that's Vallby too."

I have become accustomed to this set-up by now. No houses clump together or line the sides of the roads next to each other. To me, nothing about Vallby resembles a village at all. Instead, farms scatter across vast stretches of land. No stores, churches, or buildings of any kind other than houses and barns can be found in Vallby. Bumpy, nameless roads that wind around in no particular direction connect the houses.

When Nils and Lisbeth were born in the late 1700s, homes didn't sprawl across the countryside this way. But Vallby probably looked similar to this by the time of their deaths. During their lives, a tremendous change occurred in the very fabric of rural life in Sweden, wiping out village centers, and moving peasants away from one another. The cause was the *enskifte,* or enclosure, movement.

By the mid-1700s, it had become obvious that the frequent land divisions had produced a system of incredible inefficiency. Despite the high quality of the land, productivity remained scarcely above what it had been in the Middle Ages.

One of the most important steps toward a solution took place only a few miles from where my ancestors lived. Baron Rutger Maclean, a wealthy estate owner whose vast landholdings included four villages, had grown frustrated with the low productivity on his land. So, in 1783, just a few years before Nils was born, he took a drastic step. He re-divided all his land into rectangular-shaped plots of about sixteen hectares (or forty acres).

The peasants on Maclean's land didn't exactly greet the change with open arms. For one thing, they viewed the land assignments as unfair. More importantly, the new system disrupted their way of life. Long narrow strips had allowed peasants to live near one another in small villages, which formed tight-knit social supports for the people. The obliteration of the strip-fields also meant the obliteration of the villages. Most of the houses in the village centers were torn down. Families had to move to their new plot of land and rebuild their homes far away from one another.

The peasants in the affected villages resisted with all the energy and power they had. Those who could move, did so. A number of Maclean's tenants revoked their contracts. Some had to be forcibly relocated to the new farms. A few even committed suicide. In the end though, the reformation went forward. And the result was astounding. Within a decade, Maclean reported significant increases in production.

By the 1790s, when Nils was a child, nearby large landholders began enacting similar changes. Many landlords were impressed by the jump in production on Maclean's lands. Others were inspired by the very condition that caused the peasants' distress — the destruction of the village. In the closing years of the eighteenth century, social unrest was spreading throughout Sweden. The land reforms offered the perfect way to thin out population centers, minimizing the likelihood of peasants banding together. More than just a land reform, *enskifte* worked as a means of social control.

The forced rearrangements didn't affect Nils directly until several years later. In 1803, King Gustavus IV passed the Enskifte Decree. Under the decree, the consolidation process would begin at the request of one or more village residents. A surveyor then appraised the land in the village and divided it into plots, preferably square-shaped. Peasants drew lots to assign the plots.

Once again, the law was met with great resistance. In most villages, at least one landowning peasant was willing to initiate the process. Often, few besides that one initiator supported it, though. The mayor of Malmö recorded that the Enskifte Decree descended like "an enemy bomb" on the peasants in the area. Some people emigrated to Denmark. Surveyors went about their jobs carrying loaded pistols for protection.[3]

Because the *enskifte* process was begun at the request of individual villagers, it followed a different timeline in each village. In Vallby, surveyors drew the new *enskifte* maps in 1814. By the time Nils and Lisbeth married nine years later, little remained of a village in Vallby.

Nils and Lisbeth lived on one of those square-shaped plots (or at least a portion of it). Their neighbors were scattered out in the distance. It must have seemed lonely compared to what they had known as children. Maybe Lisbeth sometimes looked out her window at night, longing for the reassuring glow of lights in someone else's windows.

Nils and Lisbeth probably shared the resentment their neighbors felt toward *enskifte*. Perhaps they resented not only the disintegration of their village, but their inability to influence the course of the change. In retrospect, historians view the *enskifte* movement as an important innovation. But for the people of the time, it deprived them of their way of life—of the camaraderie, support, and convenience of a village. It also deprived them of the feeling of control over their own lives—of the power to make choices.

Yvonne explains the addresses in Vallby as I drive her home. Each house has two numbers. The first number corresponds to a section of land, numbered one through fifteen. The location of these sections isn't necessarily sequential. Four and eleven are as likely to be next to one another as four and five are. These numbers represent the fifteen farms or divisions I saw in the old records. My family lived at No. 1, Vallby—but so did a number of other families.[4] That's what makes the second number important. Each house also has its own number, such as 1.1, 1.2, and so on. Unfortunately, the records I collected don't give the second number. Yvonne concludes that without this information, finding the exact plot of land where they lived will be difficult. I decide to worry about that later. For now, I'll just concentrate on finding No. 1, Vallby.

After saying good-bye to Yvonne, I pull back onto the main road in Kyrkheddinge, catching sight of the church not far ahead in the distance. Suddenly, I know I must make one more stop before heading to Vallby.

As I park my car in the lot again, the significance of this little white church strikes me. This church symbolizes the old ways—the life Karsti and generations before her had been born into. Karsti would walk away from it all—into a life she chose.

Nils and Lisbeth had been born into a particular religion, social class, and location. Making even small alterations to these was difficult. But this changed during Karsti's lifetime. Choices that had never existed before opened up. This happened most dramatically in two areas: emigration and religion. These two movements threaded into Karsti's life to finally present her with a choice of magnificent proportions, a choice that would have been nearly unthinkable to her parents.

Nils and Lisbeth probably hadn't considered religion a choice when they were growing up. The Swedish Lutheran Church had long been the dominant, and basically only, religious presence in the country. Opting out of religion wasn't possible either. Both strong social norms and laws kept religion firmly planted in people's lives.

Despite the lack of religious freedom, people had dissented from the state church for years. While Nils and Lisbeth were beginning their family, religious dissidence began to grow from a small and insignificant trickle into an undeniable stream. Swedish historians would later label this period as the Religious Awakening. Many of the early religious movements came from within Sweden. By the 1830s, not only American ideas, but Americans themselves, penetrated the country. The Swedish civil and religious leaders reacted immediately and forcefully. Often, they arrested these missionaries, put them in prison on diets of bread and water, or exiled them. But, repression didn't stop the growing restlessness.[5]

Just as few people dissented from the Lutheran Church, few emigrated in this period. In the 1830s, emigration from Sweden and Norway combined reached just over one thousand.[6] Emigration from Skåne was even lower than that from some of the middle and northern Swedish provinces where population density was greater and land quality was poorer.

But the trickle of emgration was about to burst into a stream. While land in Sweden was becoming a difficult-to-come-by commodity, rumors spread about miles of open land available for free in America. The *enskifte* movement combined with other government actions such as forced military service also frustrated the peasants, making them more acutely aware of their lack of freedom. Finally, weakened social links due to the breakup of villages left people with fewer ties to their hometowns.[7]

Yet in 1843, when Karsti was born, these movements that would shake Sweden and my family to the core were nothing more than a far-off rumbling.

Lisbeth and Nils were seasoned parents by the time Karsti joined the family. Nils had reached the age of fifty-six. Lisbeth was forty-three. One brother, Nils (Nils Jr. here—are you confused yet?), and four sisters: Anna, Karna, Hanna, and Elna who ranged in age from twenty to four-and-a-half, were also there to welcome their new sister to the home. Two other sons, both named Pehr, had died and Nils's oldest daughter from his first marriage had moved out.

As the youngest, Karsti had plenty of people to watch over her. One of her older sisters probably took care of her while her mother attended to other chores. Aunts and uncles, many of whom lived nearby, also made regular appearances in her life. But Karsti never knew her grandparents. All four of them had died by 1830, thirteen years before she was born.

I often think of Karsti as a three-year-old girl. Karsti's life then differed in many ways from the life of my three-year-old daughter. Nils and Lisbeth were busy with their time-consuming responsibilities. They had little time for games and child-centered outings. Karsti didn't attend preschool, mommy-and-baby swimming lessons, or music classes as Rachel has.

Still, I have no reason to believe that Karsti was less loved or less happy. Karsti probably spent a lot of time by the sides of family members. Even as a toddler, she likely followed her mother and sisters around as they did chores. She may have played in the grass as Nils worked outside or sat at the feet of one of her sisters as she knitted. Lisbeth may have hugged and sang to Karsti. Nils might have told her stories or joked with her.[8]

If Karsti did have idealistic memories like these of her family, they were only the hazy, vague memories of a very young child. Karsti's life took a drastic turn when she was still just three years old. Karsti lost her mother and two older sisters in a matter of weeks. Her twenty-four-year-old sister Anna, fifteen-year-old sister Karna, and her mother died from typhoid fever in January of 1847.

Although premature deaths were a common occurrence, that would have done nothing to ease its cruel sting for a child. Karsti spent the rest of her life without a mother. Nils, who had now reached sixty, didn't remarry. Several of his children were old enough to help, easing the burden of not having a wife at home. The oldest remaining child, Nils Jr., was twenty years old. Hanna was twelve and Elna turned eight one month after Lisbeth's death.

Before this, the Nilsson family had hired farmhands and maidservants rarely — only when their children were very young. In 1847, a young girl lived at the home briefly. She helped the family during and immediately after the deaths of Lisbeth and her two daughters when sadness must have made the added responsibilities that fell on the other family members overwhelming. No other farmhands or maidservants lived at the house again until 1854, after the farm had passed to the next generation.[9] This small fact hints of the grief that swept through their home.

I pull on my coat, gloves, and hat before opening the car door, but the sharp March wind makes me gasp anyway. I decide to explore outside the church first. I open the iron gate that leads to the churchyard lined with gravestones. Starting in one corner, I walk up and down the rows looking for family names. I see many stones for people whose lives were cut short, including numerous children. I even see a couple of gravestones for people who lived at No. 1, Vallby. But I don't see my family. Few of the gravestones date back that far.

I walk to the front door of the church, take a deep breath, and push on it. It opens. My steps are slow as I think of my family filing in through this same door—not for a Sunday meeting as I had first pictured, but for funeral services for Lisbeth and her two daughters.

I sit down on a bench in the back. I stare at the simple altar and christening bowl at the front of the church, surprised by the emotion that wells up inside me. Five minutes pass. Then ten. I find it hard to move. No note on the death records explains the effect on a little girl of having her family ripped apart. No paper I've collected tells of the devastation this family felt. But, as I sit in their church, I can feel it.

I think of three-year-old Karsti, huddled on the bench next to her father, his big arm pulling her close to him. Her head buries in his side, her eyes scrunched closed, trying to shut out everything around her—trying to make it all not real. As she leans against him, she can feel his uneven breaths and knows he is crying. He lost his own mother when he wasn't much older than Karsti is, and he knows the pain it brings his children. Karsti opens her eyes to look down the pew. Her whole family weeps together, their shoulders bent under the weight of their staggering loss.

Here, as they sit so near to me, I cry with them.

Back in my car, I turn down the little gravel road to Vallby. I think about the details I've learned about Karsti and her family.

I must see where she lived. The thought hits me forcefully. Although in Germany I gave little thought to finding the exact residences of my ancestors, now that I'm in Vallby, my desire to find Karsti's home is intense.

I drive up and down the meandering roads, stopping at each mailbox to read the address, trying to keep track of which roads I've already taken. As I drive down these dirt roads with fields on both sides, I feel the calmness in the air. The approaching twilight makes even the glow of the sun soft. As far as I can see, the only movement is the rustling of the grass in the breeze. I can hardly imagine controversy being a part of Vallby. Yet I know that in the 1850s, the introduction of a new religion created more than a small stir in this tranquil little village. Although Karsti and her family may have remained unaware at first, eventually this stirring would reach in too close for them to ignore.

Franklin Scott, a Swedish historian, called the 1840s the "intolerant decade."[10] Intolerance, of course, lasted beyond the close of that decade. But despite valiant efforts from authorities, the Religious Awakening continued to expand through Sweden.

In 1850, another new religion entered Sweden. John Forsgren, the first missionary from The Church of Jesus Christ of Latter-day Saints, arrived on June 19th of that year. Elder Forsgren (Elder is the title all male Mormon missionaries use) left Utah for his hometown of Gefle (now Gävle), Sweden, about one hundred miles north of Stockholm, where he baptized the first Swedish LDS converts. His success was short-lived. Local authorities first limited his travel. Then, all the printing presses in the area refused to print his Swedish translations of LDS literature. Not long after that, Elder Forsgren was arrested when he refused to stop preaching publicly. After releasing and re-arresting him a couple of times, authorities put him on a ship heading back to America.

The experiences of Mikael Johnson, the lone missionary sent the next spring, followed the same pattern. As soon as he began baptizing people in Gefle, the local authorities arrested him and took him to Stockholm. Elder Johnson demanded a trial, but authorities refused. Instead, they transported him the nearly four hundred miles to Malmö in chains, with only bread and water for nourishment. When he wouldn't denounce his religion, he was taken to the police in Copenhagen, Denmark.

The turning point came with Anders Winberg, the third missionary to come to Sweden—and the first one not to be evicted from the country. Elder Winberg began teaching in Lund, his hometown, which was located only about seven miles northwest of Vallby. By the end of the year, he had baptized thirteen people, making the total number of converts for Sweden thirty-four. Slow but steady success after repeated failures in northern Sweden eventually led Skåne to become the Swedish "cradle of Mormonism."[11]

After driving around aimlessly for thirty minutes, I consider giving up. I have followed every little dirt road I've encountered, but I still haven't found No. 1, Vallby. Daylight is fading, and I don't want to be lost in the countryside in the dark. I turn the car around and head back toward the highway. As I drive, I see a house I hadn't noticed before. A man wearing high work boots is walking out to the road. *Might as well ask,* I think.

I stop the car and roll down the window. "Do you know where number one, Vallby is?" I ask. With a closer look, I can see that he isn't much older than I am.

He regards me for a minute. "Number one what?"

"I don't know," I admit.

"Well, this is number 1.4, Vallby," he says.

"Really?" My voice is eager.

"Who are you looking for?"

I explain the situation. He listens and then smiles. "So you've come all the way from America to find number one, Vallby? Or is Vallby just a side-trip from the main destination?"

"I've come to find number one, Vallby," I reply.

His smile broadens. "Well, if you've come this far, you can't go home empty-handed."

A few minutes later, I stand out behind No. 1.4, Vallby, the house of Göran and his girlfriend, Jenny. Though Jenny is new to the area, Göran grew up here. Jenny talks to me in perfect English while Göran calls his parents and neighbors, trying to trace down my ancestors.

"We tore down an old house that was standing here and just finished building this one," Jenny confides, then laughs. "I hope that wasn't your ancestors' house!"

After we shiver in the cold for a while, Göran and Jenny invite me to join them for dinner. We talk about Jenny's internship in New York City, Göran's work experience in Dallas, and my plan to write a book about all of this. After dinner, they pull out some old maps of Vallby. Jenny suggests I go to the Lantmäteriet office, the office that keeps land records. She believes they can help me find my ancestors' land. She offers to meet me there tomorrow at noon. I'm overwhelmed by their help.

Jenny and Göran also let me use their phone to call home. When David answers, I give him their phone number and he calls back.

"How are the kids?" I ask anxiously.

"Fine," he says. "They've had fun with their grandma." Then sensing that I might be looking for another answer, he adds, " — but I'm sure they'll be very glad to have you back home."

I feel an initial sense of relief. My vision of crying children wasn't correct. But as I hang up the phone twenty minutes later, another feeling stirs inside me. I feel surprised, and maybe even disappointed, at how well they are faring without me.

Several hours later I say good-bye to Jenny and Göran and make my way back to Blentarp. The darkness feels thick around me as I steer the car towards the highway. I remember that Göran told me this highway follows the path of an old dirt road that had been used by peasants in the area for generations. Karsti may have come down this road with her father when he went to do business or buy supplies in Malmö. After 1853, she would have made the trip to town with her brother instead.

In 1853, Karsti's father, Nils, passed the farm along to Nils Jr., his only surviving son. He gave up his position as *åbo,* or farmer and head of the household, and became listed in the records as simply *änkeman,* or widower. Karsti's father was sixty-seven at this exchange, and her brother was twenty-seven. As was the custom, Nils remained living at the house, effectively in retirement. Nils Jr. likely had a legal obligation, as well as a family responsibility, to care for his father until his death.[12]

That same year, Karsti's older sister, Hanna, left to work at a larger farm in a nearby village.[13] Hanna didn't return home again. The "woman's work" of the farm now fell on Karsti and her older sister, Elna. By the age of nine, Karsti probably spent long hours in the field when her help was needed. She was likely responsible for feeding sheep, chickens, geese, and pigs and may have also had the unpleasant task of cleaning their stalls. Elna was probably in charge of preparing meals for the family, with Karsti assisting her.[14] Karsti must have crawled into bed at night exhausted.

Karsti's schooling didn't interfere much with her duties at home. If Karsti received an education beyond the Bible and Luther's Catechisms, it was sparse. The Riksdag (the Swedish parliament) passed a landmark act in 1842 requiring every parish to establish a common school. This took time, though. Before the act, only about half of the parishes had schools and, typically, only boys attended them. Although most people learned to read in order to study the Catechisms, writing among females was less common.[15] In the 1900 US census, one year before her death, Karsti would report that she could read, but not write.[16]

It was probably around the time the land passed to Karsti's brother that the Nilsson family first learned about the LDS Church. In April of that year, in the late hours of the night so they wouldn't be noticed by anyone, missionaries established the first branch (or small congregation) in Sweden. The branch, located in Skönabäck, a large estate thirty miles east of Malmö, consisted of thirty-six members. Missionaries soon organized additional branches nearby in Malmö, Lomma, and Lund. As in other places, missionaries encouraged new converts to begin preparations to emigrate to Utah. [17]

Later that year, the LDS Church moved even closer to the Nilssons. Despite its small size, missionaries chose Karsti's hometown to support one of the first branches of the Church. Perhaps initial interest in Vallby was strong. Perhaps it was chosen for its proximity to other places. Perhaps it was random.

The Vallby branch lasted only ten years. Today, no signs of the LDS Church remain in Vallby or the nearby area. Despite its short-lived presence, the Church still impacted a handful of lives in an extraordinary way. My family was among that handful.

I don't know how the family learned about the LDS Church. Maybe Karsti went with her father to some of the first, secret meetings held in Vallby. Or maybe the family shunned this new church initially. Maybe they took pains to avoid the missionaries, not wanting to hear the unusual teachings of dissidents from America. But maybe her father had been searching for understanding that the Lutheran Church couldn't provide. Maybe her brother longed for something different — something more. Maybe something inside Karsti made her wonder if this new message could answer the questions that burned inside her.

By 1854, some of the farmhands working at the Nilssons' home had joined the LDS Church.[18] These young men might have been the people who first introduced the Nilsson family to the Church. Or it could have been more than coincidence that Nils Jr. employed so many Mormons. Perhaps the family already sympathized with the new religion.

With a branch so close to them, the Nilsson family also witnessed firsthand the increasing persecution the Church faced. Missionaries were arrested, transported from one prison to the next, and fined. Captors held one missionary all night, roughing him up and trying to force him to drink whisky. Local leaders throughout Skåne arrested or fined people for holding, or even attending, meetings. Authorities imprisoned one missionary for twenty-five days on only bread and water. In Malmö, city leaders broke up meetings and warned LDS members that they could only assemble with ten or fewer people. Mobs stoned, knocked down, or attacked missionaries so violently that they ripped their clothes to shreds.[19]

As the little branch was struggling to get started in Vallby, important changes continued in the structure of the Nilsson family. In February of 1856, twenty-nine-year-old Nils Jr. married Karna Hansdotter. That same year, Elna left to work on a nearby farm.[20] Karsti was twelve years old at the time of her brother's marriage and she remained at home. She probably continued in a similar role — only now assisting Karna as the female head of household, instead of her sister.

On May 29, 1858, Karsti's seventy-one-year-old father died of "old age." Just fourteen years old, Karsti was essentially an orphan, dependent on her older brother. For the next two years, she stayed in the family home, now occupied only by her brother and his growing family. Karsti probably received part of the title of the farm, which she "loaned" to her brother. Nils Jr. would've been expected to repay her when he was able.

Karsti ventured away from home for the first time in 1859 to work as a maidservant on a farm in nearby Orup.[21] Unlike her sisters, who never returned home again once they had left to work for others, Karsti moved back to Vallby after only a few months in Orup.

Not long after returning to Vallby, Karsti made two decisions that changed the course of her life and affected all who would come after her. First, on September 5, 1860, Karsti was baptized a member of The Church of Jesus Christ of Latter-day Saints.[22] Then, seven months later, she set sail to America.

The next morning, I arrive at Jenny's office in Malmö at five minutes before noon. We've planned to meet here and walk the few blocks to the Lantmäteriet office together. But when I arrive, Jenny isn't there. The secretary offers to call her cell phone.

"I'm at Lantmäteriet right now," Jenny explains when the secretary hands me the phone. "I found out this morning that they close at noon, so I came an hour ago to get the maps for you. I'll meet you in the lobby in ten minutes." I'm amazed she left work to do this for me.

A few minutes later, Jenny walks in with a stack of copies of documents and maps. We find a table and she spreads the papers out across it.

"I found the house," she tells me excitedly. "It was down the road — where our neighbor's house is now." After flipping through the papers, I'm convinced she's right. The land records, dated 1860, show the property that now belongs to Jenny's neighbor under Nils Jr.'s name.

This is my last day in Sweden. I must go back to the house tonight.

I spend the rest of the day doing research and visiting nearby churches and villages. It's nearing dusk before I begin my drive towards Vallby. I turn on the dirt road, and follow it past Göran and Jenny's house. Not much further down, the road ends at a U-shaped barn across from a little house on the top of a slight hill. From what Jenny and I could deduce, the Nilsson family didn't live in this particular house — this house was built later. But this house sits on the exact spot where the Nilsson homestead once sat.

I pull on my coat and grab my camera. I consider knocking on the door, but decide against it. I want to keep my vision of the past uncluttered by the present.

I take a few pictures of the house and the surroundings. Then I stand still, breathing in the air and listening to the stillness around me. I wonder if Karsti ever stood in this very spot, breathing the air and listening to the stillness as she struggled with the decision before her.

Death had severed many ties for Karsti already. Soon, distance would pull apart the rest. An ocean would separate her from what remained of her family. I think of my own family, now an ocean away from me. My separation is brief. But, Karsti would never return. Later she must have longed for those ties. Maybe she knew that ties don't just hold people down; they bind them together.

I wonder, as I often have before: *Why did she do it? Why did she make this choice?*

For reasons I can't fully explain, the answer to this question is deeply important to me. This decision, made 116 years before I was born, has shaped my life. I want to know if it was faith or simply circumstances that prompted her to start her journey.

No record provides a straightforward answer. No diary or letter has been passed down that gives insights into Karsti's thoughts and motivations. Instead, I rely on the scanty records about the family and historical information about the place and time period to find an answer.

In some ways, going to America made sense. By 1860, Karsti didn't have a solid place in a family anymore. Her mother and father were both dead. Her siblings had died or established families of their own. Karsti lived in her childhood home, yet probably didn't feel like she belonged. Perhaps there wasn't much left to keep Karsti in Vallby.

Karsti might have felt the excitement of American fever growing all around her. Emigration had, by this time, swept the countryside. Twenty-one thousand Swedes and Norwegians left their homes in the 1850s. And, the movement was just warming up. After the close of the Civil War, the numbers jumped. By the 1880s, nearly four hundred thousand emigrants left from Sweden alone—almost seven percent of the population.[23]

Karsti had watched others plan, prepare, and then depart on this adventure. Perhaps she also felt that America extended the promise of a better life. And, by joining the LDS Church, Karsti could ensure a community and home to welcome her when she arrived.

But there was another side. For a young girl who had hardly traveled beyond the borders of her parish, setting sail to a new country with a new language, a new culture, and where everything would be unfamiliar was frightening and intimidating at the very least. The trip itself, known to be harrowing and even dangerous, presented another major drawback. In 1861, it was rare for people her age, only seventeen years old, to undertake such a journey alone. And the decision would be irreversible. Saying good-bye to family members and friends usually meant good-bye forever.

Besides, there were easier ways of getting to America than becoming a member of the LDS Church. Prejudice and shunning, although declining by 1860, still existed. Other Scandinavian converts wrote that immediately after joining, their friends would have nothing to do with them. One convert reported that when she saw her former pastor in the street, he struck her with his cane. Family members sometimes did all they could to prevent children or siblings from joining the Church and leaving the country.[24]

I don't know how Karsti's family reacted to her conversion to the LDS Church. I have reason to believe that at least Nils Jr. was supportive. He would later follow in her footsteps, joining the LDS Church and coming to Utah. Yet, Karsti still made her choice—and trip—alone.

Karsti probably didn't have much support in her community. The branch records from Vallby show that during that three-month quarter, Karsti was the only person baptized into the little branch. The branch seldom experienced more than a handful of baptisms during any quarter. It remained small, constantly struggling for its every breath. There were only twenty-six members at the time of Karsti's baptism.[25]

The one thing the Church did offer new members sometimes was financial assistance in emigrating to America. This wasn't a motivating factor for Karsti, though. Karsti paid her way, probably with money she inherited when her father died.[26] Karsti could have gone to America without joining the LDS Church.

I don't have anything Karsti wrote that describes her feelings. But, I do have a lifetime of choices. Karsti remained a part of this church that she joined less than a month after turning seventeen until the day she died. She lived according to its teachings and taught her children to do the same.

From my position at the top of this small hill, I look out at the land. Even in the dusk, I can see for miles — windmills and churches, trees and farms. Here at No. 1, Vallby, seeing the world as Karsti saw it, I know the answer to my question. My answer comes from more than a logical conclusion based on tangible evidence in the records. I feel it here.

When Karsti joined the LDS Church, she believed it to be true and committed her life to it. She left everything she knew and sailed to America because of it. Although not much more than a child, her faith was strong enough to overcome her fears.

She made her choice alone. But its consequences stretched for generations and to hundreds of people—including me.

I begin the long journey back to Madison the following morning. I go through the routine in reverse, dragging my luggage up stairs and down the street, taking the train, two planes, and a bus. Near midnight, my bus reaches its final stop in Madison where David is waiting. My week of "freedom" is over. I'm home.

When we walk into the apartment, I drop my luggage in the living room and head straight to my children's bedrooms. I quietly open Taylor's door and tiptoe into his room where he lies in his crib, snuggled under his special "night-night," unaware of my presence. I stroke his hair through the bars of the crib, then tiptoe back out.

Next, I open Rachel's door and walk softly to her bedside. She has a stuffed animal in each arm and more line the edge and bottom of her bed. I lean over to kiss her forehead.

Rachel turns over as her eyes flutter open. "Mommy..." she mumbles, smiling at me sleepily. "I missed you." Then she rolls over and goes back to sleep.

She did miss me, I think, surprised at the pleasure I feel in that.

"I missed you too," I whisper back.

I knew my children needed me. Maybe I didn't realize how much I needed them. I had focused on the weight of my ties, not on their strength.

I stand and look at Rachel for a minute, thinking of Karsti's decision. Karsti made her choice knowing that everything has a cost. A lot of hardship and difficulty would come from her decision. She hadn't chosen the easy path—she had chosen the one she believed in. I wonder if in the difficult times, she thought back to the day in Sweden when she made her choice. It must have brought her comfort and courage to know she had selected her path.

As I look down at my sleeping daughter, I'm reminded that I have made choices too. And I know, as I always have, that I would not choose differently.

TAYLOR AND RACHEL IN THE WAGON RUTS IN GUERNSEY, WYOMING

CHAPTER SEVEN

SOMETHING MORE:
KARSTI'S JOURNEY

"**M**ommy, can I bring Stitch Bear on our trip?" Rachel asks, holding up the teddy bear that someone at the hospital gave her when she had to get stitches three years ago. "He'll get lonely without me."

"Sure," I agree, glancing at her quickly before turning my eyes back to the computer. I click on one last link and push the print button.

"And can Taylor bring Spot?" She sticks out her other hand holding the stuffed Dalmatian.

"Spot wants to come," Taylor adds solemnly.

"Of course, we can't leave Spot," I say.

They both smile, satisfied.

"Stitch says, 'Thank you'," Rachel tells me, before taking Taylor's hand and returning to the living room where my mom is waiting to read their bedtime stories.

I take the papers, various printouts of hotel reservations and directions, off the printer and add them to my folder. Tomorrow I will leave on another trip, one I've been planning since I returned from Sweden over four months ago. I want to follow a part of the path that led Karsti from Sweden to Utah by driving the Oregon Trail, or Mormon Trail.

Unlike my other trips, I won't be making this one alone. I'm bringing my kids—and my mom. My friends think I'm crazy to voluntarily spend four days in a car with two preschool-aged children—for fun even. They may be right, but I'm not crazy enough to make the trip with my two children by myself. When David told me he couldn't take any more time away from school, I convinced my mom to come with us instead. She's not particularly interested in the Oregon Trail—or Karsti for that matter (Karsti, as she keeps pointing out, is my dad's ancestor—not hers), but she would do almost anything to spend more time with her grandkids—and to help me.

Despite the long miles ahead, I'm excited about the trip. I have lived not far from Karsti's home in Utah and have visited her childhood home in Sweden. Now I can follow part of her journey. I need to take this trip to feel complete.

Although Karsti couldn't know exactly what lay ahead on her journey to Utah, she would have received warning enough to give the faint of heart second thoughts. The length of the trip alone was daunting. While the Albrechts had steam ships and trains to take them to Utah in a matter of weeks, Karsti had far less convenient options available. She would travel for over five months by sailing ship, trains, smaller boats, and then covered wagon. LDS Church leaders and literature given to travelers at the time warned of the dangers and risks that accompanied the long trip. Shipwrecks, seasickness, cholera, frostbite, starvation, dysentery, and measles had claimed the lives of many travelers before her.[1]

Yet, it was the cost of the trip—not the risks—that proved to be the greatest deterrent to most people. The trip to Salt Lake City for a family could easily total more than the family's earnings for an entire year. Many Scandinavian members had to rely on Church loans through the Perpetual Emigration Fund (PEF) to finance the trip. Karsti, though, was among those who paid in advance.[2]

Karsti prepared carefully for her journey. For one thing, she had to decide what to bring. The *Skandinaviens Stjerne,* a Mormon publication, warned emigrants not to bring more than one hundred pounds of luggage per person. Taking anything above the weight or space allotment on boats or trains increased the cost of travel significantly. Karsti had to fit a lot into that one hundred pounds. She needed clothing for both the hot summers and the cold winters she would find in Utah. She also needed to bring eating and cooking utensils, bedding, five days worth of food for the first leg of the trip to Liverpool, towels, a comb, and soap among other things.[3]

Another important part of Karsti's preparations was to learn English. She relied on contact with English-speaking missionaries and Church materials published in English. Missionaries held English classes on Sunday mornings. They considered the classes almost as important as religious worship.

I finish our preparations the following morning. I arrange a big bag of snacks, various toys, some music tapes for the kids, and a few books between the two car seats in the backseat of our small sedan. Then, I head back inside to get the one suitcase that I've managed to stuff all our clothes into. As I walk out of my apartment pulling the suitcase behind me, an image comes into my mind.

I see Karsti with her bags in hand, standing in front of her childhood home—on the same spot I stood only a few months ago. She hugs her brother and sister-in-law tightly, trying to keep her emotions under control. She looks past them at the house that has been her home since she was born. Beyond it, she sees the land she knows so well. Each gentle rise and fall is etched in her mind. She closes her eyes to make sure it's there—every tree, every detail of the house—clear and perfect. From now on, she will only be able to see it when she closes her eyes.

Karsti gives her brother one last hug. Her heart is pounding so loudly in her chest that she thinks he must be able to hear it too. She has never felt so small, so vulnerable. And yet, she has never felt so independent, so strong. She takes a deep breath to steady herself. Then, before the first tear can escape, she turns and walks away.

Karsti's moving out record gives another glimpse into her departure. On that day in April, 1861, when Karsti said good-bye to her family, home, village, country, and way of life, the parish register shows that six unrelated people from the nearby area also left. Other groups left a few days later, presumably to travel the great distance together. In the place for remarks for each departure from the parish, the pastor wrote only "Mormon."[4]

Traveling with a Mormon company made some aspects of Karsti's experience unique. She had more guidance and support than other emigrants. Yet, the majority of her circumstances were no different than those of the thousands of other people who also took the journey around this time. She had to face the same seasickness, cramped quarters, inclement weather, and other trials they did.

Most travelers from southern Sweden started their journey by passing through the city of Malmö. For Karsti, it was a journey of only a few miles. In Malmö, Karsti and her fellow travelers boarded a boat to make the short trip across the Sound that separates Sweden and Denmark to reach Copenhagen. Here, Karsti joined 373 Danes, 128 Swedes, and 61 Norwegians—all LDS converts making their way to America. Over the next few days, this group took a series of boats and trains, stopping in Germany at Kiel and then Altona located near Hamburg. In Altona, on May 11, the group divided to cross the North Sea to England—one half of the travelers headed to Hull and the other half to Grimsby.[5]

Karsti may have found the two-day ride across the rough waters of the North Sea to be the worst part of the entire journey. Many travelers vomited during the day then buried their vomit in the thick sand of the holds in order to sleep on this same sand at night.[6] After spending one night in either Hull or Grimsby, Karsti took a train across England to Liverpool where the two groups were reunited.

In Liverpool, Karsti boarded her sailing ship, the *Monarch of the Sea*. Others joined her traveling group, for a total of 960 people representing ten different nationalities. It was one of the largest groups of Mormons to ever cross the ocean.[7] Before the ship could leave, a medical practitioner conducted an inspection to ensure that the passengers didn't have any contagious diseases and that the medicines on board were sufficient. Mormon leaders also came to address the passengers, giving them last-minute advice.

On May 16, 1861, the *Monarch of the Sea* set sail. As the ship left the dock, cheers erupted from all around.[8] Perhaps Karsti joined in, celebrating the new life that awaited her. Maybe her heart pounded in her chest, just as it had in Vallby — but this time, with excitement.

It probably wasn't long after the celebrations died down that the tedious, and even grim, nature of life on board a ship hit. Karsti slept in a narrow bunk packed closely with other bunks, making space and privacy hard to come by. The sleeping quarters were on three levels located below deck with only a small door to allow fresh air and light to penetrate.[9]

Passengers passed the time on board by sharing stories of home, describing their dreams for the future, singing, dancing, and playing games. Karsti probably attended prayer meetings every morning and evening, as well as classes on a variety of topics. On Saturday, May 18, perhaps Karsti listened to Elder Woodard and Elder Harrison, two Church leaders, lecture on geography. Or maybe she heard their "ox-team discourse" on Sunday, June 2.[10]

During her month at sea, Karsti ate simple, but adequate, meals. The New Passenger Act of 1849 required the captain to provide the passengers with at least two-and-a-half pounds of bread or biscuit, one pound of wheat flour, five pounds of oatmeal, two pounds of rice, two ounces of tea, one-half pound of sugar, and one-half pound of molasses per week. Food had to be issued in advance and not less often than twice a week. The captain also had to ensure that each passenger received three quarts of water daily.[11] Passengers could bring additional provisions, and many did. Church leaders supplied LDS emigrants with two-and-a-half pounds of sago (a type of starch), three pounds of butter, two pounds of cheese, and a pint of vinegar for each adult.[12]

Preparing—and even eating—the food was difficult. The ship didn't have enough room for 960 people to cook every night. Because of this, each family could only cook five times per week, which sometimes caused disagreements. Karsti probably ate many of her meals using her trunk as a table. In rough waters, she struggled to prevent her makeshift table from sliding back and forth across the deck.[13]

Maybe Karsti was one of the travelers who suffered from a more vexing problem—seasickness. For some passengers, their seasickness improved when the weather was calm. For others, it became a constant, terrible part of life at sea. These people spent much of their time in bed, their stomachs never settled, in a relentless struggle to keep their food down.

Worse than illness, poor food, or crowded conditions for many emigrants was the terror of being at the mercy of the sea. Everyone had heard stories of shipwrecks. When an inevitable storm struck the ship, and the winds howled and the boat rocked violently, passengers trembled with fear.

When I think of Karsti's voyage across the ocean, one image stands out in my mind.

Karsti hurries down the steps leading below deck in the semi-dark as the massive, angry sea tosses the ship back and forth. Behind her, she hears the hatch door slam shut with a resounding thud. She reminds herself that this is to protect the passengers—to keep the water out, not to make them miserable. A few lanterns give off a dim glow, the only light available. She searches for something to hold on to in order to steady herself against the relentless motion of the ship. Around her, she sees other passengers gripping their beds, their faces white.

The hours drag on down here in her dark prison. Karsti hears the sounds of crying, praying, and violent heaving piercing the air from time to time. Seasickness spreads among the passengers, yet nobody can go above deck to empty the buckets. The stench of vomit and used chamber pots makes her stomach lurch more than the motion does.

The arrival of night does nothing to calm the waves. Karsti knows they could be shut in like this until the storm subsides—possibly for days. She can feel the noise, the smells, the stifling air, and the people closing in on her. Her breathing becomes more rapid; her pulse starts to race.[14]

Then, she remembers. Karsti closes her eyes. Suddenly, she's in Vallby with the fresh air and blue sky, with the light sound of her brother's children laughing.

When she opens her eyes, she doesn't feel the suffocating closeness of people anymore. She feels alone.

My mom returns from the short walk to pick up Rachel and Taylor from their summer preschool and we buckle them in their car seats. We're leaving at noon in the hope that they will nap through the afternoon. But as we pull out of my apartment's parking lot, they show no signs of sleepiness. Instead, Rachel bubbles over with excitement.

"Mommy, I told my teacher I had to leave early because I was going to drive the 'Regon Trail and learn more about my ancestors," she tells me happily.

I smile at the thought of her teacher's reaction to this. I've been telling my children for weeks how exciting the trip will be, trying to brainwash them into believing it. Apparently, my propaganda worked.

"Mommy, will I see a wagon?" Rachel asks. "What are we looking for?"

I explain that we don't meet up with the start of the trail until tomorrow. Rachel seems satisfied and pulls out a book to "read" to Taylor. As the road rushes by, I find myself mulling over her question. What *am* I looking for? I'm looking for trail ruts and historical markers. But, I'm also looking to find what Karsti found, to see what she saw. I want to understand her—her feelings, her thoughts, her motivations.

The *Monarch of the Sea* reached New York on June 16, 1861. Karsti's first glimpse of this land of liberty and freedom probably didn't make it seem at all like what she was looking for. At that time, the US oozed with troubles. The Civil War had broken out only a couple of months before. One of the first things Karsti saw was "the military parading the streets of New York, and drumming up for volunteers to go and fight the south," as one fellow traveler described.[15]

Karsti's group headed to Castle Garden, located on the water's edge in lower Manhattan. Castle Garden, the predecessor to Ellis Island, served as the station to examine and process new immigrants until 1890. Scores of immigrants crowded through its doors, hundreds each day, thousands each month.

Here, Karsti and the other immigrants reported their names and destinations. Government officials informed them that they could purchase train tickets, exchange money, get directions, learn about employment opportunities, and use other services. Immigrants could also sleep on the floor at Castle Garden for a couple of nights. These services were provided partly in an effort to shield the immigrants from the thieves and opportunists who hung around the harbor waiting to prey on the ill-informed, and sometimes desperate, people that flowed into the country. Physical exams given at Castle Garden also served as a way to screen people and keep out those with contagious diseases.[16]

Karsti and her group stayed at Castle Garden for a few days. They rested while their leaders secured the travel arrangements for the rest of the journey. A few, particularly those with small children, opted to stay in hotels instead. Most of the travelers couldn't afford this option. Karsti most likely made her bed on the "greasy, dirty floor," as someone in her group wrote.[17]

Sometimes I imagine Karsti at Castle Garden. She stacks her luggage, which represents all her possessions, around her. She rolls up a piece of clothing and places it under her head. Then, she lies down on the hard floor. Around her, strangers and other people from her group stretch out in a similarly uncomfortable way. Their combined voices, a jumble of unfamiliar languages, drift through the room. Karsti tries to shut everything out, to sleep.

When she closes her eyes, the picture of Vallby floats into her mind. In the thrill of setting foot on American soil for the first time, Karsti had felt joy—a pure, simple emotion—not the complicated mix of emotions that has been with her through the trip. But now the memory of her home, instead of lulling her into a peaceful sleep, rekindles the ache inside her.

In New York City, Karsti boarded the first of a series of trains. Traveling by rail was no luxury, especially for emigrants who traveled in the cheapest cars, known fittingly as "emigrant cars." These dirty, crowded cars didn't provide much in the line of eating or sleeping accommodations, sanitary facilities, or drinking water. The ceaseless jerking and bouncing made the trip even more miserable. Still, emigrants preferred these to sheep and cattle cars, which they sometimes had to take, particularly during the Civil War when many passenger cars were burned and damaged. In the sheep cars, people didn't dare sit down because of the filth around them.[18]

Karsti stopped first in Dunkirk, a town in northwestern New York along Lake Erie. After that, her group stopped in Cleveland and then Chicago before finally reaching Quincy, Illinois, where the Mississippi River greeted them. Here, Karsti rested overnight with her group on June 25. The next day, she boarded the steamship, *Blackhawk*, and headed twenty miles down and across the river, landing in Hannibal, Missouri.[19]

If the United States had issued travel advisories back then, they would have surely issued one for traveling in Missouri in 1861. Although the Civil War made travel in much of the country dangerous, Missouri was particularly affected. Missouri had entered the war on the side of the Union, but with the support of only part of its population. This split loyalty led to intense internal tensions. Its strategically important location within the country magnified the conflict even more.

Southern sympathizers in Missouri did all they could to destroy the railroad tracks rather than let them be controlled by the Union. They tore up tracks, burned and weakened bridges, and even shot at trains which were known to sometimes carry Union soldiers. In an effort to protect the tracks, Union soldiers were stationed at railroad bridges. Occasionally, guards stopped trains and conducted inspections to ensure they weren't transporting any rebels or arms.[20]

After driving for a few hours, we stop to eat dinner and switch drivers. While my mom drives, I stare out the car window. I think of Karsti as I watch the landscape fly by. She also sits by the window, her head resting against the side of the train. She can't watch the changing scenery as I do. Her window has been boarded up. The train conductor felt it would be safer this way. But for Karsti, it serves as a constant reminder of the danger.

Karsti sits back in her seat, trying to swallow the nervousness that fills her stomach and climbs into her throat. She hears the shrill wailing of a baby and remembers the conductor's warning to remain quiet in order to decrease the chance of an attack. With so many children on board, this isn't an easy task. Karsti watches the mother desperately trying to calm the baby. At last, the mother succeeds in soothing the child to sleep.[21]

With the crying now quieted, Karsti can again hear cannons booming and guns firing in the distance. She has nothing to look at and nobody to talk to as the hours crawl by.

Darkness surrounds us when we get to our hotel in Council Bluffs, Iowa, located just across the Missouri River from Omaha, Nebraska. The railroad ended and the wagon trail began at the town of Florence, now nothing more than a section of Omaha. Karsti arrived here at the beginning of July after taking the train through Missouri and a steamboat up the river.

I get my first glimpse of the area the next morning. Green, rolling hills create a tranquil backdrop as we drive into Omaha. Our first stop will be in Florence at the Mormon Trail Center which depicts the early presence of the LDS Church in this area.

As soon as we pull into a parking spot, my children clamber out of the car and take off running down the sidewalk. I follow closely behind Taylor, trying to prevent him from yanking out the flowers from the carefully tended flowerbeds.

Inside, a tour guide shows us the displays. They tell the story of the winter of 1846–1847 when Mormons first flooded into this area after being forced to leave their homes in Nauvoo, Illinois. With nowhere to go, the ten thousand Mormons trudged westward across slushy, muddy Iowa. The trek took over four months. Realizing they weren't equipped to continue their trip westward, the group stopped here at the banks of the Missouri River. The Mormons called their temporary settlement Winter Quarters. The weakened group battled hunger and disease throughout that bitter winter. Many people, particularly children, didn't survive. Finally, in the early spring of 1847, they left to make their way to the Salt Lake Valley.

The Trail Center focuses on the Winter Quarters part of the story. But there's more. By the time Karsti arrived fourteen years after that first winter, the town of Florence replaced Winter Quarters. Florence, the juncture to the last phase of the trip west, functioned as the outfitting place for Mormons continuing across the plains to Utah.

A bustling scene of preparations greeted Karsti when she arrived in Florence. Few permanent buildings lined the streets. Since the residents usually lived here for only a few weeks, they made their homes in tents and other temporary dwellings. The *Monarch of the Sea* passengers swelled the population to twenty-five hundred, nearly all of whom were Mormons preparing to head west.[22]

Although Florence lacked buildings, it had an abundance of other things. When Karsti entered the stores, she found mountains of basic provisions. In one outfitting season, 13,000 pounds of sugar, 3,186 pounds of apples, 3,707 pounds of coffee, 6,155 yards of tent cloth, 3,300 pounds of ham, 15,121 pounds of bacon, 6,700 pounds of side meat, and 2,900 pounds of shoulder meat passed through Florence and into the wagons. Other goods such as bar soap, candles, pickles, baking powder, corn, rice, yeast, rope, twine, needles, thread, and tobacco also lined the shelves. Stores sold flour, but only in small quantities. Advanced parties cached large amounts of flour along the way so wagon trains could pick it up as they needed it.[23]

The year Karsti arrived in Florence, LDS Church leaders were experimenting with a new approach to westward travel. Brigham Young, the leader of the Church, had become concerned about the growing number of impoverished Mormon converts scattered overseas, and especially from New York to Florence, unable to finance the trip to Utah. The war had heightened his sense of urgency. The Church needed a cheaper way to get converts to Utah.

An earlier experiment with handcarts had proved this method wasn't the solution they were looking for. So, Brigham Young decided to try the "down and back plan." He believed the plan would not only reduce the cost to the Church and allow more people to make the trip to Salt Lake City, but it would also help stimulate the Utah economy. Under this plan, wagon train leaders, or teamsters, would come from Utah to Florence early in the spring of the year. They would bring extra cattle and other surplus goods that were produced in Utah to sell to the new members for their journey or to be taken east and sold. They would also bring oxen and wagons belonging to people in Utah that they had allowed the Church to "borrow." The poorer converts would use these. The teamsters would then lead the wagon trains to Utah. The plan got its name from the wagon train leaders who traveled down to Florence and back again to Utah in one season.[24]

Many converts depended on wagons supplied by the Church, but that didn't mean that they made the trip for free. Church leaders kept careful records, adding the costs to the travelers' PEF accounts. The converts were expected to eventually pay the money back in full. Karsti traveled with an independent company, meaning she bought her own provisions and paid for her wagon.[25]

Church leaders assigned Karsti a wagon train as well as a particular wagon. Leaders tried to keep people who spoke the same language together. Sharing a wagon required Karsti to interact with her traveling companions on an intimate level, although not because of time spent riding together in the wagon. Karsti knew from the beginning that the wagon wouldn't carry her across the plains. Only the old, young, and the disabled or sick rode in the wagons. Wagons carried provisions, not people.

On July 13, after nearly two weeks of preparations, Karsti's wagon train started off along the trail, following the Platte River westward. The group consisted of 338 people in 61 wagons, nearly all of whom had traveled with Karsti on the *Monarch of the Sea*. Scandinavians, particularly Danes, dominated the group. Samuel Woolley, a thirty-five-year-old LDS convert originally from Pennsylvania, led the wagon train with captains appointed for every ten wagons.[26]

Although Karsti and her group journeyed into the frontier, they didn't follow a lonely, forgotten path. By 1861, the trail was a busy highway, flooded with people moving west. The trail that became known as the Oregon Trail, Mormon Trail, or California Trail (the trails were basically identical until travelers reached western Wyoming, except that the Mormon Trail was on the opposite side of the Platte River) had been used for thousands of years. Animals and American Indians were the first to follow the Platte River. Fur trappers, mountain men, and explorers came in the early 1800s, but only in small numbers. Then missionaries, hoping to convert the American Indians, followed suit. Not until 1841 did the first group of people intent on migrating west set off across the faint tracks. One thousand migrants completed the trip in 1843, and the numbers continued to grow throughout the 1840s.

The floodgates opened in the 1850s as gold fever drew scores of people west. Between 1840 and when Karsti crossed the plains in 1861, three hundred thousand people followed these trails. Fifty-three thousand went to Oregon, mostly in hope of finding fertile farmland. Two hundred thousand headed for California, often in search of gold. Forty-seven thousand sought religious freedom in Utah.[27]

This heavy traffic left its mark on the trail. Discarded belongings littered the sides for miles. Travelers sometimes found their wagons too loaded down, and deposited the "extras" as they walked. Pioneers saw food, stoves, cooking tools, dead animals, and a long list of other items that earlier travelers had thrown aside. Some travelers picked up a few of these that they found useful and added them to their own wagons.

Besides leaving their mark on the trail, these travelers also left their mark on history. In many ways, they epitomized the American dream as they took risks to make their ideals a reality. Each group of people had their own reasons for going west. Yet, in many ways, their motivation was the same. They were each looking for a better life— for something more.

After looking around the Trail Center in old Florence, we're also ready to "begin" our trip, although by now twenty-four hours have passed since we left Madison. The lack of sleep catches up with my children at last. They both drift off in the backseat within minutes of leaving.

We now continue west toward Fort Kearney, a rudimentary fort about two hundred miles down the trail from Florence that offered weary travelers a place to purchase provisions and to rest. Following I-80 would be the fastest route, but I'm determined to stick to the actual trail route as much as possible. So instead, we arch north, following the Platte River as we drive on a state highway that passes through dozens of little towns.

A constant line of trees along the bank that shield the river from our view are the only evidence that we're following the Platte. These trees also provide the only variety in the otherwise flat, dull landscape that stretches out around us. Even the river itself proves unspectacular. The few times we cross it, I'm surprised by its lack of vigor. Instead of roaring along, it trickles and meanders lazily over a wide, muddy bottom. Despite its unimpressive appearance, the river had an impressive job. It led, and provided life support for, thousands of people heading west.

As I strain my neck to watch the trees marching steadily along, I can almost see the line of wagons strung out next to them. Karsti walks beside one of the wagons, her head bent. The sun beats down relentlessly as she trudges forward, surrounded by dust stirred up by the wagons, the oxen, and her own feet. The uneventful scenery blurs the days together for her as it blurs the hours for me.

Monotony and tedium filled the pioneers' days. Peter Nielsen, one of the captains overseeing ten wagons, described the general feeling when he wrote on July 27, "We continued our journey in good order and continued thus the following days, and nothing extraordinary happened."[28]

Mundane details such as the weather, trail conditions, and starting times each morning pervade the diary of Nielson as well as Samuel Woolley, the wagon train leader. A typical entry like the one in Woolley's diary on July 23, reads: "Started at 7 o'clock. Drove along the river for 9 miles. Stopped to bathe, then another 6 miles and camped some distance from the water. Clear and warm."

The diaries contain little flavor of the emotion of the trip—the frustration and excitement, the interactions of the people, or even a clear picture of what a day on the trek was like. But, they do give a daily log of Karsti's life. There's no other time when I know something about what she did every day. For me, even the trivialness of the journals is an exhilarating discovery.

"Started at 5 1/2 o'clock" reads one entry in Woolley's journal. "Started at 6 o'clock to Green River," reads the next entry. Days began early. "Traveled 1/2 mile over heavy sand bluff to river…3 miles…7 miles over sand… 8 miles and camped." Travelers carefully noted the distance covered every day. Each mile behind them meant one mile closer to their destination. From morning until evening, Karsti walked, often covering around seventeen miles in a day. By nightfall, she was hot, tired, and dirty. Some pioneers wrote of sore and bleeding feet from endless walking in poor quality—and for the Scandinavians, often wooden—shoes.

On July 13, Nielsen wrote, "12 miles, excellent water and grass." Water was essential, both for the people and their livestock. When they followed the Platte River, water was easily available. Once they left the river's side, the quest to find water became a driving force. On September 4, Nielsen wrote, "Drove 10 miles before we reached good water and grass." Four days later, he recorded, "Drove 14 miles before we reached water."

Trail conditions were also of vital importance since they determined how fast the wagons could move. "The road has been sandy and hilly, and in consequence of this we have not traveled as much in the last seven days, but according to the circumstances we make pretty good progress," Nielsen wrote on August 11.

Weather affected their journey, and both Woolley and Nielson regularly recorded it. Nielsen noted "heavy rain" on July 14, and then added the next day, "Bad weather for several days." A hailstorm on August 17 scared some of the oxen and sent them running. Walking all afternoon in the middle of July was obviously "very warm" as Woolley wrote. By the beginning of September, as the group passed through the canyons and mountains, the nights sometimes turned unpleasantly chilly. Nielsen wrote on Saturday, September 7, "The night was very cold." Karsti and the others had nothing to shield them from weather extremes.

The diaries also describe encounters with American Indians—all peaceful. Immediately after setting out, several American Indians approached Karsti's group and asked for food. Nielsen wrote in the middle of August: "We have come across quite a few Indians and they have been very kind to us…Yesterday [during a hail storm], nearby Indians took off their hats and held them over the heads of the [women] camped near them. In the evening, they came over and got some bread, flour and pork."

Other challenges confronted the group. At least two people died along the trail—an older woman and an eighteen-year-old girl. Problems with oxen disrupted their progress. "This morning a lot of the oxen [are] lost," Woolley wrote on August 29. On September 6, he noted they had lost sixteen oxen and two cows. Two days later, he again recorded, "Several oxen died."

Still, the pioneers made time for fun. Karsti talked with other women as they walked while the children ran beside them, sometimes playing tag or other games. One Swedish traveler who sailed with Karsti remembered: "As a child, this had been a delightful pleasure jaunt and I remember it only as fun. We children would run along as happy as could be. My older sisters used to make rag dolls as they walked along, for us little children to play with."[29]

Often at night, the pioneers sang and danced by the campfire.

We reach Fort Kearney close to 5:00 p.m. and make a brief stop to let the kids run off some energy. Then we return to the road. By now the Platte River has met up with the interstate, making our travel much faster. We speed along, singing "Bingo" (Taylor's favorite song) repeatedly, intermixed with the extended version of "The Wheels on the Bus" which includes many verses Rachel has composed herself.

We leave the interstate again a couple of hours beyond Fort Kearny and follow the Platte River north. After some time, the flat countryside gives way to rolling hills. This signals to me that we are nearing Ash Hollow, a respite of natural springs and ash trees, 180 miles west of Fort Kearny.

I catch sight of the historical marker, and pull the car off the road. To save time, I leave the kids in the car with my mom and jump out. I follow a little sidewalk until I come to a sign and display. Here, the sign says, are some of the few remaining wagon ruts along the trail. I glance down to see the deep marks carved into the rock.

In the warm breezy twilight air, the sight of these original marks makes me catch my breath. The wagon train's presence looms so near that I reach out my hand, almost expecting to touch the wagons in the semi-darkness.

As I stare at the ruts, I imagine Karsti and her wagon train making their way down the hill. They have chained the wheels to prevent the wagons from speeding out of control. The animals and men sweat and strain as they use all their strength to keep the pace manageable. Worry and concentration line everyone's faces.

My gaze moves further out as another scene fills my mind. The wagons form a large circle under the starry sky. The flames of the campfire leap into the air, casting shadows on the canvases of the wagons around them. Voices rise from around the campfire—but not voices of sorrow and drudgery. These voices laugh and sing, their words incomprehensible, but their feeling clear. Music rings in the air—the clear notes of a fiddle. Around the fire, Karsti dances along with the others, her skirts swaying and her long, blonde braids swinging. Her face, caught up in a breathless smile, shows no sign of the loneliness and worry that have accompanied her.

A few miles past Ash Hollow, we stop at a gas station. We've only been back on the highway for about five minutes when I hear a sound coming from the backseat. I glance over my shoulder to see Taylor gagging. I pull over as quickly as I can, but not in time. Taylor, who has always been prone to carsickness, throws up all over his car seat and clothes.

I jump out and run around to his side of the car.

"Uh-oh, Mama," he cries over and over again.

I strip off his clothes while my mom attempts to clean up the mess with a roll of paper towels and a box of wet wipes. We wrap his clothes in a plastic bag and set him back in his semi-clean car seat in his diaper and a blanket. Luckily, the hotel isn't far.

As the sun goes down, I sing lullabies until my children fall asleep. I had hoped we would make it to Chimney Rock while there was still some small strain of light left. Pioneers could see this distinctive rock, with its round broad base under a tall, thin pinnacle for days before they reached it. I had looked forward to seeing this important marker, but now it's obvious we won't beat the darkness there. I try to ignore the feeling of disappointment creeping up in me.

As we get close to the area where Chimney Rock should be, my mom and I see a lighted structure ahead of us. We take guesses as to what it might be. Only when it stands directly before us do we realize we're looking at Chimney Rock itself, glowing in the dark from lights installed around it shining up onto it. We pull up as close as we can and stare at it in the darkness. Although we hadn't recognized it, Chimney Rock had beckoned us for miles just as it had beckoned Karsti so many years ago.

We turn back onto the highway and drive the remaining distance to the town of Scottsbluff, about twenty-fives miles short of the Wyoming state line. As we park in front of the hotel, Taylor, now exhausted and disoriented, wakes up and cries inconsolably. We hurry into the hotel, carrying the children and dragging suitcases behind us up the stairs. My mom heads back out to the car to finish cleaning up.

In our hotel room, I hand Rachel her pajamas and lie down beside Taylor. I stroke his hair to calm him. At last, his sobbing subsides as sleep overcomes him. I glance over at Rachel, now asleep in the next bed. I close my eyes too. Despite the chaos of the day, I feel satisfied.

Rachel and Taylor both wake up before 6:00 the next morning, so we decide to start our drive early. The terrain out the window seems to get rougher by the mile. This uneven land slowed travel for Karsti's wagon train. They had to struggle both to pull the wagons up steep inclines and then to keep them from racing out of control when the trail turned downhill.

We soon cross into Wyoming where we come across frequent landmarks and historical sites. These landmarks were well known among the travelers and marked their progress as they made their way west. We choose only a few of them to explore.

We spend an hour in the morning looking around Fort Laramie, now a National Historic Site, located about thirty miles west of the Nebraska/Wyoming border. Here, pioneers restocked on goods. Then, we wind our way towards Guernsey, a little town thirteen miles west of Fort Laramie along US-26, which is known for having some of the best-preserved wagon ruts on the trail. To my surprise, no sign marks the turn-off to the ruts. We ask directions at a gas station, then follow a curvy, country road to find them. Despite their unglamorous setting, the ruts are striking. Rachel and Taylor climb over the rocks and down into them. The ruts, now over five feet deep due to erosion, swallow them.

The travelers lost the guidance of the Platte River not long after Guernsey. Instead, they relied on the bending, winding Sweetwater River. If the travelers followed all of the river's many curves, it would have added many days of travel to the trip. To avoid this, they took shortcuts, often leaving the river's side for a while, and then crossing over it again and again as they pushed forward.

After Guernsey, we stop at the landmarks of Independence Rock and then, only a little further down the road, at Devil's Gate. The highway departs from the trail temporarily after Devil's Gate, continuing up north to the town of Lander and then heading back south. The trail, on the other hand, cuts a shorter path across the steep mountains and rocks. Rocky Ridge, known to all travelers as one of the most difficult parts of the trail, lies on this shortcut.

I had hoped to follow a dirt road that runs close to the trail. After driving for some time though, it becomes obvious that we passed the turn. I hate to miss a part of the trail as important as Rocky Ridge. But there's no time to turn around. Instead, we follow the highway up to Lander, the only town within miles that has a hotel, and the place we'll be sleeping tonight.

We haven't left Lander far behind the next morning when the road begins climbing into the mountains. Near the top of the mountain, we catch sight of a sign that says "Rocky Ridge" and points down a little dirt road shooting off the main road. Intrigued, we follow it. We soon find ourselves in South Pass City. The sign at the entrance to the town proclaims, "Population: About 7." The deserted gold mining town is now a State Historic Site. We go into the small shop at the entrance to ask directions. Here, we learn that somehow we've stumbled onto the other side of the road that follows the trail across the shortcut. I ask the man behind the desk about going to Rocky Ridge.

"Oh sure, you can get there from here," he tells us, pulling out a map. As he points out the route, I suddenly remember something I read.

"Do you need four-wheel drive to go on that road?" I ask.

He looks up from the map and stares at me. "Where ya' from?"

"Wisconsin," I reply meekly.

"Well, here in the mountains of Wyoming, those are the kinds of roads we have. It's a dirt road, sure. But it's a fine road. You don't need four-wheel drive."

We take the map and set off along the road, the car jumping and jolting as we go. Every few hundred yards, the road splits. Each time, we stop and study the map, which is marked much better than the road. Then we shrug, choose one path, and continue on. Faded wooden markers that we pass occasionally read "Oregon Trail" assuring us we're still on the right path. After driving a little while, a sign tells us we have eleven miles left to get to Rocky Ridge. My heart beats faster in anticipation.

Soon after that encouraging sign though, the quality of the road begins to deteriorate. Instead of a flat, wide dirt road, we now find ourselves driving along a narrow path with deep ruts on each side for the wheels. The uneven surface, littered with large rocks, slows us to a crawl. Our surroundings look harsh and deserted. We have seen no signs of civilization since we left South Pass City.

We drive for several miles like this until my mom brings the car to a stop, then turns to look at me.

"I don't think this car can make it," she says.

I had known this even before she said it. As long as it remained unsaid, I could pretend I didn't. But now, I nod my agreement. With considerable effort, my mom turns the car around and starts back down the road the way we came.

I turn and look over my shoulder one more time. For a moment in my mind, I watch a long line of wagons continuing at their slow, steady pace. Towards the back of the group, I see the small frame of a young woman, her dress swishing as she walks, her head shielded by a plain-colored bonnet. She takes a few more steps, then turns around to survey the land behind her. Her face is smudged, her eyes weary. She knows the difficulty that lies ahead.

Not long after returning to the main road, we come to South Pass. We get out of the car at the lookout and stare off into the distance, trying to see what the markers describe. Although almost imperceptible to us, South Pass was the key to the overland trail system. All trails heading west had to pass through this approximately twenty-mile gap between the Rocky Mountains and Wind River Mountains.

Another important landmark lies only a few miles past South Pass—the separation of the trails. The Mormons parted ways with the other travelers here. Most people continued west. The Mormons turned south to follow a less-established path to Fort Bridger near the current Utah border, through Echo Canyon and Emigration Canyon and then into the Salt Lake Valley. Now, we turn south too, following their path past the fort and into the canyons.

Immigrants' diaries depict their wonder at passing through the canyons. But I find Echo Canyon unspectacular. I can see little more than parched, brown dirt all around. We drive down the interstate through much of the canyon before turning off onto a smaller road which leads us into Emigration Canyon.

The drastic beauty of this second canyon strikes me immediately. The road climbs steeply upward, taking us beyond the brown desert floor into the mountains where thick, tall pine trees line the sides of the road and hover over our car. The road winds back and forth, with periodic overlooks showing breathtaking scenes of high mountain peaks and sloping valleys covered in the thick green of the trees. Every few miles, markers provide a little information about the trek over the mountains.

After driving in the shadowy trees for some time, we emerge at a clearing known as Big Mountain Summit. We climb out of the car and take in the view, as magnificent as anything I have ever seen before. Yet, I can't help but think that these same steep slopes and thick trees that make the area beautiful created nightmares for the pioneers with their wagons.

There's little time to admire the view. My children are restless. Taylor sits on the ground and whimpers while Rachel pulls on my hand, asking me when she'll get to see her cousins. I'm also anxious to get off the mountain road before the storm brewing over us hits in full force.

We get back in the car and continue downward on the winding road. We're now within minutes of our destination. I try to imagine the thoughts and feelings that would have come over Karsti as she approached the end of her journey. Nielsen recorded that, on September 22, the group "washed and fixed ourselves and drove into Salt Lake City in the afternoon where many friends and acquaintances met us."[30]

Other journals and histories show the range of reactions. Alma Felt, who made the journey the same year, remembered: "When I saw our mother looking over this valley with tears streaming down her pale cheeks, she made this remark, 'Is this Zion, and are we at an end of this long weary journey?'" She concluded, "The arrival in the valley of desert and sagebrush must have been a heartbreaking contrast to the beautiful home she had left in Sweden."[31]

But Anders Christensen, another convert who arrived two years after Karsti, wrote: "It was a pleasant and delightful sight to see the beautiful city spread out before us… The city far exceeded my expectations, both as to extent and beauty."[32]

The miles slip behind us as our car flies down the road. I think of Karsti walking these final miles. I long to know her thoughts, to see into her heart. Yet, I feel like I almost can. Her feet ached less, the sun shone more brightly, and the miles passed more quickly on her last day of travel. Her family, her home, her country were all far behind her. But as she looked into the distant valley at the place she had sacrificed so much to see, a feeling of peace washed over her. She had made it.

The first signs of Salt Lake City are evidenced by cabins, and then houses, that dot the roadside as we approach the bottom of the canyon. We follow the road further to a statue that memorializes the words of Brigham Young when he led the first party of Mormon pioneers into the valley. Looking over the wilderness before him, he declared, "This is the right place."

We stop our car and get out by the statue. The rain sprinkles down on us as Rachel and Taylor gather rocks off the gravel road. We have also completed our journey.

Here at the end of the trail, my thoughts drift to a paper I submitted to a history journal. I wrote that by telling the story of Karsti's life, I was telling the story of the ordinary Swedish Mormon pioneer. The editor responded that she was convinced that although much remained unknown about Karsti's life, one thing was clear—Karsti was not ordinary.

The comment surprised me. Karsti didn't have money, power, or notable influence. Nothing set her apart from others around her. She didn't leave a lasting story behind that was retold to many people. No books mention her name; no memorials preserve her contribution. Just like all my other ancestors, Karsti certainly was ordinary.

After following in Karsti's footsteps for hundreds of miles, after seeing where her life began and where it ended, after getting to know her a little more—I can finally see what the reviewer saw so quickly. I was wrong about Karsti. There was something more to her. The strength of character and commitment she showed in making her momentous decision and following through with it alone when she was still just a teenager was nothing short of extraordinary.

But, more importantly, I was wrong about ordinary. I was measuring ordinary by how important, how distinguished, a person was. Perhaps a person becomes extraordinary not by becoming well-known, but by making good choices—no matter how great or small the consequences are—no matter who sees or cares what those choices are.

Like those thousands of people who headed west in the last part of the 1800s, I have been searching for something more in my life. I haven't been content with what I have—with what I have seen as ordinary. But maybe again, I was wrong about ordinary. Maybe what I have isn't so ordinary after all.

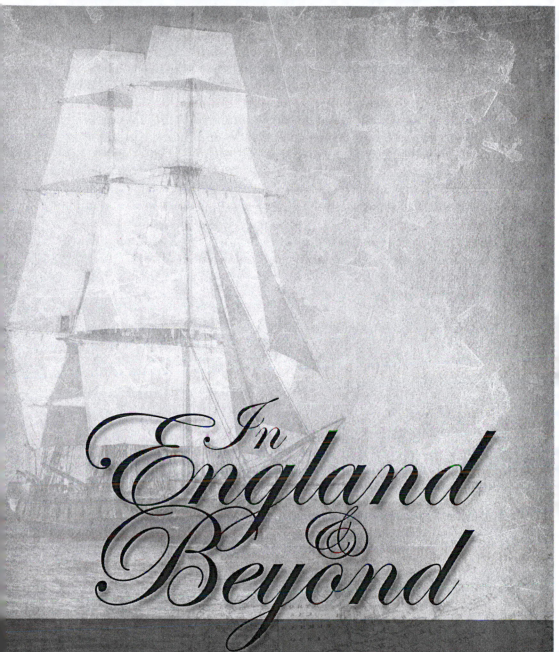

In England & Beyond

The Story of the Family of
Edmond Harris

PART THREE

English Family Tree

James Harris
b. Abt 1800 in
Buckinghamshire

Elizabeth Harris
b. Abt 1800 near
Buckinghamshire

*Edmond Harris
b. 1825 in Wingrave, Buckinghamshire

m.

m.

Eliza Barrett

Karsti Nilsdotter

*the journey taker in this section
See appendix for individual family groups

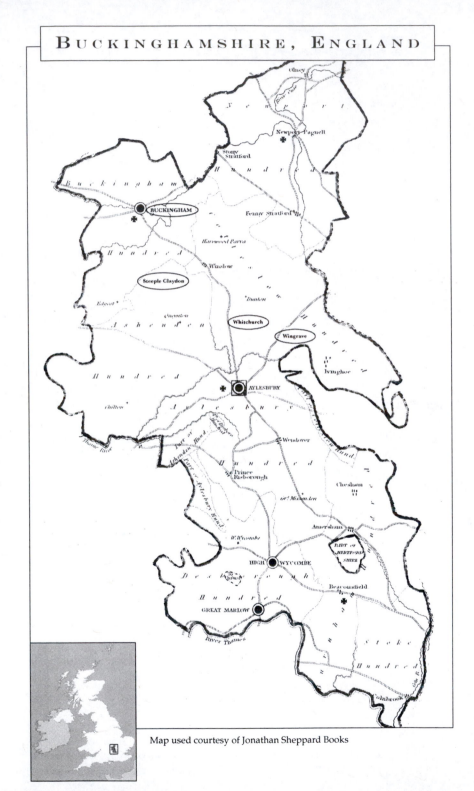

BUCKINGHAMSHIRE, ENGLAND

Map used courtesy of Jonathan Sheppard Books

MY PARENTS WITH THE PASTOR IN THE CHURCH
IN WINGRAVE, ENGLAND

CHAPTER EIGHT

MISTAKES:
EDMOND'S PARENTS

I stand in the flight check-in line at the Rome airport trying not to bite my fingernails—a habit that flares up when I'm nervous.[1] Today, I'm flying to London from Rome. My entire family has gathered in Italy for the Christmas break, courtesy of my parents who have funded the reunion. My brother, Mathew, already lives here with his wife and son. My little family, as well as my parents, my brother, Scott, and my sister, Laura, have arrived over the past couple of days.

Before we start our tour around Italy, my parents and I are taking a short side-trip to England. David will stay in Rome with our children. I saw our proximity to England while in Italy as an ideal opportunity to trace another journey taker. This time I will follow the path of Edmond Harris, my great-great-great-grandfather. His path eventually met up with Karsti's in Utah. But it started in a little village in England. And that's where I will start tracing it tomorrow.

It wasn't too difficult to talk my parents into coming with me. For one thing, my mom didn't like the idea of me "traipsing" around England by myself. I also worked a day and a half of sightseeing in London into our trip. My parents haven't been to London before and a new destination sounds fun. But, I want the trip to be more than that for them. I have spent months securing every detail to ensure we would have a smooth and meaningful trip. I want my parents to feel what I feel—or expect to feel—in looking straight into the eyes of the past.

Unfortunately, my parents' trip has already shown signs of being less than the ideal vacation I envisioned for them. They flew from Texas to Rome yesterday. Besides bringing everything they need to stay for seventeen days, my mom also brought her usual mountain of Christmas presents for the kids. Unfortunately, not one single suitcase or bag arrived in Italy. Since my parents were leaving for England the next day, they bought a few things and then borrowed what they could from David and me.

147

And now our tickets seem to be causing the airport employees distress—although I have no idea why.

The man behind the counter hangs up the phone and walks around to where I stand.

"You must come with me," he says in halting English, striding ahead of me. I dart after him as he nearly disappears into the crowd. When I catch up with him, he's standing in front of a window talking to another woman.

"Is there a problem?" I ask.

"Yes," the woman says in English, looking me over in exasperation—obviously holding me responsible for whatever the problem is. "Your flight was canceled. We sent out e-mails. Did you not receive it? You were supposed to call and reschedule your flight."

I stare at her blankly. "No, I didn't receive an e-mail like that." When she doesn't say anything else, I add, "So, what are we supposed to do?"

"There is another flight with room." She looks at her watch. "They are boarding now."

"Now?" I repeat.

"Yes. It is far. You will have to run."

"What if we miss the flight?

She shrugs. "This was not my mistake." The obvious implication is that the problem has been caused by my mistake. I clench my teeth, but decide not to waste time arguing. Instead, I grab my bags and hurry back to my parents.

We have now encountered the second stumbling block in my perfectly planned trip.

We rush through airport security as quickly as possible and dash through the corridor, suitcases bouncing behind us. As we near the terminal, we hear a voice over the loudspeaker, first in Italian and then in English, announcing the final boarding call for our flight. With a final burst of speed, we reach the gate just as the woman on duty starts to shut the door. She scowls at us, but takes our ticket. Panting and sweating, we walk onto the plane and jostle our way through the narrow aisle.

My irritation subsides once we settle into our seats. The excitement I always feel for traveling—particularly to places my family lived— returns. I have been looking forward to following the Harris family's path, or perhaps more accurately, leaping between the scattered footprints they left behind.

My information on the Harris family begins only with Edmond's parents, although I hope I will be able to learn more in the future. So far, even untangling this family has been a headache. I've run into the typical obstacles that arise in genealogical research — incomplete sources, records with minimal information, a common family name, and lack of access to the records. My problems also have another cause — a cause linked not to the records, but to the people themselves. Although I am still trying to piece the story together, I've found enough clues to conclude that some of the confusion in the family story arises from choices family members made.

I don't know when or where Edmond's parents, James Harris and Elizabeth Johns, were born. It was probably in or near Buckinghamshire, a county located slightly northwest of London, around the turn of the nineteenth century. Like my German and Swedish ancestors, they were common people who lived in small, little-known villages. Yet some unique aspects of English history created important differences in their daily lives.

During the time James and Elizabeth were raising their family, England had a relatively stable and open government. The roots of this stretched back centuries earlier to the establishment of a constitutional monarchy in 1688 during the Glorious Revolution. William III and Mary II, the new rulers, had to agree to the Bill of Rights as a prerequisite to accepting the English crown. The Bill of Rights put important limitations on the crown and began the gradual shift of power away from the monarchy and towards parliament. It also set the conditions that led to common people in England having more freedom and more voice in their government than common people in Germany or Sweden did.

A century later, another revolution began in England. This one would eventually transform the world. This revolution didn't involve politics and the military, but economics and production. Now known as the Industrial Revolution, it shifted employment patterns as people left agriculture and their small villages to head to the cities and the employment opportunities offered there.

Yet, much stayed the same for James and Elizabeth. Throughout the first half of the nineteenth century, the majority of people in England still lived in villages and still made their living in agriculture or by working as independent craftsmen.[2] James and Elizabeth saw the world changing around them, but they were still rooted in the ways of the past.

We arrive in London at 3:40 p.m. without further problems. After we get our bags, we take a shuttle to the rental agency to pick up the car I've reserved for us. We will sleep at a little bed and breakfast about an hour away—not far from where the Harris family lived. I have a map and driving directions. How hard can it be?

The novelty of driving on the left side of the road quickly fades. My dad has agreed to take over the task since he's the only one who has ever done this before (albeit many years ago). We find the road system even more confusing than turning into the opposite lane. Stoplights are nowhere to be found. Instead, we drive in loops around traffic roundabouts every few miles. Darkness wastes no time arriving, making it difficult to read the signs. All three of us focus our attention on driving. Still, we repeatedly find ourselves on the wrong road, going the wrong direction.

We finally see a sign that indicates we're nearing our destination. Just as I let out a sigh of relief, I hear a strange noise. It only takes a few seconds to identify it: the sound of the car bumping unevenly down the highway.

My parents look at each other.

"A flat tire," my mom says. "We've got to pull over."

But there's no place to pull over. In growing desperation, we spot a few feet of highway with a little extra room on the side—enough to get the car off the road. My dad stops the car and my parents climb out into the cold December night.

My dad sets to work changing the tire with my mom at his side. I can't help looking out the window from time to time at the busy highway—literally inches from where I sit. The cars and trucks whiz by, shaking our car with their momentum. I think of a story I read about a woman who had a flat tire on a freeway, got hit by a passing car, and died.

Hurry, I tell my parents silently.

Five minutes pass. Then ten.

What are they doing? I wonder.

I remember another story about a man on a highway in Utah who met an unpleasant demise when he pulled his truck over on the side of an interstate highway.

My mom opens the door. "Pray," she says before she shuts the door.

Another five minutes pass. The door opens again. This time my dad gets in. My mom climbs in on the other side.

"I can't change the tire," my dad says, a hint of stress evident in his voice. My dad, the calmest person I've ever met in my life, never gets stressed. This makes me feel even more worried. "One of the lug nuts is stuck. It won't come off."

"What are we going to do?" I ask.

"Well, we can't sit here all night," my mom answers.

My dad starts the car and we limp forward towards an exit. I dig through my folders, looking for the roadside assistance number that came with the car. After what seems like eons, we pull into the parking lot of a gas station.

Now in the safety of the parking lot, I am no longer scared. I am mad. What kind of defective car is this? I use the pay phone to call the rental car agency and the roadside assistance. I demand to know why we can't get the lug nut off. Nobody knows. Nobody cares. They promise to send someone to help us in an hour. The gas station is closing. We have no phone and no way to go anywhere else.

"An hour is not acceptable," I nearly yell into the phone. "It's cold and the gas station is closing. We can't just hang out in a dark, deserted gas station parking lot." The other people in the gas station stare at me as my voice rises. But, I don't care. I'm tired—and furious.

They promise to send help in thirty minutes. Forty-five minutes later, a truck pulls up.

"Oh," he says when we explain the problem, looking at us like we're the dumbest people he's ever seen. "The lug nut is designed not to come off. All cars here are like that. That way nobody can steal your tire. There's a key in the glove box."

"Why didn't anyone tell us?" I ask. He shrugs, then gets back in his truck and drives off.

We've now hit the third stumbling bock in my plan. And we haven't even arrived yet.

It's nearly midnight when we pull into the driveway of the bed and breakfast. We unload the car in silence. I look over at my parents who are wearily dragging in their suitcase full of borrowed clothes. My dad's coat is covered in dirt and oil. Mascara streaks down my mom's face from the cold wind. I convinced them to come—to use their time and money to make this trip. I planned all of our activities. Now, I feel responsible for the outcome. I wanted their trip to be memorable—but this wasn't what I had in mind.

I wake up early the next morning. Despite the mishaps of the day before, I have great expectations for today. Yesterday the sun set around 4:00 p.m. which motivates me to hurry so we can take advantage of every minute of daylight. First on our agenda is the village of Wingrave—the beginning of the Harris family as far as I can trace it.

James and Elizabeth began their lives together in 1821 in this village of 675 people located in Buckinghamshire in southeastern

England.[3] At that time, England was recovering from a social and economic crisis that had shaken the country to its core. England was at war with France during the early years of James and Elizabeth's lives. Instead of bringing stability, the end of war and of wartime production left England reeling. At the same time, the radical ideas of freedom and equality that had shaken mainland Europe reached England. Intellectual leaders took the opportunity to call the masses to action. Strikes and other disturbances broke out as the standard of living for most rural laborers continued to fall.[4]

Although people in England enjoyed more freedom and a higher standard of living than many others in Europe, widespread poverty and oppression still existed. This higher standard of living was mostly found in the new and growing middle class, a group not found to the same extent in other European countries. But the middle class comprised only a minority of the population. By mid-century, over eighty percent of the people in England were still working class.[5]

James and Elizabeth probably benefited little from the improving living conditions. Many working-class people continued to live in rudimentary environments. Homes of laborers were small and simple, with boarded roofs and floors remaining a novelty throughout the century. Diets consisted mostly of bread and potatoes.[6]

Downturns in the economic cycle brought hunger and suffering. Outbreaks of disease claimed many lives among the young and old alike. In the 1840s, three of every twenty infants failed to reach their first birthdays.[7] When James and Elizabeth were born, the average life expectancy remained just under thirty-six. Fifty years later, it had still failed to reach forty.[8] Despite any advantages living in England gave James and Elizabeth over my other ancestral families, their lives were still hard.

We start the drive to Wingrave as the chilly first rays of sunshine break over the landscape. Nothing awe-inspiring jumps out at me as we drive. Yet like the land of my ancestors in Germany and Sweden, a subtle, calm beauty lingers here. Sleepy sheep lie in the meadows surrounded by hedge fences. Every few miles we pass another quaint village where brick and half-timbered homes line the roads.

We stop quickly in Aylesbury, the county seat of Buckinghamshire, for breakfast. Here, we purchase a few hot, steamy "pasties," flaky pastries stuffed with different types of fillings. I nibble on mine as we drive the remaining six miles to Wingrave and turn onto one of the village streets.

It was here that James and Elizabeth's story started, I think as I peer out the window. They were both only about twenty years old when they married in Wingrave on September 1, 1821. Although ages at marriage were generally lower in England than in other Western European countries, James and Elizabeth still married a few years earlier than average.[9]

Later records complicate the story of their lives together. But perhaps everything seemed simple during those early days of courtship. As we drive down the streets of their hometown, I wonder what brought them together.

I imagine James walking down the road in front of us. Was he tall and handsome, with curly brown hair and deep-blue eyes? Maybe his good looks swept Elizabeth off her feet. Or perhaps he was short and stocky, with a nose a little too long for his face. Maybe he had a charismatic personality that made him the center of any social gathering. Maybe that's what drew Elizabeth to him. Maybe their parents were friends. Elizabeth had been born out of the county. Maybe she came to Wingrave to work. Perhaps she was lonely and enjoyed the attention James paid her.

In my mind, I can see James stopping to knock on a door. A few seconds later, Elizabeth answers. Her long, brown hair is pulled up neatly on top of her head which makes her large brown eyes stand out even more than usual. Her smile makes James's heart beat faster. Or maybe she has plain features — or is heavyset with big ears. Maybe he snaps at her to hurry — they'll be late for their appointment. Maybe it's a courtship of convenience and no real love or magic sparks in the air between them.

But that's not what I envision here on the winding, romantic roads of Wingrave. James hands Elizabeth flowers and she smiles. They walk off down the road, hand in hand, whispering and laughing together.

Maybe they really fell in love.

We park near the church and get out of the car. The blustery wind takes me off guard as we walk towards the church doors. The gray, stone building almost blends into the frowning, dull sky. I tug on the door, but find it locked. Bending down, I peek through the keyhole, hoping for a glimpse of the interior. Instead, I see people. Startled, I knock on the door. I hear footsteps and then the door swings open to show a man and a woman — clearly the pastor and his wife.

"My ancestors married and baptized their children here nearly two hundred years ago," I blurt out. "We were hoping we could look around."

The pleasant expression on the pastor's face never changes. "Of course," he says, as if this happens every day. "Come in."

My parents and I crowd in, anxious to be out of the piercing wind. Entering the church does little to warm us up, though. The walls shield the wind, but the temperature remains the same.

I walk slowly up the aisle, staring at the arches around me and thinking of James and Elizabeth on their wedding day, walking these same steps.

The pastor soon appears at my side, holding a book.

"What were their names?" he asks.

"James Harris and Elizabeth Johns," I tell him. "They married here in 1821."

He flips through some pages, then holds the book open so I can see it.

"Yes, here they are."

I look over at the transcribed entry with the names printed clearly. "Two children were also baptized here," I add after a moment.

James and Elizabeth baptized their first child in this church on the hill sixteen months after they married. They named the baby James for his father, with the middle name Johns for his mother. In August of 1825, they baptized their second son — my great-great-great-grandfather. They named him Edmond Johns.

The pastor locates these records and shows them to me. Then, he takes us around the church, pointing out some of its features. He shows us the baptismal bowl that dates back hundreds of years and explains some of the architectural changes. Finally, we get ready to leave.

"I don't suppose there's any way we could find out where they lived, is there?" my mom asks as we start toward the door.

Of course not, I think. *They wouldn't have records like that here.*

"No, I'm afraid not," the pastor answers. I pull the heavy door open.

"Wait," the pastor says. We all stop. "Did you say he was a blacksmith?"

"Yes," I answer.

"Well, the old smithy is still standing. The town blacksmith lived there for hundreds of years. The shop and house connected to it passed from one blacksmith to another. Nobody uses the shop now, of course, but someone still lives in the house. I'm sure that's where they lived."

As we climb back in the car, a rush of excitement passes through me. I had not expected to be able to see where the family lived.

Finding the old blacksmith shop proves more difficult than the pastor made it sound. We drive in loops through streets almost too narrow for our car before stopping at a gas station to ask for help.

"Sure, I know where the old blacksmith shop is," the man sitting behind the counter says, giving us a puzzled look. "But nobody has worked there for a long time. Some real nice people live in the house, but they're not home right now."

He leads us around the corner to a little brick building covered in green moss. *This is it,* I think as the man gives us one last confused glance and walks away. *This was once James Harris's shop.* I look over at my dad standing beside me. I wonder if this shop has as much significance to him as it does to me.

The building's double doors are tied shut leaving a gap just large enough for me to peer through. Inside I can see a small workroom that is mostly empty. Old bellows still hang against the back wall.

My mind reels back in time as I picture James sitting here at the bench. His brow furrows in concentration, the sweat running down his forehead from the hours spent working over the fire. He only needs a few more minutes to complete this project. Little James sits on the ground while Edmond toddles around in circles at his feet. Elizabeth had brought them with her to tell him dinner was ready. He agreed to bring them back in with him so Elizabeth could get back to the kitchen.

With one final stroke, James finishes. He leans over to pick Edmond up, tossing the toddler above his head. Edmond shrieks and giggles, before falling back into his father's arms.

"Come on boys," James says. "Let's go eat."

Edmond probably had no memories from this shop and the house behind it. He was still very young when his family moved away from here. Wingrave was Edmond's beginning, but somehow it never really became part of his past.

Back in the car, I flip through the records of Edmond's life one more time, as if expecting to see something I missed. Wingrave presents only the first incongruence in the family—the first mistake in the records.

Edmond left behind a trail of records thicker than most of my ancestors. I've collected parish records, ship records, LDS Church records, census records, and others about him. I have copies of all sorts of documents that list his place and date of birth. On most of these, Edmond himself provided the information. He was very consistent, never wavering in what he said.

The only problem was he was wrong.

Edmond told everyone he was born on July 9, 1824, (a year and a month too early) in Long Crendon, England (a village on the opposite side of Buckinghamshire).[10] As far as I can tell from the records, the family never lived there.

Sometimes I lie awake in bed and try to think of reasons why Edmond gave this wrong information. Possibly, Edmond's parents told him this, and he was simply repeating it. Maybe he didn't really know his birthplace or birth date so he made it up. I suppose it's possible that James and Elizabeth were visiting friends in Long Crendon in July of 1824 and Edmond was actually born there—but not baptized until a year later in Wingrave. Whatever the reason, the fact remains that Edmond never once indicated he had lived in Wingrave.

James and Elizabeth moved to Whitchurch, a village about five miles north of Wingrave, sometime between 1825 and 1830. Here, between 1830 and 1837, four more children were born into the family: Mary, James, William, and Thomas. Mary died at age sixteen months. Thomas lived less than a year.

Edmond may have attended school in Whitchurch when he was old enough. But, he received only a limited education, if any. At the time, one-third of children never attended school at all. Working-class children, even those who went to school, rarely went more than three years. Families usually couldn't afford to send children more than this, both because of the fees charged by the schools and because of the productivity missed by not having their help at home.[11]

As a result, many people in the countryside didn't achieve even a basic level of literacy. In 1830, less than sixty percent of adults in England could read.[12] Edmond was able to sign his name on his marriage record, showing that he had at least some ability to write. His mother signed her name with only a mark.[13]

While the Harris family lived in Whitchurch, discontent with the government began to fester throughout England again. Sweeping calls for change met with no results. Rural unrest, particularly in the southeast near where the Harris family lived, grew. Perhaps James joined other villagers in protests that sometimes erupted in violence.

The British parliament passed the Reform Act of 1832 after recognizing that compromise was the only way to avoid rebellion. This Act made important, yet limited, changes in the political system. The Act extended the vote to all adult males owning more than £10 worth of property—about one in seven. The conservatives had made concessions, but the power of the privileged still remained protected. The immediate crisis was diffused. Periods of unrest would flare up again, but England wouldn't experience the far-reaching rebellions that hit continental Europe over the next few decades.[14]

The working class also made some advancements. Yet, many felt bitterly disappointed, believing progress had not extended nearly far enough. As a skilled craftsman, James may have been among those to receive the vote. More likely, though, James shared in the frustration of knowing his voice would still not be heard.

It takes us only about ten minutes to reach Whitchurch. We locate the gray stone church and pull the car up as close as we can. My dad opts to wait in the warm car, while my mom comes up to the church with me.

My mom and I walk through the church graveyard looking for the tombstones of the two Harris children who died in Whitchurch. A few of the stones date back to the beginning of the 1800s, which gives us hope. My mom and I crouch on the ground next to them and squint. The writing has faded on many of the old stones, making deciphering even the names next to impossible.

My teeth chatter as I pull my coat tighter around me, trying to keep out the wind. I glance over at my mom. She has her black hat pulled nearly over her eyes and her arms crossed tightly across her chest. My mom hates being cold. I feel a stab of guilt for her misery.

A few minutes later, we give up and head back to the car. Before climbing in, I snap a picture of the church that once played such an important part in my ancestors' lives. They gathered here every Sunday—on warm, sunny days and on cold winter days like this one. Inside these doors, they baptized four children. And within the grounds I stand on now, they buried two of these little ones.

Religion held a central place in the Harris family's lives just as it had for the Albrecht and Nilsson families. England's most prominent denomination was the Church of England (also known as the Anglican Church). The Church of England's controversial and unusual background led religion in England in a different direction than the rest of Europe.

The origins of the Church of England date back to the reign of Henry VIII who ruled England from 1509 to 1547. Catholicism served as the state religion when Henry took power. When the Pope refused to allow Henry to divorce his first wife, Catherine of Aragon, in order to marry his mistress, Anne Boleyn, Henry decided to take matters into his own hands. First, he appointed new officials in England who would agree to annul the marriage. In 1533, the marriage was annulled and Henry married Anne. The following year, Henry passed a law declaring the king to be the supreme head of the new Church of England, completing its separation from the Catholic Church.

The Church of England vacillated in its alignment between Catholicism and Protestantism at the whim of the ruling monarch over the next centuries. This difference of opinion set the stage for a unique characteristic of religion in England—the prevalence of dissident denominations.

The state religion functioned as almost the sole religion in many Western European countries through the early 1800s. By mid-century, dissident religions remained small, scattered, and persecuted in most places. In England though, diversity existed on a much larger scale. The Church of England still occupied a privileged place in society, and other religious groups (particularly Catholics) did meet some discrimination. Still, followers of other religions enjoyed a level of freedom not experienced elsewhere in Europe.[15]

Perhaps the most significant nonconformist religion was Methodism. Founded by John Wesley in the mid-1700s, Methodism represented a homegrown derivation of the Church of England with a unique emphasis on spirituality and emotions. The religion continued to attract followers so that by the mid-1800s, over two million people attended services in over eleven thousand places of worship. Other nonconformist religions also drew sizable crowds. Baptists and Independents, both of which had been around longer than the Methodists, increased in numbers throughout the first half of the nineteenth century. Unitarians and Quakers also claimed large memberships.[16]

While James and Elizabeth raised their family in the Anglican Church, they probably had neighbors that belonged to other religions. Methodists and, to a lesser extent, Baptists had an important presence in Buckinghamshire. Members of these denominations often held a disproportionate amount of positions of power in the community.

The religious environment would have important consequences for the Harris family.

The Harris family prepared to move again after a decade in Whitchurch. This time they chose Steeple Claydon, a village about ten miles northwest of Whitchurch, as their destination. The town is the next stop on our tour too.

Events in Steeple Claydon left a tangled trail of records behind. This is further complicated by the fact that most of my research was done secondhand. The limited information that I had made it impractical to order microfilms to the Family History Center in Madison. Instead, I relied on my brother, Scott, who lived forty-five minutes from the Family History Library in Salt Lake City. I would e-mail him a list of films to search and he would e-mail me back the results. Internet databases provided my other major source of information.

As we enter the town of Steeple Claydon, all the distance, the extra steps, the extra people, are gone. Here, I can get as close to the Harris family — as close to the past — as it is possible to be. And maybe I can understand what really happened.

As we drive down some of the town roads, I consider what I already know about the Harris family in Steeple Claydon.

James Harris appears in the records of Steeple Claydon for the first time in 1840. He is listed as the father of a child, Emmanuel. But Elizabeth isn't listed as the mother. Instead, the pastor wrote the name "Sarah" in that column. No other surname is given for this Sarah, and there are none of the usual markings that indicate that a child is illegitimate.

A census of the area taken a year later adds more confusion to the situation. The record contains only a list of people, their ages rounded down to the nearest five years (except for children under ten — then exact ages are given), occupations, and notes about whether they were born in the county or not. Seven people lived in the Harris household in 1841, including: James (age forty), Elizabeth (age forty), Edmond (age fifteen), Sarah (age fifteen), James (age eight), William (age six), and Emmanuel (age one). All have the Harris surname. James worked as a blacksmith, and Edmond is employed as a laborer. Elizabeth and Sarah were both born out of the county. The children all match up with the birth records I had already found — except Sarah.[17]

Ten years later, the 1851 census lists Emmanuel again, now eleven years old, living with James and a different wife, Ann. James and William also live there. This census gives each person's relationship to the head of household. According to the record, all three boys are James's sons.[18]

The records of Steeple Claydon reveal one more event in the lives of the Harris family. In 1845, James and Elizabeth baptized a daughter, Eliza. This birth record is the last paper I have with Elizabeth's name on it.

Together, the documents don't make sense. The more I study the records, the more it feels like a choose-your-own-adventure novel — or a choose-your-own-scenario family.

When my brother first sent me the packet of papers he had copied from the Steeple Claydon records, he also sent a note. He wrote, "I'm convinced James had a child with a teenage girl who was living with the family." Scott's hypothesis was that Sarah was a neighbor girl employed by the Harris family. She had an affair with James which produced the child, Emmanuel. James was a scoundrel and a cheat.

I latched on to this theory. I envisioned the conclusion to the scenario. By 1845, Elizabeth simply couldn't stand it anymore. She took her new baby and left—maybe to live with a relative. That was why I couldn't locate anything else about her.

I felt pity for Elizabeth. No matter how heartbroken Elizabeth was, she would have had few options. Divorce was only allowed in extreme circumstances, and even then a double standard prevailed. One proviso of the law allowed a man to divorce a wife who had committed adultery, but didn't allow a divorce when the genders were reversed. Besides, the cost and time involved to divorce ensured that it remained practically impossible for the working-class people. Even when divorce was granted, husbands retained all legal rights for children over seven years of age.[19]

Women in the mid-1800s were also economically dependent on their husbands. If Elizabeth left James, she would have struggled to provide for herself and her children. Although industrialization provided more jobs for women, these jobs paid low wages and required long hours, making it nearly impossible to balance caring for small children with work.

There were some problems with the James-the-scoundrel theory, though. Why wasn't the child marked as illegitimate? Illegitimate children born to unmarried couples who intended to later marry were common, but a married, middle-aged man having a baby with a teenage girl was not. It would have been scandalous. Yet the records give no indication that there was anything out of the ordinary with Emmanuel's birth. Besides, this Sarah should have a different surname.

What else could have happened?

A trip to the library in Salt Lake City turned up another possibility. I had handed over my documents to a research consultant. She studied them carefully, obviously perplexed also. Finally, she came up with another explanation. What about James and Elizabeth's first son who was also named James? What happened to him? Maybe he married a Sarah and they had a child named Emmanuel in 1840. James Jr. died soon after, and James Sr. took in his daughter-in-law and his grandson. Instead of being a scoundrel, James was generous and kind. It seemed plausible—at first.

There were problems with the James-the-generous theory as well. It was true that I had no idea what happened to James Jr.—the eldest James Jr. anyway. My hunch was that he died as a child, which was why the family reused the name (although families didn't always wait until the death of a child to reuse a name). A search of marriage records didn't turn up any possible marriage records for a James and Sarah or death records for a James. Besides, the 1851 census said Emmanuel was James Sr.'s son.

I dismissed this scenario as less likely than the first one. That left me with my original hypothesis—the James-the-scoundrel one.

Instability also prevailed around the Harris family. Economic crisis again shook the country in 1837 to 1838, the years immediately prior to the family's arrival in Steeple Claydon. Fluctuations throughout the 1840s led to great insecurity in the lives of working-class people. Wages, along with the availability of employment, changed from year to year. Prices for other goods also bounced around. Financial security remained an elusive goal for most people.[20]

These fluctuations might partially explain the inconsistencies in James's occupation. Throughout the 1820s, records list him as a blacksmith. The pastor added "laborer" to his description in 1832. In 1835, he is just a blacksmith again. Records from 1837 until 1845 describe him as a laborer, making no mention of him being a blacksmith.[21] Later, the 1851 census again lists blacksmith as his occupation.[22] Maybe James had trouble finding employment as a blacksmith some years, or had to take on additional work to make ends meet.

The working-class population responded to the floundering economy with more protests. Some people also responded with organized action. This unrest, combined with the disastrous Irish potato famine that struck in the mid-1840s, led some government leaders to believe change was necessary again. Led by Sir Robert Peel, the British prime minister, parliament passed several reform acts, culminating with the repeal of the Corn Laws (tariffs that protected domestic British corn prices—and the interests of the wealthy landowners) in 1846. Fierce opposition caused Peel to resign.

Many demands of the working-class people remained unmet. But, like before, the reform was enough to diffuse the crisis. Even as revolution and rebellion swept through many Western European countries in 1848, a sort of stability prevailed in England.[23]

Stability hadn't found the Harris family yet, though. Sometime between 1845 and 1850, James and his family moved about five miles north to the town of Buckingham. Edmond probably didn't move with them. He had struck out on his own by this time—and had maybe even made his way to London already. James' wife, Elizabeth, might not have made the move either. She disappears from the records after the 1845 birth of Eliza—as does Eliza. The two either died or—as in my James-the-scoundrel theory—left. The move to Buckingham is the last stop I know on James's life path—and it is also our last stop today.

With a population that reached over four thousand by the mid-1800s, Buckingham was considerably larger than other places the Harris family had lived. It had little in the way of industry, but instead functioned mostly as an agricultural and market town. When the Harris family arrived, the town bustled with activity. The population was growing so fast that building could hardly keep up. Local industries emerged and new churches were erected. The railway, after originally bypassing Buckingham, arrived at last. Schools opened and a town newspaper began printing.

The Harris family had really arrived at the peak of a curve, though. Buckingham never grasped the waves of industry that transformed life for other towns around it. Soon after the Harris family arrived, Buckingham began a long and steady decline. The most prominent family in the area fell into financial ruin, with effects rippling throughout the town. Buckingham's position at the north of the county meant that many businesses and political establishments passed it by in favor of Aylesbury which was more centrally located within the county. Buckingham lost political representatives and watched many local industries go under.[24]

The town's loss turns out to be my gain. The decline served, in some ways, to freeze Buckingham. Modern changes didn't penetrate as deeply here as they did in other places, leaving Buckingham much the same as it was when the Harris family walked down these streets from their home to Market Square or to the town church.

We drive through these streets, winding our way towards the center of town. With each turn, it seems that the streets shrink narrower and narrower until I'm convinced our car must be wider than the street. Yet, not only do cars continue driving, two-way traffic manages to work its way through. We often have to drive on the curb in order for both cars to squeeze by each other. I wince and close my eyes, only to find that somehow we got by without incident.

The old brick buildings lining the street hold a charm that dances around us. Only the cars, obviously out of place and unwelcome on the tiny streets, remind me that we've only arrived in a new place, not a new century. I want to laugh at the absurdity of trying to maneuver our car, gasp for air as the endless buildings crowd together, or wander around all evening in the nearly magical maze. I take picture after picture—none of which can convey the feelings that I'm trying to capture.

After a walk around the center of town, we drive up the hill to the church. The sun has already begun to set, casting the long shadows of twilight on the building. This church and its bell tower played an important role in the lives of the Harris family. The 8:00 p.m. curfew

bell rang out daily from 1781 until 1940. The same bell also rang fo
five minutes at 6:00 in the morning. Bells rang to alert people to fires
or in honor of particular festivities. The bells also signified death. A
certain bell rang when a child under twelve died; a different one rang
for a person over twelve. Then, after a pause, nine tenor bells rang for
the death of a male, or six if the person had been female.[25]

We pull open the wooden door and enter the church. I walk slowly
up the main aisle, just as I did in Wingrave this morning. Once again,
I'm following in the footsteps of James on his wedding day. But here,
in July of 1850, it was his second wedding day. The marriage record
shows James, a widower, marrying Ann Norris Coles, a widow. Ann
would become the stepmother to three children still living with James:
James Jr. (age seventeen), William (age fifteen), and Emmanuel (age
ten). If Ann had children from her previous marriage, none moved
in with them. Edmond probably never met Ann. By the time of his
father's wedding, he had already left England.

James and Ann's life together got off to a rough start. A few weeks
before their second anniversary, James Jr. died at age nineteen. Only
eighteen months later, on March 20, 1853, Emmanuel died at age
thirteen. The laconic parish records reveal nothing except the burial
dates and ages of these two boys. Losing two teenage sons who had
made it past infancy and childhood when the risk of death was the
highest, must have been heart-wrenching. The records tell me nothing
about the causes or circumstances, emotions or reactions. Yet I do
know one detail. Twice in two years the same bell pattern rang for
the Harris family. The tenor bell sounded, paused for a moment, then
rang out nine clear tolls.

The next morning my dad drops me off at the county archive in
Aylesbury. My parents will do a little sightseeing while I do some
research. At the archive, I spread my records out in front of an
archivist there and explain the family saga. She hesitates for only a
moment before giving me her conclusion.

"Sarah is a daughter of James and Elizabeth, and Elizabeth actually
is Emmanuel's mother," she says, as if this is obvious. "The pastor
made a mistake when he wrote down the mother's name. He looked
over at the family and saw the daughter, Sarah, standing there with
them. He wasn't paying attention, so he wrote the daughter's name
down instead."

I'm still doubtful.

"Look how Sarah is listed in order with the other children in the
census record. She must be a daughter." I remember that Edmond
was born in 1825 in Wingrave and Mary in 1830 in Whitchurch.

erhaps the family moved between those years to a different home—a home in a different county since Sarah Harris was supposedly born outside of Buckinghamshire. Here, Sarah was born and the older son, James, died.

This surprisingly simple scenario seems to be the most likely explanation so far. There might even be a way to check. I send for the civil registration birth certificate of Emmanuel—the last hope at shedding light on the family.

The remainder of our trip passes in a whirlwind. We return our rental car later that day (where we cause a scene by flatly refusing to pay the £100 they claim we owe for the flat tire). The next day and a half we rush around London at top speed, trying to cram in as much sightseeing as possible.

On the morning of Christmas Eve, we board our plane to return to Rome. As the people around me find their seats, I evaluate our trip. I haven't untangled my family yet, but I am less quick to condemn James now. In fact, I feel almost guilty for my James-the-scoundrel theory.

"Well, that was quite the trip, wasn't it?" My dad asks, interrupting my thoughts. I wait for elaboration, unsure of what he means.

"It was fun to drive through those little English towns and see where the Harris family lived. I really enjoyed it," he continues.

"Me too," my mom says. I can tell they really mean it.

Our trip, with all its flaws, was a success.

Several weeks later, an e-mail with the subject heading "Certificate Request" appears in my inbox. A woman from the office that handles civil registration record requests writes that she found the birth record of Emmanuel, but wasn't able to locate the death record for Elizabeth Harris I had asked for. She asks if I would like another search instead.

I quickly type information for another couple of certificates I am interested in purchasing. "If it isn't too inconvenient," I add, "Could you tell me the name of Emmanuel's mother?" I am too anxious to wait another few days for the certificate to arrive in the mail.

Her reply is long and filled with the details of more unsuccessful searches. Almost as an afterthought, she writes at the end, "Oh, just to confirm—Emmanuel's mother was Elizabeth."

I sit back in my chair. I think of the pastor writing down "Sarah" as James and Elizabeth stood beside him baptizing their new son. He could have never known that hundreds of years later his carelessness in writing one word would have descendants and archivists on two continents forming all kinds of scenarios about the Harris family.

It was such a little mistake—for him.

PASSENGER DEPARTURE LIST FROM ENGLAND
FOR EDMOND AND ELIZA (BARRETT) HARRIS

CHAPTER NINE

DESTINATIONS:
EDMOND AND
ELIZA'S JOURNEY

I sit alone in my bedroom listening to the distant giggles of Rachel and Taylor as they play with the other neighborhood children outside. Rachel has been begging for someone to push her on the swings—one of my least favorite parenting jobs. David agreed to take over the task so I can stay inside and do something I've wanted to do for a long time.

Today, I'm going to put together Edmond's life. I pull out my binders containing copied documents, notebooks filled with scribbled entries, and file folders with research reports I wrote to myself—all focused on Edmond and his family. I have collected stacks of papers and details about his life. Yet, they lack cohesiveness. The research process has stretched out nearly four years making the information in the documents seem like disconnected events instead of parts of a continuous timeline. I feel like the time has come to put it all together, to find Edmond's story amidst all the details.

I set a large white notebook in front of me and begin leafing through its pages, looking for dates and places of any major events. Near the beginning of the notebook, I find a copy of a marriage record. As I read over the names, my mind drifts to the day four years ago when I found it.

Sitting at a computer at the Family History Library in Salt Lake City, I type Edmond's name into the FamilySearch computer program. An unexpected result appears on the screen. It says that on May 7, 1847, Edmond Harris married Eliza Barrett in the St. Pancras Church in London.

Eliza? I think. None of my family records show anyone by this name.

I hurry to get the microfilm of the original record to verify. A few minutes later, I stare down at the entry in the parish records. Here is proof of Edmond's first—and forgotten—family.

Eliza Barrett was a native of London, having been born there on October 9, 1824. By 1847, she and Edmond lived on the same street in London.[1] Edmond had likely moved to London from Steeple Claydon looking for work. As industrialization swept the country, he joined the masses of people migrating from the villages into the cities.

In the mid-1800s, London was a city bursting with sights and sounds, wealth and poverty, opportunity and misery. Over two million people lived there, many originally from other countries. Housing construction couldn't keep pace with the people pouring in, resulting in crowded, unsanitary, disease-plagued slums. The gap between the rich and the poor continued to widen, until they almost lived in two separate worlds. Pollution, grime, and filth filled the air and streets. The poet P.B. Shelley concluded, "Hell is a city much like London."[2]

Edmond and Eliza made their first home together here, joining the class of struggling urban poor. Eliza worked as a house servant. Edmond worked as a carman, transporting merchandise by driving a horse-drawn cart.[3] Including the time spent in the stable with the horses, Edmond may have worked nearly a hundred hours a week. Despite this, his pay remained low. Few, if any, occupations paid lower hourly wages. Unpleasant side effects also came with the job. Most carmen couldn't afford to clothe themselves adequately for the winter and suffered frequently from bronchitis and pneumonia. Also, as one observer pointed out, "It is admitted that carmen are largely addicted to strong drink."[4]

It was while living in London that Edmond and Eliza encountered missionaries from The Church of Jesus Christ of Latter-day Saints. Although in 1849 Mormon missionaries had not yet entered Germany or Sweden, the LDS Church already had a strong presence in England. The first Mormon missionaries arrived there in July of 1837—only seven years after the Church had been established in the US.

While the LDS Church continued to struggle at home, the British Mission was successful almost immediately. In less than a year, seven missionaries baptized fifteen hundred people in England. Missionaries and converts encountered some persecution, but they generally taught and worshipped in peace. While other countries later expelled and outlawed Mormon missionaries, in England, entire congregations converted at once. In fact, missionaries found people in England much more willing than people in America to listen to their message. Membership reached seventy-five hundred by 1842. The gathering of British converts to America began as soon as arrangements could be made. The first group set sail in 1840.[5]

The success of the LDS Church was partly due to circumstances in England. As the Industrial Revolution flung England into transition, people longed for something that provided security. The atmosphere of relative religious tolerance also helped pave the way for the Church. A religious census taken in 1851 showed just how extensive religious diversity had become. Of the over six million people who went to church services on census Sunday, forty-seven percent attended an Anglican church, four percent attended a Catholic church, and forty-nine percent attended another church (most notably Methodist and Baptist churches).[6] The widespread practice of nonconformist religions created a setting in which the LDS Church could flourish.

The expansion of the LDS Church in England slowed for a few years in the mid-1840s as crisis, including the martyrdom of Joseph Smith, gripped the Church at home. Then, reorganization and a renewed missionary push led to a period of growth. Despite the constant drain of emigration, early membership in Britain peaked at thirty-three thousand in 1851. Edmond and Eliza were baptized in January of 1849 during this period of growth.[7]

As members of the urban lower class, Edmond and Eliza fit the mold of the typical English LDS convert. Nine out of ten converts in this period claimed urban homes. Without the roots and traditions of their home villages, urban dwellers were more open to new ideas and more likely to be seeking an anchor in their lives. Poverty was almost as common with nearly eighty percent of converts coming from the lower class. Mormon missionaries urged participation and action, and told people to change their lives—something often only the poor were willing to do.[8]

I can only guess how Edmond and Eliza's families reacted to the news of their baptisms. I assume they were at least taken aback, if not totally opposed. The couple soon had more startling news for their families: they were moving to Australia.

From where I sit cross-legged on the floor, I survey the scene around me. The stack of papers spread out across the floor appears to be growing more chaotic instead of more organized. I dig through a folder, pulling out a faded copy of the passenger list from the *Blonde,* the ship which carried Edmond and Eliza to Australia in December of 1849.[9] I remember back to when I first learned about this voyage.

"Australia?" I repeat doubtfully, as David and I sit at a table in the Family History Library in Salt Lake City.

"Australia," David confirms, waving the paper he has copied as proof. He has spent the afternoon acting as my gofer and is now immensely pleased to have made a discovery of his own.

"They were probably convicts," my dad tells me the next day on the phone. "People got arrested and exiled to Australia all the time, even for small offenses. Maybe he just stole a loaf of bread because his family was hungry."

"Australia?" My grandma thinks it over for a minute when I call to ask her about it. "No, I never heard anything about that."

"Australia was not just settled by convicts, you know," a professor who is from Australia bristles when David relates Edmond's story at a conference dinner. "People came for other reasons, too."

I will never know the exact reasons Edmond and Eliza emigrated to Australia, particularly less than a year after joining a church that instructed, and even helped, its members go to America. I can eliminate a few reasons, though. They weren't convicts. In fact, by 1849 convicts weren't allowed to arrive in New South Wales, Australia.

During the first forty years of Australia's colonization, nearly all of the arrivals were convicts. The census of 1828 showed that only five thousand of the more than thirty-six thousand inhabitants of New South Wales had come voluntarily. Then, policies began to change. England had too many people for too few jobs while Australia had many jobs but too few people. So, the government did what it could to rectify the situation. Between 1831 and 1850, 170,000 free emigrants set sail to Australia from England. Those who could afford it paid for the voyage themselves. They were the minority. The government picked up the tab for two-thirds of the travelers through an assisted emigration program. These emigrants usually came from the bottom rungs of society. The leaders of England figured the country would be better off without them. Edmond and Eliza were among these.[10]

I also know that hope of striking it rich in the gold fields didn't lure them to Australia. Although gold drew many people, Edmond and Eliza left before the gold rush began. Probably, they simply believed Australia offered economic opportunities not available in London. There, work and cheap land were supposedly available to everyone. And they could make the voyage for free.

Having a prepaid ticket to Australia didn't make the trip easy. Although travel by sea was generally unpleasant in 1849, travel for assisted emigrants to Australia was particularly bad. The distance alone was intimidating. The longer travel time combined with the frequency of storms and the condition of the ports made shipwrecks for passengers traveling to Australia more common than for those traveling to other places. The English government also went to no great lengths to ensure the safety or comfort of the people whose passages they paid.

Despite the risks and discomforts of the voyage, many people remained determined to make the trip. When Edmond and Eliza set sail in 1849, they joined thirty-two thousand people who left the United Kingdom for Australia or New Zealand that year.[11]

Edmond and Eliza settled in Maitland, a community about one hundred miles north of Sydney. Maitland had been founded three decades earlier as a convict settlement. Australia, at that time, wasn't a unified nation. Instead, individual British colonies such as Maitland were scattered along the perimeter of the island. Outside the settlements stretched miles and miles of "bush," the term used to describe forests and other uncultivated land. In this new environment, the Harris family added two children to their family: Maria, born in 1853, and Lister, born at the beginning of 1855.

In many ways, the Harris family's lives turned upside down upon arrival in Australia. Seasons were backwards. Animals and vegetation were different. The sight of the Aboriginal people frightened many of them. Yet, Australia still contained familiar bits of home. Settlers paid tribute to the same monarch as they had before. A familiar language and, to some extent, culture surrounded Edmond and Eliza since nearly all the immigrants came from England.[12]

Although no new convicts landed after 1840, convicts, former convicts, and the children of convicts still made up a large proportion of the population. Many convicts had been sent to Australia for stealing and didn't constitute a threat to public safety. In fact, some people claimed to prefer the company of the convicts to the free immigrants. Since two-thirds of the free immigrants had come with the help of the government, some believed the majority of them had just as questionable characters as the convicts. After all, the government sent the people it didn't want—sometimes even loading up prostitutes, homeless, or insane people off the streets.[13]

But most free immigrants were simply destitute urban workers. Rather than being bothered by the make-up of the Australian population, Edmond and Eliza may have felt right at home.

Edmond and Eliza did differ from those around them in one way: they were some of the first Mormons in Australia. The Mormon missionaries didn't arrive in Australia until October of 1851.[14] The Harris family likely had no connection with the LDS Church for the first few years they were in Australia.

In May of 1852, Eliza read an article in the *Sydney Morning Herald* that defended Mormonism. She contacted the missionaries in Sydney and made a plea for LDS literature adding, "I care not what I pay for it." She also requested that missionaries be sent to their home as soon as possible. John McCarthy and John Jones, Mormon missionaries serving in Australia, heeded her request. Over the next months, Edmond and Eliza worked with the missionaries to establish a branch in Maitland.[15]

Neither Edmond nor Eliza left behind any written record. But others in the Maitland branch did mention them in their diaries. These records show Edmond and Eliza attending meetings, hosting guests, and participating in conversations about Church teachings. The only personal description of them comes from the diary of John Perkins, another member of the Maitland branch. He wrote that Eliza was the dirtiest woman he had ever met and that all Edmond did was "walk around grumping and growling like a bear with a sore head."[16]

I squint at my transcription of the journal entry in my notebook. The LDS Church Archives containing the diary allowed no photocopies — or even pens. As I flip through the pages in search of other insights, my mind wanders back to a scene in our kitchen.

Rachel, then two years old, sits at the table waiting for her lunch. Taylor sits in his high chair a few feet away, banging his spoon on the tray — his way of telling me to hurry. I hold the phone with my shoulder, keeping both hands free to make Rachel's peanut butter sandwich and stir Taylor's rice cereal. As I get lunch ready, I describe to my dad what I found in the archive, including the diary entry.

"A bear with a sore head?" Rachel asks as I hang up the phone. "What does that mean, Mommy?"

"I don't know," I say.

We decide to try it out. We take turns walking around the kitchen, growling and rubbing our heads. Taylor watches us from his high chair and giggles.

Although the diary entry is amusing, I also find it disturbing. I wonder if Edmond and Eliza knew that John Perkins felt this way about them. They couldn't have known that his words would be the only insight into their personalities to survive the weathering of history. His unkind remarks, now with nothing to counter them, exist as fact.

I close the notebook and pull out a binder containing papers carefully arranged in sheet protectors. A copy of a microfilmed index card lies on top. The card states that after living in Australia for less than six years, Eliza and her children set sail again. They boarded the *Julia Ann* in September of 1855 — this time headed for California.

Another scene rushes into my mind.

I sit at the computer with the index card in front of me after everyone else in the house has gone to sleep. Tonight, I have decided to see what I can learn about the family and their voyage. I want to know: What happened to Eliza? Why have I never heard of her?

Eliza and Edmond probably began making preparations to go to America several years prior to 1855. Funding a trip like this presented a serious challenge for families like theirs who had limited financial resources. The ship passage cost approximately £24. In comparison, a storekeeper earned slightly more than £2 a week. Then there was the additional cost of getting from California to Utah, another significant undertaking. In all, it cost nearly three times as much to make the journey from Australia to Utah as it did to travel from England to Utah. Many Mormon converts paid their way in advance through installments to President Farnham, the president of the Australian mission. For a short time, the Perpetual Emigration Fund also provided assistance. [17]

Despite the financial strain, about half of the Mormons in Australia in the 1800s managed to find a way to make the trip. The group of Australian converts was never large to begin with, though. About 452 Mormons emigrated from Australia during the nineteenth century. [18]

The Harris family's emigration from England blends neatly into the historical context. They represented a movement, a feeling, a vision that swept through Europe. People left their countries of origins in droves, headed toward the promise of a new land. As one of those lands of promise, Australia had people streaming in.

Their emigration from Australia was different. When the Harris family left in 1855, they traveled the wrong way on a one-way road. The tide they followed hadn't changed directions—but the Harris family had. Religion was their clear motivation. They had already come to a land of economic promise when they set sail for Australia. Now, they headed to a land of religious promise. They left to find Zion.

On the rainy, windy, dismal afternoon of September 7, 1855, fifty-six passengers boarded the *Julia Ann*. Half of the passengers were members of the LDS Church. Benjamin Franklin Pond, an experienced seaman, served as the captain. The trip was supposed to take three months, their final destination being San Francisco, California. From here, the Mormon passengers planned to continue on to Utah. [19]

Eliza must have felt some anxiety as she boarded the ship with her two-year-old daughter, Maria, and her six-month-old son, Lister. Eliza had no illusions about traveling by ship. She had done it before and she knew it wouldn't be easy. And she would make this trip without her husband. Edmond had originally planned on making the trip with his family, but Church leaders announced just before the launching of the *Julia Ann* that the Perpetual Emigration Fund could no longer assist Australian emigrants. Without help, the family didn't have enough funds for everyone to go. Edmond would have to wait.[20]

Although nothing has been passed down about Edmond's good-bye to his family, I have envisioned it in my mind many times.

Edmond stands at the pier with his family. As he looks at his wife with their two small children, he worries again about how she'll manage. Maria cries as Edmond kneels to say good-bye to his little girl. He strokes her hair and promises they will see each other soon. He pats Lister's head and comments on how big he will be the next time they're together. Then, he holds Eliza's hands and looks into her eyes which are swimming with emotion—nervousness, sadness, and excitement—as they talk about when they will all be reunited in Zion.

Later, Edmond watches as the ship leaves the port. He waves to Eliza and the children as they stand on the deck, waving back at him. They shrink little by little—and then they are gone. Perhaps in future years, he would reflect often on that day. He would remember the dress Eliza wore, the tight hug Maria gave him, and the sleepy look on baby Lister's face.

They had worked hard and prepared carefully to make the journey, scrimping and saving small amounts at a time. As the ship sailed into the distance, Edmond must have felt that Zion was a destination worthy of every sacrifice. But he never guessed the price he would pay.

From the start of the voyage, winds blew harshly, rocking the ship and causing terrible seasickness for the passengers on board. One of the passengers, Andrew Anderson, recorded that most people threw up after eating their first meal. "My family and others were sick little or much all the time," he wrote.[21] The passengers received some "Indian cornmeal," evidently useful for upset stomachs. Despite illness, most of the Mormon passengers got along with one another. In these conditions the days passed, each not much different from the one before.

By October 4, the ship had been at sea for nearly a month. Captain Pond spent the day steering through an area filled with threatening reefs. By the time nightfall arrived, it appeared that the danger had passed. Captain Pond appointed a lookout and went below to rest. The passengers began to settle down for the evening. Eliza probably went below to steerage with her children. Perhaps she nursed her baby, sang to her daughter, or held her children close as she told them stories about Zion.

Then a call rang out. "Hard down the helm." [22] With a noise so loud that is sounded like thunder, the *Julia Ann* crashed directly into a reef.

The consequences were immediate and disastrous. Captain Pond wrote, "I sprang to my feet, but my heart failed me, as I was nearly thrown upon the floor by the violent striking of the ship." [23] The heavy waves pounded the ship sideways against the reef. The stern section lifted onto the reef and the bow fell deep into the water. A large hole opened in the side of the ship and the booms swung violently across the deck.

The ship was not sinking — it was breaking into pieces. Even worse, there was no land in sight. Captain Pond "instantly saw there was no hope for the ship, and very little for the lives of those on board." [24]

The extent of the crisis soon became evident to all. The scene would haunt survivors throughout their lives. John McCarthy, the missionary who had responded to Eliza's request for LDS literature, "saw mothers nursing their babies in the midst of falling masts and broken spars while the breakers were rolling twenty feet high over the wreck." [25] The waves washed two young girls overboard. They were never seen again.

Word soon came for everyone to gather in the cabin. Parents hurried below, pulling their children out of bed as they made their way there. Esther Spangenberg, another passenger, described "mothers holding their undressed children in their arms as they snatched them from their slumbers, screaming and lamenting." [26] Amidst this chaos, Eliza managed to get her children to the cabin with the others.

Even in the cabin, water covered the deck and continued to seep in as waves pounded mercilessly against the ship. Esther Spangenberg wrote: "When I reached the cabin, the scene can never be erased from my memory. Mothers screaming, and children clinging to them in terror, furniture was torn from its lashing and all upturned, the ship was lying on her beam ends." [27]

Meanwhile, the crew began to implement a desperate plan. One crew member swam to the nearby reef and attached a rope to it. Passengers then began to make their way, hand-over-hand, slowly and painstakingly, to the highest part of the reef. Crew members assisted the passengers by carrying young children across the rope with them. As Captain Pond wrote, "The process was an exceedingly arduous one, and attended with much peril." [28] Even the relative refuge of the reef left the passengers chest deep in water and surrounded by sharks. The plan was not ideal, but it was their only chance for survival.

The crew called passengers up from the cabin one by one to take their turn crossing to the reef, beginning with the women and children. In my mind, I can see Eliza. She stands in the cabin as water splashes all around her. The boat rocks and creaks violently from side to side, the darkness pressing down against her. Soaking wet and bruised from the debris falling wildly from the boat, Eliza keeps her children close as they wait for their turn to cross. Her clothes are nearly ripped to shreds. She holds Maria's arm tightly as the little girl clings desperately to her legs. Eliza realizes there is no way she can carry a baby and cross to the reef—she will need both hands to grip the rope. With deliberate carefulness, she lashes Lister across her chest, making sure he is as tight as possible.

Someone calls Maria's name. The people below pass Maria up on deck and then to a crew member. Eliza watches anxiously, acutely feeling her own powerlessness. She waits. And she prays. The seconds seem like hours as the boat lurches and the water swells around her. At last, word comes back—Maria reached the reef safely. Eliza breathes a deep sigh of relief.

From up on deck, she hears a crew member call her name. She is ready. She kisses Lister and whispers consoling words in his ear, almost as much for her own reassurance as for his.

Then suddenly, she hears someone shouting, "Hold on all!"

And then "an awful sea struck the ship, tearing up the bulwarks, threatening death and destruction to everything within reach."[29] The ship couldn't take the pounding it was receiving any longer. The *Julia Ann* broke in two across the hatch. Captain Pond described: "The sea had stove in the forward part of my cabin and washed away the starboard staterooms, taking with it two women and a child. The poor mother had lashed her infant to her bosom."[30]

Eliza and Lister were washed away and drowned.

Here in my bedroom, I remember reading Captain Pond's words for the first time.

Several hours have passed since I started what I thought would be a quick preliminary search on the Internet for information about the *Julia Ann*. Now, I can't read any further. Captain Pond's words ring in my head. I get up and pace the floor. I want to tell someone. But there's no one to tell. It's 2:00 in the morning. Everyone is asleep.

Why didn't anyone tell me? I wonder. But there was no one to tell me. No one alive today knew about the fate of Eliza Barrett Harris.

I sit back down at my computer and cry. I cry for their tragedy and for my lack of knowledge of it. The thought that Eliza died one hundred and fifty years ago does little to console me. Through the detailed, time-consuming research I have done, I have come to know her. Now, I feel an intimate and personal loss.

Eliza isn't my blood relative. If I were to meet her, I might even be repulsed. She was poor, ignorant, and dirty. Yet now I am bound to her. I know the last actions of her life. I sense her final thoughts and feelings, her most personal and vulnerable emotions. I feel her desperate love for her children. Despite the vastly different circumstances of our lives, we share something. If I had been on the *Julia Ann* instead of her, I would have also clutched my daughter tightly and lashed my baby boy to my chest.

I quietly open the door to my children's bedroom and see them lying there peacefully, their backs rising and falling with each breath. Rachel is two years old. Taylor is six months old.

I get into bed and think of Maria and Lister, Rachel and Taylor.

Most of the passengers had made it to the reef by the time this tremendous wave struck the cabin. Five people drowned including Eliza, Lister, the two ten-year-old girls, and the mother of one of the girls. Two families remained on the boat.

The situation grew more desperate. The hauling line parted. Captain Pond begged the remaining adults to save themselves, but they refused to leave their children. Pond and Chief Officer Coffin, an experienced seaman and whaler, threw themselves on the rope in an effort to save their own lives. They made it safely to the reef.

Hope was gone. The two families had no way to cross the treacherous sea to the reef. Finally, one last powerful wave hit the boat. Instead of drowning the remaining passengers, the wave split the boat, carrying the piece on which the families stood until it knocked into the reef. The families walked off the boat and onto the reef to join the others.[31]

Through all this, two-year-old Maria Harris watched and waited with the others on the reef. The water was too deep for her to stand. Someone must have held the trembling, terrified little girl as she waited for her mother. But Eliza never came. At some point, someone explained to Maria that her mother and baby brother had drowned. Someone told her that she was now alone.

No image of the shipwreck strikes me more deeply than that of Maria alone on the reef. Sometimes I picture her, huddled in the arms of someone she barely knows, her clothing wet and torn, her thin, brown hair matted and dirty. Big tears stream down her cheeks. There is nobody now to wipe them away. The enormity of the dark sky seems to rest on her. No baby brother holds her finger. No mother hugs her close.

The surviving passengers spent the first night standing on the reef, waiting for daylight. They were cut, bruised, and nearly naked. Through the night, the sounds of the sea blended with the sounds of mourning. Maria's crying must have blended in with the crying of the others.

The next morning, the crew set off in a salvaged quarterboat, a small boat hung at the boat's quarter, to investigate an island in the distance. The other passengers gathered what provisions they could from the wreck. They stayed close together in the center of the reef, trying to discourage the circling sharks from attacking. Their lips swelled and their thirst grew desperate since there was no drinkable water available. At 4:00 p.m., the crew returned with disappointing news. The three nearby islands appeared to be only sandbars, filled with rats and "sea-fowl."

With no other option, Coffin loaded the women and children on the quarterboat and set off for one of the islands anyway. Little Maria and the other women and children spent their second night sleeping directly on the hard rocks on the little island. They did solve the most immediate crisis though. By digging deep into the sand, the women found fresh water that they scooped up in small amounts with seashells.

The men didn't arrive until the next evening, having gone two days and two nights without water. Since there wasn't time to shuttle them all back and forth on the quarterboat, the men walked around the coral reef until they reached the island. The water often rose chin high, forcing them to swim much of the distance. The weaker ones clung to a makeshift raft filled with provisions that they towed along behind them.

Once everyone arrived on the island, Captain Pond called them together and told them "a common brotherhood should be maintained."[32] The group divided into family units and built huts with roofs of pandanus leaves. Maria stayed with Peter and Elizabeth Penfold, the only Mormon couple on the voyage without small children of their own. The first week they ate mostly crabs. As they explored the island, they added coconut and turtle to their diet. Shark meat provided an occasional treat. The women learned to make a kind of pancake by mixing some flour saved from the ship with grated coconut and turtle eggs.

Once they had assured temporary survival, the group turned their attention to getting off the island. Captain Pond's calculations showed that they were too far off-course for a passing ship to discover them by chance. They would have to reach help themselves. The nearest populated island, one of the Society Islands, was three to five hundred miles to the east. Unfortunately, a strong wind had blown from this direction the entire time they had been on the island. Captain Pond dismissed that option as hopeless, believing it impossible to row their little makeshift boat so far against the wind. Instead, the thoughts and plans of the crew focused on the Navigators Islands (now known as the Samoan Islands), located fifteen hundred miles in the opposite direction. They began preparing the quarterboat, choosing the crew, and finding an appropriate departure spot.

The decision to head towards the Navigators Islands did not receive unanimous support from the survivors. According to Captain Pond, the Mormons in the group were "superstitious and bitterly opposed" to this plan.[33] John McCarthy told Captain Pond that he had had a vision in which he saw the group sailing toward the Navigators Islands. All went well for a day or two. Then, he saw the boat upside down and the bodies of the crew floating around it. Many of the Mormons accepted his vision as fact and began lobbying for the rescue mission to head the other direction.

McCarthy came to Captain Pond with a second vision several days later. In this vision, the quarterboat headed east with ten men on board. The group arrived at the Society Islands after three days and sent a vessel back to bring the others to safety in Tahiti. Captain Pond, not immune to the pressure around him, began having second thoughts. As he wrote, "a gloomy, undefined premonition of evil and disaster" had come over him since making the decision to head toward the Navigators Islands.[34]

At 3:00 in the morning on November 20, the morning of the scheduled departure, Captain Pond awoke to find the quarterboat missing. There could be no possibility of rescue without the boat. The entire group gathered on the sand. Many cried. Captain Pond calmed everyone and ordered a search. Someone finally found the boat. The wind had blown it a significant distance. It was filled with water, but not damaged.

On this beach in the early morning hours, Captain Pond abruptly changed his mind about the rescue plan. He decided to take ten men and row toward the Society Islands. Only nine crew members agreed to go. Captain Pond asked John McCarthy if he believed his own vision. If so, would he prove his faith by going with the small company? McCarthy agreed to go.

Owens, the first mate, woke Captain Pond at daybreak the next day to tell him that the wind had switched directions. It was the first westerly wind they had experienced in their eight weeks on the island. Despite drizzling rain and stormy conditions, Captain Pond decided the time had come to take their chances.

Everyone gathered on the shore to see the boat off. As the shipwrecked passengers waved good-bye, they knew there would be no second chance. Either the boat would reach the island and they would be saved, or the rescue party would die in the attempt, leaving the rest of the group stranded on the island until they also perished.

For two weeks, those left behind on the island hovered "in a state of anxious suspense, thinking continually on the success of our company," as Andrew Anderson, one of the survivors, explained. Then, on December 2, someone spotted a ship in the distance. Even little Maria must have partly understood the significance of that long-awaited moment. Anderson wrote: "I need not attempt to describe our feelings of gratitude and praise which we felt to give the God of Israel for his goodness and mercy in thus working a deliverance for us; for I have no language to express my own feelings, much less the feelings of those around me."[35]

They later learned how near disaster their rescue mission had come. The men on board the quarterboat started out making good progress. On their third day at sea, their greatest fear came true—the wind switched back to its original direction and a storm developed. Exhausted from their constant rowing, despair overwhelmed the group of men. They pulled a tarp over their heads, their only protection from the storm, as the waves tossed them about for hours. Destruction seemed certain.

Then, someone cried, "Land! Land!" Captain Pond wrote, "Tears of gratitude filled our eyes."[36] They had made it to Bora-Bora, one of the Society Islands. Some of the crew members immediately took a letter describing the situation to the British consul, who then sent a message on to Captain Latham of the *Emma Packer*. The *Emma Packer* set sail directly to rescue the survivors still on the island, stopping only briefly along the way to pick up Captain Pond. Captain Pond later noted that the events had unfolded exactly as McCarthy had described.

A week's journey on the *Emma Packer* brought the newly rescued *Julia Ann* survivors to Huahine, one of the Society Islands. The group stayed here for three days before continuing on to Tahiti. In Tahiti, they hoped for support from the British or American consuls until they resumed their journey to the US. Both consuls refused to assist. (The American consul argued that the group consisted of English citizens while the British consul said they were on an American ship.) Fortunately, the United Board of Masonic Lodges intervened, providing the passengers with desperately needed food and lodging. The majority of the Mormon passengers stayed under their care for over a month, until January 16, 1856, when the Freemasons could no longer help them. Another desperate petition to the British consul secured provisions through February. Finally, at the end of February, Maria and the others set sail to San Francisco.

The news of the shipwreck traveled slowly. Andrew Anderson wrote a letter from Tahiti to President Farnham in Australia dated February 22, 1856. In the letter, Anderson described the events of the last few months, including a brief narrative of the wreck and an accounting of who had drowned. On March 31, President Farnham received the letter. Soon after reading it, he must have called Edmond into his office and told him that his wife and young son had been dead for nearly six months.

The community's reaction to the news of the wreck was probably dramatic. Besides being tragic, the news was also startling. Everyone knew the journey to America was fraught with danger, but shipwrecks were relatively rare. From 1840 to 1890, eighty-five thousand Mormon converts crossed the ocean to gather in Utah. Of all the "Mormon" vessels that carried them to America, only the *Julia Ann* wrecked.[37]

The *Jenny Ford* was the next Mormon ship to leave Australia. It departed in May of 1856, stopping in Tahiti to pick up the surviving passengers of the *Julia Ann*. But, by the time the *Jenny Ford* got there, the survivors had already left for California.

Edmond didn't sail aboard the *Jenny Ford* though. Finances were probably the deciding factor again. Edmond finally left Australia for America on June 27, 1857, aboard the *Lucas*.[38]

Sometimes I think of him boarding the ship. No family waves good-bye from the pier. And, no family will greet him when he arrives. Edmond has lived with the knowledge of his family's fate for over a year now. It almost feels normal to be alone, although the empty hole inside him still gapes open so wide that he's certain he will never feel truly normal again. He finds comfort in one thought: he will see Maria soon.

He gives one last look behind him at this country that has been just another stop along his life journey. Then, he pulls his trunk onto the ship.

While the accounts of the *Julia Ann* kept me riveted to my computer, the same can't be said for the ship log of the *Lucas* (although I'm sure the absence of exciting developments didn't disappoint the passengers). The account is dry and tedious, full of descriptions of the weather and lists of who led the prayers or taught the classes. The record mentions Edmond's name a few times in insightful statements such as "Prayer by Elder Harris, attended by singing."[39]

Seasickness struck on the *Lucas* by the end of the first day and "was very unpleasant" according to the ship journal.[40] By the second day, rain poured down. On Sunday, July 12, a heavy wave struck the ship and shook it from end to end. The upper deck filled with water. But no lasting damage occurred. The Church leaders on board, Presidents Wall and Dowdle, calmed everyone and the passengers returned to bed.

The ship journal provides glimpses into daily life. The days began and ended with prayers, usually accompanied by singing. Passengers attended meetings, especially on Sundays, when anyone could address the group, expressing his or her feelings on the "truthfulness of the gospel of Jesus Christ and the restored Church." Often one of the Church leaders spoke to the passengers, providing counsel on a range of religious topics. On June 30, President Dowdle "made a few remarks on being united and obeying the orders of the Church." Presidents Wall and Dowdle "gave instructions to the Saints on cleanliness, order, and government of families" on the third of July.

The *Lucas* passengers struggled to get along with each other. Cramped quarters, seasickness, lack of privacy, and other inconveniences strained the good will of even the most polite passengers. On July 20, the ship journal reads, "There is a want of unity among us and not the best of feelings among us." Other entries record a "slight disturbance with two of the brethren" and later "a difficulty arose between two families which was not settled before going to bed."[41]

Church leaders spent a significant amount of time quieting these disputes and trying to make peace. On August 4, "President Wall restored peace between two brethren." In fact, the only time Edmond's name appears as more than just offering a prayer is in relation to a squabble. The passengers chose Elder Roberts, another one of the Church leaders on board, to teach at a school established for the children. When he asked for some help with this assignment, Edmond volunteered. But on August 18, Edmond refused to teach anymore because "some of the parents found fault with him."

The *Lucas* docked at San Pedro, California, on October 12. The next day, Edmond and the other passengers set off by wagon on the eighty-mile journey inland to San Bernardino. They arrived there four days later. San Bernardino, although not Zion itself, was its representative. As such, it delivered a memorable, if unexpected, first impression.

San Bernardino was a Mormon colony that had been founded in 1851. By 1857, more Mormons lived there than any other place outside of Salt Lake City. Yet, San Bernardino had a precarious existence because it was one of the farthest colonies from Utah and was known to be viewed unfavorably by Brigham Young.[42] At the time Edmond arrived, San Bernardino had other problems besides Brigham Young's lack of enthusiasm. Animosity towards the Mormons was building in the area. Many of the critics were disaffected Mormons, who now devoted a great deal of time to stirring up contention. Rumors of a looming clash between the US Army and the residents of Utah over replacing Brigham Young as governor also reached the colony about this time, which heightened tensions further. News of the conflict impacted the Mormons in San Bernardino deeply. Some wanted to return to Utah both because of fear for their safety in California and out of a desire to support the main body of members in Utah.

But there were also persuasive reasons to stay in San Bernardino. Many of its residents had strong emotional and economic attachments to the city. The group had also incurred a large debt when they bought the land. Most of the Mormon residents had not yet paid off their personal debts. Some leaders felt strongly that, even if the settlers returned to Utah eventually, they at least needed to stay in San Bernardino until they fulfilled their financial commitments.

A few days after the *Lucas* passengers arrived, the San Bernardino group of about three thousand settlers voted to accept the new arrivals into their congregation. Probably some of the Australians planned to stay in San Bernardino, at least temporarily, in order to save money to pay for the rest of the journey. Others hoped to continue to Utah immediately. But soon their options were altered.

Numerous letters had arrived from Brigham Young indicating his growing desire for the settlers to return to Utah. Some Church leaders in San Bernardino tried to prevent the people from finding out about these letters. In early November of 1857, their contents reached the residents and instantly caused strong reactions among the settlers.

The first few weeks of November passed in a flurry of preparations as a large group of people began preparing to make the difficult journey to Utah. Many felt intense loyalty to the leaders of the Church and never questioned the direction to return to Utah. The decision wasn't so easy for everyone. Nearly one-third of the Mormon population of San Bernardino stayed behind. Most of those who left did so at great personal loss. In their hurry to leave, they sold their land for a fraction of its value.

After all that had happened over the previous few years, arriving in San Bernardino in its moment of crisis must have been disturbing, if not disheartening, for Edmond. I can only guess at his reaction, though. His life between his arrival in October of 1857 in San Bernardino and his later presence in Utah in 1864 remains a mystery. Two census records provide my only clues.

My brother copied a page from the 1860 San Francisco census which lists a man named Edmond Harris who lives alone and works as a laborer. The man, who the census claims is from Wales (which could be an error or this could be a different Edmond Harris), is living over four hundred miles from San Bernardino—but very close to someone important to him.[43]

The second census record I have came from a woman who took an interest in little Maria's fate after she read a magazine article I wrote about the family. In her e-mail, she provided a list of extractions of possible census records. Beyond 1870, the records become tangled. But, the 1860 census clearly shows Maria Harris living in Oakland, California, with Peter and Elizabeth Penfold, the couple who were assigned to take care of Maria after the shipwreck.[44]

I have formed a scenario from these records. As soon as possible after arriving in San Bernardino, Edmond made preparations to head north to San Francisco where another Mormon colony was located. More importantly, Maria's ship had landed in San Francisco. Edmond went in search of his daughter—a daughter he hadn't seen in two years. When he arrived in San Francisco, perhaps someone directed him to Maria's home in Oakland.

Sometimes, I imagine Edmond knocking on the Penfolds' door. I imagine the adults talking and pacing the floor, Maria looking from one to the other in confusion. Maybe Edmond wanted to bring Maria with him. Maybe the Penfolds convinced him it was best for her to stay with them—the people she now viewed as family. Maybe Maria didn't want the trauma of losing people she loved again in order to be reunited with a father she hardly remembered. Besides, how could a single man care for a little girl? Maria had to stay. It was the best solution. Or at least that's what Edmond kept telling himself.

I think of Edmond walking out the Penfolds' door, then turning around for one last glimpse of his daughter. I think of Maria sitting at the window and watching him disappear.

I can only speculate about their meeting, about the discussion, about the decision. But one thing I do know: when Edmond arrived in Utah, it was without Maria.

I sit at the computer, with papers spread out around me, preparing to write the Harris family's story. I continuously check the papers to verify the details. Although the particulars slip away, the feeling stays clear. My emotional attachment to the family is strong—almost embarrassingly so. I hardly dare repeat their story. Every time I do, a lump forms in my throat and my voice wavers. Their tragedy overwhelms me.

The Harris family was willing to sacrifice, but they hadn't known how much would be required. If they had known that seeking Zion would cost them their very lives, would they still have embarked on their journey? Was Zion a destination worthy of the journey when Edmond arrived alone?

This is how I have always thought about it. But as I begin to type, a different impression fills me.

I find it hard to believe that Gunnison, Utah, the place where Edmond would eventually settle and die, was worth the terrible price. Yet, I believe Edmond and Eliza didn't consider this literal place their goal. After all, it wasn't Utah they were seeking, but Zion.

Today, Utah is no longer considered Zion. The gathering was discontinued a hundred years ago. Church leaders no longer encourage converts to come to Utah. But they still encourage them to find Zion. Zion is not a place—it's a state of being, a frame of mind, a feeling within. It's a belief in something beyond one's self, a devotion to a greater cause.

Zion is not a destination. It is a journey.

Perhaps Edmond and Eliza understood that. Perhaps they weren't looking for a destination at all, but for a journey. Perhaps their real journey had little to do with moving from England to Australia to America. Maybe it was a more ambiguous kind of journey—a journey of character. Edmond and Eliza knew there could be no guarantee of their destination. They could only control the journey, their path, and their choices.

Edmond experienced a tragic and heartbreaking loss, one that probably nearly paralyzed him. But now I realize that the story of Edmond's first family isn't a story of a destination never reached. Edmond's story isn't about a destination at all. It's about a journey.

GUNNISON, UTAH

CHAPTER TEN

STARTING OVER: EDMOND AND KARSTI IN UTAH

Edmond's arrival in Utah was the end of a journey, but in many ways it was also a beginning. In Utah, Edmond Harris met Karsti Nilsdotter and they began a new life together.

I don't know, and I'll probably never know, exactly when Karsti and Edmond married. No record, to my knowledge, has survived of the event. This isn't particularly surprising since many Utah records from this period are spotty—if they exist at all. There are a few pieces of information that help me to narrow the date down to a small window. Karsti arrived in the Salt Lake Valley in September of 1861. Presumably, their first child, Mary Elizabeth, was born on New Year's Day of 1864.[1] Karsti and Edmond must have married sometime between these two dates.

I probably will also never know *why* Karsti and Edmond married. My family tree contains few less likely matches. In 1862, when they may have met, Karsti was eighteen years old. Edmond was thirty-seven. Karsti was a peasant farm girl from small-town Sweden. She had only lived in the US a short time, and likely still struggled with her English. Edmond came from the working class of big-city England, and certainly didn't speak any Swedish. He had already been married and fathered two children. Karsti had been three years old when Edmond married Eliza.

Yet, they did have one thing in common: they were both alone in a new country. Karsti had left everything behind to come to Utah. Edmond had lost everything along the way. They were far from home with nothing familiar around them. As a young woman, Karsti had few options available to support herself. Edmond was reaching middle-age, an old man to be single in the Mormon world.

Edmond and Karsti were both starting over.

I'm in bed reading a book about the early history of Utah when the phone rings. Since it's after 10:00 p.m., I assume it must be David.

"So, how did it go?" I ask him.

"I think it went well," he says, his voice sounding tired. "I'm just glad this is the last interview." David is in Oklahoma interviewing for a professor position—his sixth and final interview in the past two and a half months.

"So am I," I say. While he has been away interviewing and flying across the country, I have endured many long days of single parenthood. Under any circumstances this would be less than ideal, but now that I'm nearly eight months pregnant with our third child, I find it exhausting.

This has been a pregnancy filled with so much morning sickness that I have been barely functional. My other pregnancies seem nearly pleasant in comparison. Only in the last couple of weeks has the worst of it lifted. I feel as if I'm waking up from a long sleep—waking up back into my life. Yet just as it seems that I am getting my life back together, I'm preparing for it to be yanked out from under me again.

David will finish his PhD in a couple of months. Then, we'll pack up all our belongings and our three children and head off to some unknown destination—wherever David gets a job. First, there will be one detour. We have already committed to spend the next year in Valencia, Spain, where David will work for a professor at a university. Although I originally encouraged the move abroad, now it intimidates me. It's an opportunity too perfect not to snatch up, and yet a change too tremendous not to fear.

"So, now we just wait," David concludes after describing the town and university to me.

I have never been good at waiting. And I certainly don't like it. In fact, I'm already tired of it. David's first interview was at the end of January. Some of the schools said they would get back to us in the middle of March. Now, a week into April, we're still in the dark.

Two universities have contacted us. One called to say they wouldn't make a decision for a few more weeks. Another e-mailed with the tantalizing news that they wanted to hire David, but weren't sure if they could get funding for the position. This second piece of information came from the University of Massachusetts, the school we had both quickly assigned the number one spot on our list. That e-mail was like a carrot being dangled right in front of our faces, but just out of reach.

Although we've been working toward this for a long time, I feel overwhelmed now that the future seems so near. The changes ahead are exciting — and terrifying. We will have a new baby, a move abroad and back again, a new job, a house (at last, hopefully), a new community — a new life.

Edmond and Karsti began their new lives together in Millcreek, Utah (or technically what would become Utah), located just a few miles south of Salt Lake City. Their first child, Mary Elizabeth, was born there in January of 1864. Their stay in Millcreek was short and, in the chronology of their lives, seemingly unimportant. Perhaps it was only a stage of transition, never a permanent home. Many immigrants resided briefly in, or around, Salt Lake City until they chose, or were assigned, another place to live.

Within two years, Edmond and Karsti moved to Spring Lake Villa (known simply as Spring Lake), a new and sparsely populated town about sixty miles south of Salt Lake City. Even today, Spring Lake is an inconspicuous and overlooked, although not unpleasant, town. It's located a few miles off the main highway, halfway between the towns of Payson and Santaquin. During my five years in Utah, I lived only a few miles north of Spring Lake and never knew it existed.

Spring Lake had been founded as part of the colonization system. Under this system, Brigham Young established organized Mormon settlements throughout a large area in an effort to lay claim to the land. Church leaders would first send an exploration party into a new place. Then, they selected families to move there who had the range of skills they believed necessary to form an effective community. Often leaders even provided specific instructions on the economic focus of the new settlement.

Church authorities oversaw the establishment of many communities, but non-directed colonization also flourished in the first few decades of the Church's presence in Utah. Adventurous settlers began communities on their own. Church leaders encouraged these settlements, and then helped to support them as soon as possible.

Mormon settlers spread at a rapid pace. Not only did they found many towns throughout what is now Utah, they also expanded to form settlements in California, Arizona, Mexico, and other places. They abandoned some of them in 1857 when Brigham Young called the settlers back to Utah in wake of a looming clash with the federal government. Still, colonization persisted as communities grew in population and number. By 1900, Mormons had established 325 permanent and 44 abandoned settlements.[2]

One of the earliest colonization sites was in Utah Valley, where Spring Lake is located. In 1849, thirty families settled the valley.

Within a year, the population had grown to over two thousand. Some of these people came to Spring Lake in 1850. An early settler to the area, Joseph E. Johnson, converted a house surrounded by an adobe wall into "an adobe mansion" which became the center of town life. Over the next few years, a handful of families arrived and built homes in the area.[3] By the early 1860s, the initial leadership-directed push for settlers had passed. Edmond and Karsti likely made the decision to come to Spring Lake independently.

Sometimes I think of Edmond and Karsti arriving in Spring Lake, their few possessions piled in the back of their wagon. Edmond stops the horses in the middle of a field of sagebrush and jumps off the wagon. He runs his fingers through his thinning, dark brown hair as he walks around to help Karsti down from the wagon. He studies Karsti's face, trying to guess what she's thinking, trying to read her first impression of their new home. He follows her gaze as she looks around at the scattered houses, the sparkling man-made lake, and the mountains towering behind it all. Her eyes scan the distance—the blue-gray sky and the wild, fierce grass with hardly a sign of settlement interfering with its freedom. Edmond knows it's not Vallby—and it's certainly not London—but he hopes they can be happy here.

Edmond takes Karsti's hand without saying a word. She climbs down, her grip tight as she balances their baby in one arm.

Standing beside him, Karsti's eyes meet his at last. "So this is it," she says in her simple way. Edmond thinks he can hear the slightest trace of weariness in her voice.

Then she nods, as if satisfied that she has taken it all in, and smiles. "We're here."

Karsti and Edmond might have found life in Spring Lake to be even more different than they had expected. Their biggest surprise may have been their new neighbors. The small, isolated community was also home to a number of Ute Indians.

Mormon doctrine taught that American Indians were descendants of the Lamanites, an ancient people in the Book of Mormon. Prophecies declared that the day would come when these people would "blossom as a rose" and prosper in the land.[4] Prosperity, in the Mormon view, was closely linked to conversion to Mormonism. So, Mormons took seriously the call to teach and baptize the American Indians.

Because of their duty to help the American Indians "blossom," Mormons were eager, at least at first, to make friends and avoid conflict with them. Brigham Young proclaimed that it was "better to feed the Indians than fight them." Mormons and American Indians lived side by side, sometimes genuinely becoming friends and working together. This provided a stark contrast to many other settler-Indian relationships throughout the West.[5]

From the beginning, this friendship required great effort and patience on both sides. Small skirmishes broke out frequently. A few horror stories as well as the unfamiliar appearance of the American Indians were enough to make many settlers nervous. Although Karsti may have become acquainted with some of the Utes, she probably still trembled when she encountered a Ute man. Many of the Mormon women, probably including Karsti, disliked giving food to the Utes who appeared more and more frequently begging on their doorsteps.

Although the Mormons came with a different approach, in the end, the result was much the same. As in other places, the settlers altered the environment and used the resources, destroying the American Indian way of life. This brought suffering, dependence, and resentment to the American Indian population. The positive relationship that existed when Karsti and Edmond first arrived didn't last long.

Their new neighbors were not the only difference in their lives. The Utah government was nothing like government in their home countries. In fact, it was really not much like any government anywhere else either.

When the Mormons first arrived in the Salt Lake Valley in 1847, they brought their own form of government with them—the well-organized hierarchy of the LDS Church. Separation of Church and State did not exist. This Mormon government made gaining statehood—as the State of Deseret—one of their first orders of business. In their petition to the federal government, they provided nominees for the major state governmental positions, including Brigham Young for governor and Church leaders for the other positions. Fearful of persecution and domination, Mormons held self-rule as the ultimate importance in the process.

Congress turned down the request for statehood in what would become an often-repeated scenario. Instead, the Compromise of 1850 formed a Utah Territory. Although President Fillmore did give Brigham Young the governor's seat, he appointed non-Mormons to most of the other positions.

Brigham Young served as the governor of the territory of Utah until 1857 when President Buchanan forcibly installed a new governor, with the US military as his escort. It soon became apparent that it would take more than removing Young as governor to effectively remove him as the leader of the people in Utah. While non-Mormons continued to officially govern the territory, Young and the Church organization kept the real power throughout the 1860s, operating through what became known as the Ghost State of Deseret.[6]

Polygamy lay at the root of the strain between the federal government and the LDS Church. Karsti and Edmond never participated in polygamy, but they still lived with its consequences. Only a minority of the members of the Church ever married into polygamy, but its very existence was enough to disturb people throughout the country. While polygamy may have topped people's list of concerns about the Mormons, it was at the top of a long list of concerns. The close ties of Church and State, Utah's preference for isolation, the amount of foreign-born people arriving there, and the reluctance of Utah pioneers to sponsor and enroll their children in free public schools all led others to conclude that Utah—and the Mormons—were distinctly un-American.

I'm so engrossed in reading about the Utah government that the sound of the phone ringing makes me jump. I reach over and pick it up.

"They have a position. They're offering me a job," David's voice is breathless, excited.

"Who?" I ask, smiling already.

"UMass says they're putting together an offer for me. The department chair will call about it tonight."

That night, we talk about nothing else. When will he call? What will he say? What will we say?

But the phone doesn't ring. David checks the phone five or six times to make sure the ringer is on. He checks to make sure the phone is plugged in. He picks up the receiver to make sure he can hear a dial tone. Then he paces around the living room. We eat dinner and put the kids to bed—but still nobody calls. It's 9:00 p.m., then 10:00 p.m.

"He won't call this late," I say finally.

"But he said he'd call tonight," David says, confused. "Maybe something happened. Maybe he sent me an e-mail saying he'd call another time."

He goes into our bedroom to check.

"Oh no." His voice sounds very small.

"What?" I ask, walking in to where to he sits staring at the computer screen.

"I e-mailed him the wrong phone number."

"You did what?"

"He asked for my phone number so he could call me. I typed it in wrong." David doesn't say anything for a minute. "He is going to think I'm an idiot. What kind of person tells their future boss the wrong phone number when he wants to call and make a job offer?"

I try not to laugh. Then I notice his wording. "Your future boss?"

He looks at me. "I thought you wanted to go to Massachusetts."

"I do," I say, my heart starting to pound. The decision that has lingered just out of our reach for so long now dances right in front of us. We just have to reach out and grab it.

A few days later, after he sends the correct phone number and talks with the department chair, David signs his name on the line. It's official. We are moving to Amherst, Massachusetts, in a year.

I have never been to Massachusetts. Actually, I've never been anywhere near it. I wonder what our lives will be like there.

If Karsti and Edmond had harbored any fantasies about what their new lives in Zion would be like, these illusions disappeared quickly. Life in frontier Utah was harsh, primitive, and filled with lots of hard work.

Hard work wasn't new to them, of course. Yet on the frontier, common tasks had an unusual twist to them. Karsti and Edmond had lived in established communities in Sweden and England. Towns, complete with homes and functioning farms, already existed. Cities were located nearby. Peasants in nineteenth-century Europe were self-reliant by today's standards, but self-reliance took on a whole new meaning in Utah. Utah pioneers had no choice; there wasn't anyone else to rely on. Before the railroad was completed in 1869, Utah settlers had no way to get many of the goods to which people in the eastern US had access.

Church leaders emphasized self-reliance as not only necessary, but beneficial to the LDS people. After the persecution Mormons had endured in other places, Young wanted them to establish their own communities, separate from the outside world and its harassments. If a local person couldn't be found that could perform a particular trade, the settlers either learned to do it—or did without.

Besides using the skills they brought with them, Karsti and Edmond learned new skills. This may have even included their new livelihood—farming. No matter what other contributions a family made to the community, nearly all families farmed at first. Edmond had grown up as the son of a blacksmith. He spent the first part of his adult life working as a low-wage laborer in a city. Unless he had farmed while living in Australia, the details of farming may have been somewhat unfamiliar to him. Although Karsti had grown up farming, the experience on the desert land of Utah was nothing like what she was accustomed to on the fertile plains in Skåne.

The Harris family probably tried to grow a little of everything on their farm. Many people grew corn, sugar cane, and potatoes. Some later added tobacco, hemp, and flax. Edmond and Karsti may have had peach and apple trees as well. Most of the settlers owned a few animals such as cattle, horses, mules, and pigs.[7]

As Karsti and Edmond adjusted to life in Utah, back in Sweden, Karsti's brother, Nils Jr., made a decision that Karsti had probably not even dared hope for. Nils Jr. was baptized into the LDS Church in August of 1862.[8] Nine months later, Nils Jr., his wife, Karna, and their children began their trip to Utah. They arrived in New York on June 1, 1863. Following Karsti's path of two years earlier, they continued on to Utah.[9]

I have often thought of the scene that must have occurred.

Karsti scans the group anxiously. She shifts her baby from side to side as she stands on tiptoe to peer over the crowd again.

"I don't see them," she whispers to Edmond, who stands beside her.

Before he can respond, he hears a gasp from his wife. Without a word, she begins to run, pushing her way through the people in front of her. Edmond hurries behind her, trying to keep up.

"Nils!" she calls. A man about the same age as Edmond, with brown hair and tired-looking eyes turns to look at them.

"Karsti!" he exclaims, the tiredness melting from his face. He drops the hands of his two children and engulfs his sister in a big hug.

For weeks she has thought of all the things they would talk about. She would introduce him to Edmond—and her baby. She would tell him about the American Indians and about Spring Lake. She would ask about her sisters and about their farm, about his family and about their trip.

She pulls back and studies him more closely. There will be time to talk. First, she just wants to look at him—at all of them. She had thought she would never see her family again, and now her brother stands here in front of her with his wife and children. She laughs as she hugs him again, the tears running down her cheeks.

In November of 1864, Karsti and Edmond added their second child, Moroni Johns, to the family. Karsti was twenty-one years old. A few months later, war broke out around them.

Tension between the settlers and the American Indians had been growing for some time. Relationships deteriorated as the American

Indian population plummeted, largely due to starvation. In April of 1865, some Mormon settlers and Ute representatives met in Manti to discuss cattle that some desperate and hungry American Indians had stolen. When one of the settlers jerked one of the Utes off of his horse, Black Hawk, a young Ute from Spring Lake, promised retaliation. He was true to his word. Black Hawk proved to be an effective and influential leader, uniting numerous American Indian tribes together in a loose coalition against the settlers.

The first two years of what became known as the Black Hawk Indian War were the most intense. American Indians attacked settlements sporadically throughout much of Utah. Their main purpose was to capture cattle, a task at which they were immensely successful.

Tragedies occurred on both sides as emotions escalated. By the end of the war, the Utes and their allies had killed seventy settlers. In a few instances, American Indians ambushed families in their homes. In response, Mormons deserted the small settlements so that they would be less vulnerable. They also struck back. Friendly American Indians, as well as women and children, occasionally became victims as frustrated settlers reacted in anger and confusion. Fear spread its long, bony fingers into nearly every Utah community.

Perhaps what made the Black Hawk Indian War different from American Indian conflicts that occurred in other parts of the country was the role of the federal government. In other places, federal troops quickly entered and squashed the American Indian resistance. Not in Utah. For one thing, Mormons were reluctant to ask for help, fearing the government's interference more than they feared the American Indians. Mormons tried to keep the events of the war hidden from outsiders, rarely even writing about them in the newspapers. In turn, the federal government, which harbored ambiguous or even antagonistic feelings towards the Mormons, was happy to look the other way. Besides, the government had its hands full at that time with the Civil War and its aftermath.[10]

The impact of the Black Hawk Indian War, if not the battles directly, reached Spring Lake. In 1865, Brigham Young became concerned about the safety of the families living there. He encouraged the settlers to move to Santaquin. The people of Spring Lake were reluctant to leave their homes and farms. The local leader, Benjamin Franklin Johnson, wrote to Brigham Young requesting permission for them to stay. He proposed that instead they turn his home into a temporary fort in which all the settlers could live.

On January 30, 1866, Young replied: "You are at liberty to stay where you are for the present season at your own risk, if in your judgment it is safe. I cannot warrant you in so doing, but by taking such precautions as you have proposed, there would be no particular danger perhaps from Indians."[11] The Harris family and their neighbors probably moved into the Johnson home during the worst part of the conflict.

Edmond may have joined the Nauvoo Legion, a private militia, to fight Black Hawk and his warriors. More likely though, his participation in the war was limited to community defense measures. He probably kept watch or built barriers to protect the community against attacks. Karsti surely worried over the safety of her children as they played in the fields or helped on the farm. Yet, life had to continue.

In October of 1866, when the family might have still lived within the fort, Karsti's third child, Ephraim, was born. That winter, sickness ravaged the community. Severe weather struck, leaving deep snow on the ground well into March.

Karsti and Edmond were probably grateful that at least their worst fears of a severe attack by the Utes weren't confirmed. Minor incidences did reach them, though. In a report made in March of 1867 to Church officials in Salt Lake City, leaders in Spring Lake revealed that they "had Indian troubles last season."[12]

Events took a major turn for the better that fall. Black Hawk made peace with the Mormons. The next year, he signed a peace treaty. Without his leadership, the organization of the American Indians crumbled. Much of the fear subsided. People in Spring Lake left the fort and returned home. Still, the war stumbled on — although with much less vigor — until 1872, when two hundred federal troops entered the scene to fight the American Indians.

One of the concluding events of the war took place in Spring Lake. On September 27, 1870, Benjamin Johnson wrote a letter to share some news: "I hasten to tell you — Black Hawk, the Indian desperado is dead."[13]

Black Hawk had been ill for some time. He returned to his birthplace to die. The morning of his death, Karsti and Edmond likely heard the wail of a Ute squaw echoing through the town. The other members of the tribe killed a horse and buried Black Hawk's body in it. Then "Indian Joe," another Ute leader, came to ask Benjamin Johnson to pass the information on to Brigham Young.

With the worst of the war over in 1867, some degree of normalcy returned to Karsti and Edmond's lives. In this nearly peaceful atmosphere on June 25, 1868, my great-great-grandmother was born. They named her Chasty after the Americanized form of her mother's name.

In 1869, the Harris family faced a severe attack—not by American Indians, but by grasshoppers. Grasshopper and cricket invasions had periodically wreaked havoc on the farmland since the pioneers arrived in the Salt Lake Valley. The insects sometimes swarmed in groups so large and thick that they made the entire sky hazy. As they approached in massive clouds, some people compared the noise from their wings to the sound of a passing train. The insects descended on the crops, eating everything and sometimes leaving the settlers hovering near starvation. One observer noted that the insects had caused more suffering to the Utah pioneers than all other trials combined. [14] The Harris family probably went hungry some of the time in 1869 because of the damaged crops.

A historical milestone occurred that same year: the transcontinental railroad was completed. Goods arrived from the East, ending the need to self-produce everything. Also around that time, the theocratic State of Deseret quietly died out. Although the unique flavor of Utah would continue, the movement away from isolationism had begun.

Another daughter, Rosann, was born to Edmond and Karsti in 1870. This swelled the family to include five children. Although I have no record of any other children born in Spring Lake, it's likely that at least a sixth child was born there. The next child I know of was born in 1876—six years after Rosann.

The existence and identities of these children will forever remain a mystery to me. Churches in Germany, Sweden, and England kept fairly complete records of births starting as early as two hundred years or more before this. But, no records document births consistently in Spring Lake, or many other western US communities, until after the beginning of the 1900s. Only one record provides more evidence that the Harris family had additional children. In the 1900 census, Karsti reported that she had had eleven children, five of whom were living. [15] My family group sheet lists eight. Edmond and Karsti probably buried these other three as babies.

In 1874, Edmond turned forty-nine and Karsti turned thirty-two. They had lived in Spring Lake for about eleven years. They had battled drought and grasshoppers, assimilated into a new culture, made a home from nothing, hid from the Utes in a makeshift fort, and probably buried a few children. Life in Utah hadn't been easy.

Sitting on the living room floor, I fold another tiny outfit and set it in front of me. I had decided to get the boxes of baby clothes out of the storage unit—just in case. Rachel and Taylor were both born a few weeks early, so I can't help thinking that, despite my due date being a month away, the baby could come at any time.

It's late and I'm worn out. My nausea, although milder than in earlier months, continues to dominate my life. Coupled with the size of my huge belly, I feel like even small tasks require an enormous amount of energy. *I'm getting old and tired*, I think, smiling to myself. If I'm old and tired at twenty-eight, I'm in trouble.

I feel the baby moving inside me. Subconsciously, I rub my protruding stomach. As I do, my mind jumps to Karsti at age thirty-two. She is only four years older than I am now, but she has lived through so much more than I have.

Standing in the middle of her floor — in a room much more basic than the one I sit in now — Karsti rubs her own protruding stomach. The skin is pulled so tight that she feels like it might burst. The children are in bed. She has decided to straighten the house a little before she sits down to knit some socks — a task that seems to be never-ending in their household.

She bends over to pick some things off the ground, but finds her awkward stomach to be in the way. Her back aches more with each pregnancy. A feeling of weariness sweeps over her. Walking over to the table, she drops into a chair. She runs her fingers through her straggly hair and then over her face — as if checking for premature wrinkles.

Just then, the door swings open and Edmond walks in, his feet dragging, exhaustion etched on his face. He sits down and tugs at a boot before glancing up at his wife.

"What's wrong?" he asks.

"I'm getting old," she tells him.

He bursts out laughing. "You? I'm the old one."

"Well, that's true. But, I'm getting old too — and tired."

He succeeds in getting his boots off and moves his chair closer to his wife's, patting her large tummy. After a moment, Karsti starts to stand up.

Edmond grabs her hand and gently pulls her back into her chair.

"What's the rush?" he asks. "Maybe us two old people should just sit here for a minute."

She smiles, allowing her body to relax into the chair.

They sit in silence — too tired to make conversation.

In March of 1874, Benjamin Johnson wrote that they had "passed winter pleasantly" and that "good peace and cheerfulness prevail." Life was stabilizing in Spring Lake.[16]

Life wasn't stabilizing for the Harris family, though. After more than a decade in the little town, the family relocated. This time, they chose Gunnison, Utah, a town sixty miles south of Spring Lake in Sanpete County, as their destination. Chasty, my great-great-grandmother, was six years old. The other four children ranged in age from four to eleven.

Gunnison, although much larger than Spring Lake, was still a small, rural community. In 1870, a few years before their arrival, a postmaster recorded that ninety families lived in the town which was surrounded by "barren and desolate" fields.[17] This desert environment created challenges. As a local history reported, "In addition to caring for her family and helping with the hard work, each pioneer mother waged a constant war on the lizards, snakes, and rodents that would share her dwelling in spite of all she could do."[18]

Sanpete County offered Karsti an element of familiarity. No other place in Utah had such a high concentration of Scandinavians. In 1870, Scandinavian immigrants comprised eighty percent of the population. Although Danish settlers predominated, plenty of Swedish people lived there as well. Elements of their old cultures survived in language, celebrations, and food. Yet, there was still intense pressure to assimilate into the Utah Mormon culture. Even in Sanpete County, ties to the old country didn't survive long.[19]

The people of Gunnison were still reeling from war when the Harris family arrived. The Black Hawk Indian War had hit Sanpete County hard. Many of the communities there were temporarily abandoned. The settlers built forts in some of the more prominent towns, including Gunnison, where they gathered with their livestock. The raids and attacks of the war didn't end until the treaty in 1872. Not until then could settlers return to their homes and resume their lives.

Gunnison entered a period of growth when the war finally ended. The people turned their energies to building the community. They implemented new projects, improved irrigation, and erected new buildings. The community also started their own United Order, an all-encompassing effort at communal living. This new United Order was launched at about the same time Edmond and Karsti moved to Gunnison. Almost immediately after arriving, the Harris family, along with about three hundred other people, joined it.[20]

The United Order movement, revitalized under Brigham Young in 1874, drew on ideas from earlier LDS history. This idealistic system sought to eliminate personal wealth and instead encouraged people to live with all things in common. Participants devoted their resources to the Church. In return, leaders assigned each family a "stewardship" over which they had control. Church leaders hoped the Orders would strengthen cooperation and promote equality in communities as well as counteract the materialism and selfishness they felt had been growing since the completion of the railroad.

Two hundred local United Orders were established by the fall of 1874 — at least on paper. From the beginning, Young emphasized that participation was voluntary and that the Orders should only go as far as the individual communities wanted. Because of this, and a general lack of commitment, many of the United Orders barely went beyond the initial organization.[21]

The Gunnison United Order did manage to get off the ground. In their first meetings, which Edmond and Karsti may have attended, the members declared their goals of "building up the Kingdom of God" as well as raising the standard of living "dividing with each other until all had plenty of this world's goods." Committees directed a range of activities including farming, herding, salt boiling (boiling salty water in order to separate out the salt), and harness making. The United Order also took over the gristmill and the cooperative store, purchased large farm equipment, and built new buildings.[22] Without a lot of assets, the Harris family's contribution of "stock" to the Order was one ox.[23]

The United Order in Gunnison did not last for long. According to the bishop (the leader of the ward or congregation), it failed because too much "pride and folly... stood in the way."[24] Living communally and in perfect equality proved to be a difficult task.

As time passed, farms in Gunnison became more successful, meaning that it wasn't necessary for everyone to farm. Leaders began encouraging people to consider other occupations. One report given at the end of the 1870s stated: "At least forty percent of the people ought to be occupied by something besides farming. In addition to what we now have, home industry ought to include the manufacture of sugar, rope, brooms, glass, china, linseed oil, and silk, woolen, and leather goods."[25] Perhaps the Harris family left farming behind to make their living in one of these areas.

Comfort and prosperity never became part of the Harris family's lives. At least three more children were born while they lived in Gunnison, including Rachel (born in 1876), Joseph (born in 1879), and Sarah (born in 1881). The growing number of children surely strained the family's tight resources. Chasty described her childhood by writing: "I spent most of my time helping Mother weave rag carpets. We were very poor and sometimes didn't have all the dry bread we needed to eat. When I was twelve, I started to hire out anywhere I got a chance. I earned my own clothes and helped Mother and Father all I could."[26]

Chasty turned thirteen in 1881. When I think of her then, I see a tall, lanky girl with knobby knees and skinny arms, her long, stringy, dishwater blonde hair tied back out of her face, making its square shape and her deep-set eyes even more apparent.

I don't picture Chasty running and laughing with her friends. Instead, I see her working—helping with chores in someone else's house. I imagine her late at night, sitting beside her mother weaving those carpets to sell—doing the work of an adult. And sometimes I think of her lying awake in bed, wondering if her family will have enough food for tomorrow—her young mind weighed down by the thoughts of an adult.

I don't picture Chasty unhappy. But I always picture her somber. At age thirteen, Chasty was as much an adult as she was a child.

During their years in Gunnison, Karsti and Edmond must have felt the increasing political tension which affected every Utah community. After Brigham Young's death in 1877, polygamy continued among a small, but influential, minority of the LDS Church members. The practice also continued to draw the attention and wrath of the rest of the nation. US presidents and other leaders came under increasing pressure to do something about the "Utah problem." So, they began to take action.

Congress rejected Utah's petition for statehood six times between 1849 and 1887. They consistently stipulated that the Mormons must first forsake the "un-American" practice of polygamy. In 1882, Congress passed the Edmunds Act. This new bill gave the courts power to fine and imprison polygamists. Anyone who practiced or believed in polygamy couldn't serve on a jury. Polygamists couldn't vote or hold public office. As the non-Mormon court system got more efficient at prosecuting polygamists, the Church found a new strategy. Polygamists, including numerous Church leaders, went into hiding.[27]

Karsti and Edmond were also facing changes of their own. After growing for two decades, the Harris household began shrinking. First, in June of 1884, Edmond and Karsti's youngest son, Joseph, died at age four. The next year, Chasty married Johann (now John), Mina and Georg Albrecht's son. His family lived nearby in the town of Dover at the time. John and Chasty settled there and had their first child less than a year later.

Then in 1886, Edmond died at age sixty-one. No death record explains the cause. Only the Gunnison cemetery records provide the date.[28]

I always feel an illogical surprise at Edmond's death whenever I review the family papers. The deaths of my other ancestors give no more warning and look no different on the family charts than his does. Yet, somehow Edmond's death always seems sudden. It's almost as if, after all he had been through, his vulnerability to something as common and mundane as death is unexpected.

Karsti was left a widow at age forty-three with six children still living at home. The youngest child, Sarah, was only five years old. From then on, Karsti raised her children alone. For a family who was already struggling financially, the death of the breadwinner must have been a crippling blow. There was little opportunity for a woman to earn a living on her own. Karsti had to rely heavily on her children, particularly the older ones, for the family to survive.

Sitting here at my computer, entering the source for Edmond's death, I remember an afternoon a year ago.

The sun scorches my arms and neck as I walk in and out of rows of gravestones in the Gunnison cemetery. When I'm in Utah, I often feel as if the sun is so close it might consume me.

"Do you see it?" I call to my brother, Scott, who has stopped to squint more closely at an inscription.

He pauses. "No."

I continue walking as David tries to entertain our children. Taylor whimpers and Rachel runs along behind me hollering, "Wait for me, Mommy!"

An hour passes. We've covered all the logical sections of the graveyard, but to no avail. We have to leave. This cemetery detour has already used much more time than I planned.

As we drive out of Gunnison, I stare out my window. Of all my ancestors, there are few, if any, with more dramatic lives than Edmond Harris. There's also probably no other ancestor in whom I've invested so much time learning about. My research has been filled with wrong turns, unexpected jolts, and frustrating stumbling blocks.

The town quickly fades behind us as we drive down the road, surrounded by monotonous scenery. Gunnison is a plain town, brown and bare from the relentless sun. There is nothing dramatic or even that interesting about it. Somehow, a burial in the Gunnison cemetery seems a disappointing end to his life. And a walk through this cemetery that fails to locate his grave seems a disappointing conclusion to my search.

Now at my computer, I check the date and print off the family group sheet. The document is complete—each blank filled in. Yet, this one-page document reveals so little of what I know about Edmond. I have binders and stacks of papers that fill in much more about his life. Still, much is missing. Some information I will never know. And some of what I know about Edmond doesn't come from these papers.

Thinking about the close of Edmond's life in Gunnison, I add a final piece of information like that. Although there was nothing glamorous about Edmond's life in Gunnison, he didn't want more than what he had there—a community that supported him and a family who loved him.

The year after Edmond's death, Karsti saw the situation around her reach a crisis point. Realizing that the Mormons still weren't abandoning polygamy, Congress passed the Edmunds-Tucker Bill of 1887. Its goal was to not only end polygamy, but to destroy the economic and political power of the LDS Church. Later that year, the United States Attorney General confiscated the real and personal property of the Church, including numerous Church buildings. The Mormons were forced to pay rent in order to use them. Thirteen hundred Mormons were fined or sentenced to six months in prison for practicing polygamy or even claiming to believe in the doctrine of polygamy, and foreign converts were denied citizenship under the claim that the Church was a subversive institution.[29]

In April of 1887, Chasty and John moved with John's family to Fremont, a new community about sixty miles south of Gunnison. Karsti probably moved with them. If not, she made the move soon afterwards. County records show that by 1890, she had arrived in Fremont.[30] Several of her children came too. Mary Elizabeth and Rosann had already married. This left Moroni, Ephraim, Rachel, and Sarah who could have possibly made the move with Karsti to Fremont.[31]

I know little about Karsti's life in Fremont. But I do know some of the events that occurred around her. In 1890, Wilford Woodruff, the president of the LDS Church, issued what is known as the Woodruff Manifesto. Explaining that he was acting for the temporal salvation of the Church, Woodruff wrote, "I publicly declare that my advice to the Latter-day Saints is to refrain from contracting any marriage forbidden by the law of the land." LDS President Joseph F. Smith followed up on this over a decade later with the so-called "Second Manifesto" in which he reiterated that polygamy was forbidden and that any member involved in it would be excommunicated.[32]

The federal government reacted to the Woodruff Manifesto cautiously at first, concerned that it was only a ploy. After witnessing it put into practice over the next few years, they began to accept it.

Run-ins between the LDS Church and the federal government over polygamy were far from over, as the end of polygamy did not come as neatly as some hoped. Overall, the quirkiness of Utah's early existence was declining as its people moved closer to the mainstream. Finally, in 1896, Utah was granted statehood. Many of the towns and communities held celebrations. Karsti may have joined in the rejoicing.

This is one of the last events I can even guess at in Karsti's life. Besides her name in the county history, I have only two other records of Karsti after she moved to Fremont. The 1900 census shows Karsti in Fremont with Moroni, age thirty-six, and Sarah, age eighteen.[33] Rachel had married in 1891, but then died only seven years later. Ephraim had disappeared from the records.

Two years after the census, on March 14, 1902, Karsti died. She was fifty-eight years old, even younger than Edmond had been at his death. But just as with Edmond, I have never found her death record.

Even for an ancestor in this time period, I have relatively little information about Karsti's life. I don't have a diary, any letters, or anything at all that she wrote. I don't have a photograph or a description of what she looked like. I don't even have a marriage or death record for her.

My insights into her life are more abstract, and yet, more personal. I have seen the church in which Karsti was christened, stood on the land where she once helped her parents farm, followed in her footsteps across the western US, searched out the village of Spring Lake where her little family grew, and stared at the mountains in Gunnison that must have been so familiar to her. I have followed Karsti's journey.

Despite my lack of sources, I feel like I know Karsti better than any other ancestor.

I sit outside on the bench by the playground near my apartment watching my children go down the slide and play in the sand. Other kids crowd the area, the sounds of their giggles and shrieks filling the air. Several women sit near me, on the bench, on lawn chairs, or on a blanket spread out on the grass. We talk and laugh, the discussion ranging from the upcoming graduation to how to get children to eat vegetables. The day is no different than a hundred days before it.

Yet today, I have a hard time focusing on the conversation. I look around at my children with their friends and at my own friends gathered here spontaneously on a sunny, if slightly chilly, spring day. These friends have been the constants in my life — the ones who ate my

Easter rolls even though they managed to be both dense and yeasty at the same time, the ones who helped carry in my groceries when I was pregnant and sick, the ones I've laughed with and cried with for the past five years. I have seen them as the roots and ground below me — firm and stable. Now that ground seems more like a sandy beach, the grains being washed away into the ocean. What will help me keep my balance now?

I feel a growing panic inside me as our time in Madison ticks away. I was sad to leave Provo, but my feelings for Provo can't compare to Madison. I love living here. I love our neighborhood and the close-knit community that has become so ingrained in our lives. Spain promises adventure and Massachusetts seems a perfect fit for us, but I still feel in my heart that they won't be Madison. We are so happy here. Why do we have to leave and start over?

My thoughts return to Karsti and Edmond. When they came to Utah, they had to start over. There is one important difference between their move and mine: they both arrived in Utah alone — without family. When I leave Madison, my friends will stay here. But my family will go with me.

And that should make everything different.

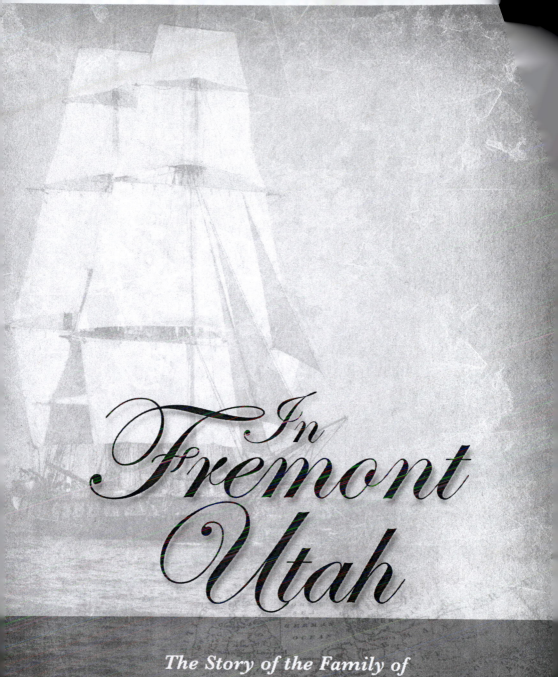

In Fremont Utah

The Story of the Family of
Earl Albrecht

PART FOUR

UTAH FAMILY TREE

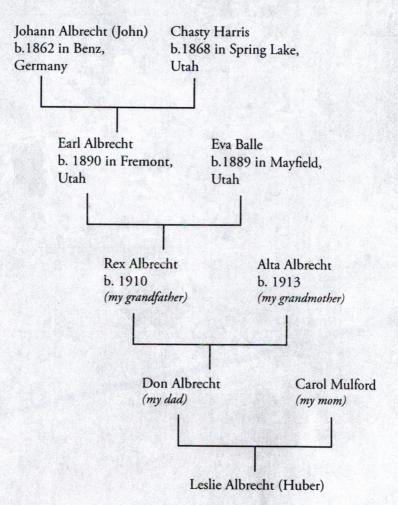

Johann Albrecht (John)
b.1862 in Benz,
Germany

Chasty Harris
b.1868 in Spring Lake,
Utah

Earl Albrecht
b. 1890 in Fremont,
Utah

Eva Balle
b.1889 in Mayfield,
Utah

Rex Albrecht
b. 1910
(my grandfather)

Alta Albrecht
b. 1913
(my grandmother)

Don Albrecht
(my dad)

Carol Mulford
(my mom)

Leslie Albrecht (Huber)

See appendix for individual family groups

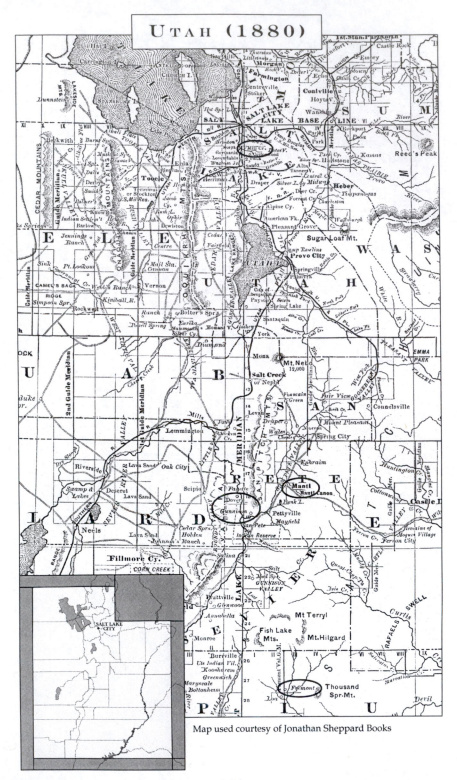

Utah (1880)

Map used courtesy of Jonathan Sheppard Books

THE TOMBSTONE OF JOHN AND CHASTY
(HARRIS) ALBRECHT

CHAPTER ELEVEN

CONNECTIONS: EARL'S PARENTS

John Albrecht and Chasty Harris, my great-great-grandparents, are the earliest generation of my family where I know someone who remembers them. With the exception of a few stories about Georg and Mina, all of my information about my earlier ancestors comes from documents—simple, lifeless facts recorded on paper.

The family stories that have survived don't paint a vibrant, or even a kind, picture of John and Chasty. They live on in people's memories only as old people, their health and abilities declining. Nobody remembers John fixing up the house, playing with his children, or going to church. His granddaughters remember that he ate peas with a knife. Besides that, they mostly remember him sitting in an old chair on the porch, doing nothing. One Sunday, his family went to church without him. When they returned home, John was sitting in that same chair, dead. Nobody even recalls him being sick.

More people have memories of Chasty, who outlived her husband by seventeen years. My Aunt Joyce remembers that Chasty had long, bony fingers. My grandma remembers Chasty taking the babies at church who screamed because she frightened them. When Chasty ate dinner at my grandparents' house, she took out her teeth and put them in her apron pocket before beginning the meal. Chasty's grandchildren remember that for Christmas she gave each of them a dime wrapped in a handkerchief.

Chasty and John left behind little to preserve their lives. Chasty, with the help of her granddaughter, wrote a short life history. It condenses her eighty-one years into one page. Chasty describes growing up poor, going to school, getting married, and filling various responsibilities at church. At the time her granddaughter wrote the history, Chasty had forty-two grandchildren and fourteen great-grandchildren.[1] Her simple history has been copied dozens of times for her great-great-grandchildren who now number in the hundreds as well as her ever-growing number of great-great-great-grandchildren.

John's daughter, Minnie, wrote a history of him. His history is just over two pages long. The first sentence gives his place of birth incorrectly. The history tells about John going to school to learn how to make shoes, getting sick on the boat to America, helping build the Manti temple, finding odd jobs to support his family, and dying in the old chair.[2] The insights are invaluable, and yet so small. I wonder if Minnie realized that her words would someday be the only history that survived of her father. I wonder if she knew that, based on those few paragraphs, generations of descendants would form their impression of John Albrecht.

I've only seen one picture of John and Chasty.[3] In it, Chasty's face is grim. Her staunch expression borders on a frown. Her hair is pulled back so tightly that it almost looks like she doesn't have any. Her deep set eyes show up as little more than shadows in the scratchy photograph.

John stares out from his picture with a deep and serious gaze. The black-and-white photo doesn't do justice to his features—curly blonde hair, light mustache, and eyes the color of the sky on a clear spring day. Perhaps it's the slant of his eyebrows, or perhaps only my imagination, but when I look at the picture, I feel that he's asking me for something—requesting my help in something only I can do.

If I only rely on other people's memories, John and Chasty remain forever weathered, worn down from the trials of life. But even if no one remembers it, John and Chasty once stood at the beginning of their journey, looking toward the future with excitement and nervousness. They built their lives, experienced triumphs and tragedies, and struggled to find happiness amidst hardships.

Since I can't recreate their lives solely from personal stories and memories, I turn to the documents once again. The documents tell me that John and Chasty met in Sanpete County, tying together the two diverse branches of my family tree. In June of 1885, the year they married, Chasty turned seventeen. That same month, John celebrated his twenty-third birthday. Chasty had been born and raised in Utah and was living with her family in Gunnison. John, who lived with his family nearby in Dover, had arrived in Utah from Germany five years earlier. After they married, John and Chasty made their home in Dover, near John's parents. Less than a year later, their first child, Rosetta, was born.

When Rosetta was seven months old, the little family packed up their belongings and left Dover. They were probably following John's parents who made the move at the same time. Chasty's mother, Karsti, and those of her children who still lived with her may have also left Gunnison to travel with John and Chasty and the Albrecht family.

Maybe they were all weary of the poor crops and constant struggle for survival. Perhaps they believed this new location offered them a more promising future. Maybe they were drawn by the excitement of being some of the first people in a recently settled community. Whatever their motivations, they loaded their wagon and began the eighty-mile trip south to Fremont, located in what was later known as Wayne County.

John and Chasty brought only a few possessions—and their family. Family had probably anchored them through changes in the past, and they must have expected family once again to be their support.

"Where should we put all this stuff?" I ask my mom as I balance a bin of genealogy papers with several framed photographs stacked precariously on top of it. David walks in behind me, his arms also full.

"Oh, I don't know. Just stack it in a corner of my bedroom, I guess," my mom replies.

I hesitate. "Are you sure?"

"Yeah, why not?" She shrugs, looking up from where she sits at the table helping Rachel and Taylor manage the ribbon, beads, paper, and glue she has taken out for them.

Despite my mom's nonchalance, I still feel a twinge of guilt as I carry a second and then a third load of our stuff into her room. We've left most of our possessions in storage in Wisconsin while we spend our year in Spain. But, I brought some of our most precious things to my parents' house where I know they will be safe.

Taking over my parents' bedroom is only one on a long list of inconveniences we're inflicting upon them. We have also extended our visit with them indefinitely. Although we originally intended to stay for a week before flying to Spain, we've run into a little flaw in the plan. Our Visas haven't arrived. We were told they would definitely be here by the end of July, but now it's the middle of August and we have yet to receive anything. David's work is completed, our two-month notice on our apartment expired, and we have nowhere to go—except to my parents' house.

My family has spent the past year coming to our rescue. When I was pregnant and sick, my mom first flew to Wisconsin, then she flew Rachel, Taylor, and me to Texas. My parents also came to Wisconsin a week after our new baby, Sarah Ann, was born while David attended a conference in New York. My mom cooked and cleaned while my dad moved boxes from our storage unit, trying to minimize the damage caused by a sewage flood. My sister, Laura, arrived as my parents flew out and picked up where they left off. Finally, my brother, Scott, spent our last week in Wisconsin with us—scrubbing the shower and taking my kids out for ice cream while we packed our belongings.

I stack the last load of bins and papers in the corner of my parents' room. Glancing around, I remember that I gave them a framed family tree to hang on their bedroom wall for Christmas last year. But I don't see it anywhere. Their walls are still blank. My parents, who are always incredibly busy, have never worried about details like decorating.

Out of the corner of my eye, I catch sight of the framed family tree leaning against the wall, half-hidden behind the dresser. I walk over and pull it out. I look over the rows of familiar names and dates. I notice the variety of places that play a role in my family story—Germany, Sweden, and England on my grandpa's side, as well as Denmark, Ireland, Scotland, Massachusetts, Rhode Island, New York, and Kentucky on other branches of the family tree. Yet one place, more than any of the others, is my family's home—our roots. That place is Fremont, Utah.

When John and Chasty arrived in Fremont, the area was known as Rabbit Valley. The first settlers to the area came to Fremont, building the first home in 1876. During the next few years, more families trickled in. The town was officially organized in 1884 with twelve blocks marked off. John and Chasty arrived soon after.[4]

The view of the landscape that unfolded before John and Chasty when they got to Fremont was probably not much different than the one that unfolds in front of me when I visit. Fremont is in the desert, alone and cut off from the world. Short, stubby, prickly bushes cover the ground without a drop of green anywhere in sight. The scenery is dry and brown, harsh and almost menacing.

But there's another side to Fremont. Jagged, stark mountains and chalky, bare rocks striped with faded shades of pink, yellow, and blue fill the horizon. On a clear night, an intricate display of stars spreads across the clear, unhindered sky.

My parents say Fremont is beautiful. To me, it's too raw, too barren to deserve an adjective as grandiose—and yet as dull—as beautiful. It's stunning, breathtaking perhaps, but not beautiful. Sometimes I think of John and Chasty arriving in Fremont and wonder what their first impression of it was.

I picture their wagon bumping over the parched ground as John guides the horses along the dirt trail lined with sagebrush. The scenery remains much the same as their destination comes into view. John tries to fight off his feelings of doubt. His father had seemed so calm about the change, so certain that Fremont offered a better life for all of them. John had taken it for granted that he was right. But now the barren surroundings make him wonder what promise this new place could hold—what it could offer different from what they had before.

Chasty walks beside the wagon with baby Rosetta strapped closely to her body. She couldn't bear the shaking and rattling of the wagon any longer so she decided to leave her seat beside John to walk for a while. Now, her shoulders grow weary with the weight of the baby. Yet, she knows they're almost there. She can see the scattered homes of the newly settled town ahead of her, growing larger with each step.

At last, the wagons roll to a stop.

"We're here!" calls Meta, John's ten-year-old sister, as she skips up to Chasty, her braids bouncing up and down. She leans her head close to Rosetta and makes a face at her. Rosetta smiles at her young aunt as she reaches up to grab one of her braids.

"This is your new home," Meta informs Rosetta solemnly. "What do you think?"

"Dadada," Rosetta answers cheerfully.

"Rosetta likes it," Meta tells Chasty. "How about you?"

Chasty glances up at John who has been watching their exchange with a distracted expression on his face. Then she looks around her again. At first glance, she feels as if they walked in a big circle and ended up back in Dover. The dry ground below her and the feeling of being nearly alone on the earth are the same.

Yet, there is something else here. Maybe it's the mountains. They seem to demand respect, bringing a touch of beauty, or at least drama, to the surroundings. Or maybe it's the feeling of a new beginning— for them and for the town—that she senses in the air.

"Well, I suppose it's as good a place as any to start a home," she says at last.

"Yes, I suppose so," John says. "If you're not opposed to a lot of hard work."

To John and Chasty, Fremont was a new destination, a place that held their future. But for me, Fremont holds the past, the history of my family. John and Chasty would raise their children in Fremont. Then, their children would raise their children there. My dad grew up in Fremont, and my grandma still lives there today. Fremont, more than anywhere else, is my family's home.

My family traveled to Wayne County—to Fremont and to Torrey, my mom's hometown—every couple of years when I was growing up. It was almost the only vacation destination we had. As a teenager, I thought it was the end of the earth. At the same time, although I would have never admitted it then, I've always been drawn to Wayne County. Wayne County offers a doorway to another world, a whimsical look into a past we've chosen to leave behind. It's a place I want to bring my children and their children.

As a child, I associated Wayne County with people hugging us and telling us they missed us and that we had gotten so big. They were people I didn't know very well. My parents, though, said they were "going home" when we went to Wayne County. My mom cried when we left. I found this bewildering. There seemed little home-like to me in Wayne County. My home was in Bryan, Texas, where I had lived since I was four years old. It seemed to me it was my parents' home too.

Wayne County seemed so... different. I saw a sharp disconnect between my parents and my grandparents. My grandparents ate roast for dinner on Sundays while I don't remember my parents ever fixing a roast once. My grandparents lived in one place most of their lives, but my parents had left home far behind. Between the four of them, my grandparents had one semester of college, while my parents both have PhDs. My grandparents earned their living with their hands; my parents type at computers in their offices.

Now I can see that in many ways Wayne County is still a part of my parents. My mom pronounces roof as "ruff," creek as "crick," both as "bolth," and favorite as "favoright." Although she has traveled around the world, she still gets nervous in airports and big cities. My dad retains the ambivalent feelings towards doctors that he learned in Wayne County. When he broke his finger, he strapped it to a Popsicle stick himself instead of going to see a doctor.

Wayne County also affected my parents in less tangible, but more meaningful, ways. It instilled its values and philosophies in them. When my dad goes to the grocery store, he smiles and says "hello" to everyone he sees. He knows the gas station attendant's life story and is on a first name basis with the workers at the pizza place. He says he learned this in Wayne County.

My mom has no tolerance for anything that even hints at dishonesty because in Wayne County all you ever needed was someone's word. Wayne County left them with an aversion for flashy spending and inequality. My parents also claim that their near-obsession with hard work originated in Wayne County. There, no excuses, complaints, or feet dragging were tolerated.

Wayne County will always be part of my parents. Because of that, it's also part of me. I have never lived in Wayne County and I will never live there. But, I have come to see it almost as my parents did — as home, as my roots.

I sit on the floor in my parents' bathroom as the water rises higher and higher in the enormous tub. Rachel and Taylor have already climbed in — and dumped the big bag of jumbo-sized Legos in there too. They giggle as they splash around in their mini-swimming pool filled with toys.

David has taken Sarah Ann with him into the other room as he searches on the computer for temporary housing in Spain. His Visa has arrived, but there's still no word on Visas for the rest of us. David and I have both tried calling the Spanish Consulate in Chicago to find out what happened to the Visas, but we are only told that they don't know anything and would prefer us to quit bothering them.

So, David will leave without us in one week. We have no choice. He has to start work. The kids and I will continue to wait at my parents' home for our Visas to arrive. David tried to assure me that he will be able to find us an apartment, register the kids for school (tasks that have proved impossible to do from the US), and get everything else set up for us.

Still, I hate even the thought of it. It's not that I mind staying with my parents. It's the uncertainty I hate — the feeling of my life being stuck while I wait for something I have no control over. I also don't look forward to being without my husband for an undetermined amount of time.

I try not to think about this now. Instead, I open up my copy of *Rainbow Views* — a book whose pages are filled with the stories and history of Wayne County. I flip to the chapter about Fremont and begin to read.

The first order of business for the Albrechts in Fremont was getting a place to live. Relying on his skills as a mason, Georg built his family a stone home outside of town. John may have built a stone home nearby or stayed with his parents at first. Eventually John and Chasty moved into a small, simple home in "downtown" Fremont. The downstairs consisted of a front room and a kitchen as well as a small master bedroom in the back. The upstairs only had one large room, divided in half. Later, their sons would sleep on one side of the room while their daughters slept on the other.[5]

Next, the family had to find a way to support themselves. As in other new Utah communities, nearly everyone turned to farming.

Before he could farm, John needed to clear off the land and prepare it. In the meantime, he helped his father run a sawmill.

John and Chasty and the other families struggled to grow crops on the marginal land. As the county history explains: "Wayne County is not considered a good farming area. Much of the surface is rugged; the valleys are small; the water supply insufficient; and the growing season in at least half of the inhabited portion is too short."[6]

It doesn't take an expert to deduce this. The suitability — or lack of suitability — of the land for farming must have been obvious to the Albrechts and other settlers from the time they first looked over the land. Yet, they still selected this area as their new home. No colonization process compelled them there. Fremont's settlers chose to come.

The success of farming in Fremont depended on getting water. Settlers immediately turned their attention to finding a way to supplement the meager rainfall. In the same year they arrived, the townspeople began digging ditches and building canals that allowed them to access the water of the Fremont River. In 1889, the community formed the Fremont Irrigation Company to oversee water rights and improve the accessibility of water.

The settlers also had to carefully select which crops to grow. Fremont had an average of about eighty days without frost, which meant only certain types of crops could survive. The settlers found that hay and hardy grains and vegetables grew fairly well there, and focused on these.[7]

Farming alone wasn't enough for many families. Throughout his life, John took on other odd jobs to help support his family. Soon after arriving in Fremont, he drove the milk truck. Later, he herded sheep. He also accepted temporary jobs such as plastering or helping on a ranch for a couple of weeks.

John and Chasty's family grew rapidly in Fremont. The first seven children were two years apart each, born between 1886 and 1898. After Rosetta came John Jr., then Earl LeRoy (my great-grandfather), born in 1890. Next came Claude, Charles, Levern, and George. Charles and George both only lived a few months. At the time of this second baby's death, Chasty was already expecting their eighth child, Minnie, born in 1899.

I know almost nothing of Earl's childhood years. But, I imagine his first memories were chaotic — memories of children running and working, yelling and laughing, and of tired and overworked parents who worried about how to feed and clothe them all.

Like John and Chasty's family, Fremont grew rapidly during its early years. It was the largest town in the area until 1895.[8] The early settlers all contributed to the community. John and his brothers and father built some of the first buildings, including the school, the church, and a store.

As Fremont grew, John and Chasty soon had neighbors from all over the world. In fact, there were few places with a higher concentration of diversity than Wayne County. In 1900, forty-six percent of the working-age adults living there were born outside the US.[9]

Wayne County wasn't the only place with a rising immigrant population. Immigration was transforming the character of the country's population. The percentage of foreign-born people in the US peaked around 1890 at nearly fifteen percent, or more than one in seven people.[10]

Immigrants typically didn't choose small towns like Fremont as their destination. By 1920, over three-quarters of foreigners lived in cities, and often in very specific cities.[11] People of the same ethnicity tended to settle in the same cities and even in the same neighborhoods. Here, in these ethnic enclaves, they continued to speak in their native languages and their cultures thrived. In Fremont, on the other hand, Danish, German, and English people all became next-door neighbors.

The multicultural background of Fremont's residents failed to create much of a multicultural community. The mixture of diverse ethnic heritages couldn't survive the intense pressure it encountered. With nobody to reinforce their culture, and with the pressing need to find common ground among neighbors, people quickly let go of ties to their home countries. A unique, but homogeneous, Fremont culture soon dominated, squelching out diversity. In basically one generation, the entire community "Americanized," or more specifically, "Fremontized."

Although John lived in Germany until he was nineteen years old, his son, Earl, couldn't speak German. Earl also couldn't speak Swedish, the native language of his maternal grandmother. Nobody passed down recipes of English, German, or Swedish food or words to traditional songs. Not even stories of the homeland survive.

Acculturation occurred throughout the country, although at different rates. More accommodating conditions existed elsewhere. In a few communities, families taught their native languages in their homes into the fourth and fifth generations. Foreign language newspapers and magazines flourished in many cities. Churches often served as venues of language and cultural preservation.

A backlash against cultural retention, and immigration in general, began to spread throughout the US by the end of the nineteenth century. In the 1880s, many states passed laws that specified that all instruction in public schools had to be done in English. Congress began passing restrictive immigration legislation, culminating in the National Origins Act of 1924. This Act, which established a quota system based on the population of the 1890 census, drastically reduced immigration, particularly among races deemed less desirable.

Since my family's cultural connections were cut off so abruptly, I feel no surviving strands reaching into my life. While my family all feels the bond to Fremont, we don't feel the same bond with Germany, England, or Sweden. I didn't feel the first pull of my tie to earlier ancestral hometowns until I arrived in Germany as a college student. It was a connection I developed, not one I inherited.

By 1911, John and Chasty had added a final five children to the family—Leonard, Owen, Edwin, Arlo, and Cleo. The grand total was an impressive thirteen. Two of the children died in infancy, one (Arlo) died at age three, and one (Edwin) died before his fifteenth birthday. Given a nine-month pregnancy, Chasty spent 117 months, or almost ten years of her life, pregnant. Between ages seventeen and thirty-eight, she never went longer than one year and nine months without being pregnant.

Thirteen children didn't only mean more months of pregnancy. It meant more of everything else too—many of these things, unlike months of pregnancy, incalculable. I can only wonder at how many times she woke in the middle of the night to feed a baby, how many hours she spent at the bedside of a sick child—some who never recovered—how many scrapes and bruises she cared for, how many punishments she laid out, or how many hugs she gave. But, I can be reasonably certain that she did all of these things much more than I have or will.

Although families were bigger then than they are today, not many were as big as John and Chasty's. In fact, by the time Chasty began to have children, fertility rates had been steadily decreasing for some time. In 1800, women in the US had an average of about seven children each. That number had fallen to 4.24 by 1880. Average family size continued to shrink during the two decades when John and Chasty had their children, settling at 3.56 by the turn of the century.[12]

The reasons for the decline also explain why it didn't affect John and Chasty. Many families had fewer children because the changing economic conditions made having children more expensive. As more families moved to urban areas, children became an economic liability instead of an asset. Rural families, like the Albrechts, could still use their children's labor on their farms. Changing attitudes towards large families and improvements in contraception were other major causes of shrinking family size. More women could choose how many children to have—and chose to have fewer. In the Mormon environment in Utah though, large families were actively encouraged.

The amount of time it took to run and support their family must have almost consumed John and Chasty. John continued doing a variety of work, increasingly away from home. At one point, the Ford Company hired him as an interpreter and sent him to Germany. He mailed back packages filled (at least according to my grandma) with nice dresses and other things mostly for Cleo, his youngest daughter and his favorite. When John returned home from Germany, his hair was dyed jet-black or, as two of his granddaughters say, almost purple. ("You've never seen anything so ridiculous," my grandma always tells me at the end of the story.)

Chasty spent her time cooking, cleaning, and caring for the children. She sewed shirts, knitted socks, and crocheted hats. She planted a vegetable garden and probably a flower garden, too. She peeled, chopped, boiled, fried, mashed, and did many other things to hundreds of potatoes—a staple crop in Fremont. In the mornings, she milked cows and then later skimmed the cream off the top to churn into butter. She made soap and candles by hand, chopped heads off chickens and plucked their feathers which she used to make pillows. At church gatherings and at home, she spent many hours quilting, talking to other women as they took turns working on each other's quilts.

I set the cups down on my parents' kitchen table as my children and I prepare to eat alone again. I've been doing the single-parent thing for two weeks now, and I'm feeling frazzled. My parents help when they're around. But they work long hours many nights and often don't return until about the time my children go to bed.

"Mommy, you gave me juice and I wanted milk!" Taylor hollers.

"Do I have to eat green beans? They make me gag," Rachel tells me.

From her bouncy seat on the floor, Sarah Ann is fussing. I can't pick her up yet. I still have to get the pasta off the stove.

"I don't want juice!" Taylor repeats.

I grab the pasta off the stove and dump it into the colander over the sink. The boiling water splashes onto my hand. I gasp and quickly stick my hand under the cold water intended for the pasta.

"Mommy!" Rachel's voice is urgent. "Taylor just spilled his juice and now the carpet is all red." As if voicing her concern for the carpet, Sarah Ann's whimpers suddenly turn into a full-out cry.

I stop, momentarily frozen. I consider going in my bedroom and closing the door. My children stare at me, confused by my lack of reaction—or motion at all. Finally, I take a deep breath, pull my stinging hand out of the water, grab Sarah Ann, and hold her with one hand while I attempt to wipe up the juice with a rag in my other hand.

As I scrub, I think of Chasty with her houseful of children during the times when John was working in Germany or out herding sheep.

How did she do it? I wonder.

In my mind, I imagine them at mealtime.

"Rosetta, can you watch the potatoes?" Chasty asks her daughter over her shoulder, as she wipes off a knife and begins to chop vegetables.

The front door slams shut as John Jr. and Earl, the two oldest sons, walk in. They've spent the afternoon on the small farm, trying to run things in their father's absence. They are tired and covered in dirt, grass, and sweat.

"Boys, go wash up. We're about to have dinner," Chasty tells them without glancing up from the vegetables. "Claude, put the cups and plates on the table—and the cheese and bread, too," she continues.

"There's no more bread, Mother," Claude answers as he pulls the cheese out of the fridge. "Levern ate the rest of it this morning."

"No, I didn't!" Levern interjects. "Earl did."

Chasty sighs. "No matter. We'll do without bread."

A squawk erupts from across the room, where Leonard has crawled under a chair and gotten stuck. Chasty hurries over to him and pulls him out with one firm yank.

"Levern, go check on Minnie, please. I haven't heard anything from her for a while. I hope she hasn't gotten into something she shouldn't. And tell your brothers to hurry. I think we're almost ready."

"Hurry!" Levern yells, not budging. Chasty raises her eyebrows at him. He gets up and runs back to complete his tasks.

Levern, John, Earl, and Minnie soon emerge. The older boys find their seats, while Minnie follows her mother and Rosetta as they set the soup, potatoes, milk, and vegetables on the table.

"Mama, I'm hungry." She repeats it several times before Chasty notices.

"Minnie!" she exclaims, looking at her for the first time. "You're covered in dirt. Were you playing outside again? Please ask one of your brothers to help you wash up."

Five minutes later, they all sit around the table. "Claude, could you please say a blessing on the food?" Chasty asks. They all bow their heads. Chasty sits down for the prayer—possibly the only time she will sit during the meal.

Still holding Sarah Ann, I finish draining the pasta. Then, I sit down at the dinner table with my children.

Perhaps motherhood connects me to Chasty also.

While John and Chasty's family was growing, the frontier was closing in around Utah. By the turn of the century, only Arizona, Oklahoma, and New Mexico (of the forty-eight contiguous states) weren't part of the Union. Settlers took over more American Indian land. Geronimo surrendered in 1886 — one of the last American Indian leaders to hold out. Frederick Jackson Turner made his claim that the frontier had fundamentally shaped American character.

The average employed person made just less than $13 a week for nearly sixty hours of work during the first decade of the 1900s. High infant and child mortality rates kept life expectancies low, with women living about forty-seven years and men living one year less on average. At the same time, the standard of living was improving and people began enjoying more leisure activities.[13]

With thirteen children and a tight budget, Chasty and John didn't have a lot of time for leisure. But, they did do things besides herd sheep and wash clothes. *Rainbow Views* reports that "during the boom days (before 1895), a spirited choir and band were organized."[14] John was the assistant director of this group that traveled to nearby communities to perform. In 1904, John served as the Justice of the Peace of Fremont.[15]

The family's major activity besides work was church. Although nobody seems too sure about how much John went to church, Chasty went faithfully. Besides going to the Sunday service, the family attended other church meetings one day during the week. On this day, all the members of the family went to different classes geared towards children, teenagers, adult men, or adult women. When Chasty wasn't helping with one of the children or youth groups, she joined in the women's meetings, known as Relief Society.

The LDS Church demanded much more than showing up twice a week to meetings. Chasty nearly always had some assigned responsibility, or calling, in the ward. She served in several different Relief Society presidencies over the years. In these callings, Chasty met often to discuss the needs of women in their group. She organized meals for families when a new baby was born or a parent was sick and likely cooked and delivered plenty of meals herself. She probably also assisted with funerals and weddings. She sewed quilts for others and may have helped organize activities for Christmas, Easter, or just for fun.[16]

Religion didn't just hold a central position in the Albrecht family; it occupied a central position in Fremont. Religion was what had brought these settlers to Utah in the first place and it continued to serve as the common ground between them after they arrived. It shaped their new community and served, perhaps, as *the* defining characteristic in their lives.

Because of the singular influence of the LDS Church, religion played a uniquely strong role in Fremont. Yet, across the country, religion held an important place in both the individual lives of people and in society as a whole at the turn of the century. Many people went to church every Sunday and talked about God in ordinary conversations.

In the past one hundred years, religion has slipped from this place. Even in Fremont, religious fervor has mellowed. Still, religion remains a centerpiece of the community. The ward continues to serve as the basic unit of organization. Church leaders function as community leaders. No churches for other denominations exist there, although supposedly a few people in town do belong to other religions.

Religion also remains a defining characteristic of my family. Although little in the way of language or culture was passed down through the generations, religion is the one family tradition that survived. John and Chasty's parents taught them their beliefs, and they taught them to their children and so on for a hundred years now. The chain of faith continued when almost nothing else did because religion never just belonged to the past for my family. It was, and still is, an integral part of the present. It has always been more than a heritage to preserve. It's a set of values, a way of life that binds my family together.

"Mommy, I'm bored," Taylor tells me in a not-so-quiet voice from his position next to me on a pew near the front of the chapel. On my other side, Rachel focuses intently on peeling the backs off little foam stickers and pressing them onto her paper. Just beyond her, my mom shakes baby keys and anything else she can find in front of Sarah Ann to keep her happy.

I try to listen to the speaker as I hand Taylor a piece of paper and some more foam stickers. Peeling the backs off presents a challenge for a three-year-old. We work out a system. He hands the stickers to me, I peel them, and then give them back to him. In contrast to his sister who pauses before attaching each sticker, carefully selecting its position, Taylor plasters them haphazardly all over his paper.

The speaker concludes and my dad walks up to the podium. He now serves as the bishop, or lay minister, of the ward. He thanks the speakers and announces the closing song. Luckily, it's one I know well. That way I won't have to use my hands—needed for sticker-peeling—to hold the songbook.

The organist plays the opening stanzas and the ward members join in singing. Although I'll never win any awards for my voice, I love to sing. Today, as we sing one of my favorite hymns, I enjoy it even more than usual. The words, which speak of faith and peace, reach inside me, stirring my emotions.

As the congregation begins the last verse, I notice my dad sitting on the stand, singing along. He doesn't use his hymnbook either. Like me, he probably learned the words as a child, while he sat with his own parents in church. With this realization comes another one: generations of my ancestors have sat in buildings similar to this with their families, singing the words to this same song.

My eyes move to the front of the chapel where the first pew sits empty. In my mind, I see people there—two parents with a long trail of children between them. The younger children squirm or stare at the people in the room. The older ones, with bored expressions on their faces, hold their books as they sing. But John and Chasty don't need their songbooks. Chasty bounces the baby on her lap and John watches the conductor as their voices, rich with feeling, join the others in the room.

Perhaps religion is the strongest connection I have to John and Chasty.

John and Chasty were still adding children to their own family when their oldest children began to get married and leave home. Their oldest daughter, Rosetta, married one month before her little brother, Edwin, was born—the eleventh of John and Chasty's thirteen children. By the time the last child was born, both John Jr. and Earl had married, too.

As the years passed, more children married. But many of them stayed nearby. The expanding family continued to get together for holidays. John and Chasty hosted Thanksgiving dinner. They also held other dinners for holidays or just for fun at their house. Chasty often made chicken noodle soup from scratch—down to killing one of their chickens to use in it.

Their grandchildren would later remember all the adults sitting around the big table talking and laughing while they ate. The grandkids had to wait until the adults finished before they got a turn.

Sometimes, they claimed, they would think they would starve to death before the adults quit eating and talking.[17]

John died March 2, 1933, in the chair on his front porch in Fremont. Death records give his cause of death as heart disease. After John's death, Chasty stayed at the center of her family. She came to visit on her grandchildren's birthdays, ate dinner with family, and helped out when she could.

In the following years, two of Chasty's adult children died. Owen died in 1938 and Claude died four years later. In all, Chasty had seen six of her children buried. The last few years of her life, Chasty moved a few miles south to Loa, also in Wayne County, to live with her daughter and family.[18] Chasty died there on February 14, 1950.

"My stomach hurts," I tell my dad as we walk into the airport, dragging five suitcases weighing seventy pounds each, three children—one in a baby backpack and one in a stroller, one car seat, three "special blankets" (one for each child), one pink princess suitcase, one diaper bag, one backpack full of art activities, and, of course, Stitch Bear and Spot (the prized stuffed animals) with us.

"Are you sick?" my dad asks.

"No, just nervous."

"About flying alone or about Spain?"

"About Spain," I answer without hesitating

My parents both offered to make the long flight to London and then Valencia with me. I seriously considered it for a while. In the end, I couldn't justify them spending so much money just to sit with me for a total traveling time of thirteen hours and thirty minutes. I knew it would be hectic—but it would be over quickly.

Living in Spain, on the other hand, won't. As we set off on our journey, the idea of relocating our family to a foreign country where we don't speak the language seems less adventurous—and more just plain scary.

My dad and I are both out of breath by the time we arrive with the luggage at the check-in line. As we wait, my dad notices that the computer screen shows my flight is delayed.

"What does this mean?" I ask the airline attendant behind the counter when it's our turn.

"It means you'll miss your connection in London," she tells me. "There are no later flights out of London to Valencia that day, either. It would be best if you go tomorrow."

I stare at her, unable to respond as I look over our pile of luggage. It was a two-hour drive to the Houston airport and another hour before that of jamming everything into my parents' car. It's also been emotionally draining. I don't want to do this all again tomorrow.

After some negotiating and many phone calls, the airline arranges for us to stay the night at a nearby hotel. My dad and I lug the suitcases and children into the shuttle and then into our hotel room.

"I'll come back in the morning to help you," my dad says when we're settled. "I have to teach at ten o'clock, but I'll leave right after my class."

"Oh Dad, you don't need to come back. I'll just take the shuttle to the airport," I tell him.

"It's too much for you by yourself. I'll be here by one o'clock."

"Really, you don't need to," I insist. "I can do it."

"Maybe so." He smiles. "But there's nothing in the world I'd rather do." It's a statement I've heard my dad make many times when one of his children needs him. Coming from anyone else, it might sound sarcastic. But from my dad, it's sincere.

"I'll see you tomorrow." He leaves before I can protest again.

The night passes slowly. We use the airline voucher to eat at the hotel restaurant for dinner. My children order ice cream for dessert and are immensely pleased. Afterwards, I search through the suitcases until I locate pajamas. I read stories, sing songs, and do everything else that goes along with the nighttime routine, feeling distracted the whole time—the reality of our trip still looming in front of me. At last, I turn the lights out. Rachel and Taylor giggle and then fight before falling asleep. Sarah Ann sleeps fitfully on my arm. When morning comes, I feel less rested than when I got into bed.

"Happy birthday, mommy!" Rachel jumps on top of me.

"Oh yeah, it's my birthday," I mumble. I purchased the tickets so we'd arrive in Spain on my birthday. Instead, I'm waking up in a hotel in Houston alone with my children.

Several hours later, we arrive at the airport with my dad. The airline attendant takes pity on us and lets my dad accompany me to the gate. My dad walks up and down the halls with my children, trying to use up their energy. I pretend to read a book, trying to think calm thoughts.

Finally, it's time to board. My dad helps me strap everything and everyone on. Then, he walks us to the gate.

My children each hug him. Then, it's my turn.

I can't think of the words to express what I feel. "Thank you for everything," I say simply as I hug my dad.

"We loved every minute of having your family at our house."

"You can have peace and quiet now," I tell him.

"Peace and quiet are overrated."

I turn and begin pushing the stroller towards the plane.

"Bye Grandpa!" Taylor shouts, leaning out of the stroller so he can see my dad. "Bye!" He waves his arms furiously.

I feel the lump in my throat growing. I remember how anxious I was for our Visas to come. Now, I realize, I will always be glad that they were late.

Point of Convergence:

Earl's Family

MY BROTHER MATHEW (RIGHT) AND ME (LEFT) WITH EVA BALLE ALBRECHT

Earl LeRoy Albrecht, John and Chasty's third child and my great-grandfather, died eight years before I was born. In the enormity of time, eight years seems very small, as if our paths just missed each other. My path did cross with Eva, my great-grandmother. She died when I was three years old. But this crossing has little meaning to me—I don't remember her.

Although I never met Earl and I don't remember Eva, I feel as if, through my long process of research and writing, our journeys have converged. Filing cabinets filled with papers and bookshelves crammed with books help me understand Earl's background and family, the influences that shaped his life. The masses of information I have gathered over the past ten years culminate with Earl.

I think of Earl as the center of an hourglass. From above, grains of sand from the wide top funnel through. The sands are of a variety of colors and textures representing his rich heritage. After the narrow center, the hourglass widens again as the sands spread out to land at the base. The bottom of the hourglass holds Earl's descendants, increasing in number and diversity with the passing of time. Earl is the convergence point of it all.

"*Un besito, por favor* (a little kiss please)," I tell Rachel and Taylor as we reach the gate to their school. They each give me a kiss on the cheek. Then they kiss Sarah Ann, who bounces in front of me in the baby pack.

"*Hasta luego* (see you soon)!" I call after them as they walk into the courtyard. I watch them disappear inside their classrooms before I turn to leave. I'm relieved there were no tears this morning.

David and I decided our kids could only learn Spanish and make friends by going to school. Despite all the comments we got before we left about how quickly kids pick up foreign languages, it has been a hard adjustment for them. I've spent many nights lying awake in bed wondering if we're doing the right thing.

I look at the city around me as I walk home with Sarah Ann. We've been in Valencia for six weeks. The kids' school has been only one of many adjustments. We live in a big city in a high-rise apartment building surrounded by other high-rise apartment buildings as far as I can see. There is no grass anywhere—only streets. Orange trees line the center medians between the streets, adding a touch of green. Walking is our main mode of transportation with an occasional trip on the bus or metro. And I am still working to expand my vocabulary of numbers, colors, and food that I arrived with.

I found the changes stimulating at first. I love the old city center, the colorful market, the nearby beach. I am fascinated by the cured pig legs hanging at the grocery store, how the restaurants are packed at 2:00 p.m. for the biggest meal of the day, and how the people drive, talk, and dress.

But some of the novelty has worn off. At first, I found it amusing to hang my groceries on the stroller and try to maneuver the whole load through the double doors (that for some reason open towards each other) of our apartment building and up the stairs into the tiny elevator. Now, I only find it exhausting. I used to find it soothing to sit on our front balcony and listen to the chatter and laughter on the street below me. Now, I find it infuriating to lie awake in bed because of that same noise outside my bedroom window. Lately, instead of noticing what is different about my life here, I mostly notice what is missing.

Back inside our apartment, I lay Sarah Ann down for her morning nap. I turn on the computer and sit down next to it. This is my time of peace—my time for writing. Yet, even this activity done alone in my own apartment is so different. And today, the differences feel almost painful.

In Wisconsin, I had to guard my writing time carefully. I turned off the ringer on the phone, ignored knocking on the door, and refused any requests of favors or invitations that fell during that time. In Spain, there is nothing to guard my time from. My calendar, filled to overcapacity in Wisconsin, now sits empty and unopened on my bookshelf. My phone that once rang constantly, now sits quietly in the corner. I don't even bother to turn the ringer off.

The changes have swept away the important along with the trivial from my life. As I sit staring at my blank computer screen in my apartment surrounded by mint green walls and the sounds of traffic out my window, I realize I must find what still remains.

More remains of Earl and Eva's lives than any of my ancestors before them. My dad lived down the street from them and saw them nearly every day while he was growing up. Many other people who are still alive knew them well. They can share personal stories about them, stories filled with emotions and character. Details abound, just waiting to be gathered.

Yet with each passing day, Earl and Eva slip deeper into the past. The events and memories must be recorded, summarized and evaluated or it won't be long until Eva and Earl become nothing more than names on a pedigree chart like all my other ancestors.

My great-grandparents' story ought to be the easiest to tell, but I find it the most intimidating. I have confidence in my ability to decipher genealogical records. I have less confidence in my ability to decipher people. I have the chance to know who my great-grandparents were, what they were like, and what was important to them.

For me, Earl and Eva's names always go together, their lives inseparably intertwined. There was never a time that Earl and Eva didn't know each other. Evalena Thompson Balle was born May 10, 1889 in Mayfield, a small town in Sanpete County, near Gunnison and Dover. When she was six weeks old, her family moved to Wayne County. Here, they built a little log cabin four miles east of Fremont on a ranch. The family moved twice more, ending up on a farm one mile outside of town.[1]

Eva's mother, Emma Thurstrup Balle, sometimes worked as a schoolteacher. My grandma has often told me how smart Grandma Balle was. The school superintendent in Wayne County once claimed that she could tell any child that had Emma Balle's blood in them — they were smarter than the rest. But there wasn't a lot of education available in Fremont. Eva had to move to Glenwood, a town fifty miles away, in order to complete eighth grade. She finished in 1906, at the age of sixteen, as the valedictorian of the class.

The summer after Eva returned home from Glenwood, Eva and Earl began dating. Earl was a year younger than Eva. Eva wrote in her life history that they weren't too serious, just having fun.

The next year, Eva took a correspondence course which she finished in the spring of 1907. The next fall, with an eighth grade education plus one correspondence course, she began teaching school in Fremont.

Meanwhile, Earl worked at Farrell's Ranch, located up in the mountains about twenty miles outside of town. Earl was a ranch hand — essentially a cowboy. He lived there along with about a dozen or so other young men whose major responsibility was to take care of the cattle.

A new group of calves was born each spring. During the summer, the ranch hands would take the cows out to graze. They would spend months riding with the cows, making sure they had enough grass, taking care of any that became sick, and doing other tasks. In the fall, when new snow started to make grazing impossible, they gathered the cows in. Back at the ranch, the ranch hands continued to watch over the cows, feeding them hay grown on-site. They wanted to fatten the cows up as much as possible so they could sell them for a high price in the spring. With the new batch of calves born that spring, the cycle started again.

Earl took pride in his work. The longest description in his short life history isn't about his children or even his wife, but about Spot—his horse. "I had a special cow horse which I broke and trained by myself. He was known as the best cutting horse in the state. His name was Spot. He was born with a big white spot on the forehead and one white leg."

In the summer of 1907, a man came through, driving a car near the ranch where Earl worked. The road was so rough that the car broke down. The man had to leave the car there while he went to Salt Lake City to find someone to repair it.

Earl and Eva had never seen a car before. When no one was around, they would sit in the car parked out in the shed. Perhaps this was where their casual dating blossomed into something more. Earl wrote in his history: "Eva and I used to sit in his car and make plans for the future. It was about the first Ford we had ever been in so we rode for miles without getting out of the shed. We planned that someday we would be married and have a car of our own…We had a family of five children before we drove from the ranch to our home in a car."

"What were Earl and Eva like?" I ask my grandma on the phone one night when all is quiet in my apartment (except the music seeping in from the street).

"Eva was tiny," she tells me. "She was short, thin, and just small-boned. Earl was tall, broad-shouldered, and rather dignified looking. When they stood side by side, the difference was striking.

"I always found Earl a little hard to get close to. He was quiet and maybe a little withdrawn. But he was a good man. One year, the price of pork was really low. Earl had all these pigs and he knew he would hardly make a profit selling them. So, he killed and dressed those pigs and took one to every widow and older couple in town. That's just the kind of person he was.

"And Eva…Everyone—*everyone*—loved Eva. She was one of the

kindest people I've ever known. She always made me feel loved. And I loved her too. When my girls were little, I used to take one in each arm and walk the two blocks to Eva's house nearly every afternoon. She'd watch out the window for me and when she saw me, she'd come out and take one of them. Then, I'd spend the afternoon with her."

My grandma can't talk about Eva without her voice getting choked with emotion. She speaks more highly of Eva than she does of anyone, except for maybe her own father.

"Whenever we needed anything, Earl and Eva were there. Earl would come sometimes to drive the tractor. Eva would help snap beans. When my daughters graduated, they showed up at the door both times with $5 to help pay for their dresses. They didn't have much money either, but they wanted to help."

I talk to my grandma for an hour, asking questions. But I forget to ask what was most important to Earl and Eva.

Eva and Earl married on November 3, 1909. Eva had just turned twenty and Earl was nineteen. The LDS Church emphasized the importance of marrying in a temple. According to Church doctrine, when people married in a temple, they could be together for eternity instead of just "until death do us part." While nearly every small town in Utah had a church, temples were few and far between. The nearest temple was in Manti—the temple Earl's father and grandfather had helped build. Earl and Eva decided to get married there.

Traveling to Manti took two days in their borrowed white-topped buggy. Earl and Eva brought two big sacks of grain that they put between them when they stopped to sleep. After the wedding ceremony, they climbed up to the top of the temple where they could look out over the town and the countryside. Perhaps they held hands as they considered their lives stretched out in front of them like the valley stretched out below. Before they left Manti, they sold the grain sacks.

Eva and Earl held a reception to celebrate their wedding when they returned to Fremont. They invited people from all over the county. When I read about it in Eva's history, I can see it in my mind.

Eva looks around the main meeting room of the little stone church. The decorations are simple—but just right. Her mother's friends put so much time into them. Eva has spent many days inside this room— and even attended dances and wedding receptions here. But it feels different tonight. She wonders if other people feel the sparkle in the air.

Eva hears a note on a violin and looks to the front of the room to see Johnnie Jacobs, the violinist for the night, ready to start.

"Would you care to dance?" Earl stands in front of her, extending his arm to her. She knows he feels awkward in his suit and hates to dance. But he wants her to be happy.

"Of course," she answers, taking his hand and smiling as they walk out to the dance floor. She feels as if they're floating across an elegant ballroom instead of just the Fremont church. Her dress swishes, just as a dress should, as she walks. It is satin striped, trimmed with satin ribbons. A pleated flounce lines the bottom of the skirt.

Eva feels everyone's eyes on them as they begin to dance—all the people who have come to share in their happiness. Earl holds her tight, his closeness making up for his lack of dancing skills. She closes her eyes, wanting to freeze this moment.

If life on a ranch had been difficult for a single man, it was even more difficult for a family. On the ranch, Earl and Eva were cut off from the rest of the world. When they first married, the twenty-mile trip to Fremont required that they spend the night there. It was nearly impossible to go to town and back in one day. It must have been a lonely existence, particularly for Eva who now had only her husband and a bunch of cowboys for company.

For Earl, life on the ranch meant long hours of hard, labor-intensive work as well as a lot of time away from home. In return, he received $35 a month. For Eva, ranch life also meant hard work. She cooked and did all the wash for the dirty farmhands. In return, she didn't receive a cent.[2]

The first winter Earl and Eva spent together at the ranch, it snowed so much they could only get out on horseback—and even then only by going a roundabout way. Frost stayed on the nail heads in the kitchen all day while Eva cooked. They did find some ways to take advantage of the severe weather, though. They hooked sleighs to the horses the men were breaking in. The wild horses ran as fast as they could, bucking and lunging. It made for an exciting ride. Eva wrote, "It helped pass some of my time away."

In the spring, Earl took a trip to Salt Lake City with the ranch owner, Mr. Farrell. He rode on horseback the entire way. Salt Lake was a city filled with livery stables and big barns. There, Earl bought a white-topped buggy. He hitched it together with the black-topped buggy Mr. Farrell had driven there, and brought them both back. Mr. Farrell drove his newly purchased car, the seventh car bought in Salt Lake City.

One winter at the ranch was enough for Eva. That spring of 1910, she and Earl bought a two-room, dirt-floor house in town. They decided Eva would live on the ranch in the summer and at the new house in town during the winter. Eva wrote, "We were as happy as though it were a mansion." They spent the next few months fixing up the little house, putting carpet on the floors and trying to make it feel like home. Perhaps there was something a little bittersweet about the preparations, though. The home would largely be for Eva and their future children — not for Earl. For the next sixteen years, they would spend the majority of each year living apart.

Rex LeRoy, their first child and my grandfather, was born on September 4, 1910. He had a habit of holding his breath, sometimes until his face turned red and he passed out. Eva would become frantic, putting him under cold water or doing anything else she could think of to startle him into breathing.

Several more children joined the family over the next few years. Emma was born in 1913, Nila in 1916, and Lula in 1918. Earl wrote one sentence in his life history noting the birth of each child. For the birth of Nila, he wrote two sentences: "Nila was born in August in 1916. At that time they had such a hard rainstorm there was a heavy flood which washed nearly all the hay into the lake."

Since Earl was gone most of the time, Eva learned to function alone. When Rex was only six years old, she left him to watch baby Nila so she could get the chores done.

World War I came and went, leaving farmers like Earl relatively untouched since they were needed at home. Then, when Rex was nine years old, crisis struck the home — and many homes throughout the US. As Eva wrote: "Lula was a fat healthy baby until she was one year old. When the Spanish influenza came to town, it struck our home."

By the time the Spanish Flu hit Fremont late in 1919, it was winding down. It had already unfurled most of its fury and earned itself a place in history as the deadliest epidemic ever recorded — killing more people in one year than the Black Plague did in four years.[3] The flu was unique both in its infectiousness and in its morbidity rates. By the winter of 1918–1919, it had reached nearly every corner of the world. Estimates of the total number of deaths vary, but many scientists now put it at over fifty million.[4]

When the Spanish Flu reached Fremont, the entire Albrecht family fell sick at once. Lula became seriously ill. As soon as Eva could get out of bed, she began waiting on her family. This premature activity brought on a relapse — even worse than the original illness. Earl watched in growing alarm as his wife's health declined. The doctors said they could do nothing for her. With his options dwindling, Earl pleaded with God to spare her life.

The only good thing about the Spanish Flu was its quick disappearance. The numbers infected during the winter of 1919–1920 when the flu came to Fremont, although higher than normal, were much smaller than the year before. By the spring of 1920, it had almost disappeared completely.

For the Albrechts, it was too late. Eva recovered, but baby Lula did not. She lived a few months after the flu swept through, but never regained her strength. Earl and Eva did all they could, taking her to doctors and waiting on her day after day. Finally, Lula died on August 5, 1920, in the hospital in Salina, a larger town sixty miles north.

A little over a year after Lula's death, another baby girl came into their home. Eva's description gives a hint to her heartache: "We were blessed with health from then on. We were also blessed with another baby, on December 11, 1921. We were very glad for this baby, we had been so lonely since the death of our little girl. We called her Donna. She was the life of our home."

The growing family found it hard to fit in their small house, so they bought a new one which, according to Eva, "had plenty of room." Earl became the foreman—the supervisor of the other men at the ranch. He now earned $60 a month. Then in April of 1925, Beth, the fifth girl and last child in the family, was born.

The next addition to the family was a car. Not long after Beth's birth, Earl and Eva bought a 1923 Chevrolet—fifteen years after they had sat in that broken-down Ford and dreamed of driving a car.

I pace around my bedroom with the phone in my hand, feeling a little nervous. Finally I dial the number of Nila Carlson, my great-aunt who I don't remember ever meeting before.

"Is this Nila?" I ask when someone with a grandmotherly voice answers.

"Yes," she says. I explain who I am and what I'm doing.

"Could I ask you a few questions about your parents?" I ask.

"Of course," she says. "But, these days I don't remember much. I'll tell you what I can."

I start down my list of detailed questions, hoping to confirm exact dates and fill in missing tidbits. I want to make sure I have everything just right. As I fire question after question, Nila hesitates, struggling to remember.

"I'm sorry," she says, sighing after one question. "I just don't remember. It was so long ago."

I pause for a minute and think. Then, I put the list of questions aside.

"What were your parents like?" I ask.

"Why, my parents, they were hard workers," she starts, the hesitant concentration gone from her voice. As she starts to talk this time, her words flow smoothly.

"Mom basically ran the home and the little farm in Fremont by herself. Dad was away nearly all the time at the ranch. Of course, we spent the summers with him, but the rest of the year, it was just us.

"Dad worked hard out on the ranch too. He came to town when he could. We all had to help. There was nobody else to do it—just us. It was hard work. Thinking back, I just don't know how Mom did it. She was the strength of our home—running the household and practically raising us by herself. And your grandpa, being the only boy and the oldest child, had a lot of responsibility, too. We didn't have much. But, you know, we were happy."

Later that night, I pull out a taped interview I recorded almost ten years ago of Emma and Donna, two of Eva and Earl's daughters. I had started to transcribe it, but I never finished.

"What about your dad?" I ask them twenty minutes into the conversation. "What was Earl like?"

Donna answers my question, her voice staticky and far away. I have to rewind the tape three times to get the words right. "Dad was a big guy. And he had a little curl in his hair. It would come down on his forehead. He was a good-looking man. I always thought so. He had blue eyes. And he was a kind man."

For an hour, I transcribe the tape. I listen to the back and forth of questions and answers, typing each sentence as closely to the conversation as I can.

"I thought our parents were strict. Didn't you, Emma?" Donna asks.

"Yes," Emma confirms, her voice soft. "Dad wasn't around too much to discipline us. But Mother was quite strict about what she wanted us to do—and she expected us to do it. She never was cross about it."

"She never was ornery," Donna agrees. "She just had a way of doing it. I can't remember ever getting a spanking, except for one time."[5]

Eventually, the conversation wanders off. Emma gets out some genealogy sheets to show me. Donna becomes distracted by someone else in the room. I never ask my last question. I never ask, "What were the most important things in your parents' lives?"

In 1926, Earl received a surprising request. A Church leader in the area rode a horse to the ranch where Earl worked and asked him to be the bishop (or lay minister) of the Fremont ward. Earl rarely even attended church. Although his family did, he had chores to do on Sunday and the trip into town was far. He lived the life of a cowboy—a lifestyle not consistent with the life of a bishop in other ways besides church attendance.[6]

Earl was taken off guard by the request, but he took it seriously. He accepted the calling. Not only that, but he decided that in order to fulfill his duties adequately, he would have to quit working at the ranch. Earl moved to town with his family and became a farmer, reforming his life in all ways necessary to conform to Church teachings. Earl served as bishop of the Fremont ward for eight years.

If Earl had expected heavenly blessing for his service, he would have been disappointed by the events that followed. In April of 1927, the family's new home caught on fire. The neighbors tried to put it out, but the fire moved quickly, burning the roof off. The house needed extensive remodeling to become livable again. While they were rebuilding, Earl and Eva decided to make another change. The pasture where the house sat had become swampy. So, they moved the house somewhere else. They cut it in half, put it on logs, and rolled it—with the help of some horses—to its new location. In the meantime, the family moved in with neighbors.

A few months later, three-year-old Beth became very sick. Eva wrote that the cause was "infantile paralysis"—also known as polio. Beth became temporarily paralyzed in one leg and arm. For months, she couldn't walk at all. Earl and Eva, who knew the pain of losing a child, were surely gripped with fear.

Polio was a disease feared by parents—and for good reason. It often struck children, earning it its name of "infantile paralysis." Polio imposed lasting damage on scores of children, and claimed many lives. Symptoms usually began with severe headaches, along with stiff, sore muscles sometimes accompanied by fever and vomiting. Paralysis could strike within hours.

Fortunately, polio released its grip on Beth. After months without use of her arm and leg, she began to take a few steps. The recovery was slow, but eventually she regained her movement completely.

Then in October of 1929, the stock market crashed. Before long, the Great Depression spread throughout the country. The Depression hit Utah hard. By 1933, the unemployment rate in Utah rose to nearly thirty-six percent, the fourth highest in the nation. Wage levels for those still working were cut nearly in half. The gross farm income fell nearly sixty percent between 1929 and 1933. Farmers like Earl had no choice but to sell their products for low prices, barely covering their cost of production. A third of the people in Utah turned to government relief funds for basic provisions.[7]

Many families felt the pinch. They adopted new measures of frugality — practiced in creative ways. Eva probably patched up clothes over and over again, relined coats with old blankets, saved string, rags, and wire for future use, and cooked cost-cutting dinners.

Women were often excluded from the workforce in order to reserve the scarce jobs for men. But Eva worked as the Fremont postmaster, a position she held for many years. She ran the post office through a room in her home. People would come and pick up their mail during certain hours. If they needed assistance to retrieve or send a package, they rang a bell and Eva would come help them.

Earl and Eva's children were reaching adulthood by the time the Depression hit. My grandfather, Rex, was called to serve a mission for the LDS Church in 1930. Then in July of 1932, Emma married D. Fount Brian who was "a fine young man" according to Eva. Fount worked as the principal of Wayne High School and the couple lived on a nearby ranch.

One morning, when they had been married a little less than three years, Fount went out to do some work on the ranch. When he didn't return home, Emma decided to check on him. She found him dead — possibly having drowned in the stream near their house due to a seizure similar to those which struck him from time to time.

The entire family was devastated. Emma was a widow at age twenty-two. She moved home with her parents for a while. Then, she decided she needed to prepare to earn a living herself, so she left for Snow College, located a little less than one hundred miles away in Ephraim. She attended Snow College for two years, then went to Brigham Young University for one year with her sister, Nila, who had just returned from serving an LDS mission. After her year at BYU, Emma left on a mission to Michigan and Indiana.

As Earl watched his children serve missions, he began thinking more about serving one himself. It seemed a good time to go. His children were older and his grown son could run his farm in his absence. So, Earl applied to fulfill a mission. In 1934, he was called to serve in the Western States Mission, the same mission his son, Rex, had been called to at age twenty. Earl was forty-four. Rex, my grandfather, married my grandmother, Alta Fern Taylor, who was also from Fremont, that same year. They helped run the farm while Earl was gone.

Missionaries in the 1930s were given very little training or guidance. Earl spent a week in Salt Lake City learning about Church teachings and procedures as well as health and manners before departing to his assigned place. He was given a copy of *A Marvelous*

Work and a Wonder by LeGrand Richards (a book about the *Book of Mormon*) and sent on his way.

One by one, all of Earl and Eva's children left home. Nila married a widowed man with two children. Emma married for the second time in 1940. Donna went away to beauty school and then married a local boy in 1942. Beth, at only eighteen, married that same year — much to the alarm of her parents.

As their children married and left home, war fell on the world again. Eva wrote in her history, "The Second World War broke out with all its horrors." Government propaganda encouraged everyone to help by doing things like buying bonds, growing "victory gardens," recycling, and conserving particular products. Many household goods including sugar, meat, gasoline, nylon, and wool were rationed.

The Albrecht family also participated in the war in a more personal way. Emma's new husband, Jeppy, went away to fight. While there, an explosion badly burned his arm. Doctors predicted at first that he would never be able to use it again. After a lot of physical therapy and medical care though, his arm finally regained its strength and movement.

With their children grown, Earl and Eva's lives became substantially different. Eva quit her position in the post office so they wouldn't be tied down. With her extra time, she became more involved in genealogical research. She began to send money away to a researcher in Denmark to learn more about her family's past and to Germany to uncover the roots of her husband's family. Most of what I knew about the Albrecht family when I started doing research came from the German genealogist Eva hired.

Much also stayed the same for Earl and Eva. They continued running their farm and taking care of more than a thousand chickens — an important part of their livelihood. They stayed involved in church. Both of their life histories, although short, carefully record many of their church callings. They served in leadership positions and taught classes through the years.

Many specifics about Earl and Eva as parents have already faded away. Their three living children are now all nearing ninety.[8] Over sixty years have passed since any lived at home. But, Earl and Eva were grandparents to their nearly thirty grandchildren not that long ago. And perhaps it's through these grandchildren that their memory shines most brightly now.[9]

Many grandkids remember Christmas Eves spent at Eva and Earl's house. All the grandchildren gathered there after a program held at the Fremont church. Here, they would each open three presents—one from Earl and Eva, one from Aunt Emma who didn't have children of her own, and one from a cousin who had drawn his or her name in the gift exchange. Earl and Eva didn't have a lot of money—and they did have a lot of grandchildren—so the gifts were small, sometimes a pair of socks or a warm winter hat. Every year when they were young, Earl bought a little red broom for my dad's older sisters, Joyce and Karma.

Some grandkids remember Eva's fresh-baked bread. She would give her grandchildren a little honey and peanut butter to stir together as the bread baked, filling the house with its smell. When it finished at last, they would spread their mixture on the hot bread. Some also remember going with Eva to pick berries. She would put a little salt in her hand for them to dip the berries in before eating them. Any that they didn't eat, they'd sell—twelve quarts of berries for one dollar.

"What kinds of things did you do with your grandparents?" I ask my dad on the phone one night.

"We spent lots of time with them," my dad tells me. "They came to our house every week for Sunday dinner. I remember Grandpa helping on the farm. I was young and he was old, so we often had the same jobs—the ones that didn't require a lot of hard labor. I also remember my mom sending me down the street to take them a piece of pie or a loaf of bread nearly every time she baked something."

I talk to my dad for an hour. He tells me about Earl and Eva's lives—about his memories of them. Then my mom is calling him and Sarah Ann is crying.

"We'll talk more later," he promises as he hangs up. I sit on the couch, turning their lives over in my mind. Then I realize that, once again, I didn't ask the question I want to know most.

I type a quick e-mail to my dad. "What was the most important thing in your grandparents' lives?" I write.

My dad writes back the next morning. "Without question, the most important things in Grandma and Grandpa's lives were family and church."

In 1959, Eva and Earl had been married for fifty years. To celebrate, on November 14 of that year, their children held a Golden Wedding Anniversary reception for them. Eva recorded, "The children hadn't spared neither time nor expense to make it a wonderful and outstanding party." As I read the description of the party, my mind drifts to the little church in Fremont.

Earl surveys the inside of the church that has been transformed for their party. He remembers the last time it was transformed for them—their wedding reception. He can hardly believe fifty years have passed.

Looking around at the people filling the room, his emotions well inside him. Every one of their children and all but two of their grandchildren are here. Friends from Fremont and other places have come too. Some have driven long distances for the occasion.

The program, put together by their grandchildren, now draws to a close. Earl has enjoyed watching his grandchildren play the piano, dance, and sing. Rex gave a tribute to them which almost brought tears to his eyes—and had tears spilling down Eva's cheeks, of course.

"We will now start the music and turn the time over for dancing," Rex announces.

Everyone helps put away the chairs. In a matter of minutes, the floor is cleared. Someone dims the lights and Earl hears the music drifting through the room.

But nobody is dancing.

Suddenly, Earl realizes they are waiting for him. He looks over at Eva who smiles at him. In these fifty years of marriage, he has not grown any fonder of dancing. But he gets up and makes his way towards her anyway.

"Would you like to dance?" he asks her.

She pretends to be surprised for a moment. "Well, yes I would, although my feet might not move as quickly as they did once."

He takes her by the hand and leads her out to the dance floor as their children and grandchildren watch. He puts his arm around her tiny waist and looks into her eyes. Her hair is gray and her skin is wrinkled. Yet, to him she is more beautiful than the day they danced on this floor fifty years ago.

Earl's health had begun declining even before their fiftieth anniversary. From time to time, he had blackouts where he would essentially pass out without warning. In 1957, this happened while he was driving his car. When the road back from the neighboring town of Loa turned, Earl didn't. The car ran through a fence. Earl suffered severe shock, broke both dental plates, and had bumps and bruises covering his body.

The year after their big party, Eva was diagnosed with cancer. In April of 1960, she underwent surgery. No sooner had she recovered from this than she needed another surgery—this time to remove cataracts from her eyes.

Meanwhile, Earl began to struggle with heart failure, or dropsy, as they called it. It gradually grew more serious. On May 10, 1968, three days before his seventy-eighth birthday, it became obvious his life was slipping. Donna ran down the street to get my grandparents. My grandpa was out in the field so my grandma left a note for him and hurried with Donna back to the house. Earl passed away soon after with his family surrounding his bed.

Eva outlived her husband by twelve years. She had never learned to drive, could hardly see anymore, and suffered from the general aches and pains of old age. But she kept busy. She spent more time on genealogical research. She also spent a lot of time with her family. For several years, she lived in St. George, located in the southwest corner of Utah, during the winter. Her daughters would take turns driving her there in the fall and picking her up in the spring. They also brought her back to Fremont for Christmas. Here, she stayed at her daughter Donna's house since her own home was boarded up for the winter. Eva died at Donna's house on February 21, 1980.

I look through my papers one Saturday afternoon while David and the kids are at the aquarium. Today I'm sorting through my stack of notes on Earl and Eva, trying to make sense of the jumble of details.

After all the interviews are completed, I think Eva's own words tell it best: "We now have in 1965 twenty-nine grandchildren: fourteen boys and fifteen girls. We have four great-grandchildren: one boy and three girls. We will celebrate our 56th Wedding Anniversary in November. Earl has been a faithful and wonderful husband. He has helped me at all times. I am thankful for my family and for all the blessings that are mine."

My mom has a picture of my brother, Mathew, and me with Eva. I'm about three years old and Mathew is barely more than a year, but we look a little older — or at least a little bigger — sitting with this tiny, frail woman. My blonde, almost white, hair and my brother's light brown hair contrast against her faded, gray hair. Our faces are smooth, our eyes large. We are children, starting our path. Eva's face is wrinkled, her eyes showing the wear of age. She is almost ninety, completing her path. The picture captures more than my brother and me with our great-grandmother. It captures a crossroads of youth and old age, of beginnings and endings. It shows a point of convergence.

Thinking of this little, old woman in the picture, I feel a twinge of regret that our convergence was so fleeting. I wish I had known my great-grandparents. I think I would have liked them.

I've just gotten comfortable when I hear tossing and turning in the crib near our bed. I hold my breath, hoping Sarah Ann will go back to sleep. But, within minutes, she has started to cry a hoarse, angry cry. I sigh as I pull the covers off, get out of bed, and pick her up. Her little cold, barely noticeable during the day, has made it hard for her to breathe when she lies down. Last night, David or I was up with her nearly every hour. I have a feeling tonight won't be much different.

I go into the living room to rock her. She does better with her head on my shoulder, her body upright. I leave the lights out as I sit down and begin to rock back and forth in our borrowed rocking chair. Sarah Ann snuggles close to me, her head tipped sideways and her mouth open wide to get more air. A fitful, twitching sleep returns almost immediately.

As I rock her, I think of Earl and Eva. Like generations before them, they lived simple lives filled with hard work and mundane chores. They didn't have room for much more. But maybe they didn't need much more. It seems that everything was clear to them—that their lives were firmly anchored in what was important. In this, they found their happiness.

My time in Spain, while sweeping away so much clutter, has only made everything less clear to me. The months of miserable pregnancy and then frantic preparations have passed. I am left again with my restlessness, but this time with a different dimension to it. Restlessness has always been part of my nature—but not an unhappy restlessness. If peace has sometimes been a struggle for me, happiness never has been. I need to find my anchor again.

With these thoughts on my mind, my eyes close, too. In my half-asleep state, a series of memories and images drifts through my mind.

One day while I'm in college, I call to talk to my parents. I tell my dad how I had told a woman at my work my plans for the future which included getting a graduate degree, publishing a book, and doing something that mattered in the world. She smiled and patted my shoulder.

"Those are ambitious goals," she said with a patronizing smile. "But we can't all be Martin Luther King Jr. or Florence Nightingale."

My dad, without hesitating, replied, "No, we can't. But someone has to. Why not you?"

Another memory, this one a little further back, comes to my mind. I'm six years old, sitting on my bed in the middle of the night with a bad case of chickenpox. I can't sleep because I itch too much. My mom sits beside me in my bed playing my favorite game—a little Smurf card game—over and over again to try to keep my mind off scratching.

My thoughts drift to stories I have heard, images of them forming in my mind. I see my dad as a teenager with bright red hair and freckles. He warms up in the gym before a basketball game. His team has traveled a long way for their game today. He shoots basket after basket. Feeling as if someone is watching him, he looks up at the bleachers. They're completely empty—except for one person. His dad sits toward the top, watching his son practice.

I see the same redheaded boy, this time younger. He skips down the road, stopping every few minutes to pick up a rock and examine it before throwing it back, his mind wandering—his thoughts a million miles away. He reaches his front door and walks in.

"Did you get the mail?" my grandma asks. She sent him on the errand nearly fifteen minutes ago.

He looks at her sheepishly. "Oh, I forgot." He had meandered down the road and back again, completely forgetting the purpose of his excursion.

Next, I think of my grandpa—not the old man I knew as a child, but the one I know only from stories. I see him sitting anxiously outside the door while my grandma is in labor. He gets up and paces, as he is not allowed to go in the room. At last the doctor appears, smiling. "You've got a boy," he tells him. My grandpa beams.

Then I picture my grandpa younger—a lean, brown-haired teenager out on the farm with Earl, his father. I see them working side by side in the fields, sometimes talking, sometimes just feeling each other's company.

Going back further still, I think of Earl as a young man, riding his horse through the countryside. There's not another person for miles. The wind whips through his blond hair and under his clothes as he grips the horse's reins, his eyes staring into the limitless sky ahead.

Sarah Ann twitches, her eyes fluttering open momentarily as she wiggles around, adjusting herself until she finds a comfortable position again nestled against me. As I watch her, I wonder if she knew the family that came before her—the family no longer here. Did she talk to them in heaven before coming to join us? Did she bid good-bye to Earl and Eva and to my grandpa? Did they share with her words of advice before letting her go to entrust her to me?

I stand up from the rocking chair and walk out to our little front porch with Sarah Ann. I look down at the street below—so familiar and yet so foreign. I feel the lonely ache that has burned deep inside me for the last few weeks. Then, I remember something my dad told me before we left.

"Living in Spain will be hard. But it will draw your family closer together."

So much has fallen away—activities, commitments, even friends. But family remains.

I think of the question I've asked about Earl and Eva. My answer would be the same. Family is the greatest point of convergence in my life. Even if I don't always recognize its strength, it has always been there. And now with everything else gone, I must quit looking beyond it.

CHAPTER THIRTEEN

MOVING FORWARD AND LEAVING BEHIND:
EARL'S DESCENDANTS

REX AND ALTA ALBRECHT,
MY GRANDPARENTS

It has been forty years since Earl died. His great-grandchildren, like me, are adults with children of their own. His descendants number in the hundreds.

Time has continued moving forward, bringing changes with it. Earl saw the introduction of telephones, electricity, and running water into his community. He lived through two World Wars and the Great Depression. When Earl was born, people rode horses on dirt roads. When he died, they drove cars on paved highways.

Now, his grandchildren and great-grandchildren do things he could have never imagined. They have home computers and use the Internet. They cook their food in microwaves and watch DVDs. They live in cities and suburbs, own two cars, talk on cell phones, and commute to work. The way of life the older ones grew up with, and the younger ones heard stories about, is in the past now.

Earl's descendants have mostly left Fremont and their common identity behind. They live throughout Utah and the US in places such as Idaho, Colorado, Nevada, Nebraska, Texas, California, Alaska, Massachusetts, and Maryland. Their personalities, career paths, and goals are as scattered as their location. With each generation, they drift further apart, and the influence of their heritage becomes more diluted.

Earl's great-grandchildren and great-great-grandchildren have nearly lost any distinguishing characteristics that would link them together. Some are strangers to each other. Many don't know their common heritage and, perhaps, really don't care that much either. Despite what they've left behind, the past is still a part of them. Its presence exists somewhere within them.

Since moving from Provo, our trips to Utah and to Fremont have become rare. With my parents in Texas and David's parents in California, there isn't vacation time or money left over to visit

Utah. But the occasional family reunion still brings us back. I can remember the last trip we took, about two years before we moved from Wisconsin.

I sit in the backseat of our small sedan, snuggly situated between Rachel and Taylor's car seats, watching the scenery of early summer through the window. My children have fallen asleep as the hours of driving come to a close. Their breathing now rises and falls in a peaceful rhythm. David and my brother, Scott, talk softly in the front seat about their missions, about college life, about a meandering stream of subjects.

The view out the window remains much the same. After climbing to the highest point on the journey, we have now begun our descent into the valley. Short, prickly bushes fill the landscape in every direction, stretching into the distance where they meet the chalky, dull brown and red cliffs just before the view fades out of sight.

Although there may not be any discernible changes in the scenery, more than the passing miles tell me we'll soon arrive at our destination. A familiarity reaches out to me as we near Fremont. I have the feeling of going home, although I've never lived here. Fremont is my family's home; it's the "motherland" as my brother, Mathew, says.

A trip here also feels like a jump back in time. This is partly because I associate Fremont with my dad's stories of childhood, stories that seem to fit more comfortably in the historical context of the previous century than in the not-so-distant 1960s. The stories are of homemade bread and baseball in the streets, of a bloody litter of cats born on my dad's head while he slept in the backyard. His stories are of family gatherings and neighbors with doors always open, of sweat, dirt, and American Indians with big sacks of potatoes over their backs to trade for six cents each. The stories juxtapose against each other, revealing a complicated dichotomy — a dichotomy shared by many small towns across the country.

Progress has always come slowly and reluctantly to Fremont. My grandparents didn't get their first flushing toilet until the late 1940s — a few years before my dad was born. Even afterwards, with one small bathroom and six children, my dad often ran outside to use the outhouse. The family didn't get a hot water heater until my dad was a teenager. When he was young, my grandma heated water on the stove to pour into the tub for the weekly baths. The small children took baths together. The older ones took turns in the same bath water, alternating each week which one got to use the water first.

Life in Fremont required self-sufficiency. My grandparents produced nearly all of the family's food. They got meat from pigs that my grandpa slaughtered himself or from their cows. Their cows also provided the family's milk. They churned butter from the cream that rose to the top. My grandma canned enough vegetables and beans from their garden to eat all year and made bread and noodles from scratch. She made most of her children's clothes and even made her own soap.

Gender roles were strictly defined. My grandpa never once changed a baby's diaper. He never got up in the middle of the night when a baby cried. The only time he ever cooked was for lunch in the summer one day a week while my grandma worked at the bank. While my dad was on his mission for two years, my grandpa didn't write him one letter. Writing letters was for women.

My grandma was the only woman in town who worked outside the home. Although she had little fear that working would damage her children, she did fear what the neighbors thought. She woke up in the middle of the night to knead dough so her children could have homemade bread in their lunches just like all the other kids.

There were no museums or symphony orchestras anywhere near Fremont. There was only one movie theater in the county. When a movie came to town, all the teenagers went to see it on Friday night. Then, they went to see the same movie again on Saturday night. For fun, they "dragged main," driving up and down the streets of Bicknell (a nearby town only slightly larger than Fremont). High school kids from the entire county attended Wayne High in Bicknell. With graduating classes in the mid-thirties, the pool from which to choose friends or dates was small.

Just as the scenery surrounding Fremont can be both harsh and beautiful at the same time, the community also has two sides. I find Fremont old-fashioned and isolated, yet sometimes I almost long to live in a place just like it.

Connections ran deep in Fremont. Mothers, fathers, and children worked side by side, day after day. Extended family, who often lived nearby, filled in when needed. My grandpa's parents lived down the street, his in-laws down another street. He saw them every day. One of his sisters lived across the road, and another lived only a few minutes away. Several of my grandma's sisters also lived in Fremont or neighboring communities.

Connections went beyond families. The line between neighbors and family was thin. Everybody knew everybody else. They knew each other's entire families and had for generations. Fences were only to keep animals in, never to keep people out.

People in Fremont worked together. Everyone in town took turns bringing one of their cows to the butcher. Every family would get a piece of each cow, rotating the quality of that piece. This way everyone had meat throughout the year. When more advanced farm equipment began to become available, it was impractical for all the farmers to buy it. Instead, everyone went in together to purchase the equipment cooperatively.

In the summer, children ran freely down the streets. Sometimes one neighbor looked after them, sometimes another did, and sometimes they just looked after each other. They popped in at one house for cookies and another house for bread and jam. They went fishing up in the mountains, and played spontaneous baseball games in the street.

People trusted each other. Crime didn't exist. Nobody locked the front door. Nobody even had a lock installed on the door. My grandparents left their car keys in the ignition so they wouldn't lose them. Nothing was stolen and nobody was afraid of someone sneaking into their home while their family slept.

I think of these images of Fremont as we exit the main road and drive towards the rocky ledge, where the little town of Fremont sits huddled against the foot of Thousand Lake Mountain. Most of the houses cluster near the center of town, with acres of farmland sprawled out around them. Many of the homes have cows or horses fenced in the backyard. Fremont has no grocery stores, restaurants, or clothing stores. In fact, there's nothing for sale in the entire town. When my dad was growing up here, his uncle owned a small store that sold a little bit of everything. It even had a gas pump out in front. That store closed twenty-five years ago.

We turn onto Main Street and then pull in front of my grandma's little white house with its perfectly-kept bushes and flowerbeds. A short, matching white fence surrounds it. When I was a child, a big pine tree stood to the left of the house, towering above it. The roots started threatening the house's foundation, so the tree was removed. Without the tree, my grandma's house looks smaller, more vulnerable.

David stops the car and I squeeze between a car seat and the front seat to get out, almost tumbling onto the gravel road as I do. I stretch my back and legs, relieved to be out of my cramped position. Then, I gather up one sleeping child while David picks up the other. My grandma already stands at the front door, smiling at us as we make our way down the sidewalk, her eyes sparkling.

"Hi, sweetheart," she says in her soothing grandma voice, opening the door wider so we can come in. She hugs and kisses me and pats Taylor's head.

"I've been watching for you all afternoon," she tells us as David holds Rachel up for her to hug and kiss. Standing next to her, David looks like a giant, towering nearly a foot above her.

"Come in and sit down. Are you hungry? I have some soup on the stove." She shuffles towards the kitchen, her feet never leaving the ground. A variety of health problems, including a dozen surgeries on her knees, feet, and back have left her slow and unsteady. But, they haven't stopped her from waiting on the guests that flow through her home.

Scott comes trudging in with an armload of bags and dumps them in a disheveled heap by the front door. Glancing around the room, I can't help but notice our ragged appearance. Rachel's hair presses against her head in a matted mess from sleeping in the car seat, Taylor is wearing only one shoe, and my clothes are wrinkled and disorderly. We seem out of place in my grandma's spotless living room filled with homemade blankets and cutesy knick-knacks.

After a brief period of shyness, my children regain their energy and run through the house, peering at the decorations and knocking over picture frames on the low-lying shelves. I hurry after then, trying to prevent them from doing any permanent damage.

"Oh, they're fine," my grandma assures me. "They won't hurt anything." I'm not so sure, but after moving the most breakable things out of their reach, I sit down to eat anyway.

Bread, crackers, cheese, fruit, milk, and juice already sit on the table, waiting for us. Steam rises from the soup—filled with thick homemade noodles and vegetables from a neighbor's garden—as my grandma carries it with shaking hands to the table. Once, I told my grandma I had never made noodles from scratch—in fact, I'd never even seen anyone do it. She was astounded.

My grandma asks David to say a blessing on the food. Then, we all begin to eat. Every few minutes, my grandma asks if we would like anything else and urges us to eat more.

"You've hardly swallowed a thing," she tells me as I refuse a third helping of soup. I've never visited my grandma's house without being served an elaborate meal and given frequent encouragements to eat more. My dad says she used to tell them they should eat every bite of their food because "there were starving children in China."

After our meal, we carry our bags and Taylor's portable crib up the stairs to the two rooms where we'll sleep. We pass a quilt hanging on the wall that my aunt made for my grandma years ago. Each square represents a different member of the family, including all her children and grandchildren at that time. My square contains a stack of ABC blocks. My brother Mathew's square has two baby shoes. Mathew and I were the age of Rachel and Taylor now. I think of the generations that have passed through this house. My parents once carried us up these stairs when they drove here for Christmas vacations. Years before that, my grandparents carried my dad up these same stairs.

My grandparents spent all but the first few years of their lives together here.[1] For a few months after they married in 1934, my grandparents lived with Earl and Eva. My grandpa ran his dad's farm while Earl served his mission. My grandma worked at the bank. Her father, who owned the bank as well as a local store, gave her the job. After a while, she received a raise to $50 a month. She used one month's salary to buy their first washing machine.

When Earl came home, my grandparents lived for a short time in the front two rooms of an old house in town, and then in two rooms in back of my grandma's father's store. My grandma quit working in the bank temporarily and worked for her father in his store until their first child, Joyce, was born. When Joyce was three days old, my grandma contracted a serious infection that the doctor who delivered Joyce had carried with him from a sick patient. Several other women he delivered got the same infection. A few even died. My grandma stayed in the hospital for nearly three weeks. According to the story she always told, she spent much of six days frozen in ice from the waist down.

In the spring of 1936, my grandparents moved into this house where my grandma still lives. They exchanged homes with my grandma's older sister, Thora, and her husband, Worthen. Worthen had built the house himself. Thora and Worthen moved into the store.

Their second child, Karma, was born less than a year later. Around this time, my grandparents bought their first car—a red Ford. My grandma says it was the most beautiful car they'd ever seen. It cost $840. My grandparents lay awake all night worrying about making such a large purchase.

In 1942, their first son, Stan, was born. My grandpa was thrilled. He hadn't had a brother and my grandma only had one. And, after all, baby boys were more reason to celebrate than baby girls in Wayne County back then. My grandpa was so excited that he mopped every floor in the house—something he had never done before and never did again. Their second son arrived in 1946—an accomplishment neither of the families in which they had grown up had achieved. They named him David.

Soon after, Karma began developing health problems. The doctors decided she had rheumatic fever and told my grandma to keep her in bed. For fourteen months, Karma's feet never touched the floor. My grandma carried her everywhere. Later Karma was diagnosed with arthritis, a disease she struggled with throughout her life. She died at age sixty-four from complications of it.

My dad, Don, was born six years after Dave, followed by Karl a couple years after that. By this time, the oldest girls had already left for college. Joyce and Karma came home one time to see my grandma standing in the living room, ironing and crying. When they asked her what was wrong, my grandma said, "I'm pregnant and I'm too old to have a baby." She was forty-two years old at the time, and would turn forty-three before Karl was born.

My dad spent his entire childhood in this house. Pictures of him show a smiling, skinny, redheaded, freckly little boy. His face is content. His eyes gleam. The feeling that radiates from the pictures matches the feeling from his stories. My dad had a happy childhood. My grandparents were firm, but kind.

Responsibility came early for my dad and his siblings. When my dad was nine, he learned to shoot a pig in the exact right spot between the eyes to kill him instantly. At age twelve, he started driving the tractor. Throughout his childhood, my dad spent his summers and early mornings helping his father, as did most of the kids in town. He milked the cows every day. He spent hours at a time leaning over and picking potatoes until his back ached. In the winter when temperatures were well below freezing, and in the summer when the sun blazed on his back, my dad helped my grandpa on the farm.

But there was more to his childhood than chores. When my dad and my Uncle Karl get together, they tell stories about when they were growing up. They talk about the final minutes of the championship basketball game (even though my dad is only 5 feet 8 inches tall, he was still a basketball star at Wayne High). They tell us about their archenemy, North Sevier, and chant, "The wasps-sps-sps, the wasps-sps-sps are gonna get beat," repeating the old cheer against another team. My uncle reminds me that they used to call my dad "The Flash" because he was so fast.

Their favorite story is about the little lambs they named Chuck, Gus, and LeRoy. The summer they raised the lambs, their nephew Gary, who was only a few years younger than they were, was staying with them. After trying to feed Chuck a bottle, Gary came running to tell them, "Suck was chucking and the nipple fell off!" After they finish the story, my dad and uncle both laugh until tears run down their cheeks.

I step into one of the bedrooms at the top of the stairs. A quick glance around shows that if we put Taylor's portable crib on the only floor space big enough for it, it will prevent the door from opening. Taylor will sleep on the floor. As I lean the crib against the wall in the corner, I wonder if this was the bedroom where my dad slept. I know that he and my Uncle Karl shared one of these upstairs rooms for years—until my dad's older brother left home and they could each have their own room. They even shared a bed.

My dad's older sisters left home before he was old enough to really remember them living here. But my dad shared the house with three brothers—at least when he was young. They wrestled in the living room and broke the windows with baseballs and basketballs. Karl once shot the TV (he aimed at Gilligan, not knowing the gun was loaded) and Stan shot the roof. Sometimes I think the halls still echo with the commotion of four boys.

After depositing our bags, we go back downstairs to talk to my grandma. Rachel sings "Twinkle, Twinkle Little Star" and Taylor demonstrates his unsteady walking. My grandma smiles and applauds appropriately. Then, she updates us on various events in my cousins' lives. One cousin is pregnant. Another had a baby. One got a mission call. All of it is news to me, since I don't talk to any of them on a regular basis.

My children grow restless and bored with our conversation. My grandma suggests we go for a ride. Going for a ride has been a standard part of nearly every visit for as long as I can remember. My grandma used to do the driving, but now that she can't drive, we go in our car. My grandma often requests that we drive up on Fish Lake Mountain. She loves following the winding roads where the scenery, filled with quaking aspen and sparkling water, contrasts so sharply with the dry valley floor.

Today, my grandma suggests we go on a tour of Fremont. The tour won't cover any new ground. With a population of less than 200 people, and a layout consisting of only a few blocks, Fremont has no houses I haven't seen and no roads on which I haven't driven. But I know there are still plenty of stories about Fremont I haven't heard. And, perhaps nobody knows these stories better than my grandma. Now ninety years old, my grandma can claim the title of the oldest person in Fremont. She has a stronger link to its past than anyone else.

The car can't hold all of us, so David stays behind with Rachel. I buckle Taylor in his car seat then glance up to see my brother helping my grandma down the sidewalk. She grips his arm, her face set in concentration as she shuffles forward. When they reach the car, my brother helps her in, then climbs in the back as she uses her hands to pull her uncooperative legs over.

"Well," she says when she's situated. "Let's get going. I'll tell you what I know."

As I start the car, my grandma points out the old church which we can see from her front lawn. "We went to church in this old stone building until 1964 when the new church was finished. George Albrecht helped build this one. We had the Albrecht family reunion here last summer, remember?"

I nod.

"Turn right on this street," my grandma tells me. I follow her instructions, pulling onto a bumpy gravel road. She motions for me to stop. "This is where John and Chasty lived most of their lives," she says, pointing out the window to a little brown and white house.

"You see that porch?" my grandma asks, her voice taking on the same disapproving tone it does every time she talks about John. "I remember John sitting right there. That's all he ever did was sit in that chair on the porch. Then one day his family came home and he was dead — still sitting in that chair.

"Chasty used to have family dinners here. I remember us all sitting around the big table she'd pull out for special occasions." As my grandma talks, I can picture John, with his dyed jet-black hair and stocky build, sitting in a chair on the porch, while Chasty, thin and bony-fingered, rustles around in the kitchen in her apron.

"Across the street over here is Earl and Eva's old house. It doesn't look much like it did then." My grandma studies the house, as if seeing it after a long absence. "We lived down the road from each other all those years, but there were never bad feelings between us..." Her voice fades as she thinks of them.

I look across the street at their house, imagining Earl and Eva coming out the door. Eva holds onto Earl's arm. They chat as they walk down the street to my grandma's house, ready to help shell the peas or do whatever else needs to be done.

"Now turn around and drive back past my house," my grandma instructs. She directs me several blocks to a brown house located on a hill. I pull over to the side of the road and stop the car. Although I've seen the house several times, nobody ever pointed it out to me before.

"This is where I grew up," she says. Looking at the house with the brown barn and granary standing nearby, I remember my dad telling me that Robert Taylor, my grandma's father, was the most well-off person in Fremont.

"When I was growing up, my sisters and I were known as 'the

twelve o'clock girls on the hill' because we always had to be home by midnight. I remember one time I was out with a boy and he had a flat tire. By the time we got home, it was a little past midnight. I sneaked in the door and climbed up on the kitchen table to adjust the clock so my father wouldn't know I was late. While I was up there, my father walked in. He hardly said a word, but just handed me the laundry. I tried to explain, but he wasn't interested. I was up the rest of the night doing laundry. The next morning, I had to work in the store. My mother felt sorry for me so she sent one of my younger sisters up there with a pillow so I could rest."

My grandma was the second of twelve children. The first eleven were girls. Her mother wrote that her husband "had been hoping for a boy all these years and when he finally got him, we were a proud family." Two of the girls died soon after birth and one lived only a year before she died of whooping cough. Until recently, the other eight girls were alive and kept in contact.

I have a picture of my grandma's family when she was young—a crowd of girls in a range of sizes and ages, and one lone boy. Today as I sit in the car with her, I picture them coming up the hill on their way home from school. The girls talk and giggle. My grandma's mother opens the door, wiping her hands on her apron, ready to greet them.

"There's one more place I want to see. Drive out this way," my grandma says, pointing down the road. Suddenly aware of the quiet in the car, I glance over my shoulder. Taylor has fallen asleep again, his head tilted to the side. Scott sets next to him, his hand supporting Taylor's head to try to make him more comfortable.

I turn around and pull the car back onto the road. We drive a few miles until we leave the little town behind. Soon, farmland stretches out on both sides of us.

"Here," my grandma says suddenly. "Slow down."

"This was our farm," she says after a pause. I pull the car over again and look out over the land.

My grandma sighs, her eyes staring into the distance. "Whenever I come out here, I think of your grandpa. For some reason, I've missed him more this past year than any time before." She looks at me. "I've been a widow now for nearly sixteen years."

My grandpa died over a decade before any of Earl's other children (besides Lula who died as a baby). I was ten years old. Even then, I had only dim memories of my grandpa. We lived in Texas and couldn't make the long trip to Utah regularly. I didn't even attend his funeral. My parents didn't have the money to fly all six of us to Utah.

Only my dad went. My mom lay in bed and cried the night of the funeral. She had loved my grandpa and was heartbroken to miss his funeral. She often said there weren't many people in the world with more goodness in them than he had.

By the time my grandpa died, his passing was a relief. He had been sick for years. Most of my memories are of him sitting in a wheelchair, his speech slurred and difficult to understand. My grandpa first sensed something was wrong just before the summer of 1973. He described it as a blackness that had come over him. He decided to go up on the mountains that summer to ride his horse and herd the cows. He thought the fresh, clean mountain air would refresh him and clear his mind. It didn't.

Over the next few years, my grandpa got gradually worse. He never complained and, in fact, never even talked about how he felt. It wasn't the Wayne County way. Instead, my grandpa suffered silently.

It took several years and several misdiagnoses for doctors to determine that he had amyotrophic lateral sclerosis (ALS) or Lou Gehrig's disease. No cure, not even any treatment, was available. ALS, a rare and progressive degenerative disease of the nervous system, impairs the brain cells which send messages from the brain and spinal cord to the muscles. No one knows its cause. Most people only live three to five years with ALS. My grandpa lived fourteen years after the first symptoms appeared.

My grandpa lost control and sensation in his hands and arms first. Then, his coordination got worse. After several more years, he needed a wheelchair. My dad says the only time my grandpa showed any frustration was when he first got his wheelchair. Several times he tried to stand up and walk. Each time, he fell.

As time passed, he could do less and less for himself. It became hard to understand him when he talked. The burden on my grandma was excruciating. The family began to pray that my grandpa would be released from his misery. In September of 1987, he died.

I don't remember very much about my grandpa other than his illness. Most of my knowledge about him comes from what my dad has told me. My grandpa was quiet and serious. He never raised his voice. When there was a disagreement, he listened while the others argued, not saying a word until he had made up his mind. Then, he spoke his opinion clearly and solidly. Usually, everyone listened.

Besides the memory of an old, sick man, one other image stays in my mind when I think of my grandpa. My grandpa, like his father, was a cowboy. He wore a hat and rode a horse. He never went to college, probably never even considered it. He never flew on an airplane, and didn't even care for visiting Salt Lake City. Although several of his children lived out of state at various times, the only time he visited them in another state was when his oldest son moved to Washington for graduate school. He loved to ride his horse up on the mountains while the cattle grazed. He found satisfaction in a large crop or a high price for one of his calves at the auction.

My grandma's voice brings me away from my thoughts. "When your dad was growing up, we farmed forty acres," she says. "We mostly grew alfalfa, along with a little barley and potatoes. The potatoes were the only crop we sold. We fed the rest to the cattle during the winter," she pauses, remembering. "Besides this land, we had another plot of sixty acres that we just left as meadow. That's where the six or seven milk cows grazed. Your dad used to get up every morning and milk those cows."

My grandparents earned most of their income from beef cattle. They owned nearly a hundred beef cows and three bulls. In the summer, the cows grazed on the mountains. In the winter, they grazed in the desert. My grandpa took turns with other men in town riding with the cows, since they could never be left alone. Nearly all of the cows gave birth to calves in the spring. If my grandpa had grown enough alfalfa to feed the calves for the winter, he kept them until the next spring when he sold them at an auction in Salina. If the crops were poor, he sold some of the calves in the fall. My grandparents also had other animals such as pigs, chickens, and a couple of horses.

When my dad was a child, he thought he had the most boring life in the world. Now, he feels differently. He speaks almost longingly of those years — recognizing them as a past he can never return to — not just because he has grown up, but because the way of life in my dad's stories doesn't exist anymore.

Fremont's history has two transforming events, two significant, large-scale movements. These movements transformed more than just Fremont — they transformed the nation. Georg and Mina Albrecht and Karsti Nilsdotter Harris came as part of the first movement. In the second half of the 1800s, people flooded into Fremont and other communities from all over the world. Those that came to Fremont planted roots, worked on their farms, and raised their families. They stayed put. For several generations, few people moved in and few people moved out.

My dad was part of the second movement. With this movement came the disappearance of a way of life, the decline of the family farm, and the restructuring of Fremont and other towns like it. In my dad's generation, hundreds of thousands of people across the US who had been raised on farms, with families stretching back generations as farmers, decided to do something different. In Fremont too, a generation picked up and left. They went to college. They got office jobs. They settled in cities and suburbs throughout Utah and beyond.

This second movement represented a fundamental shift in our country's identity. Farming, particularly on small family farms, was in our roots. The promise of farming land of one's own was one of the main draws that brought people to America in the first place. In 1790, ninety-five percent of Americans lived on farms.

America couldn't remain this way, though. With each passing decade, the percentage of people living on farms decreased. In 1940, when my grandparents were farming, twenty-five percent of Americans lived on the six million farms across the country.[2] Sixty-five percent of the population of Wayne County worked in agriculture.[3] Sixty years later, that had all changed. By 2000, only about one percent of the population lived on farms.

These changes reflect more than a simple switch in preferences. As more mechanized farm equipment became available, the family farm made less sense. Fewer man-hours were needed to harvest more land. The cost of the new equipment made it out of reach for small farmers. At first, Wayne County farmers bought one piece of equipment to share between several farmers. As time passed, some of the farmers began buying out the land from their neighbors, resulting in fewer and larger farms.

For my dad's generation, the career path laid out for their parents was no longer available to them. From 1930 to 1985, nearly five hundred thousand people left the farm every year.[4] The drain hit Wayne County hard. The population fell as more and more young people fled.

My grandparents saw what was happening. Although they were content in Fremont, they knew it had little to offer their children. They knew their children had to leave. They also knew their children would have to be prepared to leave successfully. From the time my dad was a child, his parents told him he would go to college. They didn't suggest he should go—they told him that he *would* go. Just as Tuesday followed Monday, college followed high school.

This strong push to attend college came from two people who hadn't attended a day of college between them and in a community with few college graduates. Although my grandpa supported his children going to college, my grandma was the real push. She had wanted to go to college very badly herself. But her father had believed sending girls to college was a waste of time and money.

My grandma said there were two things that she would have in her life—all her children would graduate from college and all her sons would serve missions. She had her wish. Two of her children received PhDs, two received Master's degrees, and the other two received Bachelor's degrees. One has worked as a college professor, one as a university president, one as an environmental scientist, one as a social work administrator, one as a nurse, and one as an elementary school teacher.

Not everyone who grew up on a family farm did so well. Many moved to cities and took labor-intensive jobs there. Some prospered. A lot didn't. In general, they lagged behind those who had grown up in urban areas. Those who stayed behind did even worse.

The face of America was changed forever as my dad and others like him poured out of farming communities. Small farming towns throughout the US experienced declines in population. Some have withered to only a shadow of their former existences. Others have managed to flourish, but in a different way. For Wayne County towns, the breathtaking scenery provided redemption. But, the demise of the old way of life has only been accelerated by the arrival of a new way.

Wayne County, like much of the country, has switched to a service economy. After the population dropped below fifteen hundred in 1970, Wayne County found a new focus. By 2000, a growth rate of over fifty percent pushed the population over twenty-five hundred.[5] Wayne County discovered the business of tourism. These changes have largely missed Fremont, though. Its location a few miles off the main road has meant that the tourism industry has passed it by. Perhaps more than any other town in Wayne County, Fremont still clings to its old character.

"Your uncle Stan owns this land now," my grandma says from her seat next to me. "Of course, he lives too far away to do anything with it. He just rents it out to someone here in town."

We sit in silence for a minute, watching the alfalfa blowing in the wind and listening to the steady clicks of the large sprinklers.

"Well, I believe that about covers it," she says finally. "I suppose we should be heading back." I turn the car around and start towards her house.

"See the rock up there?" she asks, pointing to a ledge near the road. "Before my legs got so bad, I used to climb up there nearly every week. I would sit and look out over the town at the houses and farms and think of all the people I've known here and all the good times I've had." She pauses, absorbed in her own thoughts for a moment.

"I'm old now. I've always wanted to be able to stay in my own home. And I've been able to do that. This is where I belong."

A strange feeling of envy creeps up in me. There's no place I belong, like my grandma belongs in Fremont. I've lived in several places throughout my life, and hesitate to call any of them home.

I park in front of my grandma's house a few minutes later. My brother helps her out of the car, while I unbuckle Taylor from his car seat. He wriggles out of my arms to toddle along the sidewalk towards her front porch. As I watch him, I wonder what significance this house will have to my children. I'm part of the first generation who has never lived in Fremont. If I were to sit on the rock ledge and look over Fremont, I would have few memories of people here.

Several hours later, I lie awake in bed in my grandma's house. Looking around in the dark, I imagine my dad, the little redheaded boy, lying in this same bed next to his brother. My grandma stands beside them. Her short brown hair frames her face—a face without one trace of a wrinkle. She pulls the large homemade quilt over them in the cold room, tucking them in snuggly. Then she kisses them each on the cheek before she turns to leave.

Then another image comes to mind—this one from my memory. I'm visiting my grandparents with my parents, brothers, and sister. After several days in Fremont, it's time to leave to drive back to Texas. We stand in the doorway, each kissing my grandma good-bye in turn—first Laura, then Scott, Mathew, me, and my mom. My dad steps up last. Even from across the room, I see the tears rolling down my grandma's cheeks. My grandma grabs hold of my dad tightly, kissing his cheek just as she did so many years ago.

But this time, it's my dad who turns to leave.

My dad left Fremont in 1970 to go to college and, with the exception of one summer, has never lived there since. After attending a year of college, he went on a two-year mission to Australia for the LDS Church. When he returned, he finished his Bachelor's degree in Forestry at Utah State in Logan.

My parents began dating soon after my dad's mission. My mother, Carol Mulford, had grown up in Wayne County also. But my parents had never really paid too much attention to each other. On a bus trip during my mom's freshman year of college, her date and my dad's date both fell asleep. My parents started talking. My mom said she wanted to get a PhD, travel around the world, and get married when she was twenty-eight. They got married the next year. My mom was nineteen. My dad was twenty-two. I was born thirteen months later.

My dad completed his Bachelor's degree in three years and also got a Master's degree at Utah State. My mom finished her degree with a double major in Family and Child Development and Sociology. My brother, Mathew, was born three months after they graduated in 1978. A few days later, my dad loaded all their belongings in the back of his father's pick-up truck and drove to Iowa. He was going to get a PhD in Rural Sociology at Iowa State in Aims. My mom followed soon after with both of us.

Leaving Utah was a major step. My mom had only been out of the state one time—on a family trip to Colorado. The flight to Iowa was her first time on a plane. My dad had gone to Australia for his mission, but hadn't really been anywhere else. Their families thought it was okay for them to go away for graduate school, as long as they came back afterwards. When they left Utah, my mom cried. She made my dad promise they would move back to Utah someday.

My parents lived in Iowa for three years while my dad got his PhD and my mom got her Master's degree. About once a year, my parents drove back to Utah to visit their families. They were students and completely broke, so they drove through the night in order to avoid paying for a motel room. My brother and I laid in the back of the car, looking out the windows at the stars.

My dad took a job at Texas A&M University when he finished school. Although they didn't say it to their families, my parents knew moving back to Utah wasn't in the plans anytime soon.

My parents arrived in Bryan, Texas, in August of 1981—not the best time of year for an introduction to the state. It was miserably hot and there were lots of bugs. My mom was nearly eight months pregnant. Scott was born six weeks later. Laura was born two and half years after that.

Gradually, Texas started to grow on them. It didn't grow on the rest of the family, though. My grandmothers both came to visit a handful of times. My mom's dad came once, and my dad's dad never came at all. A few siblings came once or twice.

Now, my parents are both college professors. My mom went back and got her PhD at Texas A&M as the mother of four children when I was in high school. She's the only woman from Wayne County to ever receive a PhD.

I spent all my childhood years in Bryan. In many ways, my childhood memories have nothing in common with my dad's childhood memories. There were no cows to milk and no baseball in the street—there were too many cars. The only time I ever rode a horse was with my dad on a visit to Fremont. I never woke up early to do chores outside—although occasionally on the weekends I had to help with the family paper route at 5:00 in the morning (which I probably complained about much more than my dad did about picking potatoes in the hot sun).

Instead, my memories are of constant running around between dance lessons, piano lessons, baseball practices, soccer games, and church activities. They're of family vacations, family planning meetings, and "family nights." My memories are of matching Raggedy Ann and Andy costumes for Halloween that my mom sewed for Mathew and me and rolling Easter eggs down a "hill" (or as close to a hill as we could find).

My memories are of eating pizza every Tuesday night and mixing Sprite and eggnog together for a special drink on New Year's Eve and Thanksgiving. They're of my mom practicing my story with me over and over again for the third grade story-telling contest, and my dad driving me and my friends to "wrap" (cover in toilet paper) someone's house so that we wouldn't sneak out alone.

My memories are of Mathew putting glue on my favorite stuffed animal, locking me out of the bathroom when I wanted to get ready for school, and sitting up late talking with me. They're memories of holding Laura's hand across the beds at night because she was afraid of the dark and making her and Scott play school—I was the teacher. They're of a house that was too small, voices that were too loud, and a feeling around it all that makes me get teary-eyed when I remember.

Perhaps, my memories really aren't so different.

Now, we are concluding another tour—this time of Spain. My entire family came to spend Christmas with us here. After a rather hectic Christmas day in Valencia at our apartment, we set off on our ten-day tour which included Madrid, Toledo, Córdoba, Sevilla, and Granada. We've ridden buses, trains, and metros, gaped at castles and cathedrals, wandered down little cobblestone medieval roads, eaten *tapas* (little dishes) and too many *bocadillos* (sandwiches), and tapped our feet along with a flamenco performance. Now, we're riding a bus from Granada back to Madrid. Here, my parents and siblings will catch a plane back to the US tomorrow, while we'll take another bus back to Valencia.

Looking around at the twelve members of my family, I think of the progression of time. A year from now, all three of my siblings and I will move to start again in a new place. Rachel will have mastered reading, Taylor will be able to write all his letters, and Sarah Ann will not only be walking—but running and climbing. And, I will be thirty years old.

Time moves forward relentlessly. It brings exciting changes and discoveries. But with each step, it leaves something—or someone—

behind. Generations of my ancestors are now in the past. Time has placed my grandpa in the past, too. Someday it will leave my parents, and then me, behind. Each disappearing generation leaves something behind as well—sometimes voluntarily, sometimes not so voluntarily—sometimes significant and sometimes insignificant.

I think of the things my parents have left me. It's from them that I got my blonde hair, my long toes, my easily upset stomach. My siblings and I all inherited large calves—a fact I used to bemoan incessantly in high school. My parents left me with a need to learn and even an obsession for education. Good grades were expected and the label of "smart" was more important than any other in my parents' house. Just as college followed high school for my dad, graduate school followed college for us. I inherited a religion, carefully taught to me from the time I was a baby, and reinforced by years of observing my parents' behavior.

I have acquired, for better or worse, my mother's need for order and yet my father's impatience for details. My parents have left me with ambition and confidence from their constant reinforcement and honest belief that their children could do anything, and yet a lingering feeling of restlessness and lack of completion when this anything I can supposedly do isn't done.

As time moves forward some more, many of these things will fade away. I think of my great-great-great-grandparents, and even those before them. Most left almost no trace of their lives at all. After digging through forgotten, dusty records, I pulled together some small evidence of their existences—their names listed in birth, marriage, and death records.

But they did leave behind something else. They left family— generations of family. They left children, who left children, who left children. For some of them, what they have left behind has grown to number people in the thousands, who have each impacted the world in different ways. And in these children and children of children, some evidence of the ancestors still remains. Consequences of their choices still appear, even if they aren't recognized.

As time moves forward, what will I leave behind? What evidence of my life will remain for my great-grandchildren or anyone else who might care? What will be important enough to survive the passing of time? What should I teach my children about their ancestors, as the Goldebee church warden directed, or even about my own life in the hope that it will never be forgotten again?

As my mind wanders over these thoughts, I catch sight of Sarah Ann sitting on my mom's lap across the bus aisle.

"Where's Sarah Ann?" my mom coos at her in a voice reserved only for babies. Sarah Ann pulls her blanket up over her face, then pulls it down quickly.

"There she is!" my dad exclaims.

Sarah Ann looks at both of them, beaming her four-toothed grin. From the seat in front of them, Rachel and Taylor giggle, as if this game of peek-a-boo is the most entertaining thing they've ever seen. Sarah Ann laughs too, not sure what's funny, but happy to be a part of it anyway. Later on in this five-hour bus ride, there will be tired children, impatient parents, short nerves, and an inevitable crisis. But for now, Sarah Ann entertains the whole family by pulling the blanket off her face.

Suddenly I think this moment—this feeling—is what I want to leave behind.

Like my ancestors before me, the most obvious remnant of my life will be my children and their children and their children after them. Perhaps a few threads of things I teach them will stay with them. I hope I'll pass down to them the faith my ancestors passed to me. Maybe my parents' emphasis on education and hard work will trickle down into some of their lives. Maybe not. In part, they'll have the power to choose what I leave behind.

I hope they carry the past with them. I want them to feel the bond of family that reaches forward more certainly for me because of the strength I now recognize in its roots. To carry forward the legacy of their family though, my children must first know it's there. I want to teach them—to help them understand—what has been left behind for them. Then, perhaps, they can carry this forward to another generation.

Chapter One

1   Funeral Sermon for Anna Gävershagen, 21 November 1693, Garwitz, Mecklen-burg-Schwerin, (copy in author's possession).

2   Tom Crepon, *Mecklenburg and West Pomerania: Pictures of a Landscape*, translated by Patrick Plant (Rostock, Germany: Hinstorff, 1998), 20. For more information on Mecklenburg during the Thirty Years' War, see also: Sarah Scott, *The History Of Mecklenburg, From The First Settlement Of The Vandals In That Country, To The Present Time, Including A Period Of About Three Thousand Years* (London, printed for J. Newbery microfilm, 1761).

3   This condition existed throughout much of what would become Germany by the eighteenth century. John G. Gagliardo, *From Pariah to Patriot: The Changing Image of the German Peasant, 1770–1840* (Lexington, Kentucky: The University Press of Kentucky, 1969), 12.

4   James Sheehan comments that in 1810 Mecklenburg displayed "an ability to resist political reform that would persist for over a century." James J. Sheehan, *German History, 1770–1866* (Oxford: Clarendon Press, 1989), 273.

5   Funeral Sermon of Anna Gävershagen.

6   The birth record, located in the records of Garwitz, used by the genealogist stated: "On 12 May 1766, to Johann Jochen Harprecht a son was born and named Johann Jochen Christian." Christian's fourth marriage record had said that his father was Johann Daniel Harprecht, the master tailor, and his mother was Maria Pingel. After looking through birth records for a twenty-five-year period, I found the following entry: "On 25 April (1769), to the tailor Daniel Harbrecht was born a son, baptized on the 27th and named Hans Jochim Christopher." A few years earlier, I found this marriage record: "On 11 Nov (1761), the master tailor Daniel Jacob Harbrecht was married to Maria Dorothea Pingel." Evangelishe Kirche Garwitz, *Kirchenbuch, 1639-1875* (Family History Library, Salt Lake City: The Genealogical Society of Utah, 1951), microfilm #69112.

7   This statement represents the condition at the time. I have since traced the family further. For more information, contact the author.

8   The name change isn't as surprising as it might first appear. People spelled phonetically at the time. Several records confirm the connection. For example, Christoph's son, Johann, appears with the name "Albrecht" or "Apbrecht" in every record after his birth. Two of his marriage records give Johann Albrecht's birth date and place, thus linking him back to Johann Harprecht, son of Christoph.

9   Bahlke Werner, *200 Jahre Neu Brenz, 1797–1997* (Neustadt-Glewe, Germany:

privately printed, 1997), 15. All information about the history of the village comes from this history.

10   Bahlke, *200 Jahre Neu Brenz*, 15.

11   Eleonore Wolf, *Neubrandenburg: Chronological History of the City*, translated by Leslie Albrecht and Intersprachen-Service (Neubrandenburg, Germany: Neubrandenburger Stadtarchiv, 1998), 13.

12   Wolf, *Neubrandenburg*, 14–15.

13   Bahlke, *200 Jahre Neu Brenz*, 33.

14   Crepon, *Mecklenburg*, 24.

15   Wolf, *Neubrandenburg*, 20.

16   Bahlke, *200 Jahre Neu Brenz*, 34.

17   Josef Ehmer, "Marriage," in *The History of the European Family: Family Life in the Long Nineteenth Century, 1789–1913*, ed. David I. Kertzer and Marzio Barbagli (New Haven: Yale University Press, 2002), 285. See also another article in that book: Lloyd Bonfield, "European Family Law," in *The History of the European Family: Family Life in the Long Nineteenth Century, 1789–1913*, ed. David I. Kertzer and Marzio Barbagli (New Haven: Yale University Press, 2002), 145.

18   It is possible that court records contain information about the divorce. So far, I have not been able to locate any.

19   Bahlke, *200 Jahre Neu Brenz*, 34.

20   Information about Napoleon comes from: John P. McKay, Bennett D. Hill, and John Buckler, *A History of World Societies* (Boston: Houghton Mifflin Company, 1992), 817–823.

21   Mecklenburg-Schwerin Volkszählungsamt, *Volkszählungslisten 1819, Hagenow D.A., Ülitz Parish*, (Family History Library, Salt Lake City, 1951), microfilm #68887.

Chapter Two

1   Very few peasants in the eastern part of Germany, particularly in Mecklenburg, truly owned their land. I use the term "owned" simply to distinguish them from "landless peasants." Christian, and others like him, still technically lived on land controlled by large, powerful estate owners.

2   Serfdom was officially abolished in Mecklenburg in 1820, although conditions improved little. Hartmut Harnisch explains that there were two principle legal categories of peasants. Those peasants considered to be "with property" were concentrated in the West. Peasants in the eastern parts of Germany had fewer rights and were more bound to their estate lords. For more information on the plight of the peasant, read: Hartmut Harnisch, "Peasants and Markets: The Background to the Agrarian Reforms in Feudal Prussia East of the Elbe, 1760–1807," in *The German Peasantry: Conflict and Community in Rural Society from the Eighteenth to the Twentieth Century*, ed. Richard J. Evans and W.R. Lee (New York: St. Martin's Press, 1986), 41–50.

3   James J. Sheehan, *German History, 1770–1866* (Oxford: Clarendon Press, 1989), 78.

4   Sheehan, *German History*, 480–481. Examples of the living conditions for this lower class can be found in: Hainer Plaul, "The Rural Proletariat: The Everyday Life of Rural Labourers in the Magdeburg Region, 1830–1880," in *The German Peasantry: Conflict and Community in Rural Society from the Eighteenth*

15 John Nicholson, letter dated 22 November 1880 to William Budge, 1880 *Wisconsin* voyage, *Mormon Immigration Index*, CD-ROM, Family History Resource File, Intellectual Reserve INC, 2000.

16 Minnie Pierce, "History of John Albrecht: My Grandfather," (biography, copy in author's possession, circa 1942).

17 James Samuel Page Bowler, "Autobiography," 1880 *Wisconsin* voyage, *Mormon Immigration Index*, CD-ROM, Family History Resource File, Intellectual Reserve INC, 2000.

18 Nicholson, letter to William Budge.

19 Clarence Albrecht, "George Albrecht." He wrote that he remembered his grandmother, Minnie Haker Albrecht, telling him about this.

20 Emma Albrecht, "A Life Story."

21 Bowler, "Autobiography."

22 Emma Albrecht, "A Life Story."

23 Bowler, "Autobiography."

24 For more information on the settlement of Manti see: M. F. Farnsworth, *History of Manti* (Salt Lake City: Genealogical Society, 1901); as well as W.H. Lever, *History of Sanpete and Emery Counties, Utah: With Sketches of Cities, Towns and Villages, Chronology of Important Events, Records of Indian Wars, Portraits of Prominent Persons, and Biographies of Representative Citizens* (Ogden, Utah: W.H. Lever, 1898), 76–94; and Albert C.T. Antrei and Allen D. Roberts, *A History of Sanpete County* (Salt Lake City: Utah State Historical Society, 1999), 383–387.

25 Louisa Tattom, *Cemetery Records of Manti, Utah* (Salt Lake City: Genealogical Society of Utah, 1936).

26 Emma Albrecht, "A Life Story."

27 Today, Fayette remains a very small community while Dover has disappeared completely. Sanpete County's history contains more details on Dover and Fayette: Antrei and Roberts, *A History of Sanpete County*, 364–365 and 371–373 and in Lever, *History of Sanpete and Emery counties*, 565–566.

28 Emma Albrecht, "A Life Story."

29 These pictures are found here: Anne Snow, *Rainbow Views: A History of Wayne County* (Springville, Utah: Art City, 1953), 179. I was able to borrow the negative and reproduce the pictures. These are the same photos included on the cover and at the beginning of this chapter.

0 Information on the settlement of Fremont comes from: Snow, *Rainbow Views*, 181.

Information about the Albrecht family settling in Fremont comes from: "Albrecht Family History."

Wilhelmina" didn't appear as one of Mina's names in her birth record.
owever, "Mina" is short for "Wilhelmina." Even in German records, her
ne appeared in many forms including several times as "Wilhelmina
beth Friederike."

ive

Malmöhus County and Kristianstad County, the two counties that
rically in the Skåne province, were merged to form a new Skåne
th boundaries roughly similar to the historical province of Skåne.

---

to the Twentieth Century, ed. Richard J. Evans and W.R. Lee (New York: St. Martin's Press, 1986), 102–128.

5 Ute Frevert, *Women in German History: From Bourgeois Emancipation to Sexual Liberation* (New York: St. Martin's Press, 1989), 24.

6 Mecklenburg-Schwerin Volkszählungsamt, *Volkszählungslisten 1819, Neukloster D.A., Nevern parish,* (Family History Library, Salt Lake City, 1951), microfilm # 68892.

7 Sheehan, *German History,* 456.

8 Mecklenburg Government, *Grossherzoglich Mecklenburg-Schwerinschwer Staats-Kalender, 1848–1880* (Stadtarchiv Neubrandenburg, Germany).

9 Sheehan, *German History,* 457.

10 Lloyd Bonfield, "European Family Law," in *The History of the European Family: Family Life in the Long Nineteenth Century, 1789–1913,* ed. David I. Kertzer and Marzio Barbagli (New Haven: Yale University Press, 2002), 113. Another chapter in the book also explains that when a pregnancy occurred, marriage was expected to follow: Josef Ehmer, "Marriage," in *The History of the European Family: Family Life in the Long Nineteenth Century, 1789–1913,* ed. David I. Kertzer and Marzio Barbagli (New Haven: Yale University Press, 2002), 317.

11 Domialämter Neukloster, "Dorf Nevern: Haker Hauswirt Dokumenten, 1835–1867," Landeshauptarchiv Schwerin, Schwerin, Germany.

12 Johann Christian Stahlberg, *Aus der Kirchenchronik Neukloster 1870–1900,* compiled by Pastor Dr. Matthias se Boor (Neukloster, Germany: privately printed, 1996), 46.

13 Much of the setting in this imaginary situation comes from: Gesine Kröhnert, *An de Klöndör: Meußer Dorfgeschichten für Kinder* (Schwerin, Germany: Mecklenburgisches Volkskundemuseum, n.d.).

14 These numbers and the later statistic on percentage of marriages that were second or subsequent marriages are based on my own calculations using the Neukloster parish records: Evangelishe Kirche Neukloster, *Kirchenbuch, 1694–1905* (Family History Library, Salt Lake City: The Genealogical Society of Utah, 1952), microfilm #69392–69394.

15 Information in this section on marriage patterns come largely from: Antoinette Fauve-Chamoux, "Marriage, Widowhood, and Divorce," in *Family Life in Early Modern Times, 1500–1789,* ed. David Kertzer and Marzio Barbagli (New Haven: Yale University Press, 2002), 242.

16 Information about women's roles comes from: Bonfield, "European Family Law," 145–147 and Frevert, *Women in German History,* 23–24. Also read: Karin Hausen, "Family and Role-Division: The Polarisation of Sexual Stereotypes in the Nineteenth Century—An Aspect of the Dissociation of Work and Family Life," in *The German Family: Essays on the Social History of the Family in Nineteenth- and Twentieth-Century Germany,* ed. Richard J. Evans and W.R. Lee (New York: St. Martin's Press, 1986), 51–83.

17 Domialämter Neukloster, "Dorf Nevern."

Chapter Three

1 Information on education in Germany comes from: Friedrich Paulsen, *German Education: Past and Present,* translated by T. Lorenz (London: T. Fisher Unwin, 1908), 236–261.

2   For more information on guilds read: Mack Walker, *German Home Towns: Community, State and General Estate, 1648–1871* (Ithaca, New York: Cornell University Press, 1971), 73–107.

3   For information on the name change, see note #8 from Chapter One.

4   For more information on the peasants' rights and land ownership see: Hartmut Harnisch, "Peasants and Markets: The Background to the Agrarian Reforms in Feudal Prussia East of the Elbe, 1760–1807," in *The German Peasantry: Conflict and Community in Rural Society from the Eighteenth to the Twentieth Century,* ed. Richard J. Evans and W.R. Lee (New York: St. Martin's Press, 1986), 37–70 and John G. Gagliardo, *From Pariah to Patriot: The Changing Image of the German Peasant, 1770–1840* (Lexington, Kentucky: The University Press of Kentucky, 1969), 21–22 and James J. Sheehan, *German History, 1770–1866* (Oxford: Clarendon Press, 1989), 473–480.

5   Sheehan, *German History,* 491–493.

6   For more on the Revolutions of 1830 read: Sheehan, *German History,* 604–621.

7   Linda A. Polluck, "Parent-Child Relations," in *The History of the European Family: Family Life in Early Modern Times, 1500–1789,* ed. David I. Kertzer and Marzio Barbagli (New Haven: Yale University Press, 2001), 196–197.

8   Laurence William Brockliss, "Organization, Training and the Medical Marketplace in the Eighteenth Century," in *The Healing Arts: Health, Disease, and Society in Europe, 1500–1800,* ed. Peter Elmer (Manchester: Manchester University Press, 2004), 352–353.

9   Mary Lindemann, *Health and Healing in Eighteenth-Century Germany* (Baltimore: The John Hopkins University Press, 1996), 291–300.

10   David I. Kertzer and Marzio Barbagli, Introduction to *The History of the European Family: Family Life in the Long Nineteenth Century, 1789–1913,* ed. David I. Kertzer and Marzio Barbagli (New Haven: Yale University Press, 2002), xxii.

11   Loftur Guttormsson, "Parent-Child Relations," in *The History of the European Family: Family Life in the Long Nineteenth Century, 1789–1913,* ed. David I. Kertzer and Marzio Barbagli (New Haven: Yale University Press, 2002), 254–256 and 265–266.

12   Mark Jenner, "Environment, Health and Population," in *The Healing Arts: Health, Disease, and Society in Europe, 1500–1800,* ed. Peter Elmer (Manchester: Manchester University Press, 2004), 301.

13   Mecklenburg Government, *Grossherzoglich Mecklenburg-Schwerinschwer Staats-Kalender, 1848–1880* (Stadtarchiv Neubrandenburg, Germany).

14   Pier Paolo Viazzo, "Mortality, Fertility, and Family," in *The History of the European Family: Family Life in Early Modern Times, 1500–1789,* ed. David I. Kertzer and Marzio Barbagli (New Haven: Yale University Press, 2002), 179–180 and Ute Frevert, *Women in German History: From Bourgeois Emancipation to Sexual Liberation* (New York: St. Martin's Press, 1989), 45–46 and 318.

15   Lindemann, *Health and Healing,* 207 and 213.

16   Guttormsson, "Parent-Child Relations," 255–256.

17   Gemeinde Gross Laasch, *Chronologische Zeittafel der Gemeinde Gross Laasch von 1229–1997,* (Gross Laasch, Germany: privately printed, circa 1995).

18   Sheehan, *German History,* 454.

19   Evangelishe Kirche Gross Tessin, *Kirchenbuch, 1671–1934* (Family History Library, Salt Lake City: The Genealogical Society of Utah, 1951), microfilm #69180.

20   Johann Christian Stahlberg, *Aus der Kirchenchronik Neukloster 1870–1900,* compiled by Pastor Dr. Matthias se Boor (Neukloster, Germany: privately printed, 1996), 47.

21   To learn more about the Revolutions of 1848 read Sheehan, *German History,* 656–710.

Chapter Four

1   This assertion is based on the birth record of Johann Christoph Albrecht in June of 1862, which states that Georg is living in Züsow. Evangelishe Kirche Goldebee, *Kirchenbuch, 1654–1913* (Family History Library, Salt Lake City: The Genealogical Society of Utah, 1951), microfilm #69127.

2   Mecklenburg Government, *Grossherzoglich Mecklenburg-Schwerinschwer Staats-Kalender, 1848–1880* (Stadtarchiv Neubrandenburg, Germany, n.d.), 148.

3   Emma Albrecht, "A Life Story of Emma Sophia Elizabeth Albrecht Morrell," (autobiography, copy in author's possession, n.d.).

4   For a basic chronology of early LDS Church history see: Church of Jesus Christ of Latter-day Saints, "Chronology of Church History," http://scriptures.lds. org/chchrono/contents (accessed January 2010).

5   Jeffrey L. Anderson, "Mormons and Germany, 1914–1933: A History of The Church of Jesus Christ of Latter-day Saints in Germany and its Relationship with the German Governments from World War I to the Rise of Hitler" (master's thesis, Brigham Young University, 1991).

6   This hypothetical occurrence is based on a comment made in a family paper: "Albrecht Family History," (family paper by unknown author, copy in author's possession, n.d.).

7   Church of Jesus Christ of Latter-day Saints, Temple Index Bureau, *En[...] Index 1846–1969* (Family History Library, Salt Lake City, 1971), micr[...] #1059545. Georg was later re-baptized in the US, a practice that [...] at the time.

8   *Utah History Encyclopedia,* s.v. "Perpetual Emigrating Fund [...] Richard Jensen), http://historytogo.utah.gov/utah_chap[...] cowboys/perpetualemigratingfundcompany.html (acc[...]

9   Clarence Albrecht, "George Albrecht," (biography, [...] circa 1950). His paper states that he got this infor[...] Historical Office.

10   Numbers relating to Mormon immigration [...] and Germany."

11   Roger Daniels, *Coming to America: A H[...] American Life* (New York: HarperCol[...]

12   Mack Walker, *Germany and the E[...] Massachusetts: Harvard Unive[...]

13   "A Compilation of General [...] *Immigration Index,* CD-R[...] INC, 2000.

14   Daniels, *Coming to Americ[...] from Hamburg," GenWebsite [...] http://www.emecklenburg.de/[...] January 2010).

Today, the twenty-five provinces of Sweden have no administrative function, but continue as cultural and historical regions. The counties function as the more important administrative units.

2   Franklin Scott, *Sweden: The Nation's History* (Carbondale and Edwardsville, Illinois: Southern Illinois University Press, 1988), 334–335.

3   Martin Dribe, *Leaving Home in a Peasant Society: Economic Fluctuations, Household Dynamics and Youth Migration in Southern Sweden, 1829–1866* (Sweden: Almqvist and Wiksell International, 2000), 27.

4   Sverige, Länsstyrelsen (Malmöhus), *Mantalslängder, 1658–1860* (Family History Library, Salt Lake City, 1951), microfilm #337666, 337662, 337661, and 337665.

5   Allan Pred, *Place, Practice and Structure: Social and Spatial Transformation in Southern Sweden, 1750–1850* (Cambridge: Polity Press, 1986), 81.

6   Orvar Löfgren, "The Potato People: The Household Economy and Family Patterns Among the Rural Proletariat in Nineteenth Century Sweden," in *Chance and Change: Social and Economic Studies in Historical Demography in the Baltic Area*, ed. Sune Åkerman, Hans Chr. Johansen, and David Gaunt (Odense: Odense University Press, 1978), 98–99.

7   Svenska Kyrkan, Everlöv socken, *Kyrkoböcker, 1662–1894: Husförhörslängd* (Family History Library, Salt Lake City: The Genealogical Society of Utah, 1952), microfilm #145108, Items 1–2.

8   Tora District Court Records, Skåne, Sweden, vol. F II a: 31, nr. 26, Lund Archive, Lund, Sweden.

9   I've recreated the scene of the morning based on the items given in Marna's probate (listed previously) and descriptions of farm life found here: Pred, *Place, Practice and Structure*, 63–81 and 94–95.

10 Pred, *Place, Practice and Structure*, 49 and 82. Also see Scott, *Sweden*, 288–289.

11 Daily tasks are described in: Pred, *Place, Practice and Structure*, 63–81.

12 Sogner Sølvi,"Illegitimacy in Old Rural Society: Some Reflections on the Problem Arising from Two Norwegian Family-Reconstruction Studies," in *Chance and Change: Social and Economic Studies in Historical Demography in the Baltic Area*, ed. Sune Åkerman, Hans Chr. Johansen, and David Gaunt (Odense: Odense University Press, 1978), 61–63.

13 Christer Lundh, "Marriage and Economic Change in Sweden during the 18th and 19th Century," in *Marriage and Rural Economy: Western Europe Since 1400*, ed. Isabelle Devos and Liam Kennedy, CORN publication series 3 (Turnhout: Brepols, 1999), 223.

14 Nils's occupation is given in the birth records of his children. See the appendix for references.

15 Scott, *Sweden*, 220–221.

16 This source describes the changes in mortality and fertility rates: David I. Kertzer and Marzio Barbagli, Introduction to *Family Life in the Long Nineteenth Century, 1789–1913*, ed. David Kertzer and Marzio Barbagli (New Haven: Yale University Press, 2002), xix–xxvi.

17 For more information on the catechisms see: Dr. Martin Luther, *Martin Luther's Small Catechisms: Explained in Questions and Answers With Proof-Texts From Holy Scripture For The Church, School and Family* (Columbus, Ohio: The Lutheran Book Concern, 1884).

18 Scott, *Sweden*, 294–295.

19 For more information on Bernadotte and the events surrounding him read: Scott, *Sweden*, 294–318.

20 Svenska Kyrkan, Everlöv socken, *Kyrkoböcker, 1662–1894: In- och utflyttningsl* (Family History Library, Salt Lake City: The Genealogical Society of Utah, 1952), microfilm #145110.

21 Bara District Court Records, Skåne, Sweden, entry for Karna Larsdotter, Kornheddinge 1822 22/7 1821–22:80, (Family History Library, Salt Lake City, 1953), microfilm #145082.

Chapter Six

1 This characterization of Vallby as well as the amount of land that Nils Nilsson owned comes from reviewing the records for various years located here: Svenska Kyrkan, Kyrkheddinge socken, *Kyrkoböcker, 1683–1899: Husförslängd* (Family History Library, Salt Lake City: The Genealogical Society of Utah, 1952), microfilm #145783.

2 Christer Winberg, "Population Growth and Proletarianization," in *Chance and Change: Social and Economic Studies in Historical Demography in the Baltic Area*, ed. Sune Åkerman, Hans Chr. Johansen, and David Gaunt (Odense: Odense University Press, 1978), 170–171.

3 General information about the *enskifte* movement comes from: Göran Hoppe, *Enclosure in Sweden: Background and Consequences* (Stockholm: The University of Stockholm, 1981), 41–62. The following source discusses its effect on Malmöhus County specifically: Allan Pred, *Place, Practice and Structure: Social and Spatial Transformation in Southern Sweden, 1750–1850* (Cambridge: Polity Press 1986), 55–62.

4 Svenska Kyrkan, Kyrkheddinge socken, *Kyrkoböcker, 1683–1899: Husförhörslängd* (Family History Library, Salt Lake City: The Genealogical Society of Utah, 1952), microfilm #145782.

5 Franklin Scott, *Sweden: The Nation's History* (Carbondale and Edwardsville, Illinois: Southern Illinois University Press, 1988), 355–361.

6 Roger Daniels, *Coming to America: A History of Immigration and Ethnicity in American Life* (New York: HarperCollins Publishers, 1991), 165.

7 Daniels, *Coming to America*, 168.

8 Loftur Guttormsson, "Parent-Child Relations," in *The History of the European Family: Family Life in the Long Nineteenth Century, 1789–1913*, ed. David I. Kertzer and Marzio Barbagli (New Haven: Yale University Press, 2002), 257–258.

9 Svenska Kyrkan, Kyrkheddinge socken, *Kyrkoböcker, 1683–1899: Husförhörslängd* (Family History Library, Salt Lake City: The Genealogical Society of Utah, 1952), microfilm #145782.

10 Scott, *Sweden*, 357.

11 Details about the LDS Church's early presence in Sweden come from: Andrew Jensen, *History of the Scandinavian Mission* (New York: Arno Press, 1979), 11.

12 Svenska Kyrkan, Kyrkheddinge socken, *Kyrkoböcker, 1683–1899: Husförhörslängd* (Family History Library, Salt Lake City: The Genealogical Society of Utah, 1952), microfilm #145782.

13 Svenska Kyrkan, Kyrkheddinge socken, *Kyrkoböcker, 1683–1899: Husförhörslängd* (Family History Library, Salt Lake City: The Genealogical Society of Utah, 1952), microfilm #145782.

14   Pred, *Place, Practice and Structure*, 78.

15   Scott, *Sweden*, 352.

16   United States Census Office, "1900, Fremont, Utah Census" (Family History Library, Washington DC, National Archives, 1967), microfilm #124168, ED 214, p. 2A.

17   Jensen, *History of the Scandinavian Mission*, 80–81.

18   In the columns for "comments" next to the names of these farmhands, the parish priest wrote "Mormon." Svenska Kyrkan, Kyrkheddinge socken, *Kyrkoböcker, 1683–1899: Husförhörslängd* (Family History Library, Salt Lake City: The Genealogical Society of Utah, 1952), microfilm #145782.

19   Jensen, *History of the Scandinavian Mission*, 103–110.

20   Svenska Kyrkan, Kyrkheddinge socken, *Kyrkoböcker, 1683–1899: Husförhörslängd* (Family History Library, Salt Lake City: The Genealogical Society of Utah, 1952), microfilm #145782.

21   Svenska Kyrkan, Kyrkheddinge socken, *Kyrkoböcker, 1683–1899: Husförhörslängd* (Family History Library, Salt Lake City: The Genealogical Society of Utah, 1952), microfilm #145782.

22   Church of Jesus Christ of Latter-day Saints Vallby Branch, (Malmöhus), *Record of Members, 1853-1863* (Family History Library, Salt Lake City: The Genealogical Society of Utah, microfilm #82947), item 2-3.

23   Daniels, *Coming to America*, 164–165.

24   William Mulder, *Homeward to Zion: The Mormon Migration from Scandinavia* (Minneapolis: University of Minnesota Press, 2000), 118–119.

25   Skåne District, Swedish Mission, "General Minutes," LDS Church Archives, Salt Lake City.

26   Andrew Jenson, "Skåne District, Swedish Mission, Manuscript History and Historical Reports," LDS Church Archives, Salt Lake City.

Chapter Seven

1   William Mulder, *Homeward to Zion: The Mormon Migration from Scandinavia* (Minneapolis: University of Minnesota Press, 2000), 167.

2   Andrew Jenson, "Skåne District, Swedish Mission, Manuscript History and Historical Reports," LDS Church Archives, Salt Lake City.

3   Mulder, *Homeward to Zion*, 165-166.

4   Svenska Kyrkan, Kyrkheddinge socken, *Kyrkoböcker, 1683–1899: In- och utflyttningsl* (Family History Library, Salt Lake City: The Genealogical Society of Utah, 1952), microfilm #145783, item 1.

5   Details of the ship's voyage come from: "A Compilation of General Voyage Notes," 1861 *Monarch of the Sea* voyage, *Mormon Immigration Index*, CD-ROM, Family History Resource File, Intellectual Reserve INC, 2000.

6   Mulder, *Homeward to Zion*, 168-169.

7   Conway B. Sonne, *Ships, Saints, and Mariners: A Maritime Encyclopedia of Mormon Migration, 1830–1890* (Salt Lake City: University of Utah Press, 1987), 146-147.

8   "A Compilation of General Voyage Notes," 1861 *Monarch of the Sea* voyage.

9   David H. Pratt and Paul F. Smart, "Life on Board a Mormon Emigrant Ship,"

World Conference on Records: Preserving Our Heritage, August 12–15, 1980, vol. 5, series 418: 7.

10   "Minutes of the *Monarch of the Sea*," 1861 *Monarch of the Sea* voyage, *Mormon Immigration Index*, CD-ROM, Family History Resource File, Intellectual Reserve INC, 2000.

11   Pratt and Smart, "Life on Board," 3.

12   Mulder, *Homeward to Zion*, 171.

13   Alma Elizabeth Mineer Felt, "Journal," 1861 *Monarch of the Sea* voyage, *Mormon Immigration Index*, CD-ROM, Family History Resource File, Intellectual Reserve INC, 2000, 196.

14   This imaginary scene is based on descriptions of other travelers such as those found here: Dean L. May, "Rites of Passage: The Gathering as Cultural Credo," *Journal of Mormon History* 28 (Spring 2003), 19–22.

15   William Probert, Jr., "Autobiography," 1861 *Monarch of the Sea* voyage, *Mormon Immigration Index*, CD-ROM, Family History Resource File, Intellectual Reserve INC, 2000.

16   For more information on Castle Garden read: Barry Moreno, "Castle Garden: The Forgotten Gateway," *Ancestry Magazine*, (March/April 2003), http://www.ancestry.com/learn/library/article.aspx?article=7233 (accessed January 2010) or George Svejda, *Castle Garden as an Immigrant Depot, 1855–1890* (Washington, DC: National Park Service, US Department of the Interior, 1968).

17   Felt, "Journal," 196.

18   Stanley B. Kimball, "Sail and Rail Pioneers before 1869," *BYU Studies* 35:2 (1995): 30.

19   Peter Nielson, "Journal of Peter Nielson," 1861 *Monarch of the Sea* voyage, *Mormon Immigration Index*, CD-ROM, Family History Resource File, Intellectual Reserve INC, 2000.

20   Fred E. Woods, "East to West through North and South: Mormon Immigration during the Civil War," *BYU Studies*, 39:1 (2000): 16–20.

21   This hypothetical scene is based on descriptions in: Woods, "East to West," 16–20.

22   William G. Hartley, "The Great Florence Fitout of 1861," *BYU Studies*, 24:3 (1984): 361.

23   Hartley, "The Great Florence Fitout," 359–360.

24   Hartley, "The Great Florence Fitout," 344–346.

25   Hartley, "The Great Florence Fitout," 647 and 667. Independent companies were composed of those who could afford to pay for their own provisions to cross the plains instead of relying on the church teams. In 1861, twelve wagon trains which included a total of 624 wagons left from Florence, heading to Utah. Eight of the twelve were independent companies.

26   Hartley, "The Great Florence Fitout," 363.

27   Richard White, *It's Your History and None of My Own* (Norman, Oklahoma: University of Oklahoma Press, 1991), 189.

28   Quotes throughout this section from Pedar Nielsen and Samuel Woolley come from their journals: Peter Nielsen, "Diary," translated by Orson B. West, typescript, July-September 1861 entries, LDS Church Archives, Salt Lake City and Samuel Woolley, "Journal," July-September 1861 entries, LDS Church Archives, Salt Lake City.

29 Felt, "Journal," 198.

30 Neilsen, "Diary."

31 Felt, "Journal," 198.

32 Anders Christensen, "Letter to President Jesse N. Smith dated 18 September 1863," 1863 *John J. Boyd* voyage, *Mormon Immigration Index*, CD-ROM, Family History Resource File, Intellectual Reserve INC, 2000.

Chapter Eight

1   I have made a few adjustments to events in my life to make the timeline fit better with my research. I actually traveled to England one year after this chapter describes it happening. We left from Valencia, where I was living at the time, and brought Sarah Ann, my seven-month-old, with us. Everything else happened as it is described here.

2   Eric J. Evans, *The Forging of the Modern State: Early Industrial Britain, 1783–1870,* 3rd ed. (Harlow, England: Longman, 2001), 128–133.

3   *GENUKI: UK and Ireland,* s.v. "Buckinghamshire," http://met.open.ac.uk/genuki/big/eng/BKM/ (accessed January 2010).

4   Evans, *The Forging of the Modern State,* 147, 191, and 201–204.

5   Edward Royle, *Modern Britain: A Society History 1750–1997,* 2nd ed. (New York: St. Martin's Press, 1997), 89.

6   Royle, *Modern Britain,* 163–167.

7   Evans, *The Forging of the Modern State,* 163.

8   Jane Humphries, "Standard of Living, Quality of Life," in *A Companion to Nineteenth-Century Britain,* ed. Chris Williams (Malden, Massachusetts: Blackwell Publishing, 2001), 300.

9   Josef Ehmer, "Marriage," in *The History of the European Family: Family Life in the Long Nineteenth Century, 1789–1913,* ed. David I. Kertzer and Marzio Barbagli (New Haven: Yale University Pres, 2002), 302.

10 Records where Edmond gave Long Crendon as his place of birth include: New South Wales, Department of Immigration, *Assisted Immigrants Inwards to Sydney, 1828–1890* (Family History Library, Salt Lake City: The Genealogical Society of Utah, 1962), microfilm #288511, 29 December 1829; Church of Jesus Christ of Latter-day Saints New South Wales District, *Record of Members, 1852–1952* (Family History Library, Salt Lake City: The Genealogical Society of Utah, 1967), microfilm #105320 (where the birth place was given as "Crandon"); and Church of Jesus Christ of Latter-day Saints, Temple Index Bureau, *Endowment Index 1846–1969* (Family History Library, Salt Lake City, 1973), microfilm #1059545.

11 Royle, *Modern Britain,* 355–362.

12 Humphries, "Standard of Living," 300.

13 Elizabeth signed her name with a mark as the informant in the civil registration record of her son: Entry June 6, 1840, for Emmanuel Harris, *Civil Registration Records* Buckinghamshire, England (copy in author's possession).

14 Evans, *The Forging of the Modern State,* 223–224.

15 Restrictions were removed from Catholics only gradually, culminating with the Catholic Relief Act of 1829. Asa Briggs, *The Age of Improvement 1783–1867,* 2nd ed. (London: Longman, 2000), 170–174.

16   A religious census was taken in 1851. For more information on its results see: Great Britain Census Office, Horace Mann. *Census of Great Britain, 1851: Religious Worship in England and Wales* (London: G. Routledge, 1854), http://www.archive.org/details/censusgreatbrit00manngoog (accessed March 2010).

17   Great Britain Census Office, *Census Returns for Steeple Claydon, 1841* (Family History Library, Salt Lake City: The Genealogical Society of Utah, 1960), microfilm #241212.

18   Great Britain Census Office, *Census Returns for Buckingham, 1851* (Family History Library, Salt Lake City: The Genealogical Society of Utah, 1960), microfilm #241221.

19   Lloyd Bonfield, "European Family Law," in *The History of the European Family: Family Life in the Long Nineteenth Century, 1789–1913,* ed. David I. Kertzer and Marzio Barbagli (New Haven: Yale University Press, 2002), 116–117 and 124–125.

20   Derrick Murphy, Richard Staton, Patrick Walsh-Atkins, and Neil Whiskend, *Britain, 1815–1918* (London: Collins Educational, 1998), 103–104.

21   I am referring to birth records of his children which include James's occupation. See the appendix for references.

22   Great Britain Census Office, "Census Returns for Buckingham, 1851."

23   For more information about Peel and his policies read: Evans, *The Forging of the Modern State,* 256–284.

24   Muriel T. Vernon and Desmond C. Bonner, *Buckingham: A History of a Country Market Town,* 3rd ed. (Milton Keynes, England: Grillford Ltd., 1984), 113.

25   Vernon and Bonner, *Buckingham,* 93–94.

Chapter Nine

1   Their street is given in their marriage record. See the appendix for source information.

2   This quote is found on many websites including: David Cody, "A Brief History of London," The Victorian Web, http://www.victorianweb.org/history/hist4.html (accessed March 2010). Later descriptions were not kinder. Quoted on that same website, John Ruskin in 1860 described it like this: "That great foul city of London—rattling, growling, smoking, stinking—ghastly heap of fermenting brickwork, pouring out poison at every pore…"

3   Their occupations come from: New South Wales, Department of Immigration, *Assisted Immigrants Inwards to Sydney, 1828–1890* (Family History Library, Salt Lake City: The Genealogical Society of Utah, 1962), microfilm #288511, 29 December 1829.

4   Information on carmen is largely from quotes from this website: Charles Booth, *Life and Labour of the People of London* as quoted in Des Gander, "The Occupation of Carman," The Gander and Gander One-Name Study, http://www.gander-name.info/misc/carmen.shtml (accessed March 2010).

5   Information throughout this section on the rise of the LDS Church in England comes from: Ronald W. Walker, "Cradling Mormonism: The Rise of the Gospel in Early Victorian England," *BYU Studies* 27:1 (1987), 25 and 31.

6   Great Britain Census Office, Horace Mann, *Census of Great Britain, 1851: Religious Worship in England and Wales* (London: G. Routledge, 1854), http://www.archive.org/details/censusgreatbrit00manngoog (accessed March 2010).

7   Church of Jesus Christ of Latter-day Saints London Conference (London), *Record of Members, 1833–1935* (Family History Library, Salt Lake City: The Genealogical Society of Utah, 1952), microfilm #87014, p. 765.

8   Walker, "Cradling Mormonism," 29.

9   New South Wales, Department of Immigration, *Assisted Immigrants Inwards to Sydney.*

10 Ken Inglis, *Australian Colonists: An Exploration of Social History 1788–1870* (Melbourne, Australia: Melbourne University Press, 1974), 16–17.

11 *GENUKI* (UK and Ireland), s.v. "The Tide of Emigration to the United States and to the British Colonies," http://www.genuki.org.uk/big/emdesc.html (accessed January 2010).

12 Inglis, *Australian Colonists*, 30–31.

13 E.G. Hazel, *Some Came Free* (Canberra, Australia: Pirie Printer Pty. Limited: 1978), 12.

14 Marjorie Newton, "The Gathering of the Australian Saints in the 1850s," *BYU Studies* 27:2 (1987): 3. For information about the early LDS Church in Australia see also: Marjorie Newton, *Southern Cross Saints: The Mormons in Australia* (Laie, Hawaii: The Institute for Polynesian Studies, 1991).

15 John Devitry-Smith, "The Wreck of the *Julia Ann*," *BYU Studies* 29:2 (1989): 2–3.

16 John Perkins, "Diary," LDS Church Archives, Salt Lake City.

17 Newton, "The Gathering of the Australian Saints," 5–7.

18 Newton, "The Gathering of the Australian Saints," 3 and 5.

19 "A Compilation of General Voyage Notes," 1856 *Julia Ann* voyage, *Mormon Immigration Index*, CD-ROM, Family History Resource File, Intellectual Reserve INC, 2000.

20 Devitry-Smith, "The Wreck of the *Julia Ann*," 3.

21 Andrew Anderson, "Letter, dated February 22, 1856," 1856 *Julia Ann* voyage, *Mormon Immigration Index*, CD-ROM, Family History Resource File, Intellectual Reserve INC, 2000.

22 Devitry-Smith, "The Wreck of the *Julia Ann*," 5–6. See this paper for a detailed, well-documented account of the shipwreck.

23 Benjamin F. Pond, "Autobiography," 1856 *Julia Ann* voyage, *Mormon Immigration Index*, CD-ROM, Family History Resource File, Intellectual Reserve INC, 2000, 115.

24 Pond, "Autobiography," 115.

25 John McCarthy, "Letter, dated 25 April 1856," 1856 *Julia Ann* voyage, *Mormon Immigration Index*, CD-ROM, Family History Resource File, Intellectual Reserve INC, 2000.

26 Esther E. Spangenburg, "Particulars of the Wreck," as quoted in Devitry-Smith, "The Wreck of the *Julia Ann*," 7.

27 Spangenburg, "Particulars of the Wreck," 7.

28 Pond, "Autobiography," 115.

29 Pond, "Autobiography," 117.

30 Pond, "Autobiography," 117.

31 See Devitry-Smith, "The Wreck of the *Julia Ann*" for more information on this and on the account that follows of their time on the island.

32 McCarthy, "Letter."

33   Pond, "Autobiography," 125.

34   Pond, "Autobiography," 122.

35   Anderson, "Letter."

36   Pond, "Autobiography," 124.

37   Conway B. Sonne, "Under Sail to Zion," *Ensign*, 21 (July 1991): 6–14.

38   A list of passengers for the *Lucas*, as well as a description of the voyage, can be found here: "A Journal of the Company of Saints on the Ship, *Lucas*," 1857 *Lucas* voyage, *Mormon Immigration Index*, CD-ROM, Family History Resource File, Intellectual Reserve INC, 2000.

39   "A Journal of the Company of Saints on the Ship, *Lucas*."

40   "A Journal of the Company of Saints on the Ship, *Lucas*." All quotes in this section come from this source on the date indicated in the text.

41   These last two quotes come from 1 August and 4 August respectively.

42   The information on San Bernardino in this section comes from: Edward Leo Lyman, *San Bernardino: The Rise and Fall of a California Community* (Signature Books: Salt Lake City, 1996), 371-430.

43   United States Census Office, "1860, San Francisco, California Census" (Family History Library, Washington DC, National Archives, 1967), microfilm #803067.

44   Elsie Harmon, e-mail to author about possible census records for Maria Harris, March 2006.

Chapter Ten

1   The birth date of Mary Elizabeth is also unclear. Again, no birth record for her survives. Later records often list 1 January 1864, as given here. However, Edmond and Karsti's next child, Moroni Johns, is listed as being born 10 November 1864. Although these two dates are theoretically possible, they are unlikely. Other records, including Gunnison ward records, give her birth date as 31 December 1862. (These same records also give her birth date in another place as 31 December 1864.) Church of Jesus Christ of Latter-day Saints, Gunnison Ward (Utah), *Record of Members, 1861–1945* (Family History Library, Salt Lake City: The Genealogical Society of Utah, 1951), microfilm #25977.

2   *Utah History Encyclopedia*, s.v. "Colonization of Utah" (by Leonard Arrington), http://www.onlineutah.com/colonizationhistory.shtml (accessed January 2010).

3   Clara Menlove, "Spring Lake," Pioneer Memorial Museum, Salt Lake City.

4   This is quoted from a revelation recorded by Joseph Smith in LDS scripture: Doctrine and Covenants 49:24.

5   John Alton Peterson, *Utah's Black Hawk Indian War* (Salt Lake City: The University of Utah Press, 1998), 5–6. The background on Mormon and American Indian relations in this chapter come largely from this source.

6   For more on the early history of Utah, including its transition to a territory and later a state read: Charles S. Peterson, *Utah: A Bicentennial History* (New York: W. W. Norton & Company Inc, 1977) and Peter Crawley, "The Constitution of the State of Deseret," in *Life in Utah: Centennial Selections from BYU Studies*, ed. James B. Allen and John W. Welch (Provo, Utah: Brigham Young University, 1996), 68–88. Also see J. Keith Melville, "Theory and Practice of Church and State during the Brigham Young Era," in *Life in Utah: Centennial Selections from*

BYU Studies, ed. James B. Allen and John W. Welch (Provo, Utah: Brigham Young University, 1996), 89–113.

7   Descriptions of life in Spring Lake in this period are given in: Spring Lake Branch, Utah Stake, "Manuscript History and Historical reports," LDS Church Archives, Salt Lake City.

8   Church of Jesus Christ of Latter-day Saints ,Vallby Branch (Malmöhus), *Record of Members, 1853–1863* (Family History Library, Salt Lake City: The Genealogical Society of Utah, year), microfilm #82947.

9   A list of passengers for the 1862 voyage of the *John J. Boyd* can be found here: *Mormon Immigration Index,* CD-ROM, Family History Resource File, Intellectual Reserve INC, 2000.

10 Peterson, *Utah's Black Hawk Indian War,* 25–26 and 391.

11 Brigham Young, "Letter to Benjamin F. Johnson, Spring Lake Villa, 30 January 1866," LDS Church Archives, Salt Lake City.

12 Spring Lake Branch, Utah Stake, "Manuscript History and Historical reports."

13 Benjamin F. Johnson, letter to editor, *Deseret News,* September 27, 1870, quoted in Peterson, *Utah's Black Hawk Indian War,* 396 (see note #60 on that page).

14 Leland Hargrave Creer, *The Founding of an Empire: The Exploration and Colonization of Utah, 1776–1856* (Salt Lake City: Bookcraft, 1947), 340–341.

15 United States Census Office, "1910, Fremont, Utah Census" (Family History Library, Washington DC, National Archives, 1967), microfilm #1654719, ED 214, p. 2A.

16 Spring Lake Branch, Utah Stake, "Manuscript history and historical reports."

17 Centennial Committee, *Memory Book to Commemorate Gunnison Valley's Centennial, 1859–1959* (Gunnison: Gunnison Centennial Book Committee, 1959), 48.

18 Centennial Committee, *Memory Book,* 49–51.

19 Albert C.T Antrei and Allen D. Roberts, *A History of Sanpete County* (Salt Lake City: Utah State Historical Society, 1999), 47.

20 Gunnison Ward, Sanpete Stake, "Historical Record, 1874–1894," LDS Church Archives, Salt Lake City.

21 For a brief overview of the United Order experiment, see: *Utah History Encyclopedia,* s.v. "The United Order Movement" (by Dean L. May), http://www.media.utah.edu/UHE/u/UNITEDORDER.html (accessed Jan 2010).

22 Centennial Committee, *Memory Book,* 49–51.

23 Gunnison Ward, Sanpete Stake, "Historical Record, 1874–1894."

24 Centennial Committee, *Memory Book,* 49.

25 Gunnison Ward, Sanpete Stake, "Historical Record, 1874–1894," 50.

26 Chasty Margaret Harris Albrecht, "Autobiography," (autobiography, copy in author's possession, circa 1940).

27 Information on polygamy and legislation against it throughout this chapter comes from: Gustive O. Larson, "Federal Government Efforts to 'Americanize' Utah before Admission to Statehood," *BYU Studies* 10:2 (1970): 5–6.

28 Church of Jesus Christ of Latter-day Saints, Gunnison Stake (Utah), *Cemetery Records: Centerfield, Fayette, and Gunnison in Sanpete County, Utah* (Family History Library, Salt Lake City, 1934), 27.

29 Larson, "Federal Government Efforts," 6–7.

30   Anne Snow, *Rainbow Views: A History of Wayne County* (Springville, Utah: Art City, 1953), 177. The county history gives a list of all settlers who had arrived by 1890. Chasty Harris is included in this list.

31   Moroni and Sarah are both with Karsti in Fremont in the 1900 census: United States Census Office, "1900, Fremont, Utah Census" (Family History Library, Washington DC, National Archives, 1967), microfilm #124168, ED 214, p. 1B. Rachel's marriage record in 1891 says she is living in Fremont. I am unsure about Ephraim as I haven't found any records to indicate what happened to him.

32   The Woodruff Manifesto is also known as "Official Declaration–1" and is found immediately following the Doctrine and Covenants in LDS scripture. Joseph F. Smith's statement can be read in numerous places online including: *Wikipedia: The Free Encyclopedia*, s.v. "Second Manifesto," http://en.wikipedia.org/wiki/Second_Manifesto (accessed January 2010).

33   United States Census Office, "1900, Fremont, Utah Census."

Chapter Eleven

1   Chasty Margaret Harris Albrecht, "Autobiography," (autobiography, copy in author's possession, circa 1940).

2   Minnie Pierce, "History of John Albrecht: My Grandfather," (biography, copy in author's possession, circa 1940).

3   These pictures are found in: Anne Snow, *Rainbow Views: A History of Wayne County* (Springville, Utah: Art City, 1953), 180.

4   Snow, *Rainbow Views*, 177.

5   Emma Albrecht Sorenson and Donna Albrecht Blackburn, interviewed by author, in Fremont, circa 1998.

6   Snow, *Rainbow Views*, 33.

7   Snow, *Rainbow Views*, 34.

8   Snow, *Rainbow Views*, 33.

9   United States Census Office, "1900, Fremont, Utah Census" (Family History Library, Washington DC, National Archives, 1967), microfilm #124168. Calculations by Don Albrecht.

10   Roger Daniels, *Coming to America: A History of Immigration and Ethnicity in American Life* (New York: HarperCollins Publishers, 1991), 125.

11   Daniels, *Coming to America*, 185.

12   EH.Net Encyclopedia, s.v. "Fertility and Mortality in the United States" (by Michael Haines, edited by Robert Whaples), http://eh.net/encyclopedia/article/haines.demography (accessed March 2010).

13   Lone Star College—Kingwood, American Cultural History Pages, 1900–1909, http://kclibrary.lonestar.edu/decade00.html (accessed March 2010).

14   Snow, Rainbow Views, 184.

15   Wayne County (Utah) County Clerk, *Miscellaneous Records, 1901–1948* (Family History Library, Salt Lake City: The Genealogical Society of Utah, 1967), microfilm #1654719.

16   Chasty Albrecht, "Autobiography."

17   Sorenson and Blackburn, interview.

     Chasty Albrecht, "Autobiography."

Chapter Twelve

1. Much of the information throughout this chapter about Earl and Eva's lives comes from their own life histories: Eva Balle Albrecht, "My Life Story," (autobiography, copy in author's possession, circa 1966), and Erlene Blackburn, "The Story of Earl LeRoy Albrecht, My Grandfather," (autobiography, copy in author's possession, 1964).

2. Emma Albrecht Sorenson and Donna Albrecht Blackburn, interviewed by author, in Fremont, circa 1998.

3. Molly Billings, "The Influenza Pandemic of 1918," Human Virology at Stanford, June 2007, http://www.stanford.edu/group/virus/uda/ (accessed March 2010).

4. Jeffery K. Taubenberger and David M. Morens, "1918 Influenza: The Mother of all Pandemics," Centers for Disease Control and Prevention: Emerging Infectious Diseases, December 2005, http://www.cdc.gov/ncidod/eid/vol12no01/05-0979.htm (accessed March 2010).

5. Sorenson and Blackburn, interview.

6. This assertion comes from a conversation with my grandmother, Alta Taylor Albrecht, Earl's daughter-in-law.

7. *Utah History Encyclopedia, s.v.* "The Great Depression" (by John S. McCormick), http://www.onlineutah.com/colonizationhistory.shtml (accessed March 2010).

8. Since this writing, Nila has also passed away. Two children are still living.

9. These memories come mostly from informal conversations with my dad and his siblings over the years.

Chapter Thirteen

1. Information about my grandparents and their lives comes from a variety of mostly informal sources which will not be footnoted throughout the chapter. Besides conversations with my grandma and her children, I also got information from her life history and the life history she wrote of her husband, my grandpa: Alta Taylor Albrecht, "Rex Albrecht," (biography, copy in author's possession, 1985) and Alta Taylor Albrecht, "Life History of Alta Fern Taylor Albrecht as Written by Herself," (autobiography, copy in author's possession, May 1965).

2. Don Albrecht and Steve Murdock, *The Sociology of U.S. Agriculture: An Economic Perspective* (Aimes, Iowa: Iowa University Press, 1990), 44.

3. Don Albrecht, "The Mechanization of Agriculture: A Historical Case Study of the Implications for Families and Communities," *Culture & Agriculture*, 19:1-2 (1997): 24.

4. Albrecht and Murdock, *Sociology of U.S. Agriculture*, 156.

5. Albrecht, "The Mechanization of Agriculture," 29-30.

Chapter One
Foundations: Early Ancestors

Father: Hans Jochim Christopher Harprecht (Christoph)
(son of Daniel Jacob Harprecht and Maria Dorothea Pingel)
b. 25 Apr 1769   Garwitz, Garwitz, Mecklenburg-Schwerin
d. 3 Jul 1838   Neu Brenz, Brenz, Mecklenburg-Schwerin

Christoph married first: 4 Jun 1790 in Brenz, Brenz, Mecklenburg-Schwerin

Mother: Christina Maria Gienken
(daughter of Johann Gienken and Catharina Sophia)
b. Abt 1769   Brenz, Brenz, Mecklenburg-Schwerin*

Children: (born and christened in Brenz or Neu Brenz, deaths except for child #3 also occurred in Brenz or Neu Brenz)
1. Sophia Christina Maria   b. 25 Feb 1791
       m. Johann Jacob Jurgen Diehn, 29 Nov 1810 in Brenz
2. Johann Jochim Christoph   b. 10 Jun 1793   d. 20 Aug 1794
3. **Johann Jochim**   b. 12 Dec 1795   d. 28 Oct 1859 in Gross Laasch, Gross
Laasch, Mecklenburg-Schwerin
       m. three times, including Sophia Maria Elisabeth Tiedemann, 30 Dec 1833
4. Eva Sophia   b. 9 Mar 1798   d. 8 Apr 1798
5. Johann Jochim   b. 13 Apr 1800
6. Christina Maria   b. 5 Oct 1802
7. Hanna Maria Dorothea   b. 23 Aug 1805   d. 14 Apr 1807
8. Sophia   b. 31 Mar 1808   d. 23 Feb 1809
9. Catharina Sophia   b. 19 May 1811

Christoph divorced his first wife and married three other times (but had no additional children):
Christoph married second: Christina Sophia Steker
m. 27 Aug 1824   Ülitz, Ülitz, Mecklenburg-Schwerin
d. 9 Jan 1828   Brenz
Christoph married third: Elizabeth Schmalfeld
m. 23 Jan 1829   Brenz
d. 26 Sep 1830   Brenz

Christoph married fourth: Anna Catharina Elisabeth Bulls
m. 27 Nov 1832   Brenz

Family information (arranged by listed dates and places unless noted) comes from:

Evangelishe Kirche Brenz. *Kirchenbuch, 1787-1875.* Family History Library, Salt Lake City: The Genealogical Society of Utah, 1951, microfilm #69018.
Note: Includes records for Neu Brenz

Evangelishe Kirche Garwitz. *Kirchenbuch, 1639-1875.* Family History Library, Salt Lake City: The Genealogical Society of Utah, 1951, microfilm #69112.

Evangelishe Kirche Gross Laasch. *Kirchenbuch, 1640-1904.* Family History Library, Salt Lake City: The Genealogical Society of Utah, 1951, microfilm #69170 and 69172.

Evangelishe Kirche Ülitz. *Kirchenbuch, 1786-1898.* Family History Library, Salt Lake City: The Genealogical Society of Utah, 1951, microfilm #69628.

* Date estimated. Brenz records don't date back this far because of a fire. Parents' names come from marriage record.

Chapter Two
Different Worlds: Mina's Parents

Father: Johann Joachim Christian Haker (Christian)
    (son of Christian Frederick Haker and Elisabeth Dorothea Satow)
b. 24 Mar 1809   Nevern, Neukloster, Mecklenburg-Schwerin
d. 21 Apr 1844   Nevern, Neukloster, Mecklenburg-Schwerin

married: 28 Nov 1833 in Neukloster, Neukloster, Mecklenburg-Schwerin

Mother: Dorothea Maria Sophia Warning
    (daughter of Johann Hinrich Warning and Sophia Elisabeth Engel)
b. 4 Dec 1813   Nevern, Neukloster, Mecklenburg-Schwerin
d. 4 Dec 1886   Nevern, Neukloster, Mecklenburg-Schwerin

Children: (born in Nevern and christened in Neukloster)
1. Child born dead   b. 3 Dec 1833
                                  d. 3 Dec 1833 in Nevern
2. Johann Carl Christian   b. 5 Jul 1835
3. Maria Wilehlmina Elisa   b. 2 Sep 1837
        m. Johann Joachim Christian Haker, 8 Feb 1861 in Neukloster
                                  d. 3 Jul 1868 in Neukloster
4. Maria Mina Elisa Frederica b. 27 Feb 1840
        m. Georg Ernst Fredrick Albrecht, 24 Jun 1864 in Goldebee, Goldebee, Mecklenburg-
            Schwerin
                                  d. 4 Apr 1916 in Fremont, Wayne, Utah

Dorothea married second: Joachim Heinrich Engel (Heinrich)
    6 Mar 1820   Tollow, Goldebee, Mecklenburg-Schwerin
    ? Jul 1845   Neukloster
    ?p 1894   Goldebee

born in Nevern and christened in Neukloster, deaths in Nevern unless otherwise

1. Child born dead   b. 25 Aug 1846   d. 25 Aug 1846
2. Elisa Wilhelmina Anna   b. 24 Nov 1847   d. 16 May 1881 in Neukloster
    m. Johann Joachim Christian, 24 Nov 1864 in Neukloster
3. Anna Maria Sophia   b. 17 Jul 1850
4. Child born dead   b. 1 Mar 1852   d. 1 Mar 1852
5. Carl Friedrich Christian   b. 1 Mar 1853   d. 28 Oct 1856
6. Dorothea Elisa Maria Wilhelmina   b. 29 Mar 1855   d. 4 Oct 1895 in Benz, Goldebee,
                                                                 Mecklenburg-Schwerin
    m. Joachim Johann Christian Haker, 27 Oct 1882 in Goldebee
7. Johann Alexander Ludwig Wilhelm   b. 5 Mar 1857   d. 4 Mar 1858

Family information (arranged by listed dates and places unless noted) comes from:

Evangelishe Kirche Goldebee. *Kirchenbuch, 1654-1913.* Family History Library, Salt Lake City: The Genealogical Society of Utah, 1951, microfilm #69127.

Evangelishe Kirche Neukloster. *Kirchenbuch, 1694-1905.* Family History Library, Salt Lake City: The Genealogical Society of Utah, 1952, microfilm #69392-69394.

Wayne County (Utah) County Clerk. *Register of Deaths, 1898-1957.* Family History Library, Salt Lake City: The Genealogical Society of Utah, 1967, microfilm #484607.

Chapter Three
Winds of Change: Georg's Parents

Father: Johann Jochim Harprecht (or Albrecht)
    (son of Hans Jochim Christopher Harprecht and Christina Maria Gienken)
b. 12 Dec 1795   Brenz, Brenz, Mecklenburg-Schwerin
d. 28 Oct 1859   Weselsdorf, Gross Laasch, Mecklenburg-Schwerin

Johann married first: Anne Marie Louise Elisabeth Garbig
b. 28 May 1796*
m. 1819   Osterburg, Osterburg, Saxony
d. 6 May 1828   Osterburg

*Children in all three marriages were christened as Albrecht instead of Harprecht.
Children: (born and christened in Osterburg, deaths also in Osterburg)
1. Johann Carl Andreas   b. 21 Nov 1819   d. 28 Oct 1826
2. Anna Dorothea Margarita   b. 16 Nov 1821   d. 23 Nov 1821
3. Johann Joachim Gottfried   b. 1 Oct 1822   d. 4 May 1830
4. Friedrich Wilhelm   b. 5 Sep 1824
    m. Friedrika Elisabeth Maria Steints, 25 Apr 1856 in Gross Laasch
5. August Friedrich Wilhelm   b. 19 Jul 1826   d. 14 Feb 1827
6. Anna Catharina Elisabeth   b. 9 Feb 1828

Johann married second: Anna Catharina Louise Schulz
b. 18 Mar 1800*
m. 21 Sep 1828   Osterburg
d. 27 Feb 1833   Osterburg

Children: (born and christened in Osterburg, death also in Osterburg)
1. Daughter born dead   b. 22 Jul 1829   d. 22 Jul 1829
2. Augusta Louisa Wilhelmina   b. 12 Sep 1830
    m. Johann Joachim Christian Haman, 15 Jan 1864 in Gross Laasch

Johann married third: 30 Dec 1833 in Gross Laasch, Gross Laasch, Mecklenburg-Schwerin

Mother: Sophia Maria Elizabeth Tiedemann
 (daughter of Friedrich David Tiedemann and Maria Elisabeth Mietz)
b. 22 Feb 1806   Weselsdorf, Gross Laasch, Mecklenburg-Schwerin

Children: (born in Weselsdorf and christened in Gross Laasch)
1. Magdalene Sophia Maria   b. 10 Nov 1834
  m. Johann Joachim Christian Gieren, 17 Feb 1864 in Gross Laasch
          d. 10 Mar 1911 in Niendorf, Gross Laasch, Mecklen-
          burg-Schwerin
2. **Georg Ernst Frederick Ferdinand** b. 20 Dec 1837
  m. Maria Mina Elisa Frederica, 24 Jun 1864 in Goldebee, Goldebee, Mecklenburg-Schwerin
          d. 1 Mar 1914 in Fremont, Wayne, Utah
3. Sophia Dorothea Maria   b. 26 May 1841
          d. 20 Feb 1842 in Gross Laasch

Family information (arranged by listed dates and places unless noted) comes from:

Evangelishe Kirche Brenz. *Kirchenbuch, 1787-1875.* Family History Library, Salt Lake City: The Genealogical Society of Utah, 1951, microfilm #69018.

Evangelishe Kirche Goldebee. *Kirchenbuch, 1654-1913.* Family History Library, Salt Lake City: The Genealogical Society of Utah, 1951, microfilm #69127.

Evangelishe Kirche Gross Laasch. *Kirchenbuch, 1640-1904.* Family History Library, Salt Lake City: The Genealogical Society of Utah, 1951, microfilm #69170 and 69172.

Evangelishe Kirche Osterburg. *Kirchenbuchduplikat, 1654-1815.* Family History Library, Salt Lake City: Magdeburg Staatsarchiv, 1983, microfilm #1335489.

Wayne County (Utah) County Clerk. *Register of Deaths, 1898-1957.* Family History Library, Salt Lake City: The Genealogical Society of Utah, 1967, microfilm #484607.

*The birth dates from Johann's first two wives come from their respective marriage records.

Chapter Four
A New Identity: Georg and Mina's Journey

Father: Georg Ernst Frederick Ferdinand Albrecht (George)
 (son of Johann Jochem Harprecht and Sophia Maria Elizabeth Tiedemann)
b. 20 Dec 1837   Weselsdorf, Gross Laasch, Mecklenburg-Schwerin
d. 1 Mar 1914   Fremont, Wayne, Utah

married: 24 Jan 1864 in Goldebee, Goldebee, Mecklenburg-Schwerin

Mother: Maria Mina Elisa Frederica Haker (Mina or Minnie)
 (daughter of Johann Joachim Christian Haker and Dorothea Maria Sophia Warning)
 27 Feb 1840   Nevern, Neukloster, Mecklenburg-Schwerin
 5 Apr 1916   Fremont, Wayne, Utah

en: (birthplaces all in Mecklenburg except #10)

1. **Johann Christoph (John)**   b. 4 Jun 1862 in Benz, Goldebee
     m. Chasty Margaret Harris, 27 Nov 1885 in Fayette, Sanpete, Utah
            d. 2 Mar 1933 in Fremont

2. Carl Christian Johann   b. 27 Feb 1864 in Benz
     m. Annie McNiel, 6 Feb 1900 in Fremont
            d. 16 Nov 1930 in Weiser, Washington, Idaho

3. Heinrich Wilhelm Carl (Henry)   b. 19 Aug 1866 in Wismar
     m. Rosann Harris, 10 Feb 1888 in Fremont
            d. 11 Apr 1939 in Fremont

4. Anna Elise Maria Dorothea   b. 27 Aug 1869 in Wismar
            d. 10 Apr 1870 in Wismar

5. Emma Sophia Elizabeth   b. 16 May 1871 in Wismar
     m. George Morrell, 10 Feb 1888 in Fremont
            d. 9 Dec 1950 in Fremont

6. Georg Hettmuth Wilhelm   b. 30 Sep 1873 in Wismar
     m. Alice Nanny, 22 Jun 1910 in Pocatello, Bannock, Idaho
            d. 16 Oct 1956 Lava Hot Springs, Bannock, Idaho

7. Wilhelmine Caroline Christiane   b. 20 Nov 1875 in Gross Tessin
(Mina or Minnie)
     m. Hyrum Morrell, 27 Mar 1894 in Fremont
            d. 24 Dec 1942 in Fremont

8. Meta Anna Caroline   b. 6 Jul 1877 in Gross Tessin
     m. Silas Edward Tanner, 17 Aug 1897 in Fremont
            d. 29 Jan 1906 in Fremont

9. Frederick Wilhelm Carl   b. 1 Nov 1879 in Gross Tessin
            d. 16 Nov 1880 in Manti, Sanpete, Utah

10. Jacob Joseph   b. 12 Jun 1883 in Dover, Sanpete, Utah
     m. Ada Matilda Taylor, 14 Oct 1903 in Fremont
            d. 12 Jun 1944 in Loa, Wayne, Utah

Birth information comes from (arranged according to date and place listed above):

Church of Jesus Christ of Latter-day Saints Fremont Ward (Fremont, Utah). *Record of Members, 1886-1950.* Family History Library, Salt Lake City: The Genealogical Society of Utah, 1967, microfilm #25941.
     Since a birth record doesn't exist, I relied on this source for Jacob's birth.

Evangelishe Kirche Goldebee. *Kirchenbuch, 1654-1913.* Family History Library, Salt Lake City: The Genealogical Society of Utah, 1951, microfilm #69127.

Evangelishe Kirche Gross Laasch. *Kirchenbuch, 1640-1904.* Family History Library, Salt Lake City: The Genealogical Society of Utah, 1951, microfilm #69170 and 69172.

Evangelishe Kirche Gross Tessin. *Kirchenbuch, 1671-1934.* Family History Library, Salt Lake City: The Genealogical Society of Utah, 1951, microfilm #69180.

Evangelishe Kirche Neukloster. *Kirchenbuch, 1694-1905.* Family History Library, Salt Lake City: The Genealogical Society of Utah, 1952, microfilm #69392-69394.

Evangelishe Kirche Wismar Kirche Sank Nicolai. *Kirchenbuch, 1643-1894.* Family History Library, Salt Lake City: The Genealogical Society of Utah, 1952, microfilm, #69656.

Marriage information comes from (applicable person listed below each record):

Bannock County (Idaho), County Clerk. *Bannock County Births, Marriages, and Deaths,*

1905-1915. Family History Library, Pocatello, Idaho: Pocatello State Archives, 1975, microfilm #1527293.
Georg (b. 1873)

Evangelishe Kirche Goldebee. *Kirchenbuch, 1654-1913.* Family History Library, Salt Lake City: The Genealogical Society of Utah, 1951, microfilm #69127.
Georg and Mina (parents)

Piute County (Utah) County Clerk. *Marriage License Records, 1872-1966.* Family History Library, Salt Lake City: The Genealogical Society of Utah, 1983, microfilm #484608.
Note: Fremont was once part of Piute County.
Heinrich – p. 5, Emma – p. 5

Church of Jesus Christ of Latter-day Saints. Fayette Ward (Fayette, Utah). *Record of Members, 1871-1950.* Family History Library, Salt Lake City: The Genealogical Society of Utah, 1952, microfilm #25955.
Johann (John)

Wayne County (Utah) County Clerk. *Marriage License Records, 1892-1978.* Family History Library, Salt Lake City: The Genealogical Society of Utah, 1996, microfilm #484603.
Carl – p. 52, Wilhelmine – p. 14, Meta – p. 36, Jacob – p. 81

Death information comes from (applicable person listed below each record):

Church of Jesus Christ of Latter-day Saints Fremont Ward (Fremont, Utah). *Record of Members, 1886-1950.* Family History Library, Salt Lake City: The Genealogical Society of Utah, 1967, microfilm #25941.
Note: As I was unable to locate Meta or Jacob's death in the Wayne County death register, I found death dates in membership records here.

Evangelishe Kirche Wismar Kirche Sank Nicolai. *Kirchenbuch, 1643-1894.* Family History Library, Salt Lake City: The Genealogical Society of Utah, 1952, microfilm, #69656.
Anna

"Obituary for George Elmer Albrecht." *Salt Lake Tribune,* 18 October 1956, p. 29, copy in author's possession.
Georg (b 1873)

Tattom, Louisa. *Cemetery Records of Manti, Utah.* Salt Lake City: Genealogical Society of Utah, 1936.
Frederick

Wayne County (Utah) County Clerk. *Register of Deaths, 1898-1957.* Family History Library, Salt Lake City: The Genealogical Society of Utah, 1967, microfilm #484607.
Georg (father), Mina (mother), Johann (John), Carl, Heinrich, Emma, Wilhelmine

Chapter Five
Ordinary Lives: Karsti's Grandparents

RSTI'S PATERNAL GRANDPARENTS
er: Nils Jepsson
1734*
ı 1806   Svinarp, Esarp, Malmöhus, Sweden

Nils married first: Kirst Pehrsdotter
b. Abt 1741*
m. 6 Dec 1760   Esarp
d. 9 Feb 1772   Svinarp

Children: (first three born in Svinarp, christened in Esarp, last born and christened in Genarp, Malmöhus, Sweden)
1. Matta   b. 27 Sep 1762
    m. Nils, 20 May 1782 in Esarp
2. Anna   b. 9 Oct 1766
    m. Elias Andersson, 14 Jul 1799 in Esarp
3. Jeppa   b. 9 Jan 1769
4. Jeppa   b. 8 Jan 1771

Nils married second: Kirsti Olofsdotter
b. Abt 1745*
m. 10 Nov 1772   Everlöv, Everlöv, Malmöhus, Sweden
d. 29 Mar 1776   Svinarp

Child: (born in Svinarp and christened in Esarp)
1. Olof   b. 26 Oct 1772

Nils married third: 12 Oct 1777 Veberöd, Veberöd, Malmöhus, Sweden

Mother: Marna Pehsdotter
    (daughter of Par Nilsson and Anna Parsdotter)
b. 20 Nov 1755   Veberöd, Veberöd, Malmöhus, Sweden
d. 20 Sep 1791   Esarp, Esarp, Malmöhus, Sweden

Children: (born in Svinarp and christened in Esarp)
1. Pehr   b. 10 Oct 1778
                                 d. 14 Nov 1788 in Esarp
2. Anders   b. 8 Jul 1781
    m. second: Hanna Olsdotter, 13 Oct 1830 in Esarp
3. Kirsti   b. 11 Oct 1783
    m. Pehr Akasson, 29 May 1807 in Esarp
4. **Nils**   b. 12 Oct 1786
    m. first: Anna Jonsdotter in Bonderup, Bonderup, Malmöhus, Sweden
    m. second: Lisbeth Nilsdotter, 2 Nov 1823 in Kyrkheddinge, Kyrkheddinge, Malmöhus, Sweden
                                 d. 6 Jun 1858 in Vallby, Kyrkheddinge, Malmöhus, Sweden
5. Ingar   b. 28 Jan 1789
6. Pehr   b. 13 Feb 1791

KARSTI'S MATERNAL GRANDPARENTS
Father: Nils Nilsson
    (son of Nils Martensson and Lisbeth Olofsdotter)
b. 15 Jul 1763   Blentarp, Blentarp, Malmöhus, Sweden
d. 6 Mar 1830   Vismarlov, Hyby, Malmöhus, Sweden

Nils married first: 15 May 1780 in Everlöv, Everlöv Malmöhus, Sweden

Mother: Karna Larsdotter
    (daughter of Lars Johansson and Beretha Trulsdotter)

b. 10 Feb 1761   Bosarp, Blentarp, Malmöhus, Sweden
d. 11 May 1822   Kornheddinge, Kyrkheddinge, Malmöhus, Sweden

Children: (born in Östarp and christened in Everlöv, died in Östarp unless otherwise noted)
1. Matta   b. 25 Jul 1780
                       d. 7 Apr 1801
2. Bengta   b. 29 Oct 1782
      m. first: Lar Jonsson, 30 Aug 1805 in Everlöv m. second: Nils Hansson**
3. Kirstina   b. 16 Mar 1785
      m. Jeppa Ros, 18 Jun 1806 in Everlöv
                       d. 22 Nov 1844 in Torreberga, Nevishög, Malmöhus
4. Marten   b. 2 Jun 1787
      m. Anna Andersson, 10 Nov 1810 in Veberöd
5. Elina   b. 6 Jun 1790
      m. Pehr Ericsson**
6. Ingar   b. 21 Mar 1793
                       d. 19 Aug 1799
7. Anna   b. 10 Sep 1795
      m. Bengt Wall, 23 Sep 1819 in Kyrkheddinge
8. Lisbeth   b. 29 Dec 1797
                       d. 17 Jan 1799
9. **Lisbeth**   b. 11 Oct 1799
      m. Nils Nilsson, 2 Nov 1823 in Kyrkheddinge
                       d. 2 Nov 1823 in Vallby
10. Nils   b. 18 Dec 1801
11. Matta   b. 28 Mar 1804
      m. Sven Mattson, 29 Oct 1822 in Kyrkheddinge

Nils married second: Kerstina Andersdotter
      m. 27 Dec 1822   Esarp

Family information (arranged by listed dates and places unless noted) comes from:

Svenska Kyrkan, Blentarp socken. *Kyrkoböcker, 1662-1901.* Family History Library, Salt Lake City: The Genealogical Society of Utah, 1995, microfilm #144940, items 1-4.

Svenska Kyrkan, Bonderup socken. *Kyrkoböcker, 1681-1906.* Family History Library, Salt Lake City: The Genealogical Society of Utah, 1995, microfilm #144875.

Svenska Kyrkan, Esarp socken. *Kyrkoböcker, 1671-1899.* Family History Library, Salt Lake City: The Genealogical Society of Utah, 1974, microfilm #145115.

Svenska Kyrkan, Everlöv socken. *Kyrkoböcker, 1662-1894.* Family History Library, Salt Lake City: The Genealogical Society of Utah, 1974, microfilm #145111, items 1-3.

Svenska Kyrkan, Genarp socken. *Kyrkoböcker, 1692-1894.* Family History Library, Salt Lake City: The Genealogical Society of Utah, 1974, microfilm #145445.

Svenska Kyrkan, Hyby socken. *Kyrkoböcker, 1689-1894.* Family History Library, Salt Lake City: The Genealogical Society of Utah, 1974, microfilm 145528.

...ska Kyrkan, Kyrkheddinge socken. *Kyrkoböcker, 1683-1899.* Family History Library, Salt City: The Genealogical Society of Utah, 1974, microfilm #145783, items 4-6.

...yrkan, Nevishog socken. *Kyrkoböcker, 1705-1897.* Family History Library, Salt Lake

City: The Genealogical Society of Utah, 1952, microfilm #146670.

Svenska Kyrkan, Veberöd socken. *Kyrkoböcker,1675-1896.* Family History Library, Salt Lake City: The Genealogical Society of Utah, 1952, microfilm #147702.

*Nils's birth year and the birth years for his first two wives are estimated based on ages at death.

** The spouses' names for Elina and Bengta come from their father's probate record: Sverige Häradsrätt (Bara). "Bouppteckningar, Entry for Nils Nilsson." Vol F II a: 31, nr. 26. Lund Archive, Lund, Sweden.

Chapter Six
Choices: Karsti's Parents

Father: Nils Nilsson
   (son of Nils Jeppson and Marna Pehrsdotter)
b. 12 Oct 1786   Svinarp, Esarp, Malmöhus, Sweden
d. 29 May 1858   Vallby, Kyrkheddinge, Malmöhus, Sweden

Nils married first: Anna Jonsdotter
b. Abt 1788   Bonderup, Bonderup, Malmöhus, Sweden
m. 29 Nov 1817   Bonderup
d. 6 Apr 1823   Vallby

Children: (born in Vallby and christened in Kyrkheddinge, death in Vallby also)
1. Marna   b. 4 Oct 1818
2. Pehr   b. 4 Apr 1821   d. 9 Nov 1823

Nils married second: 2 Nov 1823 in Kyrkheddinge, Kyrkheddinge, Malmöhus, Sweden

Mother: Lisbeth Nilsdotter
   (daughter of Nils Nilsson and Karna Larsdotter)
b. 11 Oct 1799   Everlöv, Everlöv, Malmöhus, Sweden
d. 10 Jan 1847   Vallby, Kyrkheddinge, Malmöhus, Sweden

Children: (born in Vallby and christened in Kyrkheddinge, deaths in Vallby unless otherwise noted)
1. Anna   b. 20 Dec 1824   d. 25 Jan 1847
2. Nils   b. 14 May 1826
      m. 1856, Karna Hansdotter in Kyrkheddinge
                                  d. 3 Apr 1885 in Mt. Pleasant, Sanpete, Utah
3. Pehr   b. 28 Mar 1829   d. 2 Jan 1833
4. Karna   b. 23 Jul 1831   d. 13 Jan 1847
5. Hanna   b. 26 Dec 1834
      m. 1859, Lars Andersson in Esarp
6. Elna   b. 25 Feb 1839
      m. 15 Nov 1861*
7. Kerstina (Karsti)   b. 19 Aug 1843
      m. 1862, Edmond Harris probably in Millcreek, Salt Lake, Utah**
                                  d. 14 Mar 1901 Fremont, Wayne, Utah

Family information (arranged by appropriate date and place) comes from:

Church of Jesus Christ of Latter-day Saints Genealogical Society Library Division. *Cemetery Records, Wayne County, Utah*. Salt Lake City: Genealogical Society of Utah, 1937.

Svenska Kyrkan, Bonderup socken. *Kyrkoböcker, 1681-1906*. Family History Library, Salt Lake City: The Genealogical Society of Utah, 1995, microfilm #144875.

Svenska Kyrkan, Esarp socken. *Kyrkoböcker, 1671-1899*. Family History Library, Salt Lake City: The Genealogical Society of Utah, 1952, microfilm #145115.

Svenska Kyrkan, Everlöv socken. *Kyrkoböcker, 1662-1894*. Family History Library, Salt Lake City: The Genealogical Society of Utah, 1952, microfilm # 145111, items 1-3.

Svenska Kyrkan, Kyrkheddinge socken. *Kyrkoböcker, 1683-1899*. Family History Library, Salt Lake City: The Genealogical Society of Utah, 1974, microfilm #145783, items 4-6.

*A marriage record has not yet been located. This marriage date comes from the Esarp clerical survey. Elna had been working here as a maidservant: Svenska Kyrkan, Esarp socken. *Kyrkoböcker, 1671-1899, Husförhörslängd*. Family History Library, Salt Lake City: The Genealogical Society of Utah, 1974, microfilm #497283.

**There is no source for this marriage. This date and place represent an estimate. See chapter eight (text) for more information.

Chapter Eight
Mistakes: Edmond's Parents

Father: James Harris
b. Abt 1799   Buckinghamshire, England
d. Aft 1851   Buckinghamshire, England*

James married first: 1 Sep 1821 in Wingrave, Buckingham, England

Mother: Elizabeth Johns
b. Abt 1800   near Buckinghamshire, England*

Children: (all places are in Buckinghamshire, England unless otherwise noted)
1. James Johns   b. 3 Jan 1822 in Wingrave
2. Edmond Johns   b. 14 Aug 1825 in Wingrave
    m. first: Eliza Barrett, 9 May 1847 in London, England
    m. second: Kerstina Nilsdotter, 1862 in Millcreek, Salt Lake, Utah**
           d. 23 Sep 1886 in Gunnison, Sanpete, Utah
3. Mary   b. 19 Sep 1830 in Whitchurch
           d. 8 Jan 1832 in Whitchurch
4. James   b. 4 Nov 1832 in Whitchurch
           d. 8 Jul 1852 in Buckingham
   William   b. 10 May 1835 in Whitchurch
   homas   b. 4 Feb 1837 in Whitchurch
           d. 13 Jan 1838 in Whitchurch
     anuel   b. 12 Jul 1840 in Steeple Claydon
           d. 20 Mar 1853 in Buckingham
           b. 4 Nov 1845 in Steeple Claydon

possible other child:
Sarah Harris   b. between 1825 and 1830***

James married second: Ann Norris Coles
m. 26 July 1850   Buckingham

Family information (arranged by appropriate date and place) comes from:

Church of England, Chapelry of Gawcott (Buckingham). *Parish Registers, 1806-1898*. Family History Library, Salt Lake City: The Genealogical Society of Utah, 1995, microfilm ##1042383, item 7-10.

Church of England, Parish Church of Steeple Claydon. *Parish Register, 1575-1964*. Family History Library, Salt Lake City: The Genealogical Society of Utah, 1969-2000, microfilm #1967094.

Church of England, Parish Church of Whitchurch. *Parish Register, 1653-1991*. Family History Library, Salt Lake City: The Genealogical Society of Utah, 1995, microfilm ##1966918 and 1966919.

Church of England, Parish Church of Wingrave. *Parish Register, 1550-1965*. Family History Library, Salt Lake City: The Genealogical Society of Utah, 1995, microfilm #1966920 and 1966921.

Church of England, St. Pancras Old Church (London). *Parish Register, 1660-1916*. Family History Library, Salt Lake City: The Genealogical Society of Utah, 1995, microfilm 598339.

Church of Jesus Christ of Latter-day Saints, Gunnison Stake (Utah). *Cemetery Records: Axtell, Centerfield, Fayette, and Gunnison in Sanpete County, Utah*. Family History Library, 1934, p. 27.

* Dates for James and Elizabeth are estimates based on the 1841 (in Steeple Claydon) and 1851 (in Buckingham – James only) censuses. Censuses also indicate that James was born in the county, while Elizabeth was not. The last record found to date on James is the 1851 census.

** There is no source for this marriage. This date and place represent an estimate. See chapter eight (text) for more information.

*** A Sarah Harris is found living with them in the 1841 census. It is possible that between Edmond and Mary's births, the family relocated somewhere else where this Sarah was born.

Chapter Nine
Destinations: Edmond and Eliza's Journey

Father: Edmond Johns Harris
    (son of James Harris and Elizabeth Johns)
b. 14 Aug 1825   Wingrave, Buckingham, England
d. 23 Sep 1886   Gunnison, Sanpete, Utah

Edmond married first: Eliza Barrett
b. 9 Oct 1824   London, England
m. 9 May 1847   London
d. 4 Oct 1855   at sea

Children: (both born in Sydney, Australia)
1. Maria   b. 1853
2. Lister   b. 1855   d. 4 Oct 1855, at sea

married second: (see chapter ten for more information)
Kerstina Nilsdotter

Information for Edmond comes from:

Church of England, Parish Church of Wingrave. *Parish Register, 1550-1965*. Family History Library, Salt Lake City: The Genealogical Society of Utah, 1995, microfilm #1966920 and 1966921.

Church of England, St. Pancras Old Church (London). *Parish Register, 1660-1916*. Family History Library, Salt Lake City: The Genealogical Society of Utah, 1995, microfilm 598339.

Church of Jesus Christ of Latter-day Saints, Gunnison Stake (Utah). *Cemetery Records: Axtell, Centerfield, Fayette, and Gunnison in Sanpete County, Utah*. Family History Library, 1934, p. 27.

Other information comes from:

Church of Jesus Christ of Latter-day Saints New South Wales District. *Record of Members, 1852-1952*. Family History Library, Salt Lake City: The Genealogical Society of Utah, 1967, microfilm #105320.
Note: Eliza's birth date is found in these membership records.

Death information for Eliza and Lister is based the accounts of the *Julia Ann*, the ship they took from Australia to the US. Read: Devitry-Smith, John. "The Wreck of the Julia Ann." *BYU Studies* 29:2 (1989): 5–29.

Birth dates for the children are estimated and based on later records. For example, see the list of passengers on board the *Julia Ann*: "List of Passenger on Board." 1856 *Julia Ann* voyage. *Mormon Immigration Index*, CD-ROM, Family History Resource File, Intellectual Reserve INC, 2000.

Chapter Ten
Starting Over: Edmond and Karsti in Utah

Father: Edmond Johns Harris
        (son of James Harris and Elizabeth Johns)
b. 9 Jul 1824   Wingrave, Buckingham, England
d. 23 Sep 1886   Gunnison, Sanpete, Utah

married second: about 1862 near Millcreek*
        (see chapter nine for information about his first marriage to Eliza Barrett)

Mother: Kerstina Nilsdotter (Karsti)
        (daughter of Nils Nilsson and Lisbeth Nilsdotter)
* 9 Aug 1843   Vallby, Kyrkheddinge, Malmöhus, Sweden
  Mar 1901   Fremont, Wayne, Utah

        * (birthplaces, all in Utah, given below)

1. Mary Elisabeth   b. 1 Jan 1864 in Millcreek**
     m. Brigham Pierce, 6 Jul 1887 in Logan, Cache, Utah
                           d. 1 Jun 1930 in Juarez, Mexico
2. Moroni Jay   b. 10 Nov 1864 in Spring Lake, Utah, Utah
                           d. 9 Dec 1921 in Salina, Sevier, Utah
3. Ephraim   b. 9 Oct 1866 in Spring Lake
4. Chasty Margaret   b. 25 Jun 1868 in Spring Lake
     m. John Albrecht, 27 Nov 1885 in Fayette, Sanpete, Utah
                           d. 15 Feb 1950 in Loa, Wayne, Utah
5. Rosann   b. 19 Jul 1870 in Spring Lake
     m. Henry Albrecht, 10 Feb 1888 in Fremont
                           d. 15 Mar 1952 in Fremont
6. Rachel Rebecca   b. 23 Jun 1876 in Spring Lake
     m. Eli Curtis, 29 Jan 1891 in Manti, Sanpete, Utah
                           d. 10 Apr 1898 in Levan, Juab, Utah
7. Joseph   b. 30 Dec 1879 in Gunnison
                           d. 1 Jun 1884 in Gunnison
8. Sarah Ellen   b. 15 Jun 1881 in Gunnison
     m. Brigham Pierce, 1904 in Juarez, Mexico***
                           d. 28 Nov 1941 in Juarez, Mexico

Birth information comes from (applicable person listed below each record):

Church of England, Parish Church of Wingrave. *Parish Register, 1550-1965.* Family History Library, Salt Lake City: The Genealogical Society of Utah, 1995, microfilm #1966920 and 1966921.
     Edmond

Church of Jesus Christ of Latter-day Saints, Gunnison Ward (Utah). *Record of Members, 1861-1945.* Family History Library, Salt Lake City: The Genealogical Society of Utah, 1951, microfilm #25977.
Note: In the absence of actual birth records, the following children's births were taken from church membership records: Mary, Moroni, Chasty, Rosann, Rachel

Svenska Kyrkan, Kyrkheddinge socken. *Kyrkoböcker, 1683-1899.* Family History Library, Salt Lake City: The Genealogical Society of Utah, 1952, microfilm #145782 and 145783.
     Karsti

Note: Birth information for Joseph and Sarah Ellen come from their death records. See death information below. Birth information for Ephraim comes from family records.

Marriage information comes from (applicable person listed below each record):

Cache County (Utah) County Clerk. *Marriage Records, 1887-1966.* Family History Library, Salt Lake City: The Genealogical Society of Utah, 1966, microfilm #430301.
     Mary – vol B, p. 48

Church of Jesus Christ of Latter-day Saints. Fayette Ward (Fayette, Utah). *Record of Members, 1871-1950.* Family History Library, Salt Lake City: The Genealogical Society of Utah, 1952, microfilm ##25955.
     Chasty

Sanpete County (Utah) County Clerk. *Marriage License Records, 1888-1966.* Family History Library, Salt Lake City: The Genealogical Society of Utah, 1966, microfilm # 48112
     Rachel – vol 2, p. 10

Piute County (Utah) County Clerk. *Marriage License Records, 1872-1966.* Family History Library, Salt Lake City: The Genealogical Society of Utah, 1983, microfilm #484608.
Note: Fremont was once part of Piute County.
   Rosann – p. 5

Death information comes from (applicable person listed below each record):

Church of Jesus Christ of Latter-day Saints Genealogical Society Library Division. *Cemetery Records, Wayne County.* Utah. Salt Lake City: Genealogical Society of Utah, 1937.
   Karsti (as Chasty)

Church of Jesus Christ of Latter-day Saints, Gunnison Stake (Utah). *Cemetery Records: Axtell, Centerfield, Fayette, and Gunnison in Sanpete County, Utah.* Family History Library, Typescript, 1934, p. 27.
   Edmond, Joseph

Church of Jesus Christ of Latter-day Saints Juarez Ward (Chihuahua). *Record of Members, 1887-1948.* Family History Library, Salt Lake City: The Genealogical Society of Utah, 1952, microfilm #35130.
Note: Sarah Ellen is included in both the listing of deaths and in the membership records. Mary is found only in the membership records.
   Sarah Ellen, Mary

Juab County (Utah) County Clerk. *Register of Deaths, 1898-1905.* Family History Library, Salt Lake City: The Genealogical Society of Utah, 1966, microfilm #482020.
   Rachel

Wayne County (Utah) County Clerk. Register of Deaths, 1898-1957. Family History Library, Salt Lake City: The Genealogical Society of Utah, 1967, microfilm #484607.
   Chasty

Utah Department of Health, Bureau of Vital Records and Statistics. *Utah Death Certificates, 1904-1951.* Family History Library, Salt Lake City: The Genealogical Society of Utah, 2001, microfilm # 2259285.
   Moroni – p. 142, Rosanna – p. 01

* There is no source for this marriage. This date and place represent an estimate See chapter eight (text) for more information.

**No birth record exists for Mary Elizabeth, and birth dates in other records differ. As footnote one for chapter ten states: Some records list 1 January 1864, as given here. However, Edmond and Karsti's next child, Moroni Johns, is listed as being born 10 November 1864. Although these two dates are theoretically possible, they are unlikely. Gunnison ward records give her birth date in two different places as both 31 December 1862 and 31 December 1864.

***This date and place represent my best guess. I have been unable to find a marriage date. Juarez Ward records show that Sarah arrived in Juarez from Fremont in January of 1904. By august of 1905, she and Brigham Pierce had their first son. Likely, they married sometime in 4. Also note that this was a polygamous marriage for Brigham Pierce.

Chapter Eleven
Family Connections: Earl's Parents

Father: Johann Christoph Albrecht (John)
 (son of Georg Ernst Frederick Ferdinand Albrecht and Maria Mina Elisa Frederica Haker)
 b. 4 Jun 1862   Brenz, Goldebee, Mecklenburg-Schwerin, Germany
 d. 2 Mar 1933   Fremont, Wayne, Utah

married: 27 Nov 1885 in Fayette, Sanpete, Utah

Mother: Chasty Margaret Harris
 (daughter of Edmond John Harris and Kerstina Nilsson)
 b. 25 Jun 1868   Spring Lake, Utah, Utah
 d. 14 Feb 1950   Loa, Wayne, Utah

Children: Children: (Rosetta was born in Dover, Sanpete, Utah; the rest were born in Fremont)
1. Rosetta   b. 19 Sep 1886
     m: John Lorenzo Sampson, 12 Sep 1906 in Fremont
                                  d. 5 Feb 1977 in Delta, Millard, Utah
2. John William   b. 15 Sep 1888
     m. Clara Russell, 23 Mar 1910 in Fremont
                                  d. 22 Apr 1969 in Richfield, Sevier, Utah
3. **Earl LeRoy**   b. 13 May 1890
     m. Evalena Thompson Balle, 3 Nov 1909 in Manti, Sanpete, Utah
                                  d. 10 May 1968 in Fremont
4. Claude Milton   b. 27 Aug 1892
     m. Laprele McKnight, 6 Jan 1917 in Beaver, Beaver, Utah and
     m. Zella Ireta Fotheringham, 18 Aug 1938 in Richfield
                                  d. 22 Feb 1942 in Cedar City, Iron, Utah
5. Charles Gilbert   b. 6 Oct 1894
                                  d. 25 Mar 1895 in Fremont
6. Levern   b. 1 Jan 1896
     m. Sylvia Regina Murphy, 12 Sep 1918 in Fremont
                                  d. 6 Sep 1973 in Fremont
7. Georg Frederick   b. 28 Apr 1898
                                  d. 15 Sep 1898 in Fremont
8. Minnie   b. 15 Apr 1899
     m. Miel Edwin Pierce, 19 Dec 1917 in Fremont
     m. Thomas Nephi Sant, 8 Sep 1991 in Richfield
                                  d. 23 Feb 1994 in Richfield
9. Leonard   b. 5 Dec 1901
     m. Verda Searle, 4 Sep 1929 in Manti
                                  d. 14 Sep 1988 in Fremont
10. Owen   b. 21 Jun 1904
     m. Nola Ellett, 14 Nov 1927 in Fillmore, Millard, Utah
                                  d. 16 Sep 1938 in Fremont
11. Edwin Wesley   b. 28 Oct 1906
                                  d. 14 Jan 1921 in Fremont
12. Arlo   b. 12 Feb 1909
                                  d. 2 Jan 1913 in Fremont
13. Cleo Chasty   b. 1 Sep 1911
     m. Charles Ellett, 22 Dec 1930 in Fremont
                                  d. 12 Feb 1987 in Fremont

Birth information comes from (applicable person listed below each record):

Evangelishe Kirche Goldebee. *Kirchenbuch, 1654-1913.* Family History Library, Salt Lake City: The Genealogical Society of Utah, 1951, microfilm #69127.
John (father)

Church of Jesus Christ of Latter-day Saints Fremont Ward (Fremont, Utah). *Record of Members, 1886-1950.* Family History Library, Salt Lake City: The Genealogical Society of Utah, 1967, microfilm #25941.
Note: As I could not locate birth records, I used church membership records to verify birth information.
Earl, Claude, Levern, Minnie, Leonard, Owen, Edwin (under Wesley), Cleo Chasty

Church of Jesus Christ of Latter-day Saints, Gunnison Ward (Utah). *Record of Members, 1861-1945.* Family History Library, Salt Lake City: The Genealogical Society of Utah, 1951, microfilm #25977.
Note: Since she is not included in the births, Chasty's birth information comes from the membership records.
Chasty

Note: The births of Charles and Arlo come only from family records. Birth information for Rosetta is included in her obituary (see deaths below). John William's birth date is found on his tombstone (see deaths below).

Marriage information comes from (applicable person listed below each record):

Beaver County (Utah) County Clerk. *Marriage License Records and Applications 1887-1966.* Family History Library, Salt Lake City: The Genealogical Society of Utah, 1966, microfilm #485224.
Claude's first marriage – vol 2, p. 21

Church of Jesus Christ of Latter-day Saints. Fayette Ward (Fayette, Utah). *Record of Members, 1871-1950.* Family History Library, Salt Lake City: The Genealogical Society of Utah, 1952, microfilm ##25955.
John and Chasty's marriage

Millard County (Utah) County Clerk. *Marriage License Records, 1887-1966.* Family History Library, Salt Lake City: The Genealogical Society of Utah, 1996, microfilm #482022.
Owen - vol C, p. 329

Sevier County (Utah) County Clerk. *Marriage License Records and Applications, 1887-1966.* Family History Library, Salt Lake City: The Genealogical Society of Utah, 1996, microfilm #482037
Claude's second marriage - vol D, p. 411

Wayne County (Utah) County Clerk. *Marriage License Records, 1892-1978.* Family History Library, Salt Lake City: The Genealogical Society of Utah, 1996, microfilm #484603.
Rosetta - p. 110, John W. - p. 146, Earl - p. 132, Levern -p. 211, Minnie's first marriage – p. 210, Leonard - p. 285, Cleo Chasty - p. 293

nformation on Minnie's second marriage comes from her obituary. See death ʾion below.

ʾation comes from (applicable person listed below each record):

Delta Family History Center (Delta, Utah). *Obituaries: Millard County, Utah – Death Claims Early Pioneer.* Family History Library, Delta Utah Family History Center, 2002. CD-ROM.
> Rosetta – S-23.

"Obituary for Minnie A. Pierce." *Deseret News,* Salt Lake City. http://www.deseretnews.com/article/338822/DEATH--MINNIE-A-PIERCE.html (accessed January 2010).

Utah Department of Health, Bureau of Vital Records and Statistics. *Utah Death Certificates, 1904-1951,* Family History Library, Salt Lake City: The Genealogical Society of Utah, 2001.
> Owen – microfilm #2260363, p. 84, Claude-microfilm #2260557, p. 11

Wayne County (Utah) County Clerk. *Register of Deaths, 1898-1957.* Family History Library, Salt Lake City: The Genealogical Society of Utah, 1967, microfilm #484607.
> John (father), Chasty, Edwin

Note: Other deaths were too recent to be included in microfilmed or online death records. Dates were verified in the following sources:

Photographs of tombstones in the Fremont cemetery. Copies in the possession of the author.
> Leonard, Earl, and Cleo Chasty (as well as John, Chasty, Owen, Levern, Minnie, and Leonard)

Find a Grave. "John William Albrecht." Pioneer Cemetery, Salina, Utah. www.findagrave.com (accessed January 2010).
> John William

Note: The deaths of the three children that died young: Charles, George, and Arlo come only from family records.

Chapter Twelve
Point of Convergence: Earl's Family

Father: Earl LeRoy Albrecht
> (son of Johann Christoph Albrecht and Chasty Margaret Harris)
b. 13 May 1890   Fremont, Wayne, Utah
d. 10 May 1968   Fremont, Wayne, Utah

married: 3 Nov 1909 in Manti, Sanpete, Utah

Mother: Evalena Thompson Balle (Eva)
> (daughter of Soren Christian Thompson Balle and Emma Eugenia Thurstrup)
b. 10 Mar 1889   Mayfield, Sanpete, Utah
d. 21 Feb 1980   Fremont, Wayne, Utah

Children: (born in Fremont)
1. Rex LeRoy   b. 4 Sep 1910
> m. Alta Fern Taylor, 1 Jun 1934 in Manti, Sanpete, Utah
> > d. 5 Sep 1987 in Fremont
2. Chasty Emma (Emma)   b. 14 Feb 1913
> m. Donald Fount Brian, 24 Jul 1932 in Fremont
> m. Jeppie Sorenson, 24 Dec 1940 in Fremont
> > d. 22 Aug 2001 in Richfield, Sevier, Utah

3. Nila   b. 6 Aug 1916
       m. Glen Martin Carlson, 18 Jun 1943 in Manti
                           d. 10 Sep 2008 in Orem, Utah, Utah
4. Lula   b. 5 Dec 1918
                           d. 5 Aug 1920 in Fremont
5. Donna   b. 11 Dec 1921
       m. Lewis Goff Blackburn, 21 Apr 1942 in Manti
6. Beth   b. 6 Apr 1924
       m. Alvin Kemp Robinson, 14 Aug 1942 in Fremont

Birth information comes from (applicable person listed below each record):

Church of Jesus Christ of Latter-day Saints Fremont Ward (Fremont, Utah). *Record of Members, 1886-1950.* Family History Library, Salt Lake City: The Genealogical Society of Utah, 1967, microfilm ##25941.
Note: Since they were not found in the birth records, dates for these family members were verified in ward records: Earl, Eva, Rex, Nila

Wayne County (Utah) County Clerk. *Register of Birth and of Deaths, 1899-1948.* Family History Library, Salt Lake City: The Genealogical Society of Utah, 1967, microfilm #498432, items 2-3.
       Donna- p. 842 , Lula-p.656, Beth-p.1086, Emma p. 352

Marriages information comes from (applicable person listed below each record):
Note: Even though Rex and Donna were married in Sanpete County, their marriages are recorded in Wayne County records.

Wayne County (Utah) County Clerk. *Marriage License Records, 1892-1978.* Family History Library, Salt Lake City: The Genealogical Society of Utah, 1996, microfilm #484603.
       Earl and Eva – p. 132, Rex – p. 328, Emma's first marriage – p. 309, Emma's second marriage – p. 404, Donna – p. 411, Beth, p. 414

Sanpete County (Utah) County Clerk. *Marriage License Records, 1888-1966.* Family History Library, Salt Lake City: The Genealogical Society of Utah, 1966, microfilm #48153.
       Nila - vol 9 p. 298

Deaths information comes from (applicable person listed below each record):
Note: At the time of this writing, Beth and Donna are living.

Church of Jesus Christ of Latter-day Saints Fremont Ward (Fremont, Utah). *Record of Members, 1886-1950.* Family History Library, Salt Lake City: The Genealogical Society of Utah, 1967, microfilm #25941.
       Lula

"Obituary for Nila Albrecht Carlson." *Daily Herald*, Provo, Utah.
http://ads.heraldextra.com/articles/2008/09/12/obituaries/329835.txt (accessed January 2010).
       Nila

Obituary for Emma Sorenson." *Deseret News*, Salt Lake City.
p://www.deseretnews.com/article/883776// (accessed January 2010).
       Emma

aphs of the tombstones in the Fremont cemetery and copies of the death certificates
e author's possession) for:
      va, and Rex

Chapter Thirteen
Moving Forward and Leaving Behind: Earl's Descendants

EARL'S AND EVA'S DESCENDANTS

Earl and Eva had six children. My grandfather was one of them.

My Grandfather: Rex LeRoy Albrecht
(son of Earl LeRoy Albrecht and Evalena Thomspon Balle)
b. 4 Sep 1910   Fremont, Wayne, Utah
m. 1 Jun 1934   Manti, Sanpete, Utah
d. 5 Sep 1987   Fremont, Wayne, Utah

My Grandmother: Alta Fern Taylor
(daughter or Robert Allen Taylor and Myrtle Elizabeth Peterson)
b. 7 Apr 1913   Richfield, Sevier, Utah
d. 10 Aug 2006   Bountiful, Davis, Utah (still living in the book)

They had six children: Peggy, Karma, Stan, David, Don, and Karl. All were born in or near Fremont.

Earl and Eva had twenty-nine grandchildren. My father was one of them.

My Father: Don Earl Albrecht
(son of Rex LeRoy Albrecht and Alta Fern Taylor)
b. 1952   Salina, Sevier, Utah
m. 1975   Manti, Sanpete, Utah

My Mother: Carol Jean Mulford
(daughter of Wels Walter Mulford and Wynona Nye Mecham)
b. 1956   Richfield, Sevier, Utah

They had four children: Leslie, Mathew, Scott, and Laura. Two were born in Logan, Cache, Utah and two were born in Bryan, Brazos, Texas.

I am one of Earl's great-grandchildren.

Me: Leslie Jean Albrecht
(daughter of Don Earl Albrecht and Carol Jean Mulford)
b. 1976   Logan, Cache, Utah
m. 1998   Manti, Sanpete, Utah

My Husband: George Willis Huber (David in this book)
(son of Warren Vincent Huber and LouJean Willis)
b. 1974   Washington DC

We have four children: Rachel, Taylor, and Sarah Ann born in Provo, Utah and Madison, Wisconsin and since the writing of this book, Christian, born in Seattle, Washington.

My children are four of Earl's great-great-grandchildren.

Note: No exact dates or sources have been given for this chapter in order to protect the living.

Selected Bibliography

Published Books and Articles

Albrecht, Don and Steve Murdock. *The Sociology of U.S. Agriculture: An Economic Perspective*. Aimes, Iowa: Iowa University Press, 1990.

Albrecht, Don. "The Mechanization of Agriculture: A Historical Case Study of the Implications for Families and Communities." *Culture & Agriculture*, Vol 19:1-2, (1997): 24-32.

Albrecht, Don, Carol Mulford Albrecht, and Stan Albrecht. "Poverty in Nonmetropolitan America: Impacts of Industrial, Employment, and Family Structure Variables." *Rural Sociology*, 65:1 (March 2000): 87-103.

Anderson, Jeffrey L. "Mormons and Germany, 1914-1933: A History of The Church of Jesus Christ of Latter-day Saints in Germany and its Relationship with the German Governments from World War I to the Rise of Hitler." Master's thesis, Brigham Young University, 1991.

Antrei, Albert C.T. and Allen D. Roberts. *A History of Sanpete County*. Salt Lake City: Utah State Historical Society, 1999.

Blum, Jerome. "The Internal Structure and Polity of the Village Community from the Fifteenth to the Nineteenth Century." *Journal of Modern History*, 443 (1971) 541-576.

Bonfield, Lloyd. "European Family Law." In *The History of the European Family: Family Life in the Long Nineteenth Century, 1789-1913*, edited by David I. Kertzer and Marzio Barbagli, 109-154. New Haven: Yale University Press, 2002.

Briggs, Asa. *The Age of Improvement 1783-1867*, second edition. London: Longman, 2000.

Brockliss, Laurence William. "Organization, Training and the Medical Marketplace in the Eighteenth Cenutry." In *The Healing Arts: Health, Disease, and Society in Europe, 1500-1800*, edited by Peter Elmer, 344-380. Manchester: Manchester University Press, 2004.

Brufor, W.H. *Germany in the Eighteenth Century: The Social Background of the Literary Revival*. Cambridge: University Press, 1965.

Centennial Committee. *Memory Book to Commemorate Gunnison Valley's Centenn* 1959. Gunnison: Gunnison Centennial Book Committee, 1959.

Crawley, Peter. "The Constitution of the State of Deseret." In *Life in Utah: Centennial Selections from BYU Studies*, edited by James B. Allen and John W. Welch, 68-88. Provo, Utah: Brigham Young University, 1996.

Creer, Leland Hargrave. *The Founding of an Empire: The Exploration and Colonization of Utah, 1776-1856*. Salt Lake City: Bookcraft, 1947.

Crepon, Tom. *Mecklenburg and West Pomerania: Pictures of a Landscape*. Translated by Patrick Plant. Rostock, Germany: Hinstorff, 1998.

Crull, Richard. *Mecklenburg: Werden und Sein eines Haues*. Leipzig: Belhagen und Klasing, 1903.

Daniels, Roger. *Coming to America: A History of Immigration and Ethnicity in American Life*. New York: HarperCollins Publishers, 1991.

Davis, Richard W. *Political Change and Continuity 1760-1885: A Buckinghamshire Study*. Hamden, Connecticut: Archon Books, 1972.

Devitry-Smith, John. "The Wreck of the Julia Ann." *BYU Studies* 29:2 (1989): 5–29.

Dodge, Theodore Ayrault. *Gustavus Adolphus: A History of the Art of War From its Revival after the Middle Ages to the End of the Spanish Succession War*. Boston: Houghton Mifflin and Company, 1895.

Dribe, Martin. *Leaving Home in a Peasant Society: Economic Fluctuations, Household Dynamics and Youth Migration in Southern Sweden, 1829-1866*. Almqvist and Wiksell International: Sweden, 2000.

Ehmer, Josef. "Marriage." In *The History of the European Family: Family Life in the Long Nineteenth Century, 1789-1913*, edited by David I. Kertzer and Marzio Barbagli, 282-321. New Haven: Yale University Press, 2002.

Encyclopedic History of The Church of Jesus Christ of Latter-day Saints, s.v. "Spring Lake Ward" (Andrew Jensen). Sale Lake City: Deseret News Publishing Company, 1941.

Eriksson, Ingrid and John Rogers. "Mobility in an Agrarian Community: Practical and Methodological Considerations." In *Aristocrats, Farmers, Proletarians: Essays in Swedish Demographic History*, edited by Kurt Ågren, et al., 60-87. Stockholm: Esselte studium, 1973.

Evans, Eric J. *The Forging of the Modern State: Early Industrial Britain 1783-1870*, third edition. Harlow, England: Longman, 2001.

Evans, Richard L. *A Century of Mormonism in Great Britain: A Brief Summary of the Activities of The Church of Jesus Christ of Latter-day Saints in the United Kingdon, with Emphasis on its Introduction One Hundred Years Ago*. Salt Lake City: The Deseret News Press, 1937.

-Chamoux, Antoinette. "Marriage, Widowhood, and Divorce." In *Family Life in Early Modern Times, 1500-1789*, edited by David Kertzer and Marzio Barbagli, 221-256. New Haven: Yale University Press, 2002.

Women in German History: From Bourgeois Emancipation to Sexual Liberation. v York: St. Martin's Press, 1989.

Frost, Robert I. *The Northern Wars, 1558-1721*. New York: Longman, 2000.

Gagliardo, John G. *From Pariah to Patriot: The Changing Image of the German Peasant, 1770-1840*. Lexington, Kentucky: The University Press of Kentucky, 1969.

Gaunt, David. "Family Planning and the Pre-industrial Society: Some Swedish Evidence." In *Aristocrats, Farmers, Proletarians: Essays in Swedish Demographic History*, edited by Kurt Ågren, et al., 28-59. Stockholm: Esselte studium, 1973.

Guttormsson, Loftur. "Parent-Child Relations." In *The History of the European Family: Family Life in the Long Nineteenth Century, 1789-1913*, edited by David I. Kertzer and Marzio Barbagli, 251-281. New Haven: Yale University Press, 2002.

Harnisch, Hartmut. "Peasants and Markets: The Background to the Agrarian Reforms in Feudal Prussia East of the Elbe, 1760-1807." In *The German Peasantry: Conflict and Community in Rural Society from the Eighteenth to the Twentieth Century*, edited by Richard J. Evans, and W.R. Lee, 37-70. New York: St. Martin's Press, 1986.

Hartley, William G. "The Great Florence Fitout." *BYU Studies* 24:3 (1984): 341-171.

Hassam, Andrew. *Sailing to Australia: Shipboard Diaries by Nineteenth-Century British Emigrants*. Manchester: Manchester University Press, 1994.

Hausen, Karin. "Family and Role-Division: The Polarisation of Sexual Stereotypes in the Nineteenth Century – An Aspect of the Dissociation of Work and Family Life." In *The German Family: Essays on the Social History of the Family in Nineteenth- and Twentieth-Century Germany*, edited by Richard J. Evans and W.R. Lee, 51-83. New York: St. Martin's Press, 1986.

Hazell, E.G. *Some Came Free, 1830-1892: A Story of Early Colonial Life at the Limits of Location*. Roebuck Society publication no. 25. Canberra, Australia: Aranda A.C.T., 1978.

Hoppe, Göran. *Enclosure in Sweden: Background and Consequences*. Stockholm: The University of Stockholm, 1981.

Humphries, Jane. "Standard of Living, Quality of Life." In *A Companion to Nineteenth-Century Britain*, edited by Chris Williams, 287-304. Malden, Massachusetts: Blackwell Publishing, 2001.

Hunt, Julian. *Buckingham: A Pictorial History*. Chichester, West Sussex, England: Phillimore & Co. Ltd. in association with Buckinghamshire County Library, 1994.

Inglis, Ken. *The Australian Colonists: An Exploration of Social History 1788-1870*. Melbourne, Australia: Melbourne University Press, 1974.

Jarring, Gunnar and Cilla Ingvar. Berquist. *Skåne: A book on Scania*, edited by Sven Gullers Pictorial: Stockholm, 1988.

Jenner, Mark."Environment, Health and Population." In *The Healing Arts: Health, Dise and Society in Europe, 1500-1800*, edited by Peter Elmer, 284-314. Manchest Manchester University Press, 2004.

Jenson, Andrew. *History of the Scandinavian Mission*. New York: Arno Press, 1979.

Kertzer, David I. and Marzio Barbagli. Introduction to *The History of the European Family: Family Life in the Long Nineteenth Century, 1789-1913*, edited by David I. Kertzer and Marzio Barbagli, ix-xxxviii. New Haven: Yale University Press, 2002.

Kimball, Stanley B. "Sail and Rail Pioneers before 1869." *BYU Studies* 35:2 (1995): 7-42.

Kröhnert, Gesine. *An de Klöndör: Meußer Dorfgeschichten für Kinder*. Schwerin, Germany: Mecklenburgisches Volkskundemuseum, n.d.

Lanier, Britsch, R. *Unto the Islands of the Sea: A History of the Latter-day Saints in the Pacific*. Salt Lake City: Deseret Book, 1986.

Larson, Gustive O. "Federal Government Efforts to 'Americanize' Utah before Admission to Statehood." *BYU Studies* 10:2 (1970): 1-15.

Lee, Robert. "Family and Modernisation: The Peasant Family and Social Change in Nineteenth Century Bavaria." In *The German Family: Essays on the Social History of the Family in Nineteenth and Twentieth-Century Germany*, edited by Richard J. Evans and W.R. Lee, 84-119. Totowa, New Jersey: Barnes and Nobles Books, 1981.

Lever, W.H. *History of Sanpete and Emery Counties, Utah: With Sketches of Cities, Towns and Villages, Chronology of Important Events, Records of Indian Wars, Portraits of Prominent Persons, and Biographies of Representative Citizens*. Ogden, Utah: W.H. Lever, 1898.

Lindemann, Mary. *Health and Healing in Eighteenth-Century Germany*. Baltimore: The John Hopkins University Press, 1996.

Lipscomb, George. *The History and Antiquities of the County of Buckingham*. London: J. & W. Robins, 1841.

Löfgren, Orvar. "The Potato People: The Household Economy and Family Patterns Among the Rural Proletariat in Nineteenth Century Sweden." In *Chance and Change: Social and Economic Studies in Historical Demography in the Baltic Area*, edited by Sune Åkerman, Hans Chr. Johansen, and David Gaunt, 95-106. Odense: Odense University Press, 1978.

Lubinski, Axel. "Overseas Emigration from Mecklenburg-Strelitz: The Geographic and Social Contexts." In *People in Transit: German Migrations in Comparative Perspective, 1820-1930*, edited by Dirk Hoerder and Jörg Nagler, 57-78. German Historical Insitute in Washington DC: Cambridge University Press, 1995.

Lundh, Christer. "Marriage and Economic Change in Sweden During the 18th and 19th Century." In *Marriage and Rural Economy: Western Europe Since 1400*, edited by Isabelle Devos and Liam Kennedy, 217-241. CORN publication series 3. Turnhout: Brepols, 1999.

Lundh, Christer. "Servant Migration in Sweden in the Early Nineteenth Century." *Journal of Family History* 24:1 (1999), 53-73.

—, Martin Dr. *Martin Luther's Small Catechisms: Explained in Questions and Answers with Proof-Texts from Holy Scripture for the Church, School, and Family*. Columbus, Ohio: The Lutheran Book Concern, 1884.

Lyman, Edward Leo. *San Bernardino: The Rise and Fall of a California Community*. Salt Lake City: Signature Books, 1996.

May, Dean L. "Rites of Passage: The Gathering as Cultural Credo." *Journal of Mormon History* 28 (Spring 2002) 1-41.

McKay, John P., Bennett D. Hill, and John Buckler. *A History of World Societies*. Boston: Houghton Mifflin Company, 1992.

Mecklenburg Government. *Grossherzoglich Mecklenburg-Schwerinschwer Staats-Kalender*, 1848-1880. Stadtarchiv Neubrandenburg, Germany.

Melville, J. Keith. "Theory and Practice of Church and State during the Brigham Young Era." In *Life in Utah: Centennial Selections from BYU Studies*, edited by James B. Allen and John W. Welch. Provo, 89-113. Utah: Brigham Young University, 1996.

Michie, Ranald C. *The City of London: Continuity and Change, 1850-1990*. Basingstoke, Hampshire: Macmillan Academic and Professional, 1992.

Mulder, William. *Homeward to Zion: The Mormon Migration from Scandinavia*. Minneapolis: University of Minnesota Press, 2000.

Murphy, Derrick, Richard Staton, Patrick Walsh-Atkins, and Neil Whiskend. *Britian 1815-1918*. London: Collins Educational, 1998.

Newton, Marjorie. "The Gathering of the Australian Saints in the 1850s." *BYU Studies* 27:2 (1987): 67–78.

Newton, Marjorie. *Southern Cross Saints: The Mormons in Australia*. Laie, Hawaii: The Institute for Polynesian Studies, 1991.

Paulsen, Friedrich. *German Education: Past and Present*. Translated by T. Lorenz. London: T. Fisher Unwin, 1908.

Peterson, Charles S. *Utah: A Bicentennial History*. New York: W. W. Norton & Company, Inc, 1977.

Peterson, John Alton. *Utah's Black Hawk Indian War*. Salt Lake City: The University of Utah Press, 1998.

Petschauer, Peter. *The Education of Women in Eighteenth-Century Germany: New Directions From the German Female Perspective*. Lampeter, Wales: The Edwin Mellen Press, 1989.

Plaul, Hainer. "The Rural Proletariat: The Everyday Life of Rural Labourers in the Magdeburg Region, 1830-1880." In *The German Peasantry: Conflict and Community in Rural Society from the Eighteenth to the Twentieth Century*, edited by Richard J. Evans, and W.R. Lee, 102-128. New York: St. Martin's Press, 198

Polluck, Linda A. "Parent-Child Relations." In *The History of the European Family: Family Life in Early Modern Times, 1500-1789*, edited by David I. Kertzer and Mar Barbagli, 251-281. New Haven: Yale University Press, 2001.

Pratt, David H. and Paul F. Smart. "Life on Board a Mormon Emigrant Ship." World Conference on Records: Preserving Our Heritage, August 12-15, 1980. 5: 418, 1-34.

Pred, Allan. *Place, Practice and Structure: Social and Spatial Transformation in Southern Sweden, 1750-1850.* Polity Press: Cambridge, 1986.

Royle, Edward. *Modern Britain: A Society History 1750-1997,* second edition. New York: St. Martin's Press, 1997.

Sagarra, Eda. *A Social History of Germany, 1648-1914.* New York: Holmes & Meier Publishers, 1977.

Scott, Franklin. *Sweden: The Nation's History.* Carbondale and Edwardsville, Illinois: Southern Illinois University Press, 1988.

Scott, Sarah. *The History of Mecklenburg, From the First Settlement of the Vandals in that Country, to the Present Time, Including a Period of about Three Thousand Years.* London, Printed for J. Newbery microfilm, 1761.

Sheahan, James Joseph. *History and Topography of Buckinghamshire.* London: Longman, 1861.

Sheehan, James J. *German History, 1770-1866.* Oxford: Clarendon Press, 1989.

Spree, Reinhard. *Health and Social Class in Imperial Germany: A Social History of Mortality, Morbidity, and Inequality.* New York: St. Martin's Press, 1988.

Sogner, Sølvi. "Illegitimacy in Old Rural Society: Some Reflections on the Problem Arising from Two Norwegian Family-Reconstruction Studies." In *Chance and Change: Social and Economic Studies in Historical Demography in the Baltic Area,* edited by Sune Åkerman, Hans Chr. Johansen, and David Gaunt, 61-68. Odense: Odense University Press, 1978.

Sonne, Conway B. *Ships, Saints, and Mariners: A Maritime Encyclopedia of Mormon Migration, 1830-1890.* Salt Lake City: University of Utah Press, 1987.

Sonne, Conway B. "Under Sail to Zion." *Ensign* 21 (July 1991): 6-14.

Stahlberg. Johann Christian. *Aus Kirchenchronik Neukloster, 1870-1900.* Compiled by Pastor Dr. Matthias se Boor. Neukloster, Germany: privately printed, 1996.

Svejda, George. *Castle Garden as an Immigrant Depot, 1855-1890.* Washington DC: National Park Service, U.S. Department of Interior, 1968.

Taylor, P.A.M. *Expectations Westward: The Mormons and the Emigration of their British Converts in the Nineteenth Century.* London: Oliver and Boyd, 1965.

...lly, Charles, editor. *Historical Studies of Changing Fertility.* Princeton, New Jersey: Princeton University Press, 1978.

..., Muriel T. and Desmond C. Bonner. *Buckingham: A History of a Country Market Town,* third edition. Milton Keynes, England: Grillford Ltd., 1984.

...r Paolo. "Mortality, Fertility, and Family." In *The History of the European Family:*

Family Life in Early Modern Times, 1500-1789, edited by David I. Kertzer and Marzio Barbagli, 157-187. New Haven: Yale University Press, 2001.

Walker, Mack. *German Home Towns: Community, State and General Estate, 1648-1871*. Ithica, New York: Cornell University Press, 1971.

Walker, Mack. *Germany and the Emigration, 1816-1885*. Cambridge: Harvard University Press, 1971.

Walker, Ronald W. "Cradling Mormonism: The Rise of the Gospel in Early Victorian England." *BYU Studies* 27: 1 (1987): 25-36.

White, Richard. *It's Your History and None of My Own*. Norman, Oklahoma: University of Oklahoma Press, 1991.

Winberg, Christer. "Population Growth and Proletarianization." In *Chance and Change: Social and Economic Studies in Historical Demography in the Baltic Area*, edited by Sune Åkerman, Hans Chr. Johansen, and David Gaunt, 170-184. Odense: Odense University Press, 1978.

Wolf-Dietrich Greinert. *The German System of Vocational Education: History, Organization, Prospects*. Berlin: Nomos Verlagsgesellschaft, 1994.

Woods, Fred E. "East to West through North and South: Mormon Immigration during the Civil War." *BYU Studies,* 39:1 (2000): 6-29.

Family and Local (Unpublished) Sources
Parish Records

Church of England, Chapelry of Gawcott (Buckingham). *Parish Registers for Gawcott, 1806-1898*. Family History Library, Salt Lake City: The Genealogical Society of Utah, 1995, microfilm #1042383, items 7-10.

Church of England, St. Pancras Old Church (London). *Parish Register, 1660-1916*. Family History Library, Salt Lake City: The Genealogical Society of Utah, 1995, microfilm #598339.

Church of England, Parish Church of Steeple Claydon. *Parish Register, 1575-1964*. Family History Library, Salt Lake City: The Genealogical Society of Utah, 1969-2000, microfilm #1967094.

Church of England, Parish Church of Whitchurch. *Parish Register, 1653-1991*. Family History Library, Salt Lake City: The Genealogical Society of Utah, 1995, microfilm #1966918 and 1966919.

Church of England, Parish Church of Wingrave. *Parish Register, 1550-1965*. Family History Library, Salt Lake City: The Genealogical Society of Utah, 1995, microfilm #1966920 and 1966921.

Evangelishe Kirche Brenz. *Kirchenbuch, 1787-1875*. Family History Library, Salt Lake The Genealogical Society of Utah, 1951, microfilm #69018.

Evangelishe Kirche Garwitz. *Kirchenbuch, 1639-1875.* Family History Library, Salt Lake City: The Genealogical Society of Utah, 1951, microfilm #69112.

Evangelishe Kirche Goldebee. *Kirchenbuch, 1654-1913.* Family History Library, Salt Lake City: The Genealogical Society of Utah, 1951, microfilm #69127.

Evangelishe Kirche Gross Laasch. *Kirchenbuch, 1640-1904.* Family History Library, Salt Lake City: The Genealogical Society of Utah, 1951, microfilm #69170 and 69172.

Evangelishe Kirche Gross Tessin. *Kirchenbuch, 1671-1934.* Family History Library, Salt Lake City: The Genealogical Society of Utah, 1951, microfilm #69180.

Evangelishe Kirche Lübow. *Kirchenbuch, 1654-1875.* Family History Library, Salt Lake City: The Genealogical Society of Utah, 1952, microfilm #69308.

Evangelishe Kirche Neukloster. *Kirchenbuch, 1694-1905.* Family History Library, Salt Lake City: The Genealogical Society of Utah, 1952, microfilm #69392-69394.

Evangelishe Kirche Osterburg. *Kirchenbuchduplikat, 1654-1815.* Family History Library, Salt Lake City: Magdeburg Staatsarchiv, 1983, microfilm #1335489.

Evangelishe Kirche Ülitz. *Kirchenbuch, 1786-1898.* Family History Library, Salt Lake City: The Genealogical Society of Utah, 1951, microfilm #69628.

Evangelishe Kirche Wismar Kirche Sank Nicolai. *Kirchenbuch, 1643-1894.* Family History Library, Salt Lake City: The Genealogical Society of Utah, 1952, microfilm #69656.

Svenska Kyrkan, Blentarp socken. *Kyrkoböcker, 1662-1901.* Family History Library, Salt Lake City: The Genealogical Society of Utah, 1995, microfilm #144940.

Svenska Kyrkan, Bonderup socken. *Kyrkoböcker, 1681-1906.* Family History Library, Salt Lake City: The Genealogical Society of Utah, 1995, microfilm #144875.

Svenska Kyrkan, Esarp socken. *Kyrkoböcker, 1671-1899.* Family History Library, Salt Lake City: The Genealogical Society of Utah, 1974, microfilm #145115 and 497283.

Svenska Kyrkan, Everlöv socken. *Kyrkoböcker, 1662-1894.* Family History Library, Salt Lake City: The Genealogical Society of Utah, 1974, microfilm # 145108, 145110, and 145111.

Svenska Kyrkan, Genarp socken. *Kyrkoböcker, 1692-1894.* Family History Library, Salt Lake City: The Genealogical Society of Utah, 1974, microfilm #145445.

Svenska Kyrkan, Hyby socken. *Kyrkoböcker, 1689-1894.* Family History Library, Salt Lake City: The Genealogical Society of Utah, 1974, microfilm #145528.

Svenska Kyrkan, Kyrkheddinge socken. *Kyrkoböcker, 1683-1899.* Family History Library, Salt Lake City: The Genealogical Society of Utah, 1974, microfilm #145782 and 145783.

Svenska Kyrkan, Nevishög socken. *Kyrkoböcker, 1705-1897.* Family History Library, Salt Lake City: The Genealogical Society of Utah, 1974, microfilm #146670.

Svenska Kyrkan, Veberöd socken. *Kyrkoböcker,1675-1896.* Family History Library, Salt Lake City: The Genealogical Society of Utah, 1974, microfilm #147702 and 147705.

Other Original Documents

Bannock County (Idaho), County Clerk. *Bannock County Births, Marriages, and Deaths, 1905-1915.* Family History Library, Pocatello, Idaho: Pocatello State Archives, 1975, microfilm #1527293.

Beaver County (Utah) County Clerk. *Marriage License Records and Applications 1887-1966.* Family History Library, Salt Lake City: The Genealogical Society of Utah, 1966, microfilm #485224.

Buckinghamshire, England, Civil Registration Records. Entry June 6, 1840 for Emmanuel Harris, copy in author's possession.

Great Britain Census Office. *Census Returns for Steeple Claydon, 1841.* Family History Library. Salt Lake City: The Genealogical Society of Utah, 1960, microfilm #241212.

Great Britain Census Office. *Census Returns for Buckingham, 1851.* Family History Library. Salt Lake City: The Genealogical Society of Utah, 1960, microfilm #241221.

Cache County (Utah) County Clerk. *Marriage Records, 1887-1966.* Family History Library, Salt Lake City: The Genealogical Society of Utah, 1966, microfilm #430301.

Church of Jesus Christ of Latter-day Saints, Fayette Ward (Fayette, Utah). *Record of Members, 1871-1950.* Family History Library, Salt Lake City: The Genealogical Society of Utah, 1952, microfilm #25955.

Church of Jesus Christ of Latter-day Saints, Fremont Ward (Fremont, Utah). *Record of Members, 1886-1950.* Family History Library, Salt Lake City: The Genealogical Society of Utah, 1967, microfilm #25941.

Church of Jesus Christ of Latter-day Saints Genealogical Society Library Division. *Cemetery Records, Wayne County, Utah.* Salt Lake City: Genealogical Society of Utah, 1937.

Church of Jesus Christ of Latter-day Saints, Gunnison Ward (Gunnison, Utah). *Record of Members, 1861-1945.* Family History Library, Salt Lake City: The Genealogical Society of Utah, 1951, microfilm #25977.

Church of Jesus Christ of Latter-day Saints, Gunnison Stake (Utah). *Cemetery Records: Axtell, Centerfield, Fayette, and Gunnison in Sanpete County, Utah.* Typescript, 1934, Family History Library.

Church of Jesus Christ of Latter-day Saints Juarez Ward (Chihuahua). *Record of Members, 1887-1948.* Family History Library, Salt Lake City: The Genealogical Society of Utah, 1952, microfilm #35130.

Church of Jesus Christ of Latter-day Saints London Conference (London). *Record of Members, 1833-1935.* Family History Library, Salt Lake City: The Genealogical Society of Utah, 1952, microfilm #87014, p. 765.

Church of Jesus Christ of Latter-day Saints Manti Ward (Manti, Utah). *Record of Members, 1844-1877.* Family History Library, Salt Lake City: The Genealogical Society of Utah, 1952, microfilm #26129.

Church of Jesus Christ of Latter-day Saints New South Wales District. *Record of Members, 1852-1952.* Family History Library, Salt Lake City: The Genealogical Society of Utah, 1967, microfilm #105320.

Church of Jesus Christ of Latter-day Saints Spring Lake (Spring Lake, Utah). *Record of Members.* Family History Library, Salt Lake City: The Genealogical Society of Utah, 1967, microfilm #27326.

Church of Jesus Christ of Latter-day Saints Vallby Branch, (Malmöhus). *Record of Members, 1853-1863.* Family History Library, Salt Lake City: The Genealogical Society of Utah, microfilm #82947, item 2-3.

Church of Jesus Christ of Latter-day-Saints, Temple Index Bureau. *Endowment Index 1846-1969.* Family History Library, Salt Lake City: The Genealogical Society of Utah, 1991, microfilm #1059545.

Delta Family History Center (Delta, Utah). *Obituaries: Millard County, Utah.* Family History Library, Delta Utah Family History Center, 2002. CD-ROM.

Domialämter Neukloster. "Dorf Nevern: Haker Hauswirt Dokumenten, 1835-1867." Landeshauptarchiv Schwerin in Schwerin, Germany.

Gunnison Ward, Sanpete Stake. *Historical Record, 1874-1894.* LDS Church Archives, Salt Lake City.

Hamburg Auswanderungsamt. *Auswandererlisten, 1850-1934.* Family History Library, Salt Lake City: The Genealogical Society of Utah, 1975, microfilm #1049022.

Jenson, Andrew. *Skåne District, Swedish Mission, Manuscript History and Historical Reports.* LDS Church Archives, Salt Lake City.

Juab County (Utah) County Clerk. *Register of Deaths, 1898-1905.* Family History Library, Salt Lake City: The Genealogical Society of Utah, 1966, microfilm #482020.

Mecklenburg-Schwerin Volkszählungsamt. *Volkszählungslisten 1819, Hagenow D.A., Ülitz Parish.* Family History Library, Salt Lake City: The Genealogical Society of Utah, 1951, microfilm #68887.

Mecklenburg-Schwerin Volkszählungsamt. *Volkszählungslisten 1819, Neukloster D.A., Nevern Parish.* Family History Library, Salt Lake City: The Genealogical Society of Utah, 1951, microfilm #68892.

Mecklenburgische Auswanderer Amt. "Auswanderer Dokumenten in Mecklenburg 1800-1900." Landeshauptarchiv Schwerin, Schwerin, Germany.

Millard County (Utah) County Clerk. *Marriage License Records, 1887-1966.* Family History Library, Salt Lake City: The Genealogical Society of Utah, 1996, microfilm #482022.

...uth Wales, Department of Immigration. *Assisted Immigrants Inwards to Sydney, 1828-1890.* Family History Library, Salt Lake City: The Genealogical Society of Utah, 1962, microfilm #288511, 29 December 1829.

"Obituary for Emma Sorenson." *Deseret News,* Salt Lake City. http://www.deseretnews.com/article/883776/ (accessed January 2010).

"Obituary for George Elmer Albrecht." *Salt Lake Tribune*, 18 October 1956, p. 29, copy in author's possession.

"Obituary for Minnie A. Pierce." *Deseret News*, Salt Lake City. http://www.deseretnews.com/article/338822/DEATH--MINNIE-A-PIERCE. html (accessed January 2010).

"Obituary for Nila Albrecht Carlson." *Daily Herald*, Provo, Utah. http://ads.heraldextra. com/articles/2008/09/12/obituaries/329835.txt (accessed January 2010).

Piute County (Utah) County Clerk. *Marriage License Records, 1872-1966,* Family History Library, Salt Lake City: The Genealogical Society of Utah, 1983, microfilm #484608.

Sanpete County (Utah) County Clerk, *Marriage License Records, 1888-1966*. Family History Library, Salt Lake City: The Genealogical Society of Utah, 1966, microfilm #48153 and 481124.

Sevier County (Utah) County Clerk. *Marriage License Records and Applications, 1887-1966.* Family History Library, Salt Lake City: The Genealogical Society of Utah, 1996, microfilm #482037.

The Farmer's Oracle (Spring Lake, Utah). Family History Library, Salt Lake City: Universal Microfilming, 1987, microfilm #1486763, various issues.

Skåne District, Swedish Mission. "General Minutes." LDS Church Archives, Salt Lake City.

Sverige Häradsrätt (Bara). Bouppteckningar, 1664-1861, 1822 22/7 1821-22:80, Entry for Karna Larsdotter. Family History Library, Salt Lake City: The Genealogical Society of Utah, 1953, microfilm # 145082.

Sverige Häradsrätt (Bara). *Bouppteckningar, Entry for Nils Nilsson.* Vol F II a: 31, nr. 26. Lund Archive, Lund, Sweden.

Sverige. Länsstyrelsen (Malmöhus). *Mantalslängder, 1658-1860.* Family History Library, Salt Lake City: The Genealogical Society of Utah, 1962, microfilm #337666, 337662, 337661, and 337665.

Tattom, Louisa. *Cemetery Records of Manti, Utah.* Salt Lake City: Genealogical Society of Utah, 1936.

United States Census Office. "1860, San Francisco, California Census." Family History Library, Washington DC, National Archives, 1967, microfilm #803067.

United States Census Office. "1870, Santaquin, Utah Census." Family History Library, Washington DC, National Archives, 1967, microfilm ##25542, p. 35.

United States Census Office. "1880, Gunnison, Utah Census." Family History Library, Washington DC, National Archives, 1967, microfilm #1255337, p. 8.

United States Census Office. "1900, Fremont, Utah Census." Family History Library, Washington DC, National Archives, 1967, microfilm #124168, ED 214, p.

United States Census Office. "1910, Fremont, Utah Census." Family History Library, Washington DC, National Archives, 1967, microfilm #1654719, ED 24, p. 2A.

United States Immigration and Naturalization Services. *Passenger Lists of Vessels Arriving at New York, 1820-1897*. Family History Library, Salt Lake City: Washington DC, National Archives, 1970, microfilm #295796.

Utah Department of Health, Bureau of Vital Records and Statistics. *Utah Death Certificates, 1904-1951*. Family History Library, Salt Lake City: The Genealogical Society of Utah, 2001, microfilm #2259285.

Wayne County (Utah) County Clerk. *Register of Deaths, 1898-1957*. Family History Library, Salt Lake City: The Genealogical Society of Utah, 1967, microfilm #484607.

Wayne County (Utah) County Clerk. *Register of Birth and of Deaths, 1899-1948*. Family History Library, Salt Lake City: The Genealogical Society of Utah, 1967, microfilm #498432, items 2-3.

Wayne County (Utah) County Clerk. *Marriage License Records, 1892-1978*. Family History Library, Salt Lake City: The Genealogical Society of Utah, 1996, microfilm #484603.

Wayne County (Utah) County Clerk. *Miscellaneous Records, 1901-1948*. Family History Library, Salt Lake City: The Genealogical Society of Utah, 1967, microfilm #1654719.

Wayne County (Utah) County Clerk. *Townsite Maps and Documents*. Family History Library, Salt Lake City: The Genealogical Society of Utah, 1967, microfilm #498431.

Local Histories, Letters, Websites, Biographies and Autobiographies

Albrecht Family History. Family paper by unknown author, copy in author's possession, n.d.

Albrecht, Alta Taylor. "Rex Albrecht." Biography, copy in author's possession, 1985.

Albrecht, Alta Taylor. "Life History of Alta Fern Taylor Albrecht as Written by Herself." Autobiography, copy in author's possession, May 1965.

Albrecht, Chasty Margaret Harris. "Autobiography." Autobiography, copy in author's possession, circa 1940.

Albrecht, Clarence. "George Albrecht." Copy in author's possession.

Albrecht, Emma. "A Life Story of Emma Sophia Elizabeth Albrecht Morrell." Autopbiography, copy in author's possession, circa 1940.

Albrecht, Eva. "My Life Story." Autobiography, copy in author's possession, circa 1966.

Albrecht, Keith. Letter to author, November 2003.

Bahlke, Werner. *200 Jahre Neu Brenz, 1797-1997*. Neustadt-Glewe, Germany: privately printed, 1997.

Billings, Molly. "The Influenza Pandemic of 1918." Human Virology at Stanford, June 2007. http://www.stanford.edu/group/virus/uda/ (accessed March 2010).

Blackburn, Erlene. "The Story of Earl LeRoy Albrecht, My Grandfather." Biography, copy in author's possession, circa 1964.

Booth, Charles. *Life and Labour of the People of London* as quoted in Des Gander, "The Occupation of Carman." The Gander and Gander One-Name Study, http://www.gander-name.info/misc/carmen.shtml (accessed January 2010).

Church of Jesus Christ of Latter-day Saints. "Chronology of Church History." http://scriptures.lds.org/chchrono/contents (accessed January 2010).

Cody, David. "A Brief History of London." The Victorian Web. http://www.victorianweb.org/history/hist4.html (accessed January 2010).

EH.Net Encyclopedia, s.v. "Fertility and Mortality in the United States" (by Michael Haines, edited by Robert Whaples). http://eh.net/encyclopedia/article/haines.demography (accessed March 2010).

Farnsworth, M. F. *History of Manti*. Salt Lake City: Genealogical Society, 1901.

Funeral Sermon of Anna Gävershagen, 21 November 1693, Garwitz, Mecklenburg-Schwerin. Copy in author's possession.

Gemeinde Gross Laasch. *Chronologische Zeittafel der Gemeinde Gross Laasch von 1229-1997*. Gross Laasch, Germany: privately printed, circa 1995.

GENUKI: UK and Ireland, s.v. "Buckinghamshire." http://met.open.ac.uk/genuki/big/eng/BKM/ (accessed January 2010).

GENUKI: UK and Ireland. "The Tide of Emigration to the United States and to the British Colonies." http://www.genuki.org.uk/big/emdesc.html (accessed January 2010).

Great Britain Census Office, Horace Mann. *Census of Great Britain, 1851: Religious Worship in England and Wales*. London: G. Routledge, 1854. http://www.archive.org/details/censusgreatbrit00manngoog (accessed January 2010).

Hunt, Julian. *Buckingham: A Pictorial History*. Buckinghamshire County Library: Phillimore & Co., 1994.

Lone Star College – Kingwood. *American Cultural History Pages, 1900-1909*. http://kclibrary.lonestar.edu/decade00.html (accessed January 2010).

Longenecker, Elmer Z. *The Early Blacksmiths of Lancaster County*, Elmer Z. Community Historians Annual, Number 10, Dec. 1971. http://www.horseshoe.cc/pennadutch/people/trades/blacksmith/smiths.htm (accessed January 20

Mecklenburg Government. *Grozzherzoglich Mecklenburg-Schwerinschwer Staats-Kalender, 1848-1880.* Stadtarchiv, Neubrandenburg, Germany.

Menlove, Clara. "Spring Lake." Pioneer Memorial Museum, Salt Lake City.

Moreno, Barry. "Castle Garden: The Forgotten Gateway." *Ancestry Magazine,* (March/April 2003). http://www.ancestry.com/learn/library/article. aspx?article=7233 (accessed Jan 2010).

Mormon Immigration Index, CD-ROM, Family History Resource File, Intellectual Reserve INC, 2000.
   For the *Julia Ann's* 1855 voyage, the CD includes the following sources:
   A Compilation of General Voyage Notes
   Letter from Andrew Anderson - February 22, 1856
   Letter from John McCarthy - April 25, 1856
   Letter from John S. Eldredge
   Letter from Peter Penfold - February 17, 1856
   Pond, Benjamin F. Autobiography.

   For the *Lucas's* 1857 voyage, the CD includes the following sources:
   A Compilation of General Voyage Notes

   For the *Monarch of the Sea's* 1861 voyage, the CD includes the following sources:
   A Compilation of General Voyage Notes
   Autobiography of William Probert, Jr.
   Diary of Carl Eric Lindholm
   History of Barbara Sophia Haberli Staheli
   Journal of Alma Elizabeth Mineer Felt
   Journal of Peter Nielsen
   Letter of Elias L. T. Harrison - June 19, 1861
   Minutes of the Monarch of the Sea
   The Life of John and Barbara Staheli

   For the 1863 *John J. Boyd* voyage, I quoted from:
   Letter from Anders Christensen to President Jesse N. Smith, 18 September 1863

   For the *Wisconsin's* 1880 voyage, the CD includes the following sources:
   A Compilation of General Voyage Notes
   Autobiography of James Samuel Page Bowler
   Letter from John Nicholson - November 2, 1880

MTC Committee. *The Manti Temple Centennial, 1888-1898.* Provo, Utah: Community Press, 1988.

Nielsen, Peter. "Diary." Transcribed by Orson B. West. Typescript, LDS Church Archives, Salt Lake City.

Perkins, John. "Diary." LDS Church Archives, Salt Lake City.

⋯ierce, Minnie. "History of John Albrecht: My Grandfather." Biography, copy in author's possession, circa 1940.

⋯ Anne. *Rainbow Views: A History of Wayne County.* Springville, Utah: Art City, 1953.

Spring Lake Branch, Utah Stake. "Manuscript History and Historical reports," LDS Church Archives, Salt Lake City.

Stahlberg, Johann Christian. *Aus der Kirchenchronik Neukloster 1870-1900*. Compiled by Pastor Dr. Matthias se Boor. Neukloster, Germany: privately printed, 1996.

Taubenberger, Jeffery K. and David M. Morens. "1918 Influenza: The Mother of all Pandemics." Centers for Disease Control and Prevention: Emerging Infectious Diseases, December 2005. http://www.cdc.gov/ncidod/eid/vol12no01/05-0979.htm (accessed March 2010).

Utah History Encyclopedia, s.v. "Colonization of Utah" (by Leonard Arrington). http://www.onlineutah.com/colonizationhistory.shtml (accessed January 2010).

Utah History Encyclopedia, s.v. "Perpetual Emigrating Fund Company" (by Richard Jensen). http://historytogo.utah.gov/utah_chapters/pioneers_and_cowboys/perpetualemigratingfundcompany.html (accessed March 2010).

Utah History Encyclopedia, s.v. "The Great Depression" (by John S. McCormick). http://www.onlineutah.com/colonizationhistory.shtml (accessed March 2010).

Utah History Encyclopedia, s.v. "The United Order Movement" (by Dean L. May). http://www.media.utah.edu/UHE/u/UNITEDORDER.html (accessed January 2010).

Wolf, Eleonore. *Neubrandenburg: Chronological History of the City*. Translated by Leslie Albrecht and Intersprachen-Service. Neubrandenbrg, Germany: Neubrandenburger Stadtarchiv, 1998.

Woolley, Samuel. "Journal," July-September 1861 entries, LDS Church Archives, Salt Lake City.

Young, Brigham, Letter to Benjamin F. Johnson, Spring Lake Villa, 30 January 1866, LDS Church Archives, Salt Lake City.

ACKNOWLEDGMENTS

I have wanted to write a book since I was five years old. Of course, many five-year-olds want to write books, or be ballerinas or baseball players. They change their mind every few months (my five-year-old currently wants to be a chef, a swimmer, a ballerina, a veterinarian, and a cowgirl). But my ambition never wavered or changed in all those years.

I have even wanted to write this book since I first stepped off that plane in Germany—one marriage, four children, and three moves ago. It has been a long journey—but one I have not made alone. I am indebted to many who have made my path easier. I can never thank them all, but I want to express my gratitude to a few.

First, I am grateful to those who read various versions of the manuscript (and there were many) and gave their feedback and encouragement. My writing group in Madison, Wisconsin, *Tuesdays with Story*, helped me learn the importance of feedback and gain the courage to seek it. They pointed the emerging manuscript in new directions. Dr. Raymond Wright (who taught me nearly everything I know about German research), Dr. Katherine Daynes, and Dr. Lavina Anderson read several chapters and made important suggestions as well. Friends and fellow genealogists provided feedback: Helen Ullmann, Kay Sheldon, Linda Pelletier, Deb Belle, Andrea Newman, Lynette Rife, and Jen Simms. A special thanks goes to Alissa Hyde and Trisha Sorber. Trisha had the wisdom and insight to tell me (kindly) what was missing, while Alissa had the patience to tell me over and over, "It *is* good. Really. It is." Besides being editors, they were both unwaveringly supportive friends—something everyone should have on their life journey.

I feel very fortunate to have attended Brigham Young Universi where I was able to soak in the expertise of many professors helped me learn my way through the records. I was also fortun interact extensively with the employees of the Family History who have answered countless questions about illegible words, obscure occupations, and general research quandaries.

I benefited from the guidance of numerous others in the family history arena. I would like to thank Ed Zapletal and Rick Cree from *Family Chronicle* for steering me to the resources I needed and taking this project under the wing of their magazines. I also appreciate Diane Rapaport and Maureen Taylor who answered numerous questions about the book process. Meldon Wolfgang from Jonathan Sheppard Books went above and beyond the call of duty to hunt down the obscure maps I needed. And finally, I'd like to thank my editor, Krisitne Thornley, who endured countless e-mails about footnoting formats, fixed much more than hyphen problems, and patiently got everything in order for me.

Of course, my greatest thanks are due to my family. The astute observations of my sister-in-law, Cassy, led to great improvements. Besides reading chapters, queries, overviews, pitches, and other versions of the material, my sister, Laura, spent hours listening on the phone as I celebrated or bemoaned different phases of the process. My brother, Scott, who had the unfortunate circumstance of living close to the Family History Library when I didn't, tracked down all sorts of records for me. My parents read more versions of this manuscript than anyone should ever have to read of anything. They answered questions about Wayne County, farming, and relatives. But most of all, they never faltered in their confidence in me — and this book (which is probably why my dream of being a writer has been able to survive all these years).

I am grateful for my children. I have tried so hard not to let this project interfere with my most important job — being their mom. But of course, time is a finite resource. They have been dragged across the US and beyond in the name of family history research. And, they have endured it well.

Most of all, I thank my husband (whose name is and always has been George — not David). He has picked up countless books from the library (several more than one time); taken the kids while I typed, scrolled through microfilms, or attended conferences; read various versions of the manuscript; listened to my excited accounts of new discoveries; and endured my emotional roller coaster. All this he did without complaining. I know I have been truly blessed to have the family I do.

And finally, I am thankful for the people whose story I have tried to may have taken me a while to recognize it (I'm a slow learner), come to truly understand what an amazing legacy these nineteenth-century immigrants left for me — and for all of us.

ABOUT THE AUTHOR

Leslie Albrecht Huber has written over one hundred articles, mostly on family history and history topics. Her work has appeared in publications such as *Ancestry, American Spirit, Family Chronicle, The History Channel Magazine, Family Tree Magazine, History Magazine, Internet Genealogy* and others. She enjoys speaking to genealogy societies and other groups in New England and across the country. Leslie lives in western Massachusetts with her husband and four children. When she's not cheering on her children at basketball games and dance recitals, doing laundry, or typing on her computer, she loves studying maps and reading travel guides to plan her next journey.

Visit her website at www.understandingyourancestors.com for more information on tracing immigrant ancestors.